To: Pa

From: Elma c̄ Love.

A daily devotional
for women by women

From the Heart

Rose Otis

Editor

REVIEW AND HERALD® PUBLISHING ASSOCIATION
HAGERSTOWN, MD 21740

The authors assume full responsibility for the accuracy of all facts
and quotations as cited in this book.

This book was
Edited by Jeannette R. Johnson
Copyedited by Jocelyn Fay
                    James Cavil
Jacket design by Patricia S. Wegh
Cover photos by Joel D. Springer
Typeset: 11/12 Weiss

PRINTED IN U.S.A.

01 00 99 98 97   10 9 8 7 6 5 4 3 2 1

R&H Cataloging Service
Otis, Rose, ed.
    From the heart.

    1. Devotional calendars—SDA.   2. Devotional calendars—women.
3. Women—religious life.   4. Devotional literature—SDA.   I. Title.

                    242.643

ISBN 0-8280-1288-1

The Women's Devotional Series

The Listening Heart
A Gift of Love
A Moment of Peace
Close to Home
From the Heart

To order, call 1-800-765-6955.
Visit us at www.rhpa.org

Biographical Sketches

Betty J. Adams is a retired teacher, married, with three grown children and four grandchildren. She is active in her local church's women's ministries and community services organizations, and also serves as communication secretary and associate editor of their church newsletter. She has had articles published in *Guide* magazine. Her hobbies are reading, traveling, sewing, writing, and her grandchildren. Jan. 2, June 21.

Maxine Williams Allen is a computer systems analyst living in West Virginia. She is a "hobbyist" writer and seminar presenter who is currently developing the Follow the Leader seminar series. Maxine is active in her local church in the areas of family life, women's ministries, and ministering to missing members. She enjoys reading, writing, traveling, meeting people, and computer technology. She and her husband are the happy parents of a new son. Mar. 30.

Caroline Andrew is a mother of two and lives in Australia. She has worked for an independent publishing ministry and has had some articles published, as well as some of her artwork. She enjoys graphic arts and uses this talent for her church. Caroline also enjoys helping people, cooking, and sharing her experience and recipes with those unfamiliar with vegetarian food. July 10.

Esperanza Aquino-Mopera is a registered nurse who works for a home-care service company. Her four children have now completed their college education. Her daughter is married and has given Esperanza three grandchildren to enjoy. Mar. 29, Aug. 27, Oct. 4, Nov. 16.

Donna M. Arnold is the nurse/manager of a telemetry unit at Washington Adventist Hospital in Takoma Park. She has been an assistant leader in the cradle roll department of her church since 1983, and a member of the women's ministries committee for the past two years. Her hobbies include golfing, cross-country skiing, traveling, sewing, writing, and her grandchildren. Feb. 4.

Audrey Balderstone is the mother of two sons. She and her husband operate a garden landscaping company in England. She recently obtained her Bachelor of Arts degree from London University while maintaining her interest in church and community activities and in flower arranging. Her home fellowship group has been expanded to include a prayer group. July 18.

Jennifer Baldwin writes from Sydney, Australia, where she is an administrative assistant at a hospital. She has served in various capacities in her local church, including elder, Bible instructor, and communication secretary. She enjoys writing and has contributed to a number of church publications. Aug. 10, Oct. 6.

Mary Barrett is a pastor's wife and the mother of two daughters. She plays an active part in her husband's ministry and writes for various magazines. She loves to walk, play badminton, be with friends, and make crafts. Oct. 13.

Pam Baumgartner is a missionary in Nicaragua. Besides nurturing her family, she supervises a project to promote family worships, counsels young people, writes, and studies for her master's degree in family relationships. Mar. 23, Sept. 25.

Yvonne (Stockhausen) Bazliel, a Jamaican medical missionary to the Southern Asia Division, took a medical retirement after 33 years of service because of complications following the removal of a brain tumor. She is presently preparing her autobiography, in which the above incident will be used. Her medical condition has limited her hobbies to writing letters and the occasional article for church papers. May 26, Sept. 10.

Jessie Beard and her husband live in Pennsylvania. The mother of three grown sons, Jessie works as a customer service representative and serves as a superintendent in her local church. She enjoys writing, walking, bicycling, shopping, and public speaking. Sept. 28.

Appy Niyo Benggon is from Sabah, Malaysia. She came to America in 1992 with her husband when he enrolled at Andrews University in Michigan. She works there as a secretary to the assistant vice president of student services. She enjoys reading, floral arranging, traveling, and above all, mothering. Oct. 3.

Susan Berridge is a registered nurse and a driver's education teacher. She has a master's degree in education and teaches health occupations at a vocational school. She and her husband, Ron, enjoy living in a rural setting with their children. They have four daughters, ranging in age from preschool to college. Her hobbies include painting, gardening, and outdoor activities. Aug. 16.

Annie B. Best writes from Washington, D.C., where she is a retired public schoolteacher with two grown children. She enjoys reading, listening to music, and shopping for her two grandchildren. Annie has worked in the cradle roll and kindergarten departments of her church. **May 18.**

Coleen M. Birkett, originally from Barbados, now lives in Canada and is aspiring to be a career missionary. She enjoys reading, writing, public speaking, and track and field. She has served her local church as a youth leader and as junior and earliteen superintendent. She considers her year of teaching in the Bay Islands to be the most fulfilling year of her life. **Jan. 26.**

Karen Birkett writes from Canada. She attended Oakwood College in Huntsville, Alabama, where she earned a bachelor's degree in social work. Her hobbies include knitting, reading, embroidery, and camping. **June 23.**

Joan Bova, her husband, and two daughters live in Apopka, Florida. She directs disabilities ministries for the Southern Union Conference and Florida Conference of Seventh-day Adventists and conducts seminars on disability awareness and the Americans With Disabilities Act. **Aug. 2.**

Carol Brackett is the mother of two grown sons. She made a midlife career change, graduating in December 1995 with a bachelor's degree in nursing. She is now pursuing a master's degree in nursing, with an emphasis on family practice, and is the education coordinator for a hospital in Kentucky. She enjoys reading, scuba diving, traveling, shopping, meeting new people, and learning. **May 7.**

Carole Breckenridge is a freelance writer in Bethesda, Maryland. She volunteers at a local library and advises on several educational boards. Travel, family, books, children, flowers, friends, and chocolate delight her. **Aug. 6, Nov. 14.**

Ellen Bresee, cofounder of Shepherdess International (a support system for ministers' wives), worked with her husband in pastoral and evangelistic team ministry until they retired and moved to Oregon. The mother of four, Ellen has served as an elementary schoolteacher, marriage counselor, and speaker, and is a published writer. **Apr. 11, Nov. 22.**

Betty Brooks is an administrative secretary who commutes daily from her home in Martinsburg, West Virginia, to Silver Spring, Maryland. **Oct. 16.**

Tonya L. Brown, a single mother of one son, has a bachelor's degree in administration and accounting, and a Master of Science in administration and business education. Her hobbies include writing poems and short stories, music, and working with small children. She serves her local church as the children's church coordinator. **Mar. 15, Sept. 3.**

Andrea A. Bussue was born on the Caribbean island of Nevis. She holds a master's degree in education and works at a special education facility in Washington, D.C., with children who are developmentally delayed. She has been the children's choir director at her local church in Hyattsville, Maryland. She loves children and enjoys reading, traveling, sewing, cooking, and meeting people. **Jan. 5, May 27, Aug. 29, Dec. 2.**

Edna Barrett Canaday, a retired clerk-treasurer for the city of College Place, Washington, has held offices for various clubs and her church. She was the editor of the Blue Mountain Gem and Mineral Society's newsletter. Currently she is involved in volunteer work. **Feb. 12.**

Dorothy Wainwright Carey is a retired federal government worker who lives with her husband in Ocala, Florida. She's the mother of one son and has one grandson. Her interests include traveling, reading, being outdoors, and all furry creatures. **May 21, Aug. 3.**

Teresa Carmichael, a minister's wife and the mother of two daughters, resides at Enterprise Academy, Enterprise, Kansas. She enjoys camping, hiking, reading, and writing. **Mar. 2.**

Janice M. Carver is an inspector for SCI Systems in Colorado Springs, Colorado, where she has lived for almost 30 years. She also works as a substitute teacher for a day-care center. Janice has had several poems published and enjoys writing, sewing, quilting, and crafts. **Nov. 4.**

Terri Casey lives in southern California with her husband of 20 years. They have two grown children and two grandchildren. She and her husband operate an excavation business, and she is the safety officer for several medical practices. Terri team-teaches a children's Bible class with her husband at her church and assists him with the Pathfinder Club. Her interests include camping, quilting, storytelling, painting, and reading. **Feb. 14.**

Fonda Chaffee has a doctorate in educational administration and undergraduate degrees in dietetics, specializing in food systems management. Now a widow, she is a teacher and the mother of two children. She has served her church for more than 40 years and enjoys travel, playing Scrabble, crocheting, and gardening. **Dec. 19.**

Shari Chamberlain is the director of pastoral care at Ukiah Valley Medical Center in California. On weekends she enjoys driving along the Mendocino coast, or through the northern California redwoods near her home. Developing a fruitful garden, designing a comfortable room, and discovering a bargain are all things she likes to do. **Oct. 14, Nov. 13.**

Frances Charles is a first-time contributor. She writes from South Africa. **Mar. 17, Aug. 19.**

Birol Christo is a retired schoolteacher. During her active service she also worked as an office secretary and statistician. She lives with her retired husband in Hosur, India. She is the mother of five grown children and enjoys spending her free time in gardening, sewing, and making craft items to finance her project for homeless children. **June 3.**

Jan Clarke, a "relocated" Australian, is the finance director of Stanborough Press, a Christian publishing house in England. She is a church elder and treasurer with interests that include history, reading, writing, public speaking, genealogy, and women's ministries. **Mar. 16, Sept. 5.**

Carel Clay lives in Napa, California, with her husband and daughter. She is a nursing instructor at Napa Valley College and has taught cradle roll, youth, and adult Bible classes. Carel enjoys quilting, sewing, gardening, reading, writing, public speaking, cats, and being a mom. **Feb. 15, Mar. 5, Sept. 29.**

Arlene E. Compton is a retired nursing administrator who lives in Lincoln, Nebraska, with her husband. Arlene worked for the Department of Veterans' Affairs hospitals for 35 years. She loves to travel, write, meet people, and visit her three adult children and four grandsons. She continues to be active in professional nursing organizations, as well as in her church and community. **June 14.**

Kathy Connatser is employed as a secretary in Orlando, Florida. She is the Pathfinder director in her church and enjoys playing with her grandchildren, reading, and arts and crafts. **Jan. 23.**

Renee Copeland is a secretary at Andrews University in Michigan. She enjoys decorative painting and collectibles (dolls and figurines). **June 18.**

Elita Marlem Balogh Costa is an elementary teacher living in Goiania, Brazil, with her pastor-husband. She enjoys gardening, friends, animals, travel, embroidery, piano playing, and preaching. She is active in community service and women's ministries. **May 6.**

Judy Coulston is a nutritionist and public speaker who lives in northern California. She has hosted and coproduced a weekly television program. She enjoys traveling and presenting health seminars and has developed a line of food supplements. **Feb. 25, May 28, June 26.**

Eva Alice Covey, mother of six and grandmother of 15, was a schoolteacher before her marriage, and is now a widow living in Canada. She enjoys sewing, crocheting, playing the piano, raising flowers, and writing. She has had one book and several magazine stories published and is currently working on another children's book. **Mar. 1, Apr. 1, Apr. 21.**

Celia Mejia Cruz is the administrative secretary and assistant editor/coordinator of the devotional book project for the Women's Ministries Department at the General Conference of Seventh-day Adventists. A pastor's wife, church elder, mother of five young adults, and grandmother of one, she enjoys her family, entertaining, aerobics, teaching a baptismal class at her church, presenting seminars, and preaching. In her spare moments she enjoys needlepoint, sewing, reading, and writing. **Jan. 20, Apr. 14, May 12, Aug. 13, Dec. 24.**

Eileen Cruz is a high school student living in Maryland. She enjoys listening to music, playing her flute, reading, creative writing, dogs, and young children. **June 27.**

Jucelina Moura da Silva is a theology student in São Paulo, Brazil. She enjoys reading, listening to music, and singing. **June 30.**

Thalita Regina Garcia da Silva is a first-time contributor. She writes from São Paulo, Brazil. **Sept. 26.**

Shonna R. Dalusong, a wife and the mother of two (one living daughter and one she looks forward to raising in heaven), is an educational consultant for Creative Memories and a distributor for natural supplements. When time permits, her hobbies include reading, writing, and rubber-stamping. **May 11.**

Cecily Daly writes from Huntsville, Alabama. Her articles have appeared in several religious magazines. Her hobbies include reading, writing, music, and gardening. **Feb. 24, Mar. 19.**

Virginia Dart-Collins taught the third grade for 17 years at Spring Valley Academy in Ohio before relocating to Moreno Valley, California, where she teaches church school. She and her husband lead out in marriage commitment seminars and parenting classes in their church. They were also missionaries in Ghana and Nigeria for five years. **Nov. 3.**

Lynn Marie Davis, a sign language interpreter living in Georgia, enjoys attending—and presenting—workshops. She teaches empowerment workshops for fun. *Steps to Making Your Dreams Come True* is one of her most recent. Other hobbies include walking, creative cooking, and reading. **July 28, Nov. 8.**

Wanda Davis is the manager of the Department of Pastoral Care at a regional hospital, as well as women's ministries coordinator and elder in her local church. She lives with her husband and three children in West Virginia. **Mar. 28.**

Charlotte de Beer writes from the republic of South Africa. She is the mother of two and grandmother of five children. She works for her local church as the pastor's secretary and communication secretary, is involved with Meals on Wheels, and is a published author. Her hobbies include writing, traveling the world, and walking. **Nov. 18.**

Brenda Forbes Dickerson is a wife, mother, and homemaker who writes from Omaha, Nebraska. She enjoys writing, gardening, sewing, and teaching Bible stories to children at her church. **July 6.**

Sally Pierson Dillon is a registered nurse, mother of two boys, Bible teacher, and freelance writer. She has been published in *Guide, Insight,* and other Christian magazines, as well as *Crossroads in Time,* an archaeology activity book for children. **Feb. 5, Sept. 15, Oct. 12, Dec. 1.**

Goldie Down is a freelance writer living in Australia with her minister-husband. Both were missionaries to India for 20 years. She has volunteered at her local hospital for the past 20 years and teaches creative writing at young adult night classes. Goldie has had more than 20 books published, including a creative writing textbook used in government schools. **Feb. 16, Sept. 18, Nov. 17.**

Crystal Earnhardt is a pastor's wife, freelance writer, author of the books *Will You Still Love Me Tomorrow?* and *Annie's Secret,* and coauthor of *Power for Everyday Heroes.* She's the mother of a 2-year-old daughter, two grown daughters, and has three grandchildren. She is the women's ministries coordinator for her local church. All her hobbies are on hold for now. **Jan. 31.**

Mary C. Edmister retired from real estate in 1995 to pursue freelance writing. She has written dozens of newspaper articles and a weekly column. Her articles have appeared in various religious publications, and she has been the editor of both the *National Dental Auxiliary News* magazine and a monthly real estate newsletter. She is a member of her local writer's guild and photo club. Her husband, James, died in 1985. She has four grown children. **July 7.**

Heidi Michelle Ehlert, from Washington State, is a first-time contributor. She was a student at Southern College when she submitted her story. **Oct. 21.**

Kemba Malene Esmond is a certified public accountant who is currently employed at the Review and Herald Publishing Association. She serves her local church in West Virginia as the treasurer and enjoys reading and cooking in her spare time. **May 31.**

Jocelyn Fay collects Cat's Meow Village special collection pieces and antique blue-and-white china. She is a copy editor at the Review and Herald Publishing Association in Hagerstown, Maryland. She enjoys genealogical research, and learning more about the mid-Atlantic states is one of her new pastimes. **May 4.**

Gloria J. Felder is currently working in communications in Queens, New York, where her husband pastors a congregation. They have two daughters. Gloria enjoys singing, listening to music, writing poetry, public speaking, and practicing the guitar. She is also working on publishing her book of poetry. **Dec. 10.**

Edith Fitch taught in elementary schools for 41 years. She compiled four volumes of supplementary helps for grades 1 through 4 Bible classes for church schools in Canada and has been involved in research for church and school histories. Her hobbies include traveling, writing, cooking, hardanger embroidery, and calligraphy. **Oct. 28.**

Heide Ford is the assistant editor of *Women of Spirit,* a Christian women's magazine. A registered nurse, she holds a master's degree in counseling. Her interests include reading, learning about different cultures, nurturing friendships, and kayaking. She and her pastor husband live in Hagerstown, Maryland. **Jan. 8, Oct. 1.**

Kaarina Fordham is a first-time contributor to the women's devotional book project. She is a native of Finland who served the Lord as a missionary in eastern Africa for nine years with her husband and two daughters. A retired teacher, she writes from Austell, Georgia. She loves to walk and sings in the shower. **May 15.**

Edith C. Fraser is a wife, mother, educator, and counselor. In addition to her teaching at Oakwood

College she has provided counseling services to individuals and groups in her community and is a crisis counselor for Mothers Against Drunk Driving. She has provided services as a consultant, workshop presenter, and family educator throughout the United States and Canada. **May 24.**

Prema Gaikwad is the head of the Elementary Education Department and teaches in the Graduate School of Education at Spicer Memorial College in India. She has written lessons for the *Cornerstone*, a Bible teachers' resource. Currently she is writing a series of Bible textbooks for her denomination. Her husband is the vice president for academic affairs at Spicer. They have two teenage boys. **Jan. 9.**

Norma C. Galiza and her husband are the grandparents of three grandchildren and have two more on the way. They have four adult children. Norma is currently working as an administrative secretary-cashier. Writing has been one of her favorite activities in addition to music, reading, sewing, and organizing various events. **July 30, Sept. 17.**

Edna Maye Gallington lives in Riverside, California, and works in communications. She is a graduate of La Sierra University and has taken public relations studies at the University of California at Riverside. She enjoys playing the piano, creative writing, hiking, and working in her church. **Oct. 30.**

Margy Asher Gemmell is a retired English teacher living in California. She's the mother of three children and grandmother of six. Margy enjoys writing, reading, babies, and exercise. She is an elder in her local church in charge of senior members, is active in women's ministries, and helps conduct a weekly Bible study group for women. **May 5.**

Lila Lane George is an artist, mother of two sons, and grandmother of six. Her hobbies include reading, hiking, and swimming. She and her husband have a ministry called Arizona Evangelism. **Jan. 28.**

Marybeth Gessele and her pastor husband live in Oregon and are the parents of two young adult sons. She is a home economics major and enjoys homemaking, sewing, cooking, crafts, and her country garden. She is also a caregiver for elderly people. **Mar. 10.**

Georgette Gindi lived with her family in Kuwait until the outbreak of the Gulf War, when she returned to her native Egypt. A successful businesswoman, she is also active in her local church. Georgette is the director of women's ministries for her denomination in Egypt, a post she holds voluntarily. **Apr. 15.**

Evelyn Glass is a wife, mother, grandmother, and farmer. She is the women's ministries director for the Mid-America Union of Seventh-day Adventists and serves as an elder and clerk at her church. Her interests include folk painting, refinishing furniture, public speaking, and writing for local and state newspapers as well as Christian publications. **Jan. 10, June 12, July 19, Aug. 9.**

Kathryn Gordon at the time of this writing worked as a medical social worker. She enjoys gardening, windsurfing, and once had a close encounter with a moose in Canada. **Apr. 3.**

Sarah Boules Goudah is an Egyptian currently working in Nicosia, Cyprus. She is an active youth leader in her church and loves singing. She used to sing as a soloist with the Praise Team in Egypt and has recorded 10 albums with various groups and helped in the translating and preparing of the Arabic songbook *The Power of Praise.* **Sept. 19.**

Carrol Grady lives with her pastor husband in the Northwest. She is a secretary and edits three newsletters in her "spare" time, serves in her church as an elder and as pianist for the choir, and has started an AIDS ministry. The love of her life is Jesus, and the loves of her life are her husband, children, and grandchildren; quilting; writing; and playing the piano. **Feb. 9.**

Mary Jane Graves since retirement has started a library as part of the women's ministries program in her church and has more than 700 books, cassettes, and videos cataloged. She and her husband have two grown sons and two young granddaughters, and deliver Meals on Wheels once a week. She likes reading, writing, gardening, and trying new recipes. **July 3, Sept. 23, Oct. 29.**

Ellie Green is the president of Frederick Nursing Consultants. She's a prolific writer and full-time lecturer who enjoys speaking at Christian women's retreats. Her hobbies are oil painting, watercolors, chalk painting, crocheting, and knitting. She and her husband, a rocket scientist for NASA, have two grown children. **Dec. 30.**

Carol Joy Greene is the wife of a retired pastor, mother of three grown children, and the proud grandmother of four. She and her husband currently live in Florida. Side by side they spent almost 50 years of ministry in Jamaica, the Bahamas, Canada, and Hawaii. **May 2, July 17.**

Glenda-mae Greene is the assistant vice president for student services at Andrews University in Michigan. A third-generation educator, she has taught at all levels, from kindergarten through college, and has spoken to various church groups on women's and singles issues. Glenda-mae loves photography, making tapestry, and taking long walks along shorelines. A devoted Scrabble player, she enjoys words but most important, The Word. **Feb. 6, Mar. 20, Apr. 16, May 9, June 25, July 25, Oct. 2.**

Janet M. Greene and her husband live in Florida with their two young daughters. Janet is an avid photographer, a cardiovascular nurse, and a part-time piano teacher. She is actively involved wherever she hopes it will make a difference. **Apr. 25.**

Meibel Mello Guedes writes from Brazil, where she is the director of women's ministries for the Central Brazil Union Conference of Seventh-day Adventists. She and her husband, an evangelist and pastor, have two children. **May 25.**

Hannah A. Guerrero is a registered nurse who is in the food retailing business. She has lived with her missionary parents in Bangladesh, Sri Lanka, and Uganda. She enjoys reading, music, and collecting pig bric-a-brac, coins, and bank notes from around the world. **June 8.**

Corinne A. Gurney writes from southern California. She is married and works for a major manufacturing company. She has held many church offices and is currently active in women's ministries. An avid crafter, she especially enjoys quilting, counted cross-stitch, and knitting. **June 10.**

Alberta Hack is a wife, mother, piano teacher, music committee member, church pianist, school board member, and editor of her church's publication for women. Her interests are flowers, music, and decorating her home. She has worked in the children's departments of her church for 21 years. **Sept. 2.**

Dessa Weisz Hardin is married and has three adult children. She enjoys traveling to visit her daughters living in Europe. Other interests include volunteering in school reading programs, writing, reading, and discovering a new life in the state of Maine. **Aug. 5, Nov. 5.**

Martha Hardy-Lee is a licensed marriage, family, and child therapist in private practice. She serves as an elder in her church. She enjoys singing, gardening, reading, meeting people, and family gatherings. **Jan. 22, May 8.**

Laura Hartmann and her pastor husband live in Michigan's Upper Peninsula. They have three grown children and two "grandcats." She is the office manager for the Houghton County Fair. Laura gets to be a child again and enjoy the fair all the time. **Aug. 1.**

Ann Van Arsdell Hayward has retired in North Carolina after 30 years in the healthcare industry. She is an active worker in her church and likes reading and sight-seeing. **Feb. 20, Aug. 22.**

Helen Lingscheit Heavirland and her husband live in Oregon, where she spends her time in homemaking, Bible study, bookkeeping, gardening, birdwatching, reading, writing, songwriting, and singing. She has had more than 100 manuscripts published in a large variety of magazines and has contributed to several books. **Jan. 21, June 11, Nov. 19.**

Ursula M. Hedges is a secondary school teacher/administrator. Born of missionary parents in India, she has given 10 years of mission service in the Pacific with her Australian husband, as well as many more years in Australia and New Zealand. Involved in church activities and leadership, Ursula has also published books, stories, and articles. She enjoys interior design, reading, producing dramas, sewing, cooking, and writing. Her family provides her with great pleasure. **Feb. 11, Aug. 31.**

Edna Heise is a retired teacher and the wife of a retired minister. She has three adult children and lives in Port Macquarie, a seaside town in New South Wales, Australia. **July 16.**

Kyna Hinson, a journalist and assistant college professor, is involved in women's ministries through her local church and conference. She is a published writer and enjoys embroidery, reading, baking, and working with teenagers. **Dec. 22.**

Elaine Hoilette is a supervisor for student accounts at Andrews University in Michigan. She and her husband have worked together in pastoral ministry for more than 20 years. They have one young adult daughter. **July 12.**

Karen Holford writes from England, where she is a pastor's wife and the mother of three young children. She works part-time as an occupational therapist in a head injury rehabilitation clinic. Karen is the author of *The Loneliest Grief*, a book about miscarriage recovery, and *Please, God, Make My Mummy Nice*, a book about finding God in the crazy moments of motherhood. **Jan. 11, Feb. 19, Mar. 21, Apr. 18, June 6.**

Tami Horst is the women's ministries director for the Pennsylvania Conference of Seventh-day Adventists. She also serves in her local church as head deaconess and women's ministries coordinator. She enjoys speaking, writing, bicycling, walking, and spending time with her friends and family. She and her husband have two sons. **Feb. 28, Apr. 6, Nov. 1.**

Lorraine Hudgins is retired in Glendora, California. She is an elder in her church and writes for various publications and special projects. She has written two books of devotional poems: *Almost Home* and *Going Home Together*. **Jan. 25, Feb. 10, Mar. 9, Apr. 13, Apr. 30, May 14, June 19, Oct. 17, Dec. 23, Dec. 28.**

Ramona L. Hyman, a writer and performance artist, is also an assistant professor of English at Oakwood College in Alabama. She is the singles ministry leader at the Oakwood College church. She also enjoys creating crafts, sewing, and cooking. **May 17.**

Kathy Isaacs is a mother of four children and an LPN working in geriatrics. She loves music, and the Lord has blessed her with 44 songs. She enjoys sharing these songs with others; playing the piano, violin, and guitar; singing; and learning more about music. She also enjoys crafts and gardening. **Dec. 9.**

Charlotte Ishkanian is the editor of a series of denominational mission story magazines for adults, teens, and children. She lives in the Washington, D.C., metropolitan area and is the mother of three young adults. Charlotte is actively involved in children's ministries in her home church. **June 15.**

Anita Jacobs is an editorial assistant for *Listen* magazine, a positive-lifestyle magazine for teens. She and her husband have three adult children and two grandchildren. Her hobbies include cross-stitching, quilting, reading, and traveling. **May 1.**

Lois E. Johannes is retired from mission service in Pakistan, India, Singapore, Okinawa, and the Caribbean, as well as several institutions in the United States. Now living in Loma Linda, California, she serves as a treasurer and telephone ministry member at her local church. **Nov. 9.**

Birthe Kendel, a native of Denmark, writes from St. Albans, England. A minister's wife and the mother of two teenage daughters, she is the director of children's ministries and women's ministries for the Trans-European Division of Seventh-day Adventists. **Oct. 31, Dec. 31.**

Stacey Kennedy lives in northern California with her husband and two daughters. She has just written a vegetarian cookbook for children and enjoys spending time with friends and family, cooking, crafting, camping, and antiques. **July 26.**

Marilyn King writes from Oregon, where she and her husband live in retirement. In addition to being a wife, mother, grandmother, and great-grandmother, Marilyn is a registered nurse with a master's degree in business. She enjoys family and homemaking, music, nature, her church, teaching Bible, and working in health evangelism. **Dec. 4.**

Patty Knittel is a part-time assistant office manager in Oregon, where she lives with her husband and two children. She currently serves on the women's ministries committee of the Oregon Conference and has leadership positions in the women's ministries and children's departments at her church. Reading, gardening, and sports are her favorite pastimes. **Feb. 18, June 5, Aug. 7.**

Marion E. Knox lives in Hendersonville, North Carolina, with her retired pastor husband. They have five grown children, 11 grandchildren, and four great-grandchildren. Marion loves children and has spent many years working with the Pathfinders and children's departments of the many churches they've pastored in New England and Bermuda. She enjoys knitting, birding, raising African violets, traveling, and writing. **Apr. 2, Apr. 20.**

Hepzibah G. Kore is a minister's wife in Bangalore, India, where she is the coordinator for women's ministries and Shepherdess International, as well as the director for the children's ministries and family life departments of the South India Union Section of Seventh-day Adventists. She has a son and a daughter. Hepzibah enjoys reading and working with women. **Aug. 8, Nov. 23.**

Patricia Mulraney Kovalski has recently retired after teaching for 38 years. She teaches a Bible class and is the women's ministries coordinator at her local church. She and her husband have two adult children and three grandchildren. Her favorite hobbies are traveling, ceramics, and reading. **Apr. 27.**

Teresa Krum, a registered nurse, is a pioneer missionary on one of the outer islands of Chuuk, Micronesia. Her work involves visiting the villages, giving medical care through small clinics, and assisting her husband in church activities. She enjoys playing the guitar and spending time with her husband and two young daughters. **May 22.**

Kay Kuzma is a wife, mother of three, and the president of Family Matters, a media ministry providing services to families. A teacher for 25 years, she now has a syndicated daily radio feature, a weekly television broadcast, and a free quarterly newspaper, *Family Times*. She has written more than a dozen books. **Jan. 18.**

Eileen E. Lantry, from northern Idaho, is a librarian, teacher, homemaker, pastor's wife, and missionary. Including her latest volunteer assignment in Thailand, she has served 15 years in various Asian countries. Eileen has authored 15 books and loves nature study, gardening, hiking, and cross-country skiing. **Jan. 6, Aug. 11.**

Mabel Latsha was born in Minnesota and traveled by covered wagon to Montana, and later to California. She and her husband have one son, five grandchildren, and eight great-grandchildren. She enjoys writing and has two published books, as well as articles in numerous magazines and newspapers. Now legally blind, she lives in College Place, Washington. **Mar. 26, Nov. 6.**

Gina Lee is the author of more than 400 published stories, articles, and poems. She enjoys working at the local library, teaching a writing class, and caring for her four cats. **Jan. 24, Mar. 31, June 2.**

Gwen Lee is retired from federal employment. She enjoys traveling the world and driving around the U.S.A. in her motor home, as well as photography, quilting, and playing with her computer. She is head deaconess of her church, works with Community Services, and volunteers for other church-related projects. **Mar. 7, Aug. 12, Aug. 24.**

Gerita Liebelt writes from Pueblo, Colorado, where she is a registered nurse, pastor's wife, and homemaker. She has written a book, and is a youth and Vacation Bible School leader in her local church. Her devotional first appeared in *The Heart of the Home*, a newsletter for stay-at-home moms. **July 5.**

Bessie Siemens Lobsien is a retired librarian who served in Pakistan, Hong Kong, and Mexico, as well as in the United States. Since the age of 16 she has had her poems and articles published in several church papers and in poetry collections. **Apr. 19.**

June Loor, a retired registered nurse, has been married to a minister for almost 50 years. She greatly enjoys her five grandchildren, camping at the beach, walking in the mountains, and serving the Lord in her local church. **June 24.**

Phyllis Thompson MacLafferty is an 86-year-old retired teacher-missionary and the widow of a pastor-missionary, having spent 18 years in Hawaii and Brazil. Her son is a college computer teacher, and her daughter teaches music. Phyllis still assists in Community Services and primary Sabbath school at her church. She has five grandchildren and three great-grandchildren. **Aug. 4.**

Pat Madsen travels a lot, is superintendent at her local church, and leads an evening study group. She has been a contributor to several of the women's devotional books and to her local church paper. She was editor in chief of her school paper for two years. **Jan. 30, Mar. 6, May 19, June 7, Nov. 11.**

Hazel Malcolm, mother of two, is a retired elementary school teacher living in Maryland. She is the communication secretary and a greeter for her church and enjoys reading, her children, people, cooking, and traveling. Her hobbies are photography, her flower garden, and bird-watching. **Apr. 26.**

Ann Maloney-Halim and her husband live in Lincoln, Nebraska, where she home-schools her two children and is a full-time stay-at-home mom. Ann is the editor/producer of a newsletter, *The Heart of the Home*, for stay-at-home moms. She serves her local church as an elder and enjoys biking, camping, reading, and sewing. She is currently doing an independent study course on naturopathy. **Mar. 25, June 17.**

Sherry Manison taught school for seven years and was a Bible worker in New Orleans for three years. She is currently working at the Review and Herald Publishing Association and enjoys camping, music, gardening, and some sports. **Nov. 20, Dec. 20.**

Eunice Mason, originally from the United Kingdom, is an accountant with 16 years of mission service. She is also a Bible instructor and is currently one of the teachers of the baptismal class at her church in Pinetown, South Africa. Eunice prepares the quarterly conference newsletter on a voluntary basis. She is a grandmother who enjoys knitting, sewing, and gardening. **Mar. 22.**

Jamisen Matthews is a transcriptionist for a nursing agency in Connecticut. She is a deaconess in her church, actively working with earliteens, lay activities, women's ministries, and the hospitality committee. Jamisen's many interests include houseplants, baking, in-line skating, and archaeology. **Aug. 23.**

Mary Maxson has been in pastoral ministry with her husband for 25 years and has her own "Kleenex ministry." They have two young adult children. She enjoys traveling and understanding other cultures. Mary finds pleasure in volunteering as a hospital chaplain, reading, walking, and music, and her favorite pastimes are arranging silk flowers and working in her flower garden. She loves popcorn. **Apr. 28, Apr. 29.**

Maxine McAdoo, a retired Iowa elementary teacher, is the mother of adult twin sons. She stays busy in her home church, is past president of Iowa Community Services, and is involved in teaching adult reading through the Laubach literacy program. Maxine volunteers on the county cancer board, a nursing home committee, and serves as an historical museum tour guide. **Dec. 12.**

Wilma McClarty is an English and speech professor at Southern University of Seventh-day Adventists, a wife, and the mother of two. She is a public speaker and writer who has received many honors and awards, one of the most recent being the Sears-Roebuck Teaching Excellence and Campus Leadership Award for 1991. **Apr. 7, Apr. 8, July 15, Dec. 5.**

Maria G. McClean, originally from Barbados, lives in Canada with her husband and daughter. She is a registered nurse and an elder in her local church. She enjoys writing, reading, lecturing, music, working with youth, and spending time with family and relatives. **Mar. 3, July 23, Oct. 22.**

Patsy Murdoch Meeker has written for church papers for 25 years. Patsy was widowed for the second time in July 1996. She has three sons, three stepchildren, 10 grandchildren, and 10 great-grandchildren. Patsy lives in California and enjoys writing, reading, photography, and helping at church. **Sept. 22, Dec. 27.**

Retta Michaelis writes from Loma Linda, California, where she lives with her health educator husband and two teenage daughters. She works part-time as a medical technologist at the Loma Linda University Medical Center Blood Bank and is active in her church and community. Her interests include reading, writing, Bible study, and spending time with her family. **June 22, Oct. 24.**

Marcia Mollenkopf is a first-time contributor. She wrote these submissions while living in Klamath Falls, Oregon. **Jan. 16, July 14.**

Valerie Hamel Morikone writes from West Virginia, where she is a stay-at-home mom. She home-schools her two children and is the leader and teacher of the primary children's department at her local church. Valerie enjoys reading, crocheting, and playing the piano. **May 23.**

Bonnie Moyers likes to write, walk, curl up with a good book, and cook nutritious meals. She works as a certified nursing assistant, musician, and freelance writer. Bonnie and her husband live in Virginia, where she is active in church work. They have two grown children. **July 9, Oct. 18.**

Lillian Musgrave and her family have made their home in northern California for more than 35 years. She is actively involved with the HIV spiritual support organization in her area and has established a parents' support group. When time allows, she enjoys writing (including poetry), music, and church and family activities. **Dec. 21.**

Diane R. Musten, at the time of this writing, was the administrative secretary in the Ministerial Association of the General Conference of Seventh-day Adventists. She not only collects giraffes, but likes to read and enjoys gourmet cooking, plants, and activities associated with art and music. Diane has one grown daughter, a son-in-law, and one grandson. **June 4, Sept. 21.**

Bienvisa Ladion Nebres comes from the Philippines but writes from Zaire, where she works as an office secretary in the district auditing service of her world church. She enjoys teaching, church work, music, poetry, and stamps. **Oct. 25.**

Joyce Neergaard and her husband recently returned to the United States after serving as missionaries in the Middle East for seven years. They are living in Redlands, California, where Joyce is pursuing a master's degree in international public health. **Dec. 7.**

Anne Elaine Nelson is a retired elementary teacher living in Michigan. She now does the bookkeeping for her husband's two businesses. They have four children and 11 grandchildren. Anne, a book author, is active in her local church and teaches the teen Bible class. Her favorite activities are music, sewing, crafts, traveling, photography, and creating memories with her grandchildren. **Mar. 27.**

Julia Norcott, the assistant editor of *Ministry* magazine, is a wife and the mother of two adult daughters. She is an elder in her local church, is an avid reader, and enjoys walking and her family. **Feb. 7.**

Mabel Rollins Norman, wife, mother, and grandmother, resides in Avon Park, Florida. She has been published in a number of magazines, several newspapers, and two women's devotional books. She and her husband teach a biweekly prison Bible class. She enjoys sewing, crocheting, knitting, oil painting, reading, listening to good music, and sending encouraging cards and letters. **Feb. 17, Apr. 23, July 11, Sept. 1, Oct. 27, Nov. 12.**

Connie Wells Nowlan is a mother (biological and adoptive) and wife, has been an English teacher, a girls' dean in boarding academies, a preschool teacher and director, and always a writer. Her devotionals are the result of her experiences in her varying professions. **June 9.**

Gisele Nyembwe is a first-time contributor to the women's devotional book project. She is an English teacher in Zambia. **Feb. 27.**

Hephzi Ohal was born in India and came to the United States in 1962. She and her husband have three grown children. She is an executive secretary at the International Monetary Fund in Washington, D.C., has served her local church as a deaconess, and enjoys reading and traveling. **Sept. 24, Nov. 27.**

Erika Olfert was born in Yugoslavia and migrated to Canada as a teenager. She and her pastor husband have been missionaries in India, but now live in Washington State. They have two grown sons. She is a nurse, works as a consultant and teacher, and is the youth and women's ministries leader at her church. When time permits, she enjoys oil painting, sewing, knitting, swimming, bicycling, singing, and housecleaning. **Nov. 29.**

Edna May Olsen has lived in England nearly seven years since her husband's retirement from the United States Army. Her three daughters and her granddaughters live in California. She is involved in her small church and is a published writer. Her hobbies include reading, writing, and hiking. **July 24.**

Jemima D. Orillosa is from Africa. She is a teacher by profession, but is currently employed as an administrative secretary and is the acting children's ministries director for her denominational headquarters in Nicosia, Cyprus. Her hobbies include playing with children, visiting senior citizens, entertaining, reading, and cooking. **Apr. 22.**

Rose Otis, formerly the director of women's ministries for the General Conference of Seventh-day Adventists, is now vice president for ministries, North American Division of Seventh-day Adventists. She began the women's devotional book project and edited the first six. She enjoys water sports with her family, writing, and being home. **Jan. 1, Apr. 24, July 1, Sept. 6.**

Hannele Ottschofski is a pastor's wife and mother of four daughters. Born in Finland, she grew up in Sweden and England and has spent most of her life in Germany. She enjoys music, books, and sewing, and would like to have time for writing and other creative things. **Aug. 14, Sept. 12, Nov. 10.**

Eleanor Owen resides in Pennsylvania with her husband. She is the mother of eight children and is a grandmother. **Apr. 4.**

Ofelia Pangan has three grown children, four granddaughters, and one grandson. She helps her husband, who pastors a district of two churches in central California. Ofelia likes gardening, reading, walking, sewing, traveling, and taking care of her grandchildren. **Oct. 11, Dec. 25.**

Revel Papaioannou is a pastor's wife with four grown sons and four grandchildren. She cares for her husband's two aunts, ages 98 and 84. Hobbies include fell walking, aerobics, stamp and coin collecting, and gardening. **Nov. 26.**

Jill Warden Parchment is a retired physician's wife and a former editor of the Southeast Asia Union *Messenger*. She has taught in many countries. Besides academics, she enjoys coaching sports, synchronized swimming, and choreography. **Feb. 21.**

Gwen Pascoe is trained in horticulture, but is currently studying for an arts degree, majoring in history at the University of Melbourne in Australia. She greatly enjoys playing with words. Most of her writing has been for children; she has 15 published titles. **Oct. 15.**

Sonia Paul is a wife and the mother of two, as well as the director of student housing at Oakwood College in Huntsville, Alabama. She still manages to find time to write and enjoys literature, writing, refinishing antiques, cooking, and entertaining. **July 22.**

Julia Pearce chairs the Nursing Department at Pacific Union College, Angwin, California. A wife and community worker with interests in church and health education, she is also a consultant in women's health and gives presentations on health and women's history. She enjoys reading, sewing, writing, and traveling. **Feb. 26.**

Lori Peckham is editor of *Insight* magazine at the Review and Herald Publishing Association, Hagerstown, Maryland. She and her husband are youth leaders in their local church and live in Falling Waters, West Virginia. She enjoys jet-skiing, snorkeling, and traveling. **Feb. 3, July 21, Dec. 27.**

Eunice Peverini writes from Thousand Oaks, California. She and her husband, the speaker/director of the *LaVoz de la Esperanza* radio ministry, have three adult children and five grandchildren. She enjoys community work, gardening, sewing, flower arranging, crafts, interior decorating, reading, and accompanying her husband in his ministry. **July 8, Dec. 6.**

Kathleen Stearman Pflugrad enjoys outdoor activities and information gathering. She and her husband currently live in Grayling, Michigan. They have enjoyed God's protection in traveling to all 50 states of the U.S.A. **Sept. 13.**

Felicia Phillips is the wife of an Adventist Development and Relief Agency director and the mother of three college student sons. Felicia has a master's degree in theology and is a chaplain at Manila

Sanitarium and Hospital in the Philippines. She serves as an elder in her church and enjoys preaching, teaching, giving Bible studies, and homemaking. **June 28, July 29.**

Diana Pittenger is married and the mother of two teenage children. A former radiologic technologist, she has retrained as a certified massage therapist. She enjoys teaching the youth at church, working with women's ministries, and participating in a prison ministry. In her spare time she gardens, watches birds, reads, and collects books and porcelain birds. **Sept. 9.**

Birdie Poddar writes from northeastern India. She is the wife of a retired communication director, mother of three grown children (one of whom died in early 1997), and grandmother to three grandsons. She worked as an elementary teacher, cashier, cashier accountant, and statistician before retiring in 1991. Sewing, gardening, and composing poems are some of her hobbies. **Feb. 22.**

Jeanne d'Harimalala Rasoanindrainy is registrar, librarian, and secretary at a seminary in Mauritius in the Indian Ocean. She is the women's ministries and family life coordinator at the seminary church and has prayer meeting with children on Wednesdays. Her hobbies are reading, writing, gardening, and her grandsons. **Aug. 26.** ·

Carolyn Rathbun-Sutton writes from Hagerstown, Maryland. She taught school for 25 years before becoming the editor of *Guide* magazine. Carolyn enjoys parenting, music, and caving. **Dec. 3.**

Julie Reynolds, a registered nurse, is a full-time homemaker and mother living in North Carolina. She is the women's ministry coordinator for her area. Her favorite activities include gardening, hiking in the mountains, walking on the seashore, and playing with her children. **Nov. 15.**

Jill Hines Richards enjoys cross-stitch, bird-watching, reading, crafts, skiing, and interior design. She lives in Montana with her husband, a teacher at Mount Ellis Academy. Jill is working on her doctorate in curriculum instruction. **Oct. 5, Nov. 2.**

Lynda Mae Richardson is an office professional and freelance writer from Troy, Michigan. She enjoys computers, singing, writing, and nature. She has a 12-year-old son, Nathan. **Jan. 13, Sept. 30.**

Rowena Rick, a former Seventh-day Adventist General Conference associate treasurer, is now retired and living in Pennsylvania. Her favorite hobby is gardening. **Jan. 12.**

Kay D. Rizzo is a freelance writer living in central California. She is the author of many books; manuscripts 31 and 32 are soon to be released. She also writes a monthly column for *Signs of the Times* and *Listen* magazines and hosts *The Family Hour* on KARM-FM radio. She serves as an elder, youth leader, and minister of music in her local church. Kay and her husband have two married daughters, who are professional musicians. **Jan. 4, May 16, Aug. 15, Nov. 25.**

Barbara Roberts is a stay-at-home grandma who enjoys her grandchildren. She is the head elder and superintendent at her local church. In her spare time Barbara grows orchids, sews, and writes. **July 2.**

Sharyn Robichaux wrote her story from Louisiana. She is a secretary and the mother of three adult daughters. **Nov. 30.**

Jean Reiffenstein Rothgeb and her husband are retired, but they both work in the clinic of an orthopedic surgeon in Utah. They have two daughters, four grandchildren, and two great-grandchildren. She loves the outdoors, good music, and having guests. She also enjoys sewing and handwork. Most of all, she loves her church and being able to serve her Lord in any way He asks. Jean always has an open door for anyone who needs to use their "Elijah" room, and it is rarely empty. **Dec. 11.**

Terrie E. Ruff is an assistant professor of social work at Southern Adventist University in Collegedale, Tennessee. An active volunteer in her community, she enjoys traveling, singing, and public speaking. **May 13, July 20, Dec. 26.**

Sheila Birkenstock Sanders is a widow living in the Napa Valley, where she is a counselor for mentally disabled adults. She enjoys people, photography, music, being out in nature, and working as the school superintendent at her church. Sheila is a mother with two daughters and three grandchildren. She also has a stepson, a stepdaughter, and five stepgrandchildren. **Sept. 16.**

Susana Schulz lives in Argentina, where her husband is the president of River Plate Adventist University. She is the former women's ministries director for the South American Division of the Seventh-day Adventist Church. She is now teaching and is the director of the university counseling center. She has three daughters and enjoys art, music, traveling, reading, gardening, and walking with her husband in the evenings. **Feb. 23.**

Marie H. Seard, retired, is a second-time contributor to the devotional book. She has given many hours of volunteer service at her church's world headquarters. She edits her local church newsletter and is active in the church's women's ministries department and in civic associations. She enjoys sending cards, writing, reading, traveling, and working on the computer. Marie and her husband have one adult son. **Apr. 12, Oct. 8, Nov. 24.**

Patricia L. Shinskia lives in Denver, Colorado, with her husband. She is an intake technician with the Denver district attorney's office and works with first-time juvenile offenders. She teaches an adult Bible class in her local church and enjoys singing, listening to music, writing poetry, reading, and walking. **Jan. 27.**

Rose Neff Sikora is a registered nurse who enjoys writing, camping, helping others, and spending time with her three grandchildren. She and her husband live in Hendersonville, North Carolina. **May 20.**

Sandra Simanton, a first-time contributor, writes from Texas, where she is a social worker. **May 30, Aug. 20.**

Brenda Simnett-Pratt taught languages in high school in England and was a social worker before she immigrated to the United States in 1975. A former nursing home administrator and college professor, she left education to take up body therapy and natural healing. She is a member of Mensa. **Feb. 1.**

Carol J. Smith and her husband live in Washington State with their two sons. She works in long-term nursing care as a consultant/educator. Their family enjoys water and snow skiing, canoeing, swimming, and reading. She is active in women's ministries, Bible studies, and teaching children. **Nov. 28.**

Ethel Footman Smothers, a first-time contributor, writes from Grand Rapids, Michigan. She is a published poet and author of two children's books. Ethel is the mother of four daughters and has four grandchildren. **Aug. 18.**

Annie Souare-Ndiaye is a wife, mother of one son, and a full-time worker living in Maryland. She comes from the Ivory Coast and enjoys reading, swimming, writing, and helping others. **Sept. 14.**

Marie Spangler, founder of Shepherdess International (a support system for ministers' wives), is a retired teacher, mother of two adult children, and a minister's wife. She is a published writer whose special interests include music, memory books, people, pastors' wives, and early childhood development. **Mar. 18.**

Elva E. Springer is a retired medical assistant and X-ray technician whose hobbies are camping, boating, flying, writing, and church activities. She has three children, eight grandchildren, and six great-grandchildren. She and her husband of 53 years still take their annual 5,000-mile motorcycle trip. **Dec. 16.**

Ardis Dick Stenbakken is the associate director of women's ministries for the General Conference. She was an Army chaplain's wife for nearly 24 years until her husband "retired" to work at the General Conference of Seventh-day Adventists. They have an adult daughter, son, and daughter-in-law. Ardis enjoys church work, crafts, reading, travel, and public speaking. **Jan. 17, Mar. 4, Apr. 17, June 16, July 31, Aug. 17, Oct. 26.**

Patricia Stock is a first-time contributor. She writes from her home among the fields of ripening grain in Oklahoma. **June 20.**

Iris L. Stovall enjoys writing and videography. She is an audio-visual technician, and an elder at her church and works in women's ministries at the General Conference of Seventh-day Adventists. Several of her articles have been published in religious magazines. She is married and the mother of an adult son and a teenage son and daughter. **July 13, Aug. 21, Oct. 19, Dec. 8.**

Laura Lee Swaney is studying to be a certified alcoholism counselor and plans to counsel adult survivors of incest. Her goal is for a ministry helping battered women and people with drug addictions find freedom in Jesus. She and her husband are both new writers for Christ. **Aug. 28.**

Loraine Sweetland is a teacher for Home Study International; is a book reviewer for *Library Journal*; has her own business, Information Problem Solvers; and enjoys computers, gardening, reading, and antiques. **Dec. 13, Dec. 18.**

Arlene Taylor is risk manager at St. Helena Hospital in northern California and founder and president of her own nonprofit educational foundation. An internationally known speaker and brain function consultant, she is the creator and presenter for Brainworks Unlimited, a new four-day live-in program at the health center at St. Helena. **Jan. 14, July 4, Oct. 10, Dec. 13, Dec. 17.**

Stella Thomas is an administrative secretary at the Office of Global Mission at the General Conference of Seventh-day Adventists. She is married and has two children. Her hobbies are cooking and shopping. Stella has a great burden for the young people of her church. **Sept. 11.**

Stella Thompson is on the adjunct faculty of Cameron University in Oklahoma and teaches classes in

English composition. She also teaches Discover, a weekly young adult class. Her life goal is to learn new ways of knowing Jesus Christ and sharing His love. **May 29.**

Diane J. Thurber is a pastor's wife and the mother of two boys. She assists part-time in the Bible Labs Department of the Michigan Conference of Seventh-day Adventists, then enjoys the remainder of the day with her sons. Her hobbies include piano, flute, cooking, baking, cross-stitch, and golf. At church she coordinates the greeting ministry, visits members, and assists with children's church. **Aug. 30.**

Marguerite Thygeson, a native of Washington, D.C., lives in Maryland and works as an analyst/programmer for Information Systems Services at the General Conference of Seventh-day Adventists. During the school year she spends two evenings a week tutoring for the Prepare Our Youth program. Her hobbies include vocal and instrumental music, knitting, brainteasers, and getting near the ocean and mountains whenever possible. **July 27.**

Ella Tolliver is a professor and educational counselor at Solano Community College in California. She is one of the founders of the Women's Spiritual Koinonia, a women's group that has been coordinating weekend retreats, seminars, and training sessions for 12 years. She has three adult children and six grandchildren. She enjoys reading, traveling, presenting seminars, and organizing special events. **Apr. 10.**

Darlyn Townsend lives at Camp Au Sable in northern Michigan with her husband and two sons. She is the craft director and enjoys swimming, music, flower gardening, nautical decor, making baskets, watching the deer, and riding on her quiet golf cart through the woods. **Nov. 21.**

Lilly Tryon writes from Pennsylvania, where she is a registered nurse and pastor's wife and is the home-schooling mother of two boys. Her interests include doing things with her family, flower gardening, reading, writing, playing the piano, and singing. **Feb. 13, Mar. 24, Oct. 7.**

Olga Valdivia is a wife and mother of three. She writes from Idaho, where she and her family moved 10 years ago. She works as a secretary in the advertising department of the Pacific Press Publishing Association. Olga enjoys jogging, interior decorating, reading, and crafts, and is a published writer. **Feb. 8, Sept. 4.**

Nancy Van Pelt, a certified family life educator and family and consumer science professional, is an author and internationally known speaker. She has written more than 20 books. Her hobbies are getting organized, entertaining, having fun, and quilting. Nancy and her husband live in California and are the parents of three adult children. **Mar. 11, Dec. 29.**

Janis Clark Vance holds a Master of Science degree in educational psychology and a Bachelor of Science degree in nursing, and is a certified rehabilitation counselor. She and her husband have three young adult children. Since 1990 Janis has conducted Take Heart seminars for victims of childhood sexual abuse in the United States and Canada. She enjoys studying her Bible, travel, and needlepoint. **Jan. 29, Mar. 13, Sept. 20.**

Corrine Vanderwerff is a missionary and freelance writer. She enjoys helping others to read and understand the Bible for themselves. She lives in Lubumbashi, Zaire, where her husband is the Adventist Development and Relief Agency director. **Oct. 20.**

Nancy Cachero Vasquez is the volunteer coordinator for the North American Division office at the General Conference of Seventh-day Adventists. She is the wife of one of the division's vice presidents and the mother of three young adult children. Nancy's special interests are reading, writing, crafts, shopping, and baking. **Feb. 2, Mar. 14, June 1.**

Tammy B. Vice writes from Alabama, where she is a wife and the mother of two girls. She leads the children's choir at her church and enjoys writing children's stories and songs in her "spare" time. **Apr. 9.**

Carolyn Voss teaches nursing in an associate degree nursing program. She is married, and enjoys nature, walking, traveling, quilting, and flower gardening. Recently she has had several of her poems published. **Apr. 5.**

Donna Meyer Voth is a wife and the mother of one daughter, a part-time teacher, and the women's ministries coordinator for her church in Michigan. She is also a Reach to Recovery volunteer for the American Cancer Society. Her hobbies include sewing, writing, and traveling. **Dec. 14.**

Mary M. J. Wagoner-Jacobs, from Kingman, Arizona, is a case manager for mentally disabled individuals. She is a Make-A-Wish Foundation board member/wish granter, volunteer justice court mediator, volunteer interpreter for deaf individuals, and church newsletter editor. Mary is a member of Kiwanis and the National Association of Social Workers. Her hobbies are sports and writing. **Sept. 27.**

Celeste perrino Walker is a professional freelance writer living in Vermont with her husband, young son, and new daughter. She has authored hundreds of articles and stories, a Bible study guide, and several books. In her spare time she enjoys hanging out on the CompuServe computer forum, trying to play the violin, painting with watercolors, backpacking, and cross training. **Jan. 19.**

Elizabeth Darby Watson is an associate professor of social work and the director of Genesis, a program for single parents earning a college degree at Andrews University in Michigan. She is a local church elder and women's ministries coordinator, and presents workshops and seminars. The mother of three, she enjoys creative writing, cross-stitch, and letter writing. **Sept. 7.**

Dorothy Eaton Watts is a freelance writer, editor, speaker, and at the time of this writing was the director of women's ministries for the General Conference of Seventh-day Adventists. She was a missionary in India for 16 years, founded an orphanage, has taught elementary school, and has written more than 20 books. Her hobbies include gardening, hiking, and birding (with more than 1,000 in her world total). **Jan. 3, Mar. 8, May 10, Aug. 25, Sept. 8.**

Kit Watts was assistant editor of the *Adventist Review* when she wrote this article. She now directs the La Sierra University Women's Resource Center and is assistant to the president of Southeastern California Conference for communication. She enjoys traveling and photography. **June 29.**

Veyrl Dawn Were writes from South Australia, where she is a homemaker and the mother of an adult son. A nurse by profession, she has served as a missionary in Kenya for eight years. She has written for various religious and professional publications. Hobbies include gardening, bird-watching, cooking, and knitting. Currently sharing leadership with her husband in ADCARE (Adventist Community Care), Veyrl conducts vegetarian cooking demonstrations. **Jan. 15.**

Penny Estes Wheeler is the editor of a new women's magazine, *Women of Spirit*. She is the mother of four adult children and lives in Hagerstown, Maryland, with her husband. She has written eight books and numerous articles for religious publications. Penny enjoys storytelling, flower gardening, and spending time with her family. **Nov. 7.**

Mildred Williams and her husband live in southern California. They have two grown daughters and a granddaughter. Mildred works part-time as a physical therapist and enjoys writing, sewing, gardening, and baby-sitting. She has been published in several religious magazines and has written a book. **June 13, Oct. 9.**

Debby Gray Wilmot is a musician, author, illustrator, and registered nurse living in California with her minister/chaplain husband and two teenage sons. She has taught piano and enjoys composing music, hiking, bodybuilding, playing on a softball team, and acrylic painting. Debby has been commissioned several times to write theme songs for women's groups. She has been associated with a variety of musical groups and has cut a record with Maranatha Singers. **Jan. 7, Mar. 12, Oct. 23.**

JANUARY 1

Throwing Rocks

You will again have compassion on us; you will tread our sins underfoot and hurl all our iniquities into the depths of the sea.
Micah 7:19, NIV.

*H*er note was so full of praise and thanksgiving that I couldn't believe this was the same burdened soul I had met at a women's retreat just a few weeks before. She wrote of God working in her life to provide for her needs; how He had re-arranged circumstances to benefit her; of friends who had come to her rescue more than once. And as I read on, I praised God!

I remembered how she had wept at the retreat when I shared an illustration of a nun who was observed walking along the ocean shore. A man, walking some distance behind her, noticed that she appeared to be involved in some sort of ritual. She would walk a short distance, then stop and reach down into the folds of her habit. Retrieving something, she would turn and throw the object as far as she could into the sea. After some time, the man's curiosity got the best of him, and he picked up his pace in order to catch up with her.

"Excuse me," he said softly, not wanting to startle her. "I've been following you for some time, and I can't help asking what it is that you are doing."

A broad smile spilled across the nun's time-wrinkled face. "Sir," she said in a gentle voice, "I have lived a religious life for decades, but I have come to realize that I have never had a 'rela-tionship' with my Lord. You see, I've been carrying some rocks around in my heart all these years, and since I'm not getting any younger"—she paused, eyes twinkling—"I've decided to get rid of them."

The two strangers stood face-to-face at water's edge as she continued. "So I walk along until I recall some painful memory, past hurt, or cherished sin, and I search my habit for the right size rock to match the pain it's caused me, and then I throw it out to sea. And, sir, I'm not going home until my heart is free of rocks."

The man nodded, realizing he had invited himself along on a very personal journey. Running her fingers over a rather large rock she had taken from her garment, she continued, "This rock-throwing isn't easy. Some of these are big rocks, and others have sharp, jagged edges. But today I'm throwing my rocks in a place where I can never reclaim them again."

And now the card I was reading brought news of another sister who'd brought some rocks with her to a women's retreat. I remembered looking into her troubled face as I spoke. I could see there was a struggle going on in her heart—to throw or not to throw her rocks.

The next day, when the retreat came to a close, she was the first one out of her seat and onto the platform. Her tears dampened my shoulder when she threw her arms around my neck and wept over heartbreaking rocks. She had decided. She would throw rocks too.

Today we begin a new year. A fresh page in the book of life. And I'll dare to ask you the same question that I asked at the women's retreat. Do *you* have any rocks to throw? From personal experience I will caution you that while some rocks will come loose fairly easily, others will need some careful prying in order to avoid a hemorrhage. Still others will be small, pea-sized, gnatty little rocks—like sand in your shoe. But they all need to go! Some may even require help to dislodge. If that's the situation you find yourself in, seek the help of the always-listening Lord, a trusted friend, or a Christian therapist, but determine to start your new year free of energy-draining baggage—rock-free!

ROSE OTIS

JANUARY 2

From Old to New

Therefore, if anyone is in Christ, he is a new creation; the old has gone, the new has come! 2 Cor. 5:17, NIV.

There she lay in the bottom of a box of things my daughter and I were sorting. A once-loved doll, she had been packed away in this box and forgotten for many years. It was a wonder she had been saved at all, because she was covered with grime as if her last bed had been a mud puddle. Her cloth body was tattered and worn. Our first thought was to toss her in the discard pile, as she seemed beyond repair.

Then I thought of my friend Juanita, who has a collection of hundreds of dolls. If anyone could salvage this doll, Juanita would be the one. I dunked the doll in a dishpan of warm sudsy water to remove at least some of the dirt before heading over to Juanita's house.

"Oh, poor baby!" was her immediate reaction as she carefully examined the remains of the doll. "Leave her here and I'll see what I can do."

About three days later there was a knock at the door. When I opened it, there stood Juanita. In her arms was the most beautiful doll, wearing a pink ruffled dress, matching bonnet, and crocheted booties. "Oh, Juanita, that can't be the same doll I gave you!" I exclaimed. "You're a miracle worker!"

But indeed it was the same doll, with face, arms, legs, and hair all scrubbed and an entirely new cloth body. After Juanita finished with her, the doll was a new creation. What once would have been headed for the trash heap now had value.

Jesus can do the same with us. When we feel like a discard, unable to measure up, remember that there is a remedy. There is Someone who can see beneath the grime of sin. No one is worthless in God's sight, no matter how tattered and torn we feel, because in Him we can become new creatures. What an encouragement that Christ is there ready to help when we surrender ourselves to Him!   BETTY J. ADAMS

JANUARY 3

Unexpected Favor

Let us then approach the throne of grace with confidence, so that we may receive mercy and find grace to help us in our time of need. Heb. 4:16, NIV.

*I*t was a beautiful day and all was going as I had planned. Only one more stop to make, and I would be finished with my errands! I congratulated myself on my excellent organization as I pulled into the right lane to make a turn. At that moment I checked the rearview mirror and saw the flashing lights of a police car. *Oh, no! Surely I haven't been speeding! Had I forgotten to signal?* I pulled to the side and rolled down my window, looking up innocently at the frowning policeman.

"Your tags have expired," he announced.

"Oh, I have them," I said cheerily. "We moved here six months ago, and I have the new license plates in the back window. Won't that do?"

"No!" he said, taking out his pad and pen. "They must be displayed properly. I'll have to give you a ticket."

I knew I was at fault. The new plates had arrived three months before, but both Ron and I had been too busy to install them. *Maybe he'll let me off with a warning*, I thought hopefully.

I gulped when I saw my ticket—$130. Tears filled my eyes, and my beautiful day was completely spoiled. I bypassed my last errand and headed home, sniffling all the way. By the time I reached the comfort of my bedroom I was ready for a full-blown cry. Needing a comforting word, I phoned my husband at his office and told him what had happened.

"Charge it to tuition!" Ron laughed.

"My tuition account is overdrawn," I answered. "Could I perhaps charge half to *your* tuition account?" I figured he could take part of the blame, since the car belonged to him as well as to me. After all, I had been waiting for him to install the new plates. Of course, I hadn't bothered to remind him, so I decided half the blame probably was mine, but only half!

"Of course!" he responded. "You can charge the full amount to me! I'll take complete responsibility. You needn't worry any more about it."

I hung up feeling wonderful again! What a kind, generous, understanding, magnanimous, loving husband I had to lift the burden of guilt from my shoulders, to pay my fine. With a burst of thankfulness, I realized that Ron's unexpected favor was an illustration of grace—God's grace.

I opened my journal and wrote, "I am guilty of sins much worse than driving without tags, but the guilt is hard for me to take, the fine impossible for me to pay. Lord, You come along and say, 'Dorothy, you may charge it to *My* account!' And oh, how light and joyous I suddenly feel. Thank You, Lord, thank You!"

DOROTHY EATON WATTS

Almost Heaven

Do not let your hearts be troubled. Trust in God; trust also in me. . . . I am going . . . to prepare a place for you. And if I go and prepare a place for you, I will come back and take you to be with me. John 14:1-3, NIV.

I stepped onto the balcony of our hotel suite and breathed in fresh, clean air laced with the pungent aroma of tropical flowers. Tiny goldfinches hopped across a carefully manicured lawn. Palm branches waved in the cooling trade winds, bunches of bananas clung to trees, aquamarine blue water lapped the coal-black sand. My soul expanded. I closed my eyes and praised my heavenly Father for this breathtaking paradise.

"Thank You, Lord. This is truly heaven," I whispered, not wanting to break the magical spell. Then I heard the engine of the hotel limousine ease to a stop in front. I watched the driver climb out of the shiny silver vehicle, remove a Turkish towel from the trunk, and begin to wipe the automobile's exterior. When he held up the towel for his inspection, it was covered with black soot.

So much for heaven, I thought. My shoulders slumped. Even a tropical paradise has its soot and grime. I shook the imperfection from my mind. "This *is* paradise," I insisted. Later in the day, as I walked along a wooded walk that meandered through the flowering bushes and stately palms, I found a dead bird beneath a hibiscus bush. When I tried to walk barefoot on the sandy beach, the lava rocks cut and bruised my feet.

As I thought about the soot, the dead bird, and the cuts on my feet, I had to admit that while Hawaii, for all its tropical attributes, may be as close as we get to a Garden of Eden on Planet Earth, it still is not heaven.

As pleasing to the senses as the islands may be, no tourist bureau can eradicate the effects of sin from the place. And try as I might to blind myself to reality and focus on the island's perfection, sooner or later I must admit that in this Utopia people still contract AIDS, still die of cancer, still waste their lives on drugs and booze. Drivers still kill little children by drinking and driving. People still abuse their spouses, their children, and their aging parents.

Ever since Eve and her spouse were banished from the garden, people have searched for the perfect land. The search has taken people to the far reaches of the planet and beyond. Today, on a small scale, we search for our own vision of heaven through drugs and alcohol, through sexual liaisons, through money and material things, through age-defying creams, lotions, and surgeries.

Heaven on earth, lotusland, fairyland, Shangri-la, the land of milk and honey, Disneyland, or the land of eternal youth. Alas, humans' paradise can never be perfect.

I leaned on the balcony railing outside my hotel room and sighed. "If only . . ." And then, over the roar of the surf I heard the words of my loving Jesus saying, "Do not let your heart be troubled. Trust in God. Trust in Me. I am going to prepare a place for you."

I smiled to myself. "This place is truly beautiful. Thank You, Lord, for giving me a glimpse of what You have in store for those who love You. A place where pain and death will be history, where there will be no cause for tears, where all will be joyous and filled with light. And we will never die."   KAY D. RIZZO

JANUARY 5

A Way in the Desert

Forget the former things; do not dwell on the past. See, I am doing a new thing! Now it springs up; do you not perceive it? I am making a way in the desert and streams in the wasteland. Isa. 43:18, 19, NIV.

It's the beginning of the new year, and like so many others, I spent some time reflecting on the previous year. Like any other year, it was filled with blessings, accomplishments, problems, and challenges. God was indeed very good to me. I thought about the times when He answered before I called, the times when I received some express answers to prayer, and the times that He just seemed to be saying, "Wait awhile, Andrea." I began to wonder if God was really going to answer those prayers, and why He was taking so long to respond.

As the day progressed, and I kept thinking about those unanswered prayers and my new resolutions, I became a little fearful. There was this vast unknown ahead of me. Questions flooded my mind. Would I be able to cope? Would my plans for relocation materialize? Would I like my new job and my location? Would I be happy with my decision? Would I receive the answers to my unanswered prayers? With the Spirit's guidance I was prompted to take my Bible and read the book of Isaiah. As I read chapter 43, which was so familiar to me, our text for today leaped out at me. I read and reread it. I even read it in several versions to get a deeper understanding of it. I particularly like the paraphrased version in *The Clear Word*: "Don't just think of what I have done in the past and focus on what happened then. Watch for the new thing I'm going to do. It's already beginning to happen. Can't you see it? I will make a road through the wilderness and give you streams in the desert."

This was the reassurance I needed. I felt the peace and comfort of the Holy Spirit as I contemplated the meaning of that text for my life. I then resolved to let this be the motto for the days, weeks, and months that lay ahead. I was reassured that God has an interest in me. As a matter of fact, He has my name engraved in the palm of His hands. Yes, my prayers are in the process of being answered. He's working out everything in His time. My eyes are already discerning the changes!

May you find peace in knowing that He will do the same for you. As you face this new year, remember that the God who led you in the past will be with you in the future. He who has promised is faithful.   ANDREA A. BUSSUE

Nothing Is Impossible

Nothing is impossible with God. Luke 1:37, NIV.

While walking the hot, dusty road that borders Mission College in Thailand, I poured out my problems to God. He knew all about them, but I needed to tell Someone who understood. Maybe He had a solution.

"God, this is January, and the library is to be dedicated the second week of March. You know the librarian just had open-heart surgery. She won't be able to function for six months. Now it's up to me. How can I keep the library operating smoothly, plus all the rest? My work crew needs constant supervision as I teach them to process the new books. It takes so much time to prepare and teach the library science classes, plus cataloging every English book, and there are thousands left to be done. I know the college is short on staff and facing a crisis. I believe You arranged for us to come as volunteer missionaries for just this emergency. Now it's up to You to give me help, God. I can never catalog all those books and put the library in shape in four months by myself. Besides, You know how frustrating it is to do everything through a translator."

At lunchtime my husband announced, "Did you know the business manager's parents arrived from California last night? They'll be here till May. She wants something to keep her busy. I suggested she see you at the library."

The moment I met Wanda I knew she was the answer to my prayer. "No, I've had no training in library science, but I love books and like a challenge."

"Cataloging is difficult, but if you're willing to learn I'm sure I can teach you. How soon do you want to begin?"

"Right now!" she said.

My heart was pounding with excitement and gratitude as I got a set of cataloging books, and we headed for the stacks of waiting books.

"She's amazing!" I told my husband. "She's been cataloging for only a week, and she acts like a professional. Her work is accurate and thorough. If only I didn't have so many interruptions so that I could spend more time doing my part."

"Do you suppose you could teach me, too?" My husband had a twinkle in his eyes.

"But you're swamped with carrying on the work of college president. When could you find more time?"

"In the evenings and on Sunday. I'm interested in business, economics, and social science. I could begin on those books."

Within a few days I realized God had provided another answer right in my own home. Jay did remarkably well. He and Wanda used every spare minute, and we finished by the end of February. The library was in first-class condition, thanks to their efficient help. As I watched the cutting of the ribbon at the dedication ceremony, I praised God for specializing in doing the impossible.   EILEEN E. LANTRY

JANUARY 7

Before and After

And so we are transfigured much like the Messiah, our lives gradually becoming brighter and more beautiful as God enters our lives and we become like him. 2 Cor. 3:18, Message.

I have always enjoyed magazine articles and TV talk shows that use the theme of "before and after." You know what I'm talking about: the ones that take some dowdy, drab, tired-looking individual, and with the skills of a hairstylist, makeup artist, and fashion designer transform the lackluster person into a visual marvel.

Sometimes the change is so strikingly dramatic that it's hard to believe it's the same person. And as I watch the behavior of these made-over individuals, it's easy to see how excited they are with the changes. They not only look different, they act differently—more talkative, bubbly, self-assured. It's as though each one now possesses an inner confidence that says to the world, "If this can happen to me, it can happen to you, too."

Anyone who has experienced a makeover will also tell you that it is extremely important who helps effect the transformation. You don't give yourself over to just anyone. Oh, no! The specialists who are trusted to work on you must be true artists in their areas of expertise with proven track records of success. Thus the ones whose appearance has been changed can say with confidence, "I know someone who can make you look the best you can be. Let me introduce you." And judging from the finished product, there can be no denying that an artist was at work.

Sometimes I don't like the looks of my spiritual self too much. My face wears the lines of anxiety; my shoulders sag under the burdens of modern life; my not-too-fashionable "threads" drape in a most unbecoming fashion. When in times of quietness

I gaze into the mirror of personal reflection, I can't help crying out, "Oh, how I need a transformation!"

To make your inner self, your soul, a beautiful thing, it is important to allow the correct Person to help you. Jesus can help to wash away the sadness of life and give you a radiant inner beauty that will never fade. He can supply a spectacular and most becoming wardrobe of personal graces that will allow you to be perfectly dressed for any occasion. And most important, He will renew your mind, transforming your thinking until you sparkle and glow, a shining example of His artistic skill in the most important "before and after" transformation of all time.

Transform my heart and make me like You.
A beautiful life, Jesus, help me pursue.
I pray for the strength to be all I can be.
May others discover You, Lord, in me.

DEBBY GRAY WILMOT

JANUARY 8

All I Really Need to Know . . .

Each person is given something to do that shows who God is: Everyone gets in on it, everyone benefits. All kinds of things are handed out by the Spirit, and to all kinds of people! The variety is wonderful. 1 Cor. 12:7, Message.

You've probably heard of the book entitled *All I Really Need to Know I Learned in Kindergarten*. Well, I've discovered that all I really need to know I learned in the junior tent at camp meeting this week. The theme was "Spiritual Gifts in the Body of Christ." I was impressed that 10- to 12-year-olds could understand things many adults haven't figured out yet.

The juniors learned that at whatever age they dedicate their lives to God, all their natural or cultivated talents become spiritual gifts to be of service in the body of Christ. It was exciting to see them come forward at the end of the week and share with their peers what their spiritual gifts are.

I was thrilled that kids of this age were understanding their value in God's eyes, discovering the gifts He's given them, and realizing they are an important part of the body of Christ. Some of us "older and wiser" folk still haven't grasped this.

And we women often downplay the gifts God has given us. Some of us even think it's a virtue to deny that we did a job well, or that we have a talent in a certain area. If God has gifted us, who are we to cast a shadow on His gift? Let us graciously accept the compliments people give us, while acknowledging that our gifts are from God.

And don't worry about becoming proud or getting a big head if your self-confidence is rooted in Christ. Actually, it's to His honor and glory for you to be aware of your gifts and to recognize their value to the body of Christ. Then when a need arises, you will with humble confidence say "Here am I, use me" instead of mumbling that you have no gift, or that you would be embarrassed to use your gift because Sister So-and-so does such a better job.

It's human nature for us to compare ourselves with other women. Usually we come out the losers. We're good at criticizing ourselves. That includes underrating, downplaying, and minimizing ourselves. But as God would tell you—and the juniors would second—you are an important part of the body of Christ, and you are needed now.

So all I really need to know I learned in juniors:
1. I am spiritually gifted.
2. I am a special part of the body of Christ.
3. I am needed now.
4. I am more effective as a team member.
5. If I don't use 'em, I lose 'em.
6. Using my spiritual gifts is fun.   HEIDE FORD

My Partnership

And these stones shall be for a memorial unto the children of Israel for ever. Joshua 4:7.

*M*y precious notebooks! I have eight of them now—one for each of the past eight years. Looking at them, I muse, "What a special memorial they are of God's partnership with me!" Indeed, they are like the stones that the Israelites set up as a memorial after crossing the river Jordan.

This is how it all began. Eight years ago the pastor who conducted a Week of Prayer meeting suggested a unique method of personal devotion. He proposed that we use a notebook, along with the Bible, for personal devotion. I was impressed by the simple steps he explained:

"Read thoughtfully through the Bible passage you have selected for the day," said the pastor, "and as you read along prayerfully, you will find a certain verse or verses really 'speaking' to you. This is God's message to you for the day."

He suggested that we write down with a red pen the special verse(s) in a notebook. "Ponder and meditate over the passage that you have written down," he continued. Next was our turn to converse with God. He suggested, "Write your thoughts in another color ink just below the red writing. Thank God for the blessings, share your burdens, and ask for guidance in making decisions."

His ideas enthralled me, and I decided to try them out right away. However, I wasn't sure it would really work for me. That was eight years ago. Looking back now, I have no question that it definitely works. The time that I spent with God (usually in the early part of the morning) is not wasted. God and I are partners in all the endeavors of life.

Of course, there are days when I have not consulted Him. At the end of such a day I can hear myself saying, "I have really blown it today!" I then come back to the forgotten Bible and notebook and realize that He has not forgotten me—I am the one who has forgotten Him. I get the feeling that God is really near, talking to me, and I am talking to Him. The few lines that I log in my notebook, though belated, help me regain closeness with Him.

If you are looking for a way of boosting your relationship with God, why not try this method? Once a notebook is filled, don't discard it, keep it. To me, these notebooks are a memorial of my partnership with God and, like the Israelites' altar of stone, a memorial of God's love and guidance in my life. Sometimes I browse through the pages of an old notebook and relive these experiences. Occasionally I carry these notebooks to class and share a few episodes. My students seemed to be curious, and I hope that some of them have started this useful practice. As for me, I can't help saying, "Thank You, Lord, for Your guidance!"

PREMA GAIKWAD

JANUARY 10

Humps

Sing praise to the Lord, you saints of His, and give thanks at the remembrance of His holy name. . . . Weeping may endure for a night, but joy comes in the morning. Ps. 30:4, 5, NKJV.

While visiting our son and daughter-in-law, we enjoyed watching a video together. The story was of a family of animals. We laughed together at their antics and appreciated the care the parents lavished on their young. Afterward, as we talked about what we had watched, I said, "It's too bad there was the sad part where one of the animals died."

With the wisdom of a 7-year-old, Kyle answered, "Grandma, every good story has to have some humps in it to be good." He moved his hand along in a "humping" motion to illustrate what he was saying.

I have thought about that often when things do not go as smoothly as I think they should. Each of us has many times in our lives when things happen that are not pretty—times when we feel we have gone down a long, humpy road. It may be relationships with our family or friends. Or our financial road may not be smooth. Many things happen that make life uncomfortable—and even sad. Thankfully, there usually comes a time when life is once again smooth and we can live without so many humps. It is these smooth times that rebuild our courage and help us regain the proper perspective of who we are and what life should be. The challenge is to remember that weeping is a "hump" that endures for a night, and joy comes in the morning. Joy that lifts our spirits and gives us cause to praise the Lord and give thanks, not only for the smooth roads but also for the humps that help us grow.

EVELYN GLASS

JANUARY 11

Blossoming in the Ice

He has made everything beautiful in its time. Eccl. 3:11, NIV.

I felt broken inside. I was exhausted from moving and caring for our very active toddler. We had just moved to pastor a new church district. We had wondered why we were being given only one tiny church with fewer than 25 people attending. The reason soon became apparent.

From the very first day I felt that I could cut the atmosphere with a knife. It was a church in pain and turmoil. It was also a church with very clear ideas about the role of the pastor's wife, a role I knew I could not fulfill as a mother of young children.

This had been our third week there, and the thought of ever having to go back to that church filled my heart with horror. I knew I could never really be comfortable there, and whatever I did, someone would criticize me. I felt trapped and miserable. I had come home after the potluck lunch, where my edible contributions had been poked and prodded and hadn't met with their approval. I had inadvertently caused an uproar by taking a dessert and thereby "encouraging people to overindulge."

My husband would be staying at the church all day for one meeting or another, and I was alone. I put the toddler in the buggy and decided to go for a walk. We wrapped up warm against the January cold and started out to explore our new neighborhood. It was sort of fun taking new turns, not knowing where we would end up. We discovered a bridge over a railroad track where we could wave to friendly train engineers who would blow the train's whistle in response. We found a lovely park and some pretty lanes, but still I felt heavy and overwhelmed.

"Dear Father," I prayed, "please help me to survive here somehow." Suddenly I noticed a beautiful tree. It was covered in frothy white blossoms, even in January, even in the severe cold and the ice. Those blossoms gave me hope. I decided if that tree could blossom in the ice, then maybe I could too.

We spent several difficult years trying to minister to that challenging little church, finding ways to blossom that were unaffected by the everyday pain we encountered there. We developed strong friendships with families at other nearby churches, began evangelizing a new area close by, and started to become involved with family ministry projects. I started to write and develop a ministry that had been only a dream before. By finding other fulfilling ways to serve God, we managed to survive and even blossom in what initially appeared to be a hostile environment.

If you feel the icy blasts of rejection and criticism, if you are hurting, then remember the January blossoms and ask God to make something beautiful of your life, regardless of the hostility of your environment.   KAREN HOLFORD

JANUARY 12

Naked

Because thou sayest, I am rich, and increased with goods, and have need of nothing; and knowest not that thou art wretched, and miserable, and poor, and blind, and naked. Rev. 3:17.

few years ago I was in the city of Jakarta, Indonesia, for some meetings. One Friday afternoon I decided to walk to some nearby stores just to see what they had. I walked along the very busy and extremely crowded main thoroughfare of Jakarta. Businesspeople hurried by, intent only on reaching their destination on time. Young teenagers walked along in groups—probably coming home from school. Then there were the beggars and the street children.

Suddenly my eye caught sight of a little boy—maybe 5 or 6

years old. It was his clothing. . . . First of all, I must explain that the climate in Jakarta is very warm, hot and humid. And though clothing is not essential to keep warm, everyone these days feels the need to be covered. Apparently this little boy had no clothing and no shoes, so he improvised. Where ordinarily we would expect to see a child this age wearing at least a pair of shorts, this little boy was wearing *a newspaper* wrapped around his small waist and tucked in so that it would stay in place—more or less. But he had to keep tucking the newspaper in at the waist continually, for it was not very secure.

My heart went out to the small boy, so I went into the store close by and bought him a pair of pants and a shirt and made my way back to the street to deliver them to him. After considerable searching, I couldn't find him anywhere.

That evening as I was sitting in my hotel room I remembered Revelation 3:17, which describes the Laodicean church—a church that does not realize it is naked. This little Indonesian boy realized he was naked, and he tried in his own way to supply that need. He did not realize, however, that someone was there to give him a new outfit—he moved away too quickly. We all belong to this Laodician church. Some of us do not realize our need of the robe of Christ's righteousness and try to cover our nakedness with our own good works. Neither of these situations is what God wants. He wants to cover us with His beautiful robe of righteousness; but we must not run off. We must wait for Him to clothe us. And this robe is free, because Jesus has paid the cost for us.   ROWENA R. RICK

JANUARY 13

Gathering With the Swans

Let us not give up meeting together . . . but let us encourage one another. Heb. 10:25, NIV.

Tears sprang to my eyes when I saw a little one reading "The Ugly Duckling." I watched the child's facial expressions change from sad and concerned to happy and excited as the unfortunate, rejected little bird made his unhappy journey through ducklinghood. Occasionally I would hear a little whispered, "Oh, the poor little ugly duckling!" At the end there was a big smile as he announced, "He's not an ugly duckling—he's really a swan!"

We have all experienced rejection at some point in our lives. Some of us have had more experience with it than others! I know I have, and it always hurts. But how wonderful it is to know that even if the people of this world reject or misunderstand me, I have a Friend who is always there for me. Jesus loves me so much that He gave His life to save mine. He is so patient with me that even when I have sinned and failed Him again and again, He is always waiting with open arms to hear my prayer of repentance and to forgive me, to cleanse me from all unrighteousness, and to teach me how to live the right way. I am so important to Him that even when I get so caught up in my own problems that I become discouraged and ready to quit, He never stops pursuing me and calling my name until He has drawn me back to His loving side.

There is another place we can find love and acceptance, and that's at church. Of course, since we are human and still being perfected, there is the potential for misunderstanding. But we can all go to the same Source for our strength, for the grace to forgive, and for the wisdom to understand. After a week of being "in the world, but not of the world," it's such a relief to come together with my Christian family each week, knowing we serve the same God, we are striving toward the same heaven, and we each love the same Lord.

Oh, yes, rejection is definitely a part of this life. There have been so many places that I just didn't belong; where I just didn't fit in. I kept searching for love and acceptance in all the wrong places, getting hurt again and again. But in Jesus I have found everything I have ever been searching for. And whenever I gather together with the rest of the "swans," I feel a kindred spirit between us. We are all finding our love and acceptance in the right place.

If things can be this good on earth, I can't wait to experience heaven!   LYNDA MAE RICHARDSON

JANUARY 14

The Only Way to Fly

"Not by might nor by power, but by my Spirit," says the Lord Almighty. Zech. 4:6, NIV.

*T*he fax machine purred to life and spit out a revised schedule. Revised schedule? What a euphemism. More like a bombshell! In two days my husband and I were scheduled to board a plane in San Francisco for a three-stop lecture tour. Our 21-day advance purchase tickets had arrived in the mail weeks earlier. This new printout called for me to spend an extra half day at one of the locations. It would be tight, but my schedule could accommodate the change.

I dialed the travel agency to request a departure date 12 hours later. The agent said she could accommodate the change— for an additional $1,100 per ticket! I gulped. Twenty-two hundred dollars to fly out 12 hours later? "Isn't that a bit steep?" I wondered aloud.

"Maybe so," was the reply, "but those are the rules." And those rules specified that a change on any leg of the journey required all tickets to be reissued at current fares.

I called the airline directly and explained that I was presenting health education seminars, that I didn't have control over the schedule change, and that my nonprofit corporation bank account did not contain an extra $2,200. Certainly some rational, thinking individual would be able to help me. . . . No one could—or would. The rules were the rules were the rules. Feeling a bit desperate, to say nothing of powerless, I asked to speak with an airline supervisor and repeated my story. No luck there, either.

I left my office and walked across the parking lot to pick up the mail. On the way I reported the morning's activities to my heavenly Parent. Talking with God as to a friend has almost become second nature over the years. (It felt strange at first!) I ended with these words: "I know if You need me to be at that afternoon meeting Your Spirit can prompt the airlines to reticket that one departure time without charging me $1,100 per ticket. Of course, You may not want to do that," I added, "and that's certainly all right. But I know You *can*, if You want to."

Fifteen minutes later the telephone rang on my desk. A

breathless travel agent said, "I was impressed to call another supervisor at the airline, and would you believe it? She agreed to the new departure time for only $50 per ticket!" She added that she couldn't imagine what had prompted the change of heart. They had been so firmly unhelpful before! I knew exactly what had happened and exuberantly gave God the credit over the phone.

In some ways it's been a very long, very slow journey, this learning to place my life in God's hands, to watch the evidence of omnipotent interest, and to accept whatever happens. But it's the only way to fly! ARLENE TAYLOR

The Day I Saw an Angel

Are they not all ministering spirits, sent forth to minister for them who shall be heirs of salvation? Heb. 1:14.

I expect that most of us have had at least one experience in which we were moved to say with Jacob, "Surely the Lord is in this place; and I knew it not," when we felt there was strong evidence of providential—even angelic—intervention, and disaster was averted.

Many years have elapsed since this experience came to our family. We were on holiday, my husband, our son, and one of my sisters. We were traveling the Eyre Highway from Adelaide to Perth in Western Australia, some 1,600 miles. Much of the road traversed the inhospitable, flat, and treeless Nullarbor Plain. For many miles the "road" was little more than a track where intrepid travelers battled potholes and dust in the dry summer, and mud and slush when the rains came. In later years the road had been formed and sealed. Hence our decision to attempt this journey with a camper in tow.

We had been traveling for three days. To pass the time we read and sang gospel songs. My husband was driving on a road that was narrow and straight as far ahead as the eye could see. We hadn't seen another vehicle for many miles when suddenly, out of nowhere, a huge, heavily laden semitrailer bore down upon us, sideswiping our camper. We could hear and feel the hub caps of the semi grinding against the side of the car. Then, catching the front bumper, it threw us off track into a ditch, where the car and camper came to rest at an awkward angle, mud up to the axles and effectively bogged down.

The semi driver eventually stopped a half mile or so down the road. When he walked back, he was quite abusive and seemed not at all concerned about our predicament. In a state of shock, we surveyed the damage, picking up bits and pieces, and discussing the pros and cons of our plight. Suddenly along came an empty flatbed truck with length of heavy chain. With very little communication the driver soon had us pulled back onto the road. Barely acknowledging our thanks, he was on his way and out of sight in moments, vanishing as mysteriously as he had come.

We stood amazed, feeling we were on sacred ground, that an angel had been sent to deliver us. We continued bumping along on our journey, very conscious of the Lord's protecting care. We remember that day as the day we saw one of God's ministering spirits, sent to minister to us. — VEYRL DAWN WERE

JANUARY 16

Choices

Teach me, Lord, what you want me to do, and I will obey you faithfully; teach me to serve you with complete devotion. Ps. 86:11, TEV.

I was doing many things that I knew had to be done.
Some of it was lots of work, and some of it was fun.
But when I wasn't looking (it's embarrassing to tell),
1997 slipped right off my calendar and fell.

As I bent to pick it up, not a trace was to be found.
But I could see that something else was there upon the ground.
Carefully I lifted it and held it in my hand.
I knew that I was holding something wonderful and grand.

It could be used to help or hurt, depending on its use.
It might be wisely spent or could be subject to abuse.
It could be used to selfish end or bring to others cheer.
It all depends on what I do with this, a brand-new year.

MARCIA MOLLENKOPF

A Famine Stalks the Globe

"The days are coming," declares the Sovereign Lord, "when I
will send a famine through the land—not a famine of food or a
thirst for water, but a famine of hearing the words of the Lord."
Amos 8:11, NIV.

*T*he very fact that you picked up this book and turned to
this page means that you are part of an elite and privileged
segment of the world's population. You can read. In the world
today there are almost 1 billion adults who cannot read; two
thirds of that number are women.

You may or may not know one of these more than 600 mil-
lion women, but because of circumstances that are usually beyond her control, she cannot know the ingredients in the formula
she gives her baby, or what is in the prepared food she may purchase for her family. She cannot read the warnings on a bottle of
medicine, or even read when or how much medicine to take. She
cannot read the pamphlets available from her doctor, church, or
government meant to improve her own health or welfare. She
cannot read of her rights, privileges, or responsibilities in government, or freely participate in the plans or leadership of her
church. Neither can she help her children learn to read, nor help
them with their homework. She cannot even read a bedtime
story to her child.

Although the highest percentage of women who cannot read
live in countries of the Islamic world, illiteracy is found in developed and developing countries, north, south, east, and west.
Many of these women live even in the United States. They cannot get or hold well-paying jobs. Those who teach adults to read

say that the number one reason that adults in North America want to learn to read is to be able to read the Bible. Experts say that if you teach a man to read, you teach one person. That is good. But if you teach a woman to read, you teach a family.

Long ago the prophet Amos wrote of a famine. Not a famine of food, but a famine of the Word of God. Famine has always gravely affected women and their families. But Christian women have been active in meeting and alleviating the devastation of famine. Today you have that opportunity. One way you can defeat this famine is to make sure you partake of the Word of God yourself—fortify yourself with the Word. I recently heard someone say that the Bible is a feast of revealed truths to be shared among ourselves and with the world around us. Imagine yourself watching others enjoying a feast. You can get close to the table, and even touch the food, but you are unable to eat any of it. Jesus stated that He is the Bread of Life. There is a starving world out there, and we have Bread to share; we must help the illiterate learn to eat that Bread. ARDIS DICK STENBAKKEN

JANUARY 18

Doing It for the Lord

Serve wholeheartedly, as if you were serving the Lord, not men, because you know that the Lord will reward everyone for whatever good he does, whether he is slave or free. Eph. 6:7, 8, NIV.

What do you do when you really dislike a task you have to do? Throw up your hands and say "Yuck"? Well, there is a better way!

All her life Denise hated doing the dishes. She looked forward to marriage and kids (even messy pants didn't bother her), but dirty dishes? Three times a day? Now, that was too much! At first she grumbled her way through the dishes. Next she tried stacking them to wash once a day. But neither idea worked very well. She even tried singing, "Roll, roll your burdens away," but the only joy in the dishwashing task was the detergent.

Then one morning during her personal devotion time Denise

decided it was time to ask the Lord to change her "dirty-dish" attitude. Suddenly the words of Ephesians 6:7, 8 popped into her head: "Serve wholeheartedly, as if you were serving the Lord, not men, because you know that the Lord will reward everyone for whatever good he does, whether he is slave or free."

"As if you were serving the Lord. . . ." Doing dishes as if she were doing them for Jesus had never entered her mind before. She began to visualize the kitchen as God's palace—how beautiful and spacious! The spotless golden faucets, the pearl-like bubbles in the sink, crystal goblets, and golden plates. And upstairs was the throne room. Just imagine what it would be like if Jesus had just given a banquet, and He personally had asked her if she minded doing the dishes for Him! What an honor to be considered worthy of the task! She would do anything for her Master.

The more she prayed and thought of those heavenly dishes, the more attractive her own dishes appeared. Finally she could sit no longer. "I will do the dishes as if I'm doing them for the Lord," she said aloud as she began to stack the dirty plates and run the hot water. And instead of singing "Roll, roll your burdens away," her song became "I'm doing these dishes as unto my Lord; His banner over me is love."

So if you sometimes feel caught by having to do things you detest, it really doesn't help to grumble; and putting the task off as long as possible just increases the agony! Denise's suggestion is that you take the advice in Ephesians 6:7, 8 and with goodwill do the task as if you are doing it for God Himself.

Remember, it was Jesus who said, "Inasmuch as ye have done it unto one of the least of these my brethren, ye have done it unto me" (Matt. 25:40). KAY KUZMA

Footprints in the Snow

Because he himself suffered when he was tempted, he is able to help those who are being tempted. Heb. 2:18, NIV.

I see her almost every day along my jogging route, plodding in the opposite direction. I don't know her name, but the fact that we're out there together in the swirling snow while the rest of the neighborhood remains cloistered snugly within the warmth of their homes provides the only link we seem to need. As the wind pelts snow against our faces, we call out to each other. "We're crazy to be out here!" or "Beautiful weather today!" We laugh and plod on, our stride a little longer, strengthened by knowing we are not alone.

One bitterly cold day, when I questioned my weak hold on sanity to be outside at all, let alone jogging, I peered out of the thin slit between the top of my neck warmer and the bottom of my hat. My breath choked out blasts of frozen fog. Nothing along my route stirred. I was totally alone . . . except for her tracks in the snow ahead of me. Those frozen footprints let me know she'd been there and kept me going. I was not alone.

Recently I went through circumstances that buffeted my life as well as my faith. I sometimes felt deserted not only by family and friends, but by God as well. I looked around and saw not one friendly face. Frustrated, alone, and without hope, I looked up at the sky and cried, "God, where are You?" He directed my attention to the footprints at my feet, reminding me He is not a God who rules in aloof majesty from a cold, safe distance. He is a God who walks the walk and talks the talk. Where I was going, He had traveled first. I was not alone.   CELESTE PERRINO WALKER

Tomato Beer

He who conceals his sins does not prosper, but whoever confesses and renounces them finds mercy. Prov. 28:13, NIV.

We were fresh out of college, and it was our first church assignment in the ministry. I had been arranging furniture and unpacking boxes for a week when I heard the doorbell and went to answer it. On my porch stood two women from our church with two bushel baskets of ripe tomatoes. After coming in and visiting awhile, they gave me instructions on how to can the tomatoes.

Now, I was raised in the city and had *never* canned anything in my life! But armed with their instructions and words of encouragement that this would be a foolproof endeavor, I purchased cases of new canning jars and tackled the project. Between the tomatoes and caring for my three young sons, it took the entire day.

Late that night as I looked at my pantry shelves lined with jars of red juicy tomatoes, I felt very proud of myself and went to bed tired, but very satisfied. Every day I opened the pantry and again felt the pleasure of a job well done.

On the third morning when I opened the kitchen door, the most peculiar odor permeated the air. I first thought that perhaps there was a dead rat in the kitchen, so I started checking the cabinets. The last place I checked was my pantry. To my horror, I found that every jar lid had popped and a pinkish-orange foam was oozing out of the jars and dripping down the shelves. A puddle of fermented tomato juice covered the floor. I was so upset that I cried as I tackled the cleanup job.

At church the next week the two kind women asked how my tomato canning had gone. When I told them what had happened, they said I must have left out a step in the processing, or perhaps I had failed to cut some soft spots out of the tomatoes.

Sin is like those tomatoes. When we allow resentment, anger, unresolved conflicts, or any other sin to remain in our lives, it begins a process of fermentation—slowly destroying our connection with God. Give God permission today to cut away whatever you are hanging on to that will destroy your connection with Him.

CELIA MEJIA CRUZ

Dust Bunny Damage

Set a watch, O Lord, before my mouth; keep the door of my lips.
Ps. 141:3.

J grabbed the upright vacuum cleaner out of the closet, plugged it in, and cleaned up the wildflower seeds I'd just spilled in front of the washing machine. While I was at it, I vacuumed the bathroom and hallway. Just as I hit the off switch, I noticed a pile of dirt and a dust bunny behind the vacuum cleaner. Since I'd just vacuumed there, it seemed a little strange. Nevertheless, I turned the cleaner and angled the wand toward the dust. The machine captured the mess in one quick slurp. Satisfied, I turned toward the cleaner again and reached for the switch. But there on the floor behind the cleaner sat more dirt and another fluffy dust bunny. Again my machine slurped it up. That's when I noticed three more dust bunnies. What was going on?

A sick feeling hit the pit of my stomach. I inspected the back of the cleaner. Sure enough—the last time I'd used the vacuum I'd been hurrying. I had tossed the full disposable dust bag into the garbage can, making a mental note to put in a new bag before using the vacuum again. As I unfolded a new bag, I thought about the new messes I'd created as fast as I'd cleaned up the old ones. Then I thought about something else that needs to control output—my mouth. When I carelessly spew out whatever information I've heard, I make relationship messes that are not easy to clear up.

I vacuumed the hall and bathroom again, keeping all the dust bunnies corralled in the new bag, where they could neither multiply nor do damage. As I cleaned, I prayed, "Lord, I need You to set a watch before my mouth. Please keep the door of my lips."

HELEN LINGSCHEIT HEAVIRLAND

Make My Day

A word fitly spoken is like apples of gold in settings of silver.
Prov. 25:11, NKJV.

*I*t was a typical northern California morning in early January. The cold, damp weather outside encouraged us to stay inside and enjoy the warmth. This provided the perfect setting for my morning meditation, an activity I really enjoy.

The morning devotional reading was most inspirational and continued to remain on my mind. I felt a strong need to share the reading with someone else. A friend with whom I usually shared my inspirational readings had recently moved away, so I tried to think of someone else I could share it with. The fact that it was not quite 6:00 a.m. made it difficult to think of someone I could call. Whom would I dare awaken at this hour of the morning? Who would be receptive to sharing this reading with me *after* waking up?

No one came to mind, so I decided to continue my morning activities and went to the fitness center to work out. While I was there, the morning devotional reading kept resurfacing, and that was when I thought of calling Harriet.

When she picked up the telephone, her voice sounded as though she had just awakened from a deep sleep. Assuming that was the case, I began apologizing profusely, but she interrupted me.

"No, no, I am just here in bed trying to get enough energy to get up and get going."

Knowing that she has had periods of depression in the past, I asked if there was anything I could do to be of help to her. When she said no, I said, "I would like to share a devotional reading with you."

"Please do," she replied, and I began to read with much enthusiasm.

When I paused at the end of the reading, Harriet said with a lilt in her voice, "I really like that; I really did need that."

Later that day she left a message on my answering machine thanking me for sharing the devotional reading with her. "You made my day!" she exclaimed.

Returning from a meeting in the Bay Area later in the year, Harriet asked, "Do you remember sharing a reading with me about a pasta salad that didn't have the main ingredient?"

I was puzzled at first, because I didn't know to which reading she was referring. Then she began explaining that a pasta salad without the main ingredient, pasta, was not really a legitimate pasta salad and left something to be desired. Likewise, life without the main ingredient, *God*, could be a life unfulfilled, one of varying degrees of emptiness.

Harriet then asked, "Do you think you could make a copy for me?"

Sometimes "a word fitly spoken" is all that is required to give someone that special attention and help they need.

Dear Father, help me to be a blessing to someone each day. May I continue to allow the Holy Spirit to use my words to point others to the Saviour. Amen.   MARTHA HARDY-LEE

JANUARY 23

Fascinated by Colors

Even after these dreadful things happen to you, if, in the days that follow, you find the Lord again, then you'll gladly listen to Him and obey Him. The Lord your God is a loving and merciful God. He will never abandon you. He will not break the covenant He made with your ancestors and confirmed by an oath. Deut. 4:30, 31, Clear Word.

Living on a farm meant lots of room to use our imaginations, and on this day the fun was in seeing all the pretty colors we could mix up in little glass jars. Mom had given us some food coloring that we had taken out behind the barn, where we busily made "medicine," "perfume," and all the other important things that two little girls can dream up. The colors were so pretty as the sun shone through the bottles. Holding them close to our eyes turned the whole world into gorgeous, brilliant color.

"Janny! Cookie!" Mama called for us to come, but we were having such a great time we decided not to answer and to stay quiet. After all, the barn was quite a distance from the house, and we reasoned that she wouldn't come looking for us. Besides, she probably wanted us to help her with some chores. Our plan worked. After a few more calls all was quiet, and we continued in our make-believe world.

Soon we heard the sound of our family car. Running around the corner of the barn to peek, we were just in time to see Mama driving down the dusty road. We were terrified! Where was she going? She had never left us before. Was she ever coming back? Daddy wasn't home either; he'd gone to take the milk to town. We really panicked!

Later that afternoon when Mama returned from town, our neighbor down the road told her what had happened. He described a pitiful sight—two little girls running down the long, dusty road, tears streaming down their dirty cheeks, looking for Mama. When we didn't answer her, Mama thought we must have gone with Daddy, as we had done so many times before.

It occurred to me recently that I may be in danger of being left again, only this time it won't be for an afternoon. It will be for eternity. I traded a trip to town, which was always a special treat, for the pleasure of watching the sun shine through bottles of colored water. I don't want to trade a trip to heaven for the worthless trinkets of this world. I want the Son to shine through my life and make the world a more beautiful place. I hid from my mother and suffered the consequences of separation. I don't want to hide from my heavenly Father, or suffer the separation caused by sin. I know He is calling my name, along with the names of all His other children. Please join me in getting ready for the best trip ever!

KATHY CONNATSER

JANUARY 24

Snowfall

Have you ever visited the storerooms, where I keep the snow and the hail? Job 38:22, TEV.

I was 11 years old the first time I saw snow falling from the sky. I have never seen it since. I had seen snow on the ground before—had touched it, tasted it, played in it. I had hiked

47

in it, even camped in it. But it had always been covering the ground in a smooth white blanket, like the sand on the beach near where we lived.

It had been cold for days, with plenty of rain and hail. My sister and I spent dreary afternoons cooped up in the house, looking at the wet world outside our sliding-glass door. Then one morning it happened—white flakes falling from the sky. We rushed out into the backyard to look at it. I caught a snowflake and stared at it in disbelief. It was so tiny! Since kindergarten days we had cut snowflakes out of white paper the size of our hands. But the snowflake lying in my hand seemed dwarfed by my fingers.

We begged to stay home from school, but my mother insisted we go. The radio said there was three inches of snow, and that certainly sounded like a good reason to stay home. We told her we would probably freeze to death in our short dresses.

"The school is heated, and so is the bus," she told us, and sent us out.

At school we all kept chattering so much that the teacher finally gave us a complicated art project to keep us quiet. I was still working on it when the class left for recess. I stayed inside to complete the project, because it was due the next day and I didn't want to take it home to finish it. My friends urged me to come join them in a snowball fight.

"Later," I promised them. "I'll come out and play at lunch."

I finished the project while most of my friends were throwing snowballs and building snow figures. At lunchtime I put on my coat and went out to lie in the snow. Only by that time the sun had come out and melted it all. There were only muddy puddles to show where the snow had been.

How fragile time is! Instead of pushing constantly to get ahead, perhaps we should take more time to enjoy nature or the company of those we care about.

Have you had any first snowfalls in your life? Have you missed opportunities to tell your loved ones how much they mean to you? Next time you get a chance to experience one of life's little miracles, don't pass it up. Remember that time can be as delicate and beautiful as a snowflake—and just as quick to melt away.

GINA LEE

A Visit With the President

For the Son of Man is going to come in his Father's glory with his angels, and then he will reward each person according to what he has done. Matt. 16:27, NIV.

*M*r. President, your guests are here to see you!" our host announced, and ushered us into his office, closing the door behind us.

The visit we had so long anticipated had at last become a reality. It was all made possible by my talented young friend Eileen, who is on former U.S. President Ronald Reagan's staff in Beverly Hills, California. She had invited my husband and me to visit him in his office. A few Sabbaths later at our church potluck a hug from Eileen and another invitation gave me courage. My sister and her husband were to arrive from Salem, Oregon, in two weeks. Yes, we would make the appointment and include them! I called Eileen's office, and she graciously arranged the date. With growing anticipation we prepared and reflected on this rare opportunity—and Eileen's generosity.

Monday morning arrived sunny and bright. And so did we. At the security area we were asked to give the full names of our party and by whose invitation we had come. Our four names were verified, and the attendant keyed the elevator to go directly to Floor 34. Outside the president's office, we were invited to leave our handbags. Nothing must distract us from this all-important visit.

In spite of the recent diagnosis of Alzheimer's disease, President Reagan, looking every inch the distinguished person that he is, briskly rose from his desk and greeted us with a cordial handshake. A pleasant conversation followed, then each of us stood proudly beside Mr. Reagan for individual and group pictures—16 of them! We cherished the privilege of speaking with him face-to-face as friends, and I felt I would never be quite the same again!

And I haven't been the same. For that experience caused me to focus on the invitation graciously extended to us all—an audience with the Creator-Sovereign of the universe. With a privilege so incredible I have purposed anew to devote my whole heart to getting ready. Each day I look forward with increasing eagerness to that climactic event. Each day I find excess baggage that must be abandoned. I see imperfections in my character robe and sometimes become disheartened. But my dearest Friend has already made the appointment, and if I am faithful, He will verify my name.

One beautiful day I expect to look into the loving face of my King. I want to gaze on His nail-scarred hands made beautiful by the price He paid for me; to hear His melodious voice claim me as His child, assuring me I am worth His sacrifice. With overwhelming gratitude my tears of joy will flow as I worship at His feet. I will have seen the King, and because of Him I will never be the same! Not ever!
LORRAINE HUDGINS

JANUARY 26

What a Love!

For your Maker is your husband—the Lord Almighty is his name—the Holy One of Israel is your Redeemer; he is called the God of all the earth. Isa. 54:5, NIV.

I have the perfect Husband! He loves me with an undying, unconditional love. He knows me better than I know myself, and He still loves me.

Many do not know Him and disbelieve His existence. Others know Him, and He is their husband too.

Although He is the perfect Husband, I sometimes turn my back on Him. He promised to supply all my needs—and He has. Sometimes, though, I confuse my needs with my wants and seek others to supply these wants. Of course, He always allows me to try it my way. Then, when I come back to Him with tears and apologies, He does not condemn me. Rather, He assures me that He still loves me and explains that these experiences help me to grow in His love and come to rely on Him more. Isn't He wonderful?

There are times I feel lonely, although I have the perfect Husband. When this happens, I ask Him to put His arms around me, and He always does. The exciting thing is that in His creativity He puts His arms around me in a different way each time. Sometimes it's through nature. Other times it's a Bible verse or sermon, or through the warmth of family and friends. No matter how He does it, each time I feel a surge of warmth, joy, and peace deep within. This can come only from my Husband—my Friend.

My Husband has called me to do things and go places just for Him. Many cannot understand why I go, but I love and trust my Husband so much that I want to go wherever He leads me. Each time I go somewhere with Him, others come to know Him and love Him and my relationship with Him becomes stronger.

I am part of a group that some scorn, many pity, and some envy. They call us "singles." Well, in Jesus I am a happily married, free, complete single woman. If my Husband chooses to share me with another, I will be happy. If He chooses to keep me for Himself and His service, I will be equally as happy. It is a blessing and a joy to have the perfect Husband.

Whether single or married, may you bask in the sunshine of His love today.   COLEEN M. BIRKETT

Be Still

Be still, and know that I am God: I will be exalted among the heathen, I will be exalted in the earth. Ps. 46:10.

*I*t seems I'm constantly in motion, going to and fro. While I was hurrying to catch the bus one morning on my way to work, complaining about having to go to that job again and wishing for early retirement, a smile crossed my disgruntled face as I watched a family of ducks crossing the street, seemingly without a care. Father duck led out, baby ducks marched in a line behind, and mother duck brought up the rear. I stopped, wanting to inhale the beauty of the day before the stark reality of life in the fast lane caught up with me. Far in the distance the endless landscape of the Rocky Mountains, snowcapped with all their grandeur, stretched away. I watched birds soaring through the air with wings spread, singing their own special song. I felt the bright sun as it bathed my face with its warmth, and I heard the rush of the waterfall as it fell with spurts of clear, cool water. How involved I had gotten with the "necessary" things of life! I was missing some of the "small" things of life that assure me of God's greatness, glory, and presence.

My heart welled with gratitude and praise as I experienced those few precious moments when God beckoned me to be still. How much God wants to comfort, sustain, protect, and direct me if I stop the activity of my life just for these few precious moments.

In your troubled times, when high seems the cost,
Draw strength from above.
In your lonely hours, when all seems for loss,
Reflect on My love.
In your quiet moments, when peace is near,
Give your humblest praise.
In your simple pleasures, when joys are dear,
Give your thanks always.
Be still, be still, and know that I am God.

PATRICIA L. SHINSKIA

JANUARY 28

Slavo Bogo

I prayed to the Lord and He answered me. He delivered me from all my fears. Those who look to Him for help are radiant, and they never have to cover their faces in shame. . . .The angels of the Lord encamp around those who reverence Him and deliver them. Taste and find out for yourself how good God is. Ps. 34:4-8, Clear Word.

That Sunday morning in Siberia we didn't know our desperate need of our guardian angels' protection. Doing evangelism on the Siberian frontier was challenging, exciting, and exhausting for my husband, son, and me. Now our team (the first Americans to share Christ in Abakan) was happily on its way to play soccer with the many young people attending our crusade.

As we traveled by taxi, we practiced our newly learned

Russian words: *Slavo Bogo* (praise the Lord)! How mightily God was working as Christ was uplifted each night in the meetings. The truth of God's Word was satisfying the deep spiritual hunger of sincere Siberian seekers. *Slavo Bogo!* Our work was being blessed, and now we would play with our new young friends.

Our taxi careened down the bumpy back streets, creating concern about the skill and sobriety of the driver. His face hardened as he accelerated to pass the bus ahead. The speed of the bus also increased, and the race was on. Side by side we sped along the narrow two-lane road. To our shock, a car was coming straight toward us, but our startled exclamations in English fell on uncomprehending Russian ears. The driver couldn't pass the bus and wouldn't slow down to pull in behind the bus. Helplessly we called out, "Lord, save us!" At the last second the oncoming car dove into the ditch to avoid a head-on collision. We breathed a collective sigh of grateful relief.

We praise You, powerful Lord! How powerless we are. How fragile life is—every breath is Your gift. Thank You for guardian angels that enfold and protect us. *Slavo Bogo!*   LILA LANE GEORGE

JANUARY 29

My Little Green Book

And even the very hairs of your head are all numbered. Matt. 10:30, NIV.

Where is my green book? I always keep it with my personal books in my desk. My thoughts raced. I started worrying as I realized I hadn't seen the book for a while. More than a diary, this book held a record of divine interventions for me and my family.

Eight years before, I had made a commitment with the Lord to daily prayer intercession. Each day my prayer time was a priority, and I became aware of incidents that could not just be explained away as coincidence. Perhaps my spiritual "eyes" were becoming more focused, but the entire family seemed more in tune to the idea that life events aren't just happenstance.

So I began a journal of daily activities that seemed to be a direct result of prayer. Sometimes I would read from the book to encourage myself or a family member that God was working wonderfully in our lives.

We had moved to a new home six months before, and I was recovering from a lengthy illness. My prayer and study life was not very organized, and I hadn't written in my book since the move. In fact, I hadn't even seen the book! Since memories tend to diminish in detail with time, I'd cautioned my family to document answered prayer to keep as a family record.

And now I had lost my record. I frantically emptied my desk, looked through dresser drawers, and checked all the bookshelves. But after hours of searching, the book was still lost. I sat at my desk and cried. In genuine pain I tried to explain to God how sorry I was that I had been careless or hadn't been disciplined enough with my devotion times lately. Anyway, it didn't matter, because the book was gone.

In time, as my emotions were spent, I just sat numbly in the quietness of my study. Then something—a thought or impression—caused me to go look in my closet, back in a dark corner where my attaché case sat, forgotten for the past six months. Opening it, I discovered my green book. Coincidence? Maybe. Or maybe it had just been lying there quietly, waiting for my return. I guess if God has numbered the hairs on our head He can keep up with a little book that means so much to me.

Why not start your own book of answered prayers today?

JANIS CLARK VANCE

JANUARY 30

Do We Really Need a Prompt?

The Counselor, the Holy Spirit, whom the Father will send in my name, will teach you all things and will remind you of everything I have said to you. John 14:26, NIV.

Continuing my education has been a lifelong practice, something I truly enjoy. So when I was afforded the opportunity in my "golden years" to further my education by learning to use computers, it was a dream come true.

One of the terms the teacher started using was "prompt." In my thinking that word meant to be or do something on time, or to help me with my lines when I was in a play. It didn't seem to be a word that would help me tame a mighty computer. However, after I had gotten far enough along to comprehend a little of how the computer worked, I found that a prompt was indeed my friend.

Whenever I wanted to input new text into the computer, the friendly prompt would help me by asking me what command I wanted to give. As I was programming a series of commands, it would "prompt" me to tell it what the next one was that I wanted. It is really quite simple to look up and make a selection from the various choices that the prompt may give you.

We have a prompt in our spiritual lives that can help us to keep from doing the wrong thing, much like the prompt on the computer keeps me from going out on a limb with my own way of doing things. Following the prompt as it guides me through inputting the right data helps me to get the job accomplished.

When we listen to the prompt, it will tell us when we start to do wrong and help us to do right. How often we grieve the Holy Spirit by not listening to our conscience—that still small voice that pleads with us as we are tempted to do wrong. What a wonderful Comforter Jesus gave to us when He left this world! The gift of the Holy Spirit prompts us to know what His will is for us. Do we really need a prompt? Yes, just as I need one to help me with my computer. — Pat Madsen

---

Parable of the Busy Housewife

Cast your burden on the Lord, and He shall sustain you. Ps. 55:22, NKJV.

A busy housewife decided to spend one hour with Jesus each morning. As she sat down, Bible in hand, the thought occurred to her that the beans could be cooking for dinner while she read. She put her Bible down and walked to the kitchen cabinet to get a pot, but the pot wasn't there. It sat in the sink with the crusty remains of breakfast still in it.

"Might as well wash the dishes," she reasoned to herself. Fifteen minutes later the woman put the beans in the clean pot and carried them to the stove. But the oatmeal had bubbled over onto the burner that morning, and if she didn't wipe that up right away it would harden.

The gooey oatmeal on her dishcloth reminded the woman that the towels needed to be laundered. As she collected the dirty linen in the bathroom, she noticed that her husband had forgotten to rinse the sink after shaving that morning. While she was taking care of the sink, she saw water spots all over the mirror, and in cleaning the mirror she caught sight of her own appearance.

"Oh, dear," she groaned, "my hair looks terrible! I must style it before someone comes over and sees me. But where is my brush?"

After searching for some time, the busy housewife found the brush in her daughter's bedroom under the covers of an unmade bed. As she smoothed the sheets and fluffed the pillow, she suddenly stiffened, sniffing the air. That odor . . . Was something burning?

"The beans!" she gasped. "I forgot the beans!"

CRYSTAL EARNHARDT

Reprinted from *Bouquets* 2, No. 3 (1991). Used with permission.

A Toddler's Prayer

See that you do not look down on one of these little ones. For I tell you that their angels in heaven always see the face of my Father in heaven. Matt. 18:10, NIV.

*T*affy was a fine prizewinning parakeet, a gift from relatives in Wales. Not only was he splendid to behold, with his bright, turquoise-lemon body and white head fringed with a row of precise purple dots, but he was also blessed with a calm and quiet spirit that trusted us completely.

Taffy was given free range of our house in the north of England. Our children, ages 4 and 2, loved him dearly. We decided he deserved to have a mate. Tingling with excitement, we brought home the prettiest lavender budgie imaginable. She was sleek, delicate, and shy, and we all shared Taffy's obvious delight. We named her Scousie, a reference to her originating in Liverpool. She also had free range of the house.

On her second day with us Scousie escaped into the garden. Helplessly we watched the lavender beauty swoop in ever-widening loops between plants, willows, and tall poplars at the far end of the garden. Just beyond lay a huge city park, bristling with giant trees and unknown dangers. Scousie had had no time to bond with us, and our calls went unheeded.

Gathering the children, we each prayed that Jesus would keep Scousie safe and send an angel to bring her back home. Though very young, the children understood exactly what was happening and made their requests with trusting simplicity.

We placed the empty cage in a tree at the bottom of the garden, hoping to entice Scousie back for the seeds. We watched the trees intently, and finally saw her hanging on to the outside of the cage. I expected her to hop into the cage and start eating seeds while I discreetly closed the door on her. I silently prayed that she would not fly away as I slowly made my way toward the cage.

Ignoring the seeds, Scousie clung to the cage, not moving a muscle as I approached. She did not flinch as I clasped her warm little body in my hand. Obligingly she let go of the metal bars and allowed me to carry her back to the house in my bare hand.

"Mommy, birds don't just stand there and let you pick them up in your hand, do they? I wonder what the angel said to her," pondered our daughter.

I didn't know, but I do know that we serve a wonderful God, One who cares even about our pets.

Scousie had wandered far from her owner, but her instinct told her that she was in danger. When she spotted her home, she flew to it and clung to it until she felt the grasp of her master's hands and yielded to that touch. If you are "flying" far from the Master, come back home and rest securely in His care.

BRENDA SIMNETT-PRATT

FEBRUARY 2

I'll Never Leave You

Never will I leave you; never will I forsake you. Heb. 13:5, NIV.

I shivered as my bare back came in contact with the slab table. My arms and legs shook uncontrollably as I tried to muffle my sobs. In a strange and hostile environment, my body writhing in pain, I felt so helpless, and worst of all, so alone.

It all began around 4:00 a.m. when I awoke with a sensation of pain in my back. No matter which position I tried, I could get no relief. The pain worsened. By 7:45 I was on my way to the emergency room, where a preliminary exam pointed to possible kidney stones. Then it was back and forth to radiology.

Painful shots. Drawing blood. Seven unsuccessful attempts at putting in an IV. All these, combined with the pain that hadn't completely subsided, left me in a state of sobbing and shaking. Then suddenly the room, which had been full of people attending me, was strangely quiet. Those who had "hurt" me had left. Those who loved me were not around. My life seemed out of control, and no one was there to care in my hour of need.

Have you ever felt that way? In pain, mentally or physically, and no one seemed to notice? Those who hurt you gone, apparently oblivious to what they had done? Your life out of control, and even those who loved you not aware of it? Perhaps you wondered if anyone cared anymore.

Back on that X-ray table, I looked at my shaking hands through tear-filled eyes and prayed that God would help me stop shaking and get myself under control. I knew *He* would not abandon me, for I had His promise that He would be with me always. I began to relax, and the shaking and sobbing gradually subsided. After a long day of X-rays and exams, I was released from the hospital into the care of my husband, who drove me back to the safe and familiar surroundings of family and home. Three days and three kidney stones later, I was back to work, almost as if nothing had happened.

Recently I heard a talk on the well-known verse "All things work together for good." Recalling my recent hospital experience, I thought, *What good could possibly come of that experience? Empathy for those in pain? More emphasis on keeping healthy? Or perhaps an experience to encourage others to remember that there's always One who is right there with you through every experience, even when it seems that everyone has abandoned you and you are all alone?*

I wonder. NANCY CACHERO VASQUEZ

Up, Up, and Away

How great is the love the Father has lavished on us, that we should be called children of God! And that is what we are! 1 John 3:1, NIV.

I caught a late-night flight recently from Saint Louis back to Maryland. When I found my seat and saw that the plane wasn't very full, I was glad, because I wanted to sleep. But then a mother and her three sons, who were about 3, 4, and 5 years of age, came down the aisle and took the row in front of me—on both sides of the plane. One boy sat next to his mother, and the other two settled into seats across the aisle.

Boy, she has her hands full! I thought. *And I bet I won't be able to sleep now. They'll probably be loud. Maybe I can move to another row after the plane takes off.*

But by the time we got off the ground, I didn't *want* to move. Those kids were more entertaining than a movie! This was obviously their first plane ride, and they were excited. They immediately began to explore. They turned the lights above their seats on and off, pushed the call button (the flight attendant was patient), put their meal trays up and down, pushed the window shades up and down, and fastened and unfastened their seat belts.

Their mother finally convinced them that they had to stay in their seats with their belts fastened until they saw the seat belt light go off. As the plane rattled down the runway for takeoff, the 4-year-old looked at his brothers and said, "It's like a squeeeeeeky mouse."

During the flight the 3-year-old stood on his seat and craned his neck to look out the window. Suddenly he pointed and shouted with a big grin, "Mommy, a white pillow in the sky!"

Near the end of the flight one of the boys looked out the

window and shouted, "I saw *buildings!*" as if that were the most exciting thing in the universe.

And as the plane landed, just as it touched the ground, they began shouting, "Daddy! Daddy! Daddy!" and they pushed their way down the aisle and ran into their father's arms at the arrival gate.

As I watched the boys tell their dad all about their plane ride, I thought about our heavenly Father and the trip we'll take one day to see Him and His kingdom. Right now it's so hard for Him to help us understand what it's like—and what He's like. Just like those little boys who had never flown before, we simply can't relate. We have to use earthly images, such as mice and pillows and fathers.

But one day we'll take the trip into eternity. And I have a feeling that no matter how foreign things look to us, we'll still shout "Daddy!" when we get to that golden gate. We'll know Him, because He's been walking with us all along.   LORI PECKHAM

The Haircut

Great are the works of the Lord. . . . Glorious and majestic are his deeds, and his righteousness endures forever. Ps. 111:2, 3, NIV.

I couldn't believe my eyes when I saw her walk into the beauty shop. She was tall, and she wore loose brown corduroy slacks with a baggy dark sweatshirt. She also wore dark-rimmed glasses. But her most striking feature was her shoulder-length hair—thick, dark, and sticking out in every direction. You could barely see her face and glasses. She looked like an electrified mop! She said she had an appointment for a permanent, even though she had never had one that "took" well.

The hairdresser convinced her that she didn't need a permanent, but a good haircut was in order. The woman reluctantly agreed. It was fascinating entertainment watching the woman get her haircut. She kept telling the hairdresser that ever since she had gotten her last haircut it had stuck straight out. The hairdresser continued to talk to her and kept on cutting: a section from the back, a section from each side, and some off the top. Finally the woman sat under the hair dryer, but she kept warning everyone within earshot that when she came out her hair would stick straight out.

We all waited to see what would happen. Soon the dryer shut off and she was back in the hairdresser's chair. The beautician did a little more trimming and finished styling the last strands. What a difference! Now you could see that she had a beautiful round face and lovely eyes. Her hair was no longer the main focus of her appearance.

I never saw her again, but I have often thought of this experience. God takes us just as we are. Even though we can be so unattractive to ourselves and others, He doesn't give up on us. He stays by our side talking to us, encouraging us, and taking every opportunity to guide us. Sometimes He needs to trim just a little; other times He needs to cut a large section. We complain that we don't have the talent, time, or resources. But God is patient with us and continues His remodeling process on our characters. Just as the potter in Jeremiah 18 takes the marred pot and reshapes it into something that pleases him, so God takes our marred character and reshapes it into something that pleases Him.

My prayer is that we will allow God to trim and reshape our characters. What a difference it will make!   DONNA M. ARNOLD

FEBRUARY 5

God Is Like . . .

But seek first the kingdom of God and His righteousness, and all these things shall be added to you. Matt. 6:33, NKJV.

Many of my friends feel uncomfortable in God's presence. But He reminds me of my dad.

One day I met a girlfriend after work. We walked around shopping for a while, and then got hungry. I checked my wallet and was horrified to find I had given my last dollar to my boys for lunch money. "No problem," I said. "We're right here, near Dad's office. Let's get some from him."

My friend's mouth dropped open. "You can't just go into the General Conference and ask for money!" she protested.

"I certainly can!" I said firmly. "Come on!" I dragged her toward the imposing building. She was a church secretary in the area but had never been in the headquarters building.

"Are you sure they won't mind?" she asked timidly as I signed us both in at the security desk and pulled her on down the hall toward my dad's office. As I knocked and opened the door, I could feel her shrinking back into the hall.

Dad broke into a wide grin. "How much do you need this time?" he asked, chuckling and reaching for his wallet.

"Just $5," I answered.

He handed me $10. "Have fun, you two. See you later!"

"I can't believe it!" Sharon exclaimed breathlessly as we left the building. "He knew what you wanted before you opened your mouth, then gave you twice as much as you asked for."

I laughed. "He knew I was going out with you, and he's never surprised when I come up short of cash. He's always happy to see me, even when I'm broke, and he wanted us to have fun together."

I think God greets me with the same amused benevolence whenever I bring my requests to Him. He already knows what I need, and He meets my needs and gives me more besides . . . because He too wants me to have fun. "Fullness of joy" is the way He says it in official King James English.   SALLY PIERSON DILLON

FEBRUARY 6

Intentional Inclusiveness

There is no longer Jew or Greek, there is no longer slave or free, there is no longer male and female; for all of you are one in Christ Jesus. And if you belong to Christ, then you are Abraham's offspring, heirs according to the promise. Gal. 3:28, 29, NRSV.

*L*unch was over. The table was cleared. Sitting around the table, the adults continued their intense discussion of the implications of that morning's sermon. I followed the children as far as the front porch. Settling on the swing chair, I watched them luxuriate in the summer sunshine. Then 10-year-old Jewel came to sit with me, her brow furrowed in thought as we watched a hummingbird sip elegantly from the cleome stalks.

"Do you think that Jesus loves the boys and the men more than the girls and the women?" Her voice was troubled.

"Absolutely not." My response was vehement and automatic. "Look at Ruth and Esther. Those are Bible books named after women."

"I mean, when He was here—on earth." Her tone was as specific as her question.

Scrambling for Gospel examples to support my thesis, I began, "Remember when He left a crowd of people just so He could bring a young girl back to life, stopping only to talk to and cure a woman who had been sick for 12 years?

"And remember how He stopped to visit with a Samaritan woman one hot noonday, when nobody else would talk to her?"

"Yes!" It was Jewel's turn to answer her own question. "And remember how much He loved Mary and Martha. He cried when they cried at Lazarus's tomb!"

"And remember—"

"I get the picture," she smiled. Sliding off the swing, she skipped off to join her friends. Dilemma diffused.

Our conversation got me thinking. I was struck by the fact that although Jesus spent at least 30 years of His life in and around a carpenter's shop, most of His allusions and His parables were agrarian. I understand that He had to use Isaiah's shepherd metaphor to alert those stubbornly blinded by tradition that He was in fact the scriptural Messiah. I imagine beautiful words falling in perfect cadence from His lips—a powerful blend of audible and redemptive grace. He had to use pastoral images.

But He didn't have to create the parable of the woman searching through her house to find a silver coin to remind us that God is doing just that for us (Luke 15:8). Nor did He have to use the birthing process to parallel the joy He feels when we are reborn spiritually (John 16:21).

He didn't have to paint a word picture of the woman baking bread, using yeast in the dough to remind us of the power He placed within us to change lives (Luke 13:21). He could have told us that while we wait for His coming, some will be well-prepared while others live their lives in carefree unconcern. But He chose the story of the 10 bridesmaids to bring His point home (Matt. 25:1-12).

He had to use the shepherd visuals to declare Himself. He could have left it at that, but He chose to use all the others—women-centered pictures, family-structured parables—intentional inclusiveness. That's my Jesus!　　GLENDA-MAE GREENE

For Rent

That you and I may be mutually encouraged by each other's faith. Rom. 1:12, NIV.

A number of years ago, when I was a young mother with a 1-year-old daughter, we lived in a small apartment. My husband wanted a larger place with enough room to house his recording equipment, and we needed more space for our baby. We were literally bursting at the seams in our four-room apartment. I was a stay-at-home mother, so our budget was extremely limited.

One day I saw an advertisement for the main part of a very large house that was for rent. When my husband came home, I convinced him to go with me to at least look at it. As we toured the spacious, open rooms, brightened by the many windows, and saw the large backyard, I got so excited to think of the possibility of living there. At the same time we were looking through the house, a friend of ours was also going through it. (And I knew he could afford the asking price.) We looked in all the nooks and corners and then went home without making a commitment to rent. We discussed it late into the night. The rental price was fair. However, it was more than we could spend, even if we figured in a *future* raise. Finally, we decided that this house was just more than we could afford.

Later in the week, as I was pushing my little girl in her stroller, I happened to pass by an elderly gentleman who stopped me and asked, "Are you going to rent the house?" I recognized him as a tenant who lived with his wife upstairs in that large house. I told him that we had decided that the rent was more than we could afford, even though it was worth the asking price, and we didn't feel that we should ask for a lower price. He looked at me and said, "You'll never know unless you ask!"

I thought about it, and that night I mentioned this conversation to my husband. With the old gentleman's encouragement, we called the owner and asked if the house was still available. It was. So we offered my husband's service to take care of the yard work in exchange for a much lower rent. The owner said they received a lot of mail with checks and asked if I would be willing to take care of them and save them for him to pick up. I said yes, and he agreed to our terms!

We had a new place to live that had a fireplace and a large yard. We were so happy! Then God blessed us even more. The owner saw my baby and said that the washer and dryer were very old, and that with a baby we really needed new ones. He replaced them before we moved into the house.

This happened more than 25 years ago, but I have never forgotten the kindness of the owner, nor how God uses people like the old gentleman who encouraged me and later became like a grandpa to my daughter. I am praying that God will use me to be an encouragement to someone today. JULIA W. NORCOTT

You Are Everything to Me

I have swept away your offenses like a cloud, your sins like the morning mist. Return to me, for I have redeemed you. Isa. 44:22, NIV.

My son, the youngest, has come back home. The wanderer has returned. And with his return, a stream of joy has washed through me, clearing my mind of all negative thoughts. But it wasn't long ago that life was full of hurt.

It all started late one afternoon when our son, apparently tired of our rules and feeling that he had no liberty, hoisted his backpack and left the comfort and security of our home. I still remember the look fixed in his big brown eyes that told us of his determination to leave. Did he, as he went out from our gates, think of the pain and longing that struck our hearts when he announced he was heading to New Mexico, more than 1,500 miles away? Did he think of the shadow of anxiety that fell on us when his figure was lost to our sight as he turned the corner?

But none of that matters now! He has returned. He is safely home. I saw him come back, crestfallen, and with weary and painful steps. I wanted to reproach him, to scream at him and make him fully aware of my pain. Instead, I fell on his neck in a long, clinging, tender embrace. Tears rolled from my eyes, and my voice, broken and full of emotion, could only say, "Oh, you are everything to me!"

Yes, it is true that I should have reproached my son for his thoughtless behavior. I should have tried to make him understand his hurtful deed. But I couldn't help asking myself, Haven't we all done what he did when, professing ourselves to be wise, we became fools as we sought happiness in forgetfulness of God (see Romans 1:22, 28)? And wasn't God watching for our return? Wasn't He ever compassionate to forgive the wrong we'd done without reproaching us or even asking why we'd chosen such a course?

In fact, the only differences between my son's experience as a runaway and my own separation from God lay in the fact that he was just a boy, and instead of going to New Mexico as he had planned, he was gone for only two hours hunting butterflies in the wooded area behind our backyard.

We can deny God's right to love us. We can wander in the faraway land of sin as we try to escape Him. But our heavenly Father will never forget us nor reject us. His heart is always tender toward us.

If your feet have taken the wrong path and you're tempted to think your life of sin must bar you from the Father's house, cast the thought away. "Get up, go away! For this is not your resting place." "Return to [the Father], for [He has] redeemed you" (Micah 2:10; Isaiah 44:22). He will meet you a great way off. He will cover you with His wings and enfold you in His arms of infinite love—and all this just because you are everything to Him!

"I would never go to New Mexico without you, Mommy," I heard my son say as he asked for forgiveness.

"I know, sweetie," I said, embracing him. "Oh, you are everything to me!"

OLGA VALDIVIA

My Father's Arms

The eternal God is your refuge, and underneath are the everlasting arms. Deut. 33:27, NIV.

*D*o I really remember it? Or have I just heard the story so many times I think I do? Whatever the case, my drive to be grown-up and independent was already in evidence at the age of 3.

On a warm summer day Mother and Daddy took me shopping. We stopped to look in the window of a shoe store. Clutching my little red purse, I slowly edged away from them and around the corner, engrossed in my daydream of being a grown-up young woman shopping all by myself. Carefully I studied the various shoes displayed in the window, as if I were contemplating a purchase. Amused at my intent playacting, my parents were watching me through the store window.

Looking up to see if anyone had noticed how grown-up I was, I was startled to realize that my parents were not in sight. Suddenly I was transformed from a self-assured young woman to a terrified and lost 3-year-old. With a gasping scream of "Da-a-a-dy!" I took off down the sidewalk as fast as my short legs could carry me.

Daddy immediately followed in hot pursuit, but fear lent wings to my feet, and to his horror, I reached the corner before he did. In my blind fear I would have darted into the traffic of the busy city street had not a stranger quickly grabbed me. The man handed me over to Daddy as he arrived at the street corner, puffing and panting. In Daddy's strong arms my tears ceased, and I snuggled up to him, feeing safe and secure again. And for the moment, at least, I realized that I wasn't ready to be grown-up yet and was very happy to have a mother and father to take care of me.

How often I have repeated this experience in my spiritual life. Forgetting to focus on my need of God, I blithely sail through my busy daily activities, making decisions and carrying out plans as if I were in complete control. Then the unexpected happens; disaster overtakes me, and my world comes crashing down around my feet. Suddenly I realize that I'm *not* in control, after all. Panic-stricken, I search for my heavenly Father. With

His comforting arms around me at last, I gladly admit my helplessness and need of His guidance.   CARROL GRADY

FEBRUARY 10

Seeing God Through Orion

Seek him that maketh the seven stars and Orion. Amos 5:8.

It was early in the morning when I woke—just half
        past three.
My heart was o'erwhelmed with burdens that were
        troubling me.
    I wasn't ready yet to face appointments I must keep,
And so in darkness I prayed for one more hour of sleep.

But sometimes God says no, and sleep escaped my weary
        eyes.
    It seemed I heard Him speak to me: "My child, it's
        time to rise;
You've asked for guidance, and I'm here in answer to your plea.
    When will you be available to spend some time with Me?"

"O Lord," I said, "I thank You for this hour You've come
        to spend!"
    And so I rose to talk with Him, my never-failing Friend.
I knelt before the picture window, seeking God's reply . . .
    And then I saw it—His great token gleaming in the sky!

In all its spacious splendor, to my view Orion shone.
    I felt that God was watching me from His celestial throne.
I've seen Orion often, even in the darkest skies,
    But never had it seemed so bright! It took me by surprise.

Its radiance forced my viewing, and I knew 'twas meant to be;
    My God had something special that He wanted me to see.
With eyes wide open, watching, all my cares from me were torn.
    Hot tears rolled down my cheeks as all alone I prayed
        that morn.

God's constellation filled the sky; His goodness filled my soul.
    And peace unspeakable replaced my doubts and made
    me whole.
I've learned that in the darkness, e'er my busy hours start,
    Those blessings that He promises He'll faithfully impart.

Our God who made Orion makes our cup to overflow.
    He has so many blessings that He's waiting to bestow!
But we must give Him time to speak, so let us meet Him there
    Each morning by appointment, in our quiet place of prayer.
                                                    LORRAINE HUDGINS

I Stuck!

Surely the arm of the Lord is not too short to save, nor his ear too
dull to hear. Isa. 59:1, NIV.

*E*verything was an adventure to her. Emeline's 19-month-
old legs were short, but her aspirations were long.
Dragging a little plastic chair to the coffee table in the family
room, she climbed up two stages to her final goal, which was to
sit on the seat of the exercise bicycle standing next to the table.
With triumph on her chubby face, she swung a leg over, and
there she was, the conqueror! She had made it on her own.

And then having looked down all the way to the pedals and
beyond to the floor, she turned to me and said with consternation, "I stuck!"

Of course, I scooped her up with a hug and placed her on the
floor. Everything was fine in her world now, and she gave a giggle as she went off to play.

Sometimes I fear that I am a bit like my little granddaughter,
racing into situations that seem extremely appealing, and then I
get "stuck" when the ramifications of where I am hit me. I can so
easily find that my actions have taken me far from the safety of
the floor, and I cannot even reach the pedals. It is terrifying to
feel so helpless and at risk, to know that by my own efforts I am

in a place where nothing I can do will save me. Like Emeline, though, I know that Someone will help. Someone will extricate me from a frightening or perilous circumstance if only I call. His arms are strong, His ear is tuned to my voice, and His heart of love motivates His every move.

Thank You, Father in heaven, for Your never-ending care and for helping me to understand a little more of what you are like through the love of family.   URSULA M. HEDGES

FEBRUARY 12

A Yellow Canary

If I go and prepare a place for you, I will come again, and receive you unto myself; that where I am, there ye may be also. John 14:3.

My sister offered me a yellow canary that was not good breeding stock. His wings overlapped too much, his legs were too far apart (probably because he was not turned enough in the egg while developing), and yellow was not a popular color then. I hesitated, because I like freedom to go, often wishing I did not even have house plants. But a canary—a living, breathing, seeing, hearing creature—would require even more care.

"I'll give you a cage," she encouraged.

"Is this one named?" I was weakening.

"No, he was hatched just this summer. He is just a number."

"I'll call him Sweet Tweet. I really like his song."

Sweet Tweet is totally dependent on me for food, water, his bath, a clean cage, and protection. As I weed flower beds and mow grass, I keep moving him within view, because the neighborhood cats try to catch him, even in his cage.

Molting must be a trial. He acts listless, depressed, and does not sing a note. I feel sorry for him. As I work in another part of the house, I tell him, "I'm moving you so you can be where I am."

The phrase sounded so familiar. Suddenly I realized why God created me for His pleasure (Rev. 4:11). Sweet Tweet's relationship to me is much like my relationship to God. God loves me, provides for all my needs, pities me when trials come, misses

70

me when I neglect Bible reading and prayer, provides angels for my protection, and wants me to be with Him.

Even if Sweet Tweet's mother turned one egg twice and missed another altogether, he still gets along just fine with those legs and sings a beautiful song.

We also need to make the best use of whatever disabilities we may have and stop focusing on blame-placing. Our song of praise for our Maker may not be vocal—it may be acts of kindness, doing our work well, or maintaining a cheerful attitude. In times when we don't feel like singing our song, God does not stop loving and caring for us any more than I neglect Sweet Tweet. When the molt is over, he bursts forth in a new song that's even sweeter than before. Our trials can improve our song too.

A handful of yellow feathers taught me that I was created for God's pleasure, that He misses me when I neglect Him, that He cares for me. As I move Sweet Tweet to where I'm working, I ask him, "Do you want to be where I am?" I'm comforted remembering God's promise "Where I am, there ye may be also."

EDNA BARRETT CANADAY

FEBRUARY 13

Answering Calls

I called, but no one answered; I spoke, but they did not listen. Isa. 66:4, NASB.

Have you fallen off the face of the earth?"

"I always seem to get your answering machine."

"Looks like we are playing phone tag again!"

Answering machines. A useful tool, yet so frustrating when we need to talk with someone. I confess, I dislike the telephone. It always rings at the most inopportune times. And, I admit, I have at times let the answering machine take calls, even when I am home. I'm too busy, or I don't want to be interrupted, or maybe I just don't care to talk to anyone at that moment. Those are the times that friends leave frustrated messages. Some stop leaving messages altogether, and when I play back the tape I just hear a dial tone.

Could my prayer life sometimes be like my answering machine? Do I talk to God only on Sabbaths or at bedtime or when I feel like it? I wonder if God ever watches my busyness (or laziness) and wishes I would just talk to Him. Does He sometimes feel frustrated when I don't answer His calls? What kind of messages does He leave?

What a contrast from the way God treats us! In Jeremiah 33:3 He promises, "Call to me and I will answer you" (NIV). And in Jeremiah 29:12 He promises, "Then you will call upon me and come and pray to me, and I will listen to you" (NIV). No answering machines, no call waiting, no busy signal. Just a loving God who wants me to draw closer to Him and depend on Him for every need in my life.

Father, help me to be sensitive to Your voice. I don't want You to become just a dial tone! In my busy life, help me to put my relationship with You first. Teach me also to be sensitive to the needs of those who call me—to set aside my own busyness and feelings to take the time to listen and care. That's what Jesus would do. Make me like Him. LILLY TRYON

Going the Distance

Walk in love, as Christ also hath loved us, and hath given himself for us an offering and a sacrifice to God for a sweetsmelling savour. Eph. 5:2.

pulled into the parking lot a little before 9:00 a.m. I had come to meet a friend to begin a walking program, and this lot was at the foot of some beautiful trails. I was early, so I sat back and waited. After several moments, I noticed a couple walking toward the hills. They were engrossed in conversation and did not see me. They were older people, in their 60s I guessed, and appeared to be in great shape. Each wore a stylish running outfit and sported serious running shoes. And although they had such good-looking bodies, it was their legs that captured my attention. The man's legs were strong and very muscular; his wife's legs firm and beautifully shaped. I marveled that they belonged to older people.

As I watched, the couple stopped talking and made their way up the steep incline. The husband was going strong, but his wife was beginning to tire and fall behind. Suddenly he stopped and patiently waited until she caught up with him, then lovingly took her hand and pulled her to the top of the hill. I watched as they disappeared over the rise.

A short time later I spotted the couple again. They were much older than I had first thought, and much smaller. The man was very gray, and the woman's legs were terribly scarred. But as they strode hand in hand down the hill together, they were relaxed and laughing.

I understood their elation. I have tackled this same trail many times with my own husband. It never seems to get easier, and I could appreciate their accomplishment. I wondered about the couple all morning. How long did it take them to get into such great shape? Why were the woman's legs so scarred? What had she endured? What had they endured together? Were the protective actions of the man and the total trust on the part of the woman a result of overcoming a hardship together?

Whatever the situation, it made me see my own husband in a different light. It made me recognize and appreciate his protective nature toward me. It also gave me another reason to praise and thank my heavenly Father for the man in my life and for His infinite wisdom in bringing two people together to love and trust and grow as one. I began to see that this growth takes a lifetime to root, grow, branch, and blossom. It must be nurtured and cultivated every day.

That couple will never know the impression they left on me, or how they affected my life. But I have kept them in my prayers and thank the good Lord for the blessing I received that morning.

TERRI CASEY

The Unexpected Gift

Every good and perfect gift is from above, coming down from the Father of the heavenly lights, who does not change like shifting shadows. James 1:17, NIV.

My husband and I were attending a three-day confer-
ence at the Portland, Oregon, coliseum. Although it had proved to be interesting, I had not received the emotional boost I had expected. By the last session I felt tired and ready for the trip home. We had chosen our seats for ease of exit, so we were no longer sitting with our traveling group.

As we waited for the session to begin, my husband leaned over and pointed to the couple sitting a row in front of us. "Doesn't she look like a younger version of Helen?" he asked, referring to a woman I worked with.

I glanced over, but really paid little attention. Twice more my husband commented on this particular couple. I thought nothing more about it until two hours later when the man turned around, looked me squarely in the eyes, and said, "Carel, what are you doing here?"

I stared in disbelief. This man was one of my dearest friends from high school and college, someone with whom I had studied and prayed. We lost track of each other after we both got mar-
ried. Although he recognized me, it was not until I heard his voice that I was able to recognize him. Suddenly, here was the emotional boost I had been seeking. It was as if the four of us had been directed to this place and time. As we looked around at the 15,000 other people in the coliseum, we were humbled by the magnitude of the wonderful gift that God had bestowed upon us that day. Had we not sat apart from our group, we might have missed an opportunity to renew a very dear friendship. God wanted to pour out a special blessing that none of us could have imagined. Truly, we have a creative God who enjoys placing these surprises in our pathway.

"And God is able to make all grace abound to you, so that in all things at all times, having all that you need, you will abound in every good work" (2 Cor. 9:8, NIV).   CAREL CLAY

God Answers Small Prayers Too

Lord, teach us to pray. Luke 11:1, NKJV.

My grandson asked me to let down the hem of his jeans. It was a hard job for my old eyes. I managed to take out the stitches easily enough, but when it came to rehemming, I couldn't see to thread the machine needle. I licked my fingers and wet the end of the thread as I made a dozen futile stabs at the needle before I gave up.

There was no one at home to help me, and my grandson needed the jeans for school the next morning. In desperation I said aloud, "Lord, please help me," and poked the thread toward the needle. It went straight through the eye! I could scarcely believe it. I was so grateful I poured out my thanks as the machine whirred around, hemming the first leg of the jeans.

Then I began on the second leg—and the thread broke. My heart sank. Again I licked my fingers, wet the thread, and pushed it toward the needle. I tried and tried. I hadn't a hope when I couldn't even see the eye. In utter frustration I asked, "Lord, could You possibly do it again?" Once more, I pushed the thread at the needle, and it went straight through, just as it had before. I was amazed! I wanted to tell somebody, but I knew they would probably laugh. They wouldn't believe that God would bother about threading a needle.

The big things, oh, yes. We expect God to heal us when we're sick, to take care of us when we travel, to forgive our sins, and to provide us with all our necessities. He has promised all those big things, and we have no hesitation about claiming those promises. But if we expect God to solve our large problems, then why can't we trust Him with our little perplexities? What kind of independence keeps us stumbling on our way, fumbling with our tasks, attempting everything alone, when He is so willing to share our burdens?

Is it because God has the whole universe to control that we don't like to bother Him with trifles? After all, one can't compare threading a needle with stopping a cruel war in Palestine or a famine in Africa.

God *wants* to help us with our small problems, as well as our large ones. He says that we are the apple of His eye (Zech. 2:8), and that He knows how many hairs we have on our heads (Matt. 10:30).

Ask God for help with even your smallest problems. You'll be thrilled by His response.   GOLDIE DOWN

FEBRUARY 17

When God Spread His Wings

A thousand may fall at your side, . . . but it will not come near you. You will only observe with your eyes. Ps. 91:7, 8, NIV.

From my friend's picture window we watched ominous black clouds building. Howling winds bent trees low, and a blinding rain fell. We did not know that a twister was in progress, nor that it had touched down in my neighborhood.

When the rain slackened, I drove some two miles to my home. As I neared my street, the fallen trees, branches, twigs, leaves, and the twisted metal from utility sheds were scattered about and sent a sickening feeling of dread and fear through me.

"Lord, help," I prayed repeatedly as I saw devastation all along our block. The neighbor directly across the street from us stood staring at the fallen trees in his yard. A huge tree lay across the roof of the house next to ours.

In our front yard the trees stood straight and tall. *Perhaps the damage is inside,* I thought. However, no debris of any size was anywhere, except for a few twigs scattered in the yard. I called an elderly neighbor, who, still in mild shock, related how she huddled in the hallway during the storm because she was afraid. I attempted to console her by reading Psalm 91.

"I feel so much better now," she gratefully replied, and asked if there was any damage to our property. I assured her that God sheltered us during the storm.

Remembering the mother robin in a tall pine tree in our backyard, I went out, expecting to see the nest and its contents scattered around the yard. Through my binoculars I spied mother robin sitting calmly, undisturbed.

Peace and gratitude overwhelmed me as I realized more than

ever that our house and yard testified to God's mercy and protection. Even as the mother robin sheltered her nestlings under her wings, in the same way He covered us with His feathers and provided refuge under His wings.

Two days later we found one tree in the backyard that the storm had "beheaded," and the telephone line was down. Our telephone still worked, however.

"I will protect him, for he acknowledges my name" (Ps. 91:14, NIV). God kept His promise. He is good!

MABEL ROLLINS NORMAN

FEBRUARY 18

Disinfectant, Please!

Do not let any unwholesome talk come out of your mouths, but only what is helpful for building others up according to their needs, that it may benefit those who listen. Eph. 4:29, NIV.

My son, Jason, has to tell me everything that happens at school—good and bad. When he was in kindergarten, I would pick him up at noon, and we would have the next few hours together in which he could unload every detail.

One particular day in relating the day's events Jason stated, "Mom, Kari has caught my lying germ."

Not sure I had heard him right, I asked him how he knew this. He told me that once Kari had not told him the truth, and he found out. Of course, he didn't appreciate it at all and told her she was bad for doing such a thing!

Interestingly, Jason remembered that lately he'd been having a hard time telling the truth about little things himself. His sister and I had called him on some things we heard him say, and he had to admit they weren't the whole truth. So for him to theorize that his association with Kari had somehow influenced her to lie to him was enough to make my mother heart beat with joy at this morsel of maturity.

God also loves to see our steps toward spiritual maturity in our relationships with others. We need to remember that our in-

77

fluence on someone else can either bring them closer to God or divert them down the wrong path. In Ephesians God asks us to be careful that the things we say to others are positive and build them up. That's a sobering idea when you think of some of the rude and unkind people you encounter day by day. Jesus Himself endured treatment we can't begin to fathom, yet people who were in His presence left changed.

Lord, put kind thoughts and words within me for those times today when someone tries my patience, so that we both may experience Your love and influence in our lives.   PATTY KNITTEL

FEBRUARY 19

The Mustard Tree Friend

Though it is the smallest of all your seeds, yet when it grows, it is the largest of garden plants and becomes a tree, so that the birds of the air come and perch in its branches. Matt. 13:32, NIV.

I have a very special friend. She has faced many spiritual challenges in her life, but nothing throws her. She always seems so calm and collected, and peacefulness shines out of her, along with a lot of love and happiness. Sometimes during a difficult meeting at work I will look over at her. She is looking down, her lips gently moving, and I know she is praying.

Lots of people know she prays. She has an amazing faith, and all kinds of people are drawn to her, whether they will admit they believe or not. I often catch a glimpse of her listening to someone's problems in the hospital corridor. Often I can be chatting casually about something on my mind and she will suddenly say, "Let's pray about this right now!" Then we'll find a peaceful corner or bow our heads wherever we are, and she will wrap me in the comforting arms of her faith. I always leave stronger, happier, more serene, and with a warm glow spreading out from the center of my being.

Not long ago I was reading about the parable of the mustard seed and how such a tiny thing can grow into a bushy tree. As I read on, I noticed something else. Not only does the tree grow, but all kinds of birds come and rest in the branches. Maybe some are nibbling away at berries, leaves, or insects, finding something to take away to feed their families. Other birds are there for companionship, while still others are singing or even building nests in the tree.

As I thought of that faith-seed tree, filled with birds, I thought of my friend. She is so full of faith you can't come within a mile of her without recognizing that she is in contact with God. And because of her strong, peaceful faith, people flock to her for nourishment, comfort, rest, and direction.

It doesn't matter if you are big or small, as long as you have branches that reach out to others and upward to God. Even though you may feel insignificant, the chances are that you are bigger than you feel and that there are more birds landing on your branches than you realize. Take some time today to think of at least one bird who rests on your branches, and pray about how you can share more of God's love with that individual. One day, because of your love and faith, those you help may be able to dig a little hole and plant their own seed of faith.

KAREN HOLFORD

FEBRUARY 20

Being Prepared

To that end keep alert with all perseverance. Eph. 6:18, RSV.

They called it "The Blizzard of '93," and I know why. I lived in the path of the storm that dumped nearly two feet of snow on my North Carolina home in early March. The television gave us ample warning of the impending storm, so I went to the store and bought bread, milk, and other supplies. The winds blew, the snow came, the temperature dropped, but there I sat, warm and safe inside my house, while unprepared and panic-stricken shoppers scurried for food. That night the lines at the grocery stores were tremendous, and there wasn't a loaf of bread to be found anywhere.

The Lord tells us not to worry about tomorrow, but He does

expect us to use our common sense. The motto is: "Be prepared." Doesn't that sound like a good plan? During the blizzard, as I sat comfortably curled up with a good book, my thoughts kept returning to the fact that our Lord is coming soon. For some, that may be the disaster of their lifetime; for others, a time of great expectation. It all depends on whether or not we are prepared. I had prepared for the blizzard, but what must I do to prepare for this great event?

For heat we need the companionship of the Holy Spirit. For staples, daily bread from prayer and the study of God's Word. With this preparation we can look up with confidence and say, "Lo, this is our God; we have waited for Him, and He will save us."

I want to be ready, don't you? My preparedness will not help another. Each must make her preparations now. Waiting until the last minute may leave us standing in a very long line without the Bread of Life to be found anywhere.

ANN VAN ARSDELL HAYWARD

Power Over Serpents

Behold I give unto you power to tread on serpents and scorpions, and over all the power of the enemy. Luke 10:19.

I was a photojournalist, editor of the mission magazine, and on my way to get a scoop on a story about the tribal work in northern Thailand. My husband and 13-year-old daughter were in Singapore. He is the medical director of a hospital, and my daughter attends a Christian boarding academy there.

I took the plane to Bangkok and the train to Chiang Mai. Kind friends put me on an overloaded country bus with strict instructions to the driver to "put me off" at a certain place. After several bone-shaking hours on rough roads, he dropped me off at high noon in a dense tropical jungle. I hoisted my weekend bag and cameras over my shoulder and scouted the area for some recognizable clues. Ah! Far away on a distant hilltop were visible signs of academic life. School buildings rimmed the ridge, but I couldn't find the road leading to them.

So with a prayer on my lips, I just kept visual contact and started through the thick undergrowth. I was heartened by the sight and sounds of a gurgling jungle stream, bridged by a rickety arch of wooden planks, and the melody of an old song, "Cross Over the Bridge," beckoned me to do so.

Just then a terrifying obstruction appeared. It squeezed through the wooden planks and fully raised its mottled, pulsating body four feet high. It swayed slightly, hypnotic eyes blazing and venomous fangs clearly visible from its evil open mouth. I had met the scourge of these verdant jungles—the dreaded cobra. Quite obviously, in challenging me it was obeying that old master serpent, the devil himself.

I was furious. How dare this cobra confront me? I was on the Lord's business! I stepped onto the rickety bridge and with both feet stomped out a loud reverberating tattoo that rattled the whole bridge, with that cobra just six feet from me. That did it. The cobra slithered back between the slats and into oblivion.

My heart was full of praise to God as I continued my jungle trip and completed my assignment at the tribal mission school. I thanked Him for watching over His daughter once again.

Jesus can help you overcome whatever "cobras" Satan puts in your path. Just ask for His help, and He will give you the power.

JILL WARDEN PARCHMENT

FEBRUARY 22

Be Ye Kind

Be ye kind one to another, tenderhearted, forgiving one another, even as God for Christ's sake hath forgiven you. Eph. 4:32.

*E*lephants are animals that intrigue me. Though huge in size, they move about noiselessly and obediently under the direction of a mahout, an elephant keeper. Once I had an opportunity to visit a reserved forest. We were able to ride on a tame elephant that was guided by a mahout through the forest. The mahout told the elephant to pick some wildflowers and give them to us. Suddenly I saw the elephant's trunk right in front of me, holding a little wildflower.

I reached for the flower with great delight, exclaiming, "Thank you!" I felt like hugging the elephant. I was so impressed that such a huge animal could be so gentle and kind to a stranger like me.

There are many wild elephants in the reserved forest. A local man told me a story about one of them. An elephant was in search of food when it came across a woodcutter. The elephant tried to reach for the man's lunch packet, which he had packed in a banana leaf and hung on a tree. The furious man threatened the elephant by brandishing a knife. The elephant tried many times to ask for food, but seeing the knife, he finally moved on. The man ate his food with no thought about the hungry elephant.

That night the man and his wife and baby slept on beds near the window, opened wide because of the heat. At daybreak the parents were horrified to discover their baby missing. Frantically the man led his wife through the forest in search of the baby. As he suspected, he found the same hungry elephant—and the baby lying next to it on the ground. He begged for the baby, but the elephant paid no attention. He was not going to give that baby back. The man ran home and soon came back with a basket of paddy and some bananas. He begged the elephant to accept the food and to forgive him. The elephant gently picked up the baby with his trunk and placed him in his mother's outstretched arms. The elephant could have hurt the baby, but instead taught the man a lesson from Ephesians that he never forgot: "Be ye kind one to another."

Today's verse tells us why we should be kind and forgiving: because God has forgiven us. Jesus also told us to love even our enemies, to be kind to the unthankful and the evil (Luke 6:35). In doing this, we shall be called the children of the Highest. What a wonderful reward that will be! BIRDIE PODDAR

Metamorphosis

Though your sins are like scarlet, they shall be as white as snow; though they are red like crimson, they shall be as wool. Isa. 1:18, NKJV.

For a long time I have had a deep attraction to butterflies. Though I'm really interested in them, I cannot say it is my hobby. What I feel is sheer admiration.

Some time ago I had the rare opportunity of seeing the largest private collection of butterflies in Argentina, thanks to the cordiality of its owner. What my eyes saw on that occasion is far beyond words. A true symphony of color, brilliance, and shape. Hundreds of butterflies, so many that its owner does not know exactly how many there are! All of them are laid out within neat wooden boxes. Attached to each one is a label with its scientific name, its origin, and the date it was captured. For three hours we enjoyed looking at the butterflies and listening to an explanation of their habits, nourishment, and the process of metamorphosis.

Metamorphosis, a difficult word, identifies a true miracle of transformation. Let us imagine a lovely butterfly with yellow-orange iridescent wings, bright as though somebody had spilled gold dust on them. At the beginning it was nothing but a furry black caterpillar. Or let's have a look at this other one with phosphorescent green wings, smeared with yellow and black at the edges. It started out as a large brownish caterpillar. . . . Well, we could go on and on comparing the breathtaking beauty of a butterfly with the disgusting caterpillar it was in the early stages of its life.

Do you know that God works a similar transformation in our lives? Do you realize that even though we may appear unattractive or be rejected because of faulty personality traits, with God's help and transforming power we can be like an awesome, colorful butterfly?

If you feel sad or discouraged under the burden of your vices and sins, remember that the Lord can carry out the miracle of metamorphosis in you. Don't let go of the opportunity He gives you to turn your seemingly dull or faulty existence into a wonderful life!

SUSANA SCHULZ

Morning Mist

Now we see through a glass, darkly; but then face to face: now
I know in part; but then shall I know even as also I am known.
1 Cor. 13:12.

I thought I heard it in my sleep. I turned over to catch my
first controlled breath and heard it again—a shrill birdcall.
The persistent fellow continued his racket. By now sleep was
impossible, so I tiptoed to the window and pulled back the blinds
to peep outside.

Surprise! Beautiful! Mystical! What was that? Nature's gift!
The heaviest, thickest mist had settled over everything. The
mist was everywhere. Quickly I dressed and dashed outdoors.
I needed that walk—that something different—for I was
anxious and worried. My funds were low, and the bills were
high. It was an impossible situation. But God never forgot
me. He sent me a special gift. That morning I was to discover
the meaning of the gem "The greater the problem, the richer
the blessing."

It seemed I had walked into a storybook, a misty wonderland,
a strange world. I wandered down the familiar road close to my
home, but everything appeared to be in a vague, hazy blue. I
heard the squirrel that scampered up the tree in front of me but
saw only a moving ball. I walked on, mystified and alone, before
the world awoke on that rare morning.

Visibility was only a couple feet, and as I looked up I could
see no sun, only a certain brightness. Out and away, the trees
rose like dark shadows, and the mountains melted into the cloud
that settled over everything. I rubbed my eyes, then opened them
wide and peered deeper into the haze. Suddenly everything
seemed brighter. Shafts of light began to slice the mist and penetrate the haze. The mist was gone within a few seconds, and the
sun appeared in all its brightness.

A text slashed through my mind. I repeated it slowly. "Now
we see through a glass, darkly; but then face to face, now I know
in part; but then shall I know even as also I am known." This
misty daybreak experience was a perfect illustration of that text.
I had never really understood this text before that moment, but

then I caught the message and understood the meaning. I learned what faith is.

That very same day, when I faced my challenging situation, I handled it with a different technique. Though I had no means, I ventured out in faith to claim a promise. I recited my favorite text: "Open thy mouth wide, and I will fill it" (Ps. 81:10). I dared to believe that out of His everlasting abundance God would fill any need I had. My childlike faith was rewarded. The unexpected happened. The mailcarrier brought me a promised blessing—just the amount I needed at the time I needed it. My heart rejoiced. I sang a new song, a song of praise to the Lord, who backs up every promise He has made.

CECILY DALY

FEBRUARY 25

Sunny Side Up

Ye are the light of the world. . . . Let your light so shine. Matt. 5:14-16.

What a bountiful spiritual heritage I received from my two loving parents. My three older brothers and I were close in age. Every morning Mom and Dad would prepare an ample, nutritious breakfast for us. We each had our own place setting at the kitchen table that was situated to give us a beautiful view of the San Joaquin River winding its way through the valley below. My parents subscribed to a number of fascinating magazines. Dad had a habit of tearing out articles from these magazines, according to each of our interests. He then put them at our place at the breakfast table so that we always had something to read and discuss while the food was being put on the table.

About halfway through breakfast Dad would pull out the current year's Morning Watch book and read aloud as we finished eating. Then he'd look out our big picture window and assess the weather. I can recall his sentiment on more than one wintry morning. "Well, the sun's not out today, so you're going to have to make your own sunshine!"

By the time Mom got us out the door, we were well on our

85

way to a successful day. All the way to school Dad's pep talk continued. He would tell us how to make our light for Jesus shine all over the school, and by the time our feet hit the school grounds the four of us were convinced that we were the light of the world. We were ready to face the day because we had clearly seen "the light" reflected in our godly parents, who had found the secret to keeping their "sunny side" up.

JUDY COULSTON

FEBRUARY 26

Vanity Fair

Thus saith the Lord, What iniquity have your fathers found in me, that they are gone far from me, and have walked after vanity, and are become vain? . . . Can a maid forget her ornaments, or a bride her attire? yet my people have forgotten me days without number. Why trimmest thou thy way to seek love? Jer. 2:5-33.

Alcoholics Anonymous meetings begin with introductions. "Hello, I'm So-and-so, and I'm an alcoholic." I think I should go to a Vanity Anonymous meeting. "Hello, I'm Julie, and I'm vain." All these years of being a superior person (going to church, paying tithe, going to college, doing all the right things, not drinking or smoking) have made me think I'm OK. But I have a very big problem—little gods. Usually I'm critical of other people's little gods—cars, position, sports, and such. At the same time I'm envious of their cars and interesting lives and great reputations and travels.

I was going to write a letter to the editor of a Christian journal about our little gods, when I realized the problem is really mine. I love pretty things—especially if I can wear them. Blame it on my great-grandmother, who *loved* to dress. You could hear her coming, because she had on so many bangles and rustling dresses and petticoats.

I don't know how bad I was as a teenager, but going to college was a dress event, and I was prepared. Funds were scarce, but I could sew, and fabric was reasonable. I really felt fashionable. I have to laugh now about how ridiculous I must have seemed to the deans and other adults, but I was impressed with myself. True, I studied and worked and joined clubs, but the clothing interest didn't slack off.

Now I'm amused at older people who "primp," then I look in the mirror and here I am, wrinkles and all, thinking more about what I'm going to wear to church than what priorities are in my prayers.

People say when you point your finger, there are three more fingers pointing back at yourself. Oh, me, I need help! Is there a support group? And vanity is just one of my problems, a piece of my major self-interests. So I'm pretty good about church and the Ten Commandments, except that part about "have no other gods before me" (Ex. 20:3). Help me, God.   JULIA PEARCE

FEBRUARY 27

Trust in the Lord

Trust in the Lord with all your heart, and lean not on your own understanding. Prov. 3:5, NKJV.

*I*n April 1995 I had to take my training in a boys' school well known for the corruption and lack of discipline of its pupils. The majority of students had been expelled from other schools. I was supposed to teach English to two groups; one group was made up of nearly 70 students, the other of about 27.

As expected, things were difficult from the start. I didn't know my pupils or the other teachers very well. I had to acquaint myself with an unfamiliar program. The rudeness of the students made my days unbearable. Many times I left the classroom in tears because I failed to maintain discipline during the class. Visits to my supervisor to complain seemed worthless.

Occasionally I prayed about the problem, but I didn't really believe God would help me. Instead I tried to find solutions on my own. I sent students out of the room or failed them for misbehavior. All these proved ineffective; the students' behavior worsened. Some enjoyed spending English period outside the classroom. Others didn't care if they failed, knowing they could improve their grades by giving my supervisor a bribe at the end of the term. The situation made me ill and left me with a bad attitude.

One day while looking for an address I had left in my Bible, my eyes fell on today's verse: "Trust in the Lord with all your heart, and lean not on your own understanding." For the first time I realized how much God loved me, and that I needed to count on His wisdom and not my own. The more I prayed with the assurance that He would find a solution to my problem, the more the situation around me changed. I became more understanding and less temperamental. My students showed more respect and enthusiasm for the English class. An atmosphere of cooperation began to permeate the group.

From that time on, we enjoyed being together so much that on the last day of my teacher training some of them cried as the group sang a song for me: "If we do not meet on earth, we will certainly meet in heaven."

Truly the Lord's wisdom is above and beyond all the human wisdom in this world, for only He could have wrought such a miracle in the lives of those precious students and me. Trust in Him with all your heart. He is a miracle worker.

GISELE NYEMBWE

FEBRUARY 28

A Place of Worship

O come, let us sing to the Lord! Let us shout joyfully to the Rock of our salvation. Let us come before His presence with thanksgiving; let us shout joyfully to Him with psalms. Ps. 95:1, 2, NKJV.

We were having enchiladas for dinner. As I stood at the counter cutting the black olives, onion, and peppers, I felt tired, a little down. My mind replayed the problems of the week. Would the paycheck cover all the bills this month? How could I teach the boys to be more responsible with their things? What all needed to be done this weekend? My thoughts raced as I half listened to the music playing from the stereo.

"Do I trust You, Lord?" the voice sang.

The words of the song penetrated my thoughts. *Do I trust You, Lord? Am I trusting You to take care of these problems and concerns and struggles?*

"Lord, I'm keeping my eyes on You, following You, following You . . ."

Yes, Lord, I want to keep my eyes on You. Not on the problems that surround me. Help me to focus on You and not on the struggles. You will take care of them.

"I will glorify the Lord of lords, I will glorify the Lamb."

As I stood there chopping the black olives, my kitchen became a place of worship. My heart sang praises to my God. *I will glorify You, Lord. Teach me to trust You, to keep my eyes on You. You are my God. Lord of lords. King of kings. I love You, Lord!*

Peace filled my mind. My back no longer ached. As I stirred the bean mixture, I recommitted my heart to trusting God.

God is with us every day, in the ordinary, common things we do. He waits to turn our hearts to Him and receive our praise and worship. He desires to remove the burdens of our problems and struggles and to fill us with indescribable joy. Let your heart sing to Him today!   TAMI HORST

MARCH 1

Consider the Birds

Do not worry about your life. . . . Look at the birds of the air; they do not sow or reap or store away in barns, and yet your heavenly Father feeds them. Are you not much more valuable than they? Matt. 6:25, 26, NIV.

*E*ven as a child growing up on a prairie farm in western Canada, I had an interest in birds. I tried to learn all I could about the few that came to our treeless farm. Once I found a meadowlark nest hidden under its canopy of grass.

This summer, having decided to journey back, I visited the farm where I had lived and raised my family for more than 30 years. A good many mornings just like this one had been spent on the front porch, listening and looking.

Two mourning doves, hidden from my sight, are calling to

each other, their plaintive calls alternating back and forth. Then one voice stops, but the other continues to call endlessly. Small brown birds I do not recognize walk effortlessly up the tree trunks, pecking at the unsuspecting insects hiding there. Blackbirds flit from one grove of trees to another, winging in darting dips through the still morning air. Nearby a robin takes a hop . . . two hops . . . then pauses to listen and look around, then takes two more hops. I watch, fascinated, until the robin flies away.

But still I sit. The morning sun glistens on the raindrops from last night's shower clinging to the grass. Still the twinkling wings continue to dart back and forth, and still the mourning dove calls.

> Little birdie on a twig, tiny ball of fluff,
> With the green leaves all around, you are safe enough.
> But you're not content to stay, sitting on a limb.
> Spread your wings and fly away, through the air you skim.
> The world is large beyond your tree, and you are oh,
>   so small,
> Does your heart beat rapidly? Aren't you scared you'll fall?
> Little, tiny, feathered friend, could I be like you?
> Spread my wings and fly away, trusting as you do?
> Leave the mundane all behind, of my everyday,
> Could I spread my trembling wings and be upon my way?
> Tell me, tiny little bird, way up in the sky,
> How the Father of us all, taught *you* how to fly.

Jesus said, "Don't worry. You are more valuable than the birds."

EVA ALICE COVEY

MARCH 2

Preoccupied

Keep watch, because you do not know on what day your Lord will come. Matt. 24:42, NIV.

When my husband was pastoring in Birmingham, Alabama, my brother was pastoring about an hour's drive south of us in Clanton. We often found ourselves chatting on the telephone. There was plenty to talk about—family and friends, recreational pursuits, religious news, the trials and joys of ministry. Sometimes we talked for a long time.

One morning my brother and I conversed for about 45 minutes. When I hung up the receiver, I heard a loud roaring noise that sounded to me like the operation of a cement truck. I decided to have a look. As I proceeded to my bedroom at the opposite end of the house, the noise grew louder. Looking out the window to the driveway beneath me, I was shocked to see a fire truck. With my heart racing, I hurried out to discover what was happening. My neighbor quickly filled me in.

She had been burning trash, and the fire got out of control. She tried to put it out, but her efforts were futile. As the fire made its way to our yard, she knocked vigorously on my front door. Getting no response, she anxiously called my name. Then, realizing that I was going to be no help, she had called the fire department. Two thirds of my backyard had burned while I was visiting on the phone. Just a bit more wind and my daughter, Tressa, and I would have been in real danger. The scary thing was that I had no idea what was happening.

I could have known. I could have heard my neighbor knocking. I could have heard her call my name. I could have heard the fire truck. I could have smelled the smoke—*if* I had not been so absorbed with my phone call.

Jesus likened the time when He would return to the days of Noah, just prior to the Flood. He said that the people of Noah's day had been eating, drinking, marrying, and giving in marriage and "knew nothing about what would happen until the flood came and took them all away" (Matt. 24:39, NIV). Noah had tried to warn them, but they were so intent on getting on with their lives that their spiritual senses failed them.

Are you preoccupied today? We've been given information that will help us be prepared for Jesus' soon coming. But life can be so busy. There doesn't seem to be enough time for all that we want and need to do. It's easy to become distracted from spiritual realities. Only as we make it our highest priority will we be able to detect the significance of events about us. Will we be awake or asleep? observant or oblivious? Distraction is dangerous, perhaps even deadly.

May the Lord make us watchful!   TERESA CARMICHAEL

Consider the Lilies

Consider the lilies of the field. Matt. 6:28.

*M*y daughter reached down and picked up a piece of gravel between her chubby fingers. I hastened to pry the stone gently from her grasp. How tiny it was! I would never have noticed it, but she did.

How often we ignore life's little things. We see the truck with its load and ships with their cargo, but crush the ant underfoot. We notice the soaring rocket, but fail to observe the hummingbird. We shower gifts on those who have enough, then forget to give of ourselves and our time to those with less. Life's little things bring such pleasure. If only we would pause to appreciate them. . . .

Pause long enough to consider the lilies, feed a duck, answer a letter, call a lonely or sick church member, flash a smile.

Pause to catch the sun ushering in a new day.

Pause to hug someone dear, or to place a love note on the pillow of ones you love.

Listen to your heart beat and reflect on the gift of another day of life. MARIA G. McCLEAN

Take Off Your Shoes

He has told you, O mortal, what is good; and what does the Lord require of you but to do justice, and to love kindness, and to walk humbly with your God? Micah 6:8, NRSV.

I sat looking at my suitcase. I had brought two pairs of blue shoes—a pair of flats and a pair of high heels. I wondered which to wear. I was scheduled to preach later that morning, and

I wanted to look just right. I had never been in Bangkok before, and having arrived only the night before, I wasn't sure what the local women might be wearing. I didn't want to be overdressed or underdressed, but I knew I didn't plan to wear hose—it was much too hot and humid. I also knew the women of that area of the world always dress especially nice for church. So I decided to try heels without stockings, as it wasn't far to walk.

Later I sat in the pastor's study waiting for the other worship leaders to arrive so we could enter the platform. As the two men came through the door together, I immediately noticed that both were in their stocking feet. Then it hit me: I was in a country in which people customarily remove their shoes when entering a place of worship. I turned to the pastor and asked, "Should I remove my shoes too?"

He hesitated a moment before replying that it was the usual practice. As I slipped out of my high heels, I looked at my bare feet. Entering the church with bare feet would be so undignified—I would feel so—so—well, humbled. How I wished I had at least worn stockings. Then truth flashed through. That was the whole purpose for their custom of removing shoes. I was no longer important. I was not there to be seen. I was there only to share the Word of God. I would be showing true reverence and respect for God only when I was humble myself. I thought of Moses at the burning bush: "Take off your sandals, for the place where you are standing is holy ground" (Ex. 3:5, NIV).

We have an incredible God! He is the ruler of the universe, who deserves to be treated with the greatest awe and reverence. Angels cover their faces in His presence. But He also comes down to meet with us. Isaiah 57:15 says, "For this is what the high and lofty One says—he who lives forever, whose name is holy: 'I live in a high and holy place, but also with [her] who is contrite and lowly in spirit, to revive the spirit of the lowly and to revive the heart of the contrite'" (NIV).

This mighty God even allows us to speak for Him from time to time. What a privilege! Our speaking is not always in a formal church setting; in fact, it seldom is. We speak for Him each day in all the words we use, and in our actions as well. So we need to ask ourselves whether we are trying to draw attention to ourselves or to Him.

May He be glorified in each of our lives this day.

ARDIS DICK STENBAKKEN

Sinners

While Jesus was having dinner at Matthew's house, many tax collectors and "sinners" came and ate with him and his disciples. When the Pharisees saw this, they asked his disciples, "Why does your teacher eat with tax collectors and 'sinners'?" Matt. 9:10, 11, NIV.

I have three cats at my house. One of them is a purebred Siamese. Although I am not sure if he is show quality, he is very beautiful with his black velvet paws and ears. His eyes are the deepest blue, and his body is sleek and lovely. He walks in a distinguished way and gives his affection only to those he deems worthy. His apparent belief that he is truly an aristocrat extends further than this, however, in that he will not even eat with the other cats. He has trained my husband and me to know that he is not to be fed from the same bowl—and certainly not in the same area—as the "commoner" cats. He has his own personal shelf where he eats his daily meals, and frequently requests (demands) snacks and treats.

He also refuses to use the litter box, as the common cats do, and has taught himself to use the toilet, a feat I had heard about but had never seen until he came into our lives. The other two cats sleep together, providing companionship and warmth for each other. The Siamese, however, disassociates himself from the "lower class" and keeps to himself. Like many people, he avoids fellowship with those who appear different.

Christ set an awesome example by keeping company with a variety of people. Although no human has ever been more worthy than Jesus, He associated with all types of people. Who are your friends? We tend to choose friends who are like us. Sometimes diversity makes us uncomfortable, just as it did the Pharisees when Jesus ate at Matthew's house.

"On hearing this, Jesus said, 'It is not the healthy who need a doctor, but the sick. But go and learn what this means: "I desire mercy, not sacrifice." For I have not come to call the righteous, but sinners'" (verse 12).   CAREL CLAY

Guardian Angels

The angel of the Lord encampeth round about them that fear him, and delivereth them. Ps. 34:7.

The low warning growls of Chief, my Pomeranian, brought me back to reality and sent a shiver down my spine. I had chosen to sit in the car and wait while my husband went into his office to make some reports. Beside me roared the engine of a pickup truck. Glancing sideways, I saw the driver definitely studying me. I knew he had been around the block, casing me and my car. As another car came up, he pulled away. Summoning up my courage, I drove my car into a more lighted area.

Suddenly panic struck again. I had parked almost under a monorail, and when it drove overhead, the noise was deafening. If I blew my horn or screamed, no one could hear me. Minutes later the pickup appeared. The man got out and walked back and forth close to my car. My dog bared his teeth and created an awful fuss. I didn't look at the man; I didn't want him to think I sensed danger. I tried to keep my wits about me and prayed for deliverance.

As he paced, I was able to get a good look at him. There had been a series of female murders in this area, and later, when the murderer was apprehended, he matched the exact description of the man who had been stalking me.

How many times do you think God has kept you from harm and danger, saved your life, or even kept you from much pain and suffering? How many times have the angels kept you safe and watched over you? I long to talk face-to-face with my guardian angel someday, and it will be thrilling to hear from his own lips about how he cared for me. How thankful I am that God fulfills His promises through these wonderful heavenly beings!

PAT MADSEN

Inasmuch . . .

The rich and the poor have this in common: the Lord is the maker of them all. Prov. 22:2, NRSV.

The beauty of the mountains and deep barrancas (canyons) of Mexico foretell nothing of what I will encounter when our little group lands on the grassy airstrip at El Rincon village in the Huichol Mountains of Mexico. We taxi to a stop before 20 or 30 Huichol Indians, who hurriedly congregate when they hear the roar of the plane's engines. They know the airplane brings a doctor and other good things to them. This time we are carrying vegetable seeds, garden tools, and clothing for children.

The village has a fenced garden with about 50 peach tree seedlings and some vegetables growing in raised beds. The pilot/pastor distributes seeds and tools and gives simple planting and soil improvement instructions. The doctor treats toothaches, rashes, and internal problems, dispensing medicine along with oral instructions. The director of the sponsoring foundation talks to the people about keeping bodies and teeth clean, and she and I help the doctor distribute the clothing, estimating which garment will fit which child. Big smiles erupt as they receive a shirt or pair of pants.

This tiny village has about 12 one-room adobe-brick houses, all with grass-thatched roofs. Entry to the house is a windowlike opening, about two by three feet and 18 inches above the ground, with no other windows. Smoke from cooking fires escapes between the walls and roof. Lungs are at risk from breathing smoke in the house. From two to 10 people eat and sleep in this tiny house that has no electricity, plumbing, or even an outhouse. The nearest large city is more than 100 miles away, and there isn't a paved road within 20 miles. Chickens, turkeys, and pigs wander the village yard. Dogs dodge occasional rocks thrown by little boys.

Improving the lifestyle of these indigenous people is the goal of this organization. Direct proselytizing is not allowed; however, Christ has been accepted by a few who were curious about why anyone would come so far and take so much trouble to help them live better lives.

While the Huichol Indians seem content and may not want to leave their homes for "civilization," they readily accept help in the form of water pipes that will save them a daily three-hour trek to the spring and provide purified water for drinking, cooking, and irrigating a garden of fresh vegetables to supplement their daily diet of tortillas. Seeing the smiles is reward enough for me at the end of a journey to the beautiful mountains and pastoral lives of brothers and sisters, living in the twentieth century, but light-years away in modern terms.

Why not be extravagant today? Do something unexpected for someone less fortunate. Give away a potted plant or plant clippings, bake cookies for a lonely neighbor, take a homebound person a cooked meal, or call a shut-in or a young person and invite him or her to go shopping with you. Reach out and touch someone today!

GWEN LEE

MARCH 8

Waiting Room Encounter

He spake many things unto them in parables. Matt. 13:3.

The airport waiting lounge was empty when I arrived more than two hours early for my flight to Monterrey, Mexico. I took out my journal and wrote, *I am not alone, for You are here beside me, Lord. Each item in this room makes me think of You. Here is what I see. Each item seems to be a parable, illustrating a spiritual truth, warming my heart with Your presence.*

As I noticed each item, I sketched it, then used it as a parable conveying God's message to me for the day. Here are some of the objects I drew and the notes I wrote.

1. Trash can. "Give Me the garbage of your life—hate, bitterness, remorse, guilt, pride, evil thoughts, malice, envy. I'll remove them far from you."

2. Water fountain. "I am the Water of Life. Only I can satisfy the thirst of your heart. Without Me you cannot survive!"

3. No-smoking sign. "Do not pollute your body or your mind. Allow only that which is good into your mind as well as

into your body. Be healthy, spiritually as well as physically."

4. Telephone booth. "B.C. Tel may have a wonderful communication network, but you have access to One more awesome. It is 'Heaven Tel.' The line is never busy. Call Me anytime you wish!"

5. Chairs. "Trust Me, My child, as you trust the chair you are sitting in now. Come unto Me and rest! Relax in Me! Let Me take your full weight!"

6. Heat register. "I am the one in control of the thermostat. I know what temperature you can take. I won't let you get more heat (trials and temptations) than you can bear."

7. Door. "I am the door to salvation. You must enter My kingdom through faith in Me. I am here for all—men, women, and the disabled. The door is open, and no one can shut it. Come in; I'm waiting for you!"

8. Flight schedule board. "Your flight may be on time, or early, or late. But My purposes know no haste and no delay. I will make all things beautiful in your life in My time. My answers to your prayers always come at the right time."

9. Light fixture. "I am the Light of the world. I will light your pathway today. My Word will be a light directing your steps. Use it often!"

10. Electrical outlet. "Plug into power! Every day you need to connect with Me. Without Me you can do nothing. Without connecting to Me you will have no light to share this weekend in Montemorelos."

Ninety minutes and six pages later I had 20 items sketched in my journal. Each had a message from God, spoken to me in parables. What a precious time of communion! I felt alive, rejuvenated, ready to face a heavy weekend of speaking appointments.

DOROTHY EATON WATTS

Polishing

And they shall be mine, saith the Lord of hosts, in that day when I make up my jewels. Mal. 3:17.

Oft do we thank our Father for the sunshine
And for the glorious mountain heights we view.
How plenteous is our praise for His protection;
For fragrant roses wet with morning dew;
For butterflies and sunset's dazzling brightness;
The joy that children's happy voices bring;
For cooling breeze in evening's starlit wonder,
And dreams fulfilled that cause our hearts to sing.

But dare we recognize His sovereign goodness
In pain that seems to bring us no relief?
For storms that wash away our bright ambitions,
Or blight that devastates our souls with grief?
Can we acknowledge Him for clouds that press us,
And for the thorns that prick our fingers sore?
For disappointments in our expectations,
Or bitter loss of that which we adore?

Oh, could we see our heavenly Father's blueprint
For us, produced in exquisite design;
And trusting, watch His wisdom as He molds us
To complement His excellence divine;
How quick we would respond to heaven-sent lessons,
And master all that He would have us learn—
Accepting thorns for roses, trials for gladness,
And through our tears His loving plan discern.

Afflictions bring into our lives God's rainbow—
His promise wrought from sunshine mixed with rain.
Strong character develops best through hardship,
And sacrifice draws virtue out of pain.
So rest, dear heart, and let His testing polish
Our broken lives into His jewels rare.
The Father holds us! There's no need for doubting!

We are the precious objects of His care.

LORRAINE HUDGINS

MARCH 10

Spaces

Grace and peace be multiplied unto you through the knowledge of God, and of Jesus our Lord, according as his divine power hath given unto us all things that pertain unto life and godliness. 2 Peter 1:2, 3.

Have you ever thought about how carefully God has designed space into our world? It's the spaces that shape and define creation. Take a walk through the forest. Instead of the trees, look at the spaces between them and you'll know where the peace of the woods comes from. Think of the spaces between the notes of your favorite song. Without them there would be no music. It's the spaces between the letters in our reading and writing thatmakethemmorelegible! And the space between shower and sunshine often graces us with a beautiful rainbow.

The spaces we make in our life for God are times that bring us peace and help make sense out of life. It means stopping long enough to absorb God's presence and love. Most of us have a space of time each day for our devotions, but what about the little spaces throughout the day, while waiting at a stoplight or in a checkout line? These are little spaces that can be used for a quick thank-you prayer or remembering a Bible verse.

Susanna Wesley, mother of the famous John and Charles Wesley, lived in the 1700s in a house jammed with children. She gave birth to 19 of them! There was no way she could leave the children to spend time alone, yet she knew she had to have her times with the Lord or forfeit something special in their relationship. So she made her own private prayer closet in the midst of bedlam by pulling the outer layer of her petticoats up over her head. The children learned to respect this as a sign they weren't to interrupt—she was spending time with her God. It made a difference in her life and the lives of her children.

Without time for God, our days become like music without notes or letters without words. Using the small spaces of time during our day to reflect on God serves as a refreshing pick-me-up, a brief relief from the pressures and noise around us. God knows we need time-outs. Let's utilize our spaces today to enhance our relationship with our Maker, giving us grace and peace.

MARYBETH GESSELE

MARCH 11

And the Door Was Shut

While they were on their way to buy the oil, the bridegroom arrived. The virgins who were ready went in with him to the wedding banquet. And the door was shut. Later the others also came. "Sir! Sir!" they said. "Open the door for us!" But he replied, "I tell you the truth, I don't know you." Therefore keep watch, because you do not know the day or the hour. Matt. 25:10-13, NIV.

The plane departed Fresno on schedule. My second adventure in Brazil, bouncing from city to city teaching family life seminars, had been greatly anticipated. No one is more loving or appreciative than Brazilians!

In Miami I checked in at the gate from which my plane was to depart. A pleasant agent inspected my ticket and asked for my visa. I handed her my passport, which included an expired visa from a previous trip, hoping to bluff my way through.

"Your visa has expired," the agent stated. "Do you have a current visa?"

"No," I responded. "This is all I have."

"Then I can't let you go on to São Paulo," she said apologetically.

I explained that I was midtrip, that I had already traveled more than 3,000 miles and had no way to get a visa now. Patiently but firmly she explained that she could not allow me to go on. Not only would she be fined if she did so, but I would be taken into custody and fined when I deplaned.

Tears started flowing. "Please," I pleaded. "I am speaking at a church tomorrow where 3,000 people will gather." (Surely if she heard how important I was, that this was a missionary trip, she wouldn't dare disappoint the multitude.)

The flight was announced, and other passengers began boarding the São Paulo flight. The agent offered me two nights in the downtown Hyatt Regency, paid for by the airline. They assumed responsibility for my dilemma, since I never should have been allowed to board in Fresno without proper documentation. Instead of being reassured, I was terrified to spend the night in Miami alone.

By now the last boarding call for São Paulo had been announced. Desperation set in again. "I don't have much money," I explained in an effort to catch the agent's sympathy.

"The airline will pay all your meals and taxis to and from the Brazilian Embassy. A free shuttle will take you to the hotel," she responded.

From my vantage point I saw the jetway pull away from the plane. A few more tears slipped down my cheeks. The realization of what faced me became a reality. I was staying overnight in Miami, getting a visa by myself from a foreign embassy tomorrow, and I would not make my opening meeting. The plane taxied away from the gate. I was alone and helpless, no one to intercede for me, no second chance, no mediator to open the plane door, no one to plead my case. The door was shut.

Each of us faces a similar situation. Now is the time to get your "visa" in preparation for the trip of all trips. The hours of operation are now. The doors are open. The Consul General is in His office, willing to grant you a visa to heaven. Christ provided the passport on the cross. Your daily personal relationship with Him is a prerequisite for your visa.

Bluffing didn't work then; it won't work in trying to enter heaven, either. Now is the time to visit the consulate of heaven.

NANCY L. VAN PELT

MARCH 12

First-place Award

Behold, I am coming soon! My reward is with me.
Rev. 22:12, NIV.

*W*e used to live in the desert of New Mexico. Even though it was hot and there were things that I disliked about that environment, I enjoyed the striking colors all around us, especially at certain times of the year. It always amazed me to find so much beauty in a so-called *hostile* environment. However, its beauty was often apparent only when one paid careful attention.

Our home was situated on a large mesa. Sometimes in the evening I would sit outside and gaze at the Organ Mountains, fascinated by the shadows and colors that crept into the crags and canyons. (Years later I received a Christmas card depicting a desert scene at sunrise. It took me back in memory to the varied moods and colors I had loved.)

At the time, I was in the process of creating a series of acrylic pictures. What better idea than to include a painting of a desert scene! I began. It was my most difficult undertaking ever. I tried to be so careful, but whenever I tried to get the shadows and the color variations just *right*, it wasn't. The harder I tried, the worse it was. Finally, in desperation, I simply let the paints have their way. The desert with its subtle beauty gradually came to life on the canvas. When the painting was completed, I hung it in the living room as a daily reminder of our experience.

One day a neighbor stopped by my home. During the conversation, she suggested that I enter some of my paintings in the upcoming town and country fair. My art had been displayed in public at various times; however, I had never entered a competition. After much encouragement, I selected two paintings—the desert scene and a flower-filled window box. It was exciting to walk into the large exhibit hall and leave my paintings for review by the judges. Whether or not I received a prize was not the issue; it was rewarding to know that my paintings would be shown along with those of others who also loved this same art medium.

The day the fair opened I was out of town. Eager to see what the judges had decided, my husband stopped by the exhibit hall. When I walked into the house that evening, he greeted me with a big grin and the news that *The Desert* had won first prize in its category and the *Window Flower Box*, third prize. What a surprise! My artistic talent, newly discovered, had been validated by those who were qualified to adjudicate.

I don't picture God as a harsh judge, as some view Him. There are times, however, when I compare myself against the standard of attainment and know that He could easily discredit my efforts. But because God is also my Creator, He understands the pageant of my life. He sees both the shadows and bright spots and knows who I can become.

Metaphorically, we each hang in the gallery of life. Not everyone values us for who we are. They prefer another *picture*, as it were. I know, however, that God values each of us as an original masterpiece and will ultimately award us with first place—because *first place* is available to all.   DEBBY GRAY WILMOT

MARCH 13

Every Need Is Important

And God is able to make all grace abound to you, so that in all things at all times, having all that you need, you will abound in every good work. 2 Cor. 9:8, NIV.

*N*ot right now!" I lamented to my husband. "My concentration and memory are still so slow, and I'm out of breath just trying to speak up on the telephone."

"But you love to teach, and this will be good exercise for your mind," countered my husband.

I was recovering from a long-term, debilitating exposure to a toxic gas, and after a number of treatments, my body was slowly responding to rest and more rest. With impaired memory and concentration, plus shortness of breath and chest pain with minimal exertion, I was afraid that I would never be back to my old self, "setting goals for virtually every minute of the day." As the saying goes, I liked to have my ducks lined up in a row, but mine were all in exhausted chaos.

I was being asked to teach a Bible class, only once a month.

In previous years I had taught a class every week and knew the energy needed to stand before a large group of people for 60 minutes. And this class was in a large sanctuary with no microphone.

This won't work, I thought. But with my husband's encouragement, I finally relented and agreed to teach the class. For the next three weeks I prayed, studied, and even wrote out the entire lesson, in case my memory failed. On the appointed day I asked God to please give me a loud, clear voice, because my normal voice is soft. I needed extra volume to speak to this large group.

As I began to speak and make excuses for my soft voice, I encouraged people to move closer to me. I became aware that my voice seemed quite distinct and clear. I was speaking in a conversational mode, but the volume was definitely "turned up." My voice continued at this level for the entire class period. Afterward an elderly woman came up to me.

"I was late and had to sit in the back of the class," she said. "Usually I can't hear the teacher well unless I'm up front, but your voice is the strongest and clearest of any teacher I've heard!"

Praise God for supplying all our needs. I continue to give Him all the glory on a daily basis. How often I struggle with problems that are quite simple for Him to solve, and He has promised to give His children all that we need abundantly.

JANIS CLARK VANCE

MARCH 14

Poison

There came a woman having an alabaster box of ointment of spikenard very precious; and she brake the box and poured it on his head. Mark 14:3.

I love Poison. That word, which once evoked revolting and dreadful thoughts, now brings exciting and romantic emotions. I can't imagine whoever would have thought of giving such a terrible name to such a sweet, wonderful, and exciting perfume. Despite its name, I still wear it; to me the word "poison" has almost become synonymous with "perfume."

Before I discovered Poison, I had another favorite fragrance. I wore it all the time, even though it was called (of all things) Charlie. Why would anyone put a man's name on women's cologne, especially such a nice, feminine fragrance?

Sometimes the "world" does things like that. Something good is given a bad name. Virginity, for instance. Virginity used to be considered something pure, "holy," and desirable. But today it's called old-fashioned, something to get rid of.

Humbleness is called weakness. "You have to be assertive to make it in this world," we're told. "Honesty is situational" is another subtle lie. "You must be shrewd if you want to make it." "The means justifies the end." And so the list goes.

But if we demonstrate through our lives that the fragrance of these Christian graces is sweet despite the name the world gives them, others will begin to recognize their true value.

The other night my husband took me out to a nice restaurant. We were all dressed up, and of course I was wearing my favorite perfume, Poison. After taking our order, the waiter turned to me and asked, "Are you wearing Poison?" Surprised and taken aback by such an outright question, I stammered, "Why, uh, yes." Afterward I thought *Wouldn't it have been better if instead he had asked me "Are you a Christian?" That's the real kind of fragrance I should have been exuding.*

God, help me to remember to wear the Christian fragrance of Your love today—and every day.   NANCY CACHERO VASQUEZ

The Single Voice

And the Levite, (because he hath no part nor inheritance with thee,) and the stranger, and the fatherless, and the widow, which are within thy gates, shall come, and shall eat and be satisfied; that the Lord thy God may bless thee in all the work of thine hand which thou doest. Deut. 14:29.

*M*ommy, where do babies come from?" asks the small voice of curiosity.

"Go ask your father," the mother wants to answer in a calm and loving way. Instead she screams the answer in her mind, because she knows that her response would be of no substance at that moment. Or any other moment, for that matter.

The head of the household, the spiritual leader, the disciplinarian, the family domestic . . . all roles the single voice longs to relinquish or share at some point in time, if not permanently. Even if only for a temporary time, so that the single voice could be mentally, physically, and spiritually rejuvenated.

All the cares, all the concerns, all the worries of life that weigh heavy within the soul of the single voice . . . No backup, no immediate support, only the one-sided defense of the single voice. Of course, there is no doubt that the single voice can be strong and clear, compassionate and caring, soothing and sympathetic when necessary.

However, there is that rare and ominous occasion, if the cares of life permit, when the single voice cries out for help. If you listen very carefully, you will hear the single voice. It exists in your church, at your place of employment, and may even belong to a family member. Don't waste precious minutes trying to analyze, rationalize, or criticize the single voice; just recognize that it is a child of God who longs to be treated with the love and respect due all God's children.

Never assume for a moment that just because the single voice is either voluntarily or involuntarily alone it is not lonely and in need of genuine human outreach. For whatever reason the voice exists, never doubt that there is always a need for it to be heard.

The small voice of curiosity is wonderful and may give the single voice purpose, but the presence of a pair of genuinely tuned and sensitive ears can be beautiful.   TONYA L. BROWN

MARCH 16

Excess Baggage

Let us throw off everything that hinders and the sin that so easily entangles. Heb. 12:1, NIV.

When I transferred from my home in Australia to work in New Zealand, I became what the airlines refer to as a "frequent flyer." On average twice a year I would board a plane for the three-hour flight across the Tasman Sea to visit my family or attend a business meeting.

The more frequent my journeys, the more I learned about luggage—that essential accessory of a traveler. Standing and waiting for my suitcase to appear on the airport carousel, I would wonder at the variety of colors and shapes of the suitcases. Each piece held the items considered necessary for the owner's comfort and enjoyment. Holidays meant time for shopping, so my return luggage was increased. Once the check-in clerk even attached a label for the luggage handlers that warned "HEAVY!"

When I transferred to England, I carried with me two very heavy bags, knowing my household shipment would be some weeks behind me. It took three of us to get those suitcases closed and safely locked.

As my mother sat back recovering her strength, she asked, "What will you do if customs wants to inspect your bags?"

At first the idea was funny. I had nothing to declare, but I could see Her Majesty's customs officer examining my clothes and toiletries. It might be embarrassing to have the contents of my two bags spread out on the counter. But then I would have to repack my own luggage. How would I get them closed and locked again? Was I carrying more than I needed?

I could see a similarity in my own spiritual life. Some "excess baggage" occasionally bursts forth for all to see, and I cannot pack it away again. Maybe you have the same "luggage problem." Perhaps you are loaded down by impatience with your coworkers, jealousy of a friend, anger toward your spouse, or another pressing problem. Jesus asks us to cast that excess baggage on Him and trade it for His. "If you are tired from carrying heavy burdens, come to me and I will give you rest. Take the yoke I give you. Put it on your shoulders. . . . This yoke is easy to bear, and this burden is light" (Matt. 11:28-30, CEV).

Lord, please take away the unnecessary baggage in my life and let me carry only those attributes I need.   JAN CLARKE

MARCH 17

The Greatest Gift

Your word is a lamp to my feet and a light for my path. Ps. 119:105, NIV.

The very first gift I received from David (now my husband of 30 years) was a Bible with the following inscription: "I give you now the greatest gift I can ever give. May God bless you and heaven's light be your guide."

I must admit that I was a trifle disappointed. Although I had come from a Christian background, our beautiful, leather-bound family Bible had always been kept respectfully in a bookcase. At this frivolous stage of my life, I would have been more appreciative of something that smelled nice or looked pretty, like lace, perfume, or flowers.

A little later David enrolled me in a Bible correspondence course. It was then that I began to see the first glimmers of light penetrate the darkness of ignorance that had hitherto enshrouded my spiritual life.

Words cannot adequately describe my excitement as I ventured on this journey of discovery. Guided by my lessons, I unearthed treasures greater and more precious than those in my wildest dreams. Each time I studied, the light became brighter. I could feel God wrestling with my soul, helping me to see the errors of my previous convictions, and opening my eyes to the truth. It was surely heaven's light that helped me make my decision for baptism.

I was convinced that David had been guided by that same light to give me this particular gift. James 1:17 reminds us, "Every good and every perfect present comes from heaven; it comes down from God, the creator of the heavenly lights" (TEV).

God's Word has become my lifeline. In the periods of crisis and suffering, when death stalked the corridors of my life, my comfort and hope came from the Psalms. In my choice of a life partner and in other important decisions, my guide and inspiration have been from the Bible. When my heart has been filled with joy and thanksgiving, I have looked to the Bible to find an adequate means of expression. When I have asked, "Who am I? Why am I here?" it was the Bible that supplied the only satisfactory answers.

I am truly thankful for the many gifts I have received over the years, but of them all that first gift was the greatest and the best. My prayer is that you too will find that same joy in reading God's Word.   FRANCES CHARLES

MARCH 18

Anyone Can Witness

"You are My witnesses," declares the Lord, "and My servant whom I have chosen." Isa. 43:10, NASB.

No sooner had a new family of five moved to town than a kind neighbor brought them a freshly baked loaf of bread. Seeing there were children, she offered to baby-sit while the parents unpacked. With the many kindnesses extended to them, the newcomers began to feel a closeness to their new neighbor and wondered what sparked her generosity of spirit. Carolyn, the wife, declared she had never met another human being so kind. She asked, "Why are you so different?" The neighbor replied that she was a Christian.

A special friendship developed that led to Bible studies and church attendance. Shortly after they moved, the father, a high-ranking military officer, went to Vietnam, where he was killed within a week. Eventually the rest of the family was baptized, and today one of the children is a faithful pastor's wife, witnessing for Jesus.

This outcome would never have occurred had not a faithful follower of Jesus performed such loving deeds. What a privilege to witness for Christ by simple acts of love. We may feel timid or inadequate, thinking someone else can do better, but when God impresses us to witness, we are assured of His help. The Holy Spirit even guides our words and thoughts.

The Lord will give us courage for any task He may ask us to do. He does not expect us, however, to use abilities we do not possess. He has given to all His created beings certain gifts and talents, and it is in the use of these that God will bless our witnessing for Him.   MARIE SPANGLER

———————————————— *Ɓ* ————————————————

MARCH 19

Invisible Patrol

He shall call upon me, and I will answer him: I will be with him in trouble; I will deliver him. Ps. 91:15.

*G*od's promise of protection never fails. Each day He shields His children from dangers, seen and unseen, because His presence remains with them. This I can verify by an experience I will never forget.

It was June, and four of us packed into one car heading to attend a graduation in Michigan. All went as smoothly as clockwork until somewhere in New Jersey when we made a wrong turn and, you guessed it, we were lost at night on a deserted, unknown country road. We did what seemed best—we stopped at a gas station, where someone volunteered to show us the way.

As we followed our newfound guide, we suddenly realized that the road was getting narrower and the streetlights farther apart. We became apprehensive and strangely silent. This was prayer time. Mine was simple: "Father, we are lost in the darkness of this unknown country road. Send us the protection You have promised."

By the time our prayer session was over, we noticed that the silhouette of our guide looked different—but since we had no alternative, we kept following him. Prayer continued for another minute or two.

Almost immediately a red light appeared on the dashboard. We all knew there had to be a problem somewhere but couldn't imagine what until we heard a deafening *bang!* accompanied by a

111

loud rattle. The car swerved to the right and stopped. Ahead, the lights of our guide's car slowly disappeared from our view over the brow of the hill. We were left in the darkness without help. Alone, we thought. Yet we weren't really alone, for we were awed—and comforted—by the Presence we felt. We knew we were being guided by a special convoy of angels, an invisible patrol, and we thanked God for that.

"He's gone!" one said.

"Maybe it's a deliverance!" another broke in.

"Thank You, Jesus. We called and You answered. Thank You, Father," everyone chorused.

As we sat in the darkness, trying to figure out the cause of the red light, we were certain God was with us on the dark, lonely country road. After 15 minutes of watching the dashboard, we saw the red light disappear as mysteriously as it had appeared. Nervously we started the car without any trouble, found another guide, and resumed our journey. Upon arriving in Michigan the next morning, we checked the car but never discovered the reason for that mysterious red light, nor did we encounter any problems on our return journey.

It was by the experience of this trip that I fully understood the meaning of the text and claimed the promise: "He shall call upon me, and I will answer him: I will be with him in trouble; I will deliver him." Surely, our Protector is worthy of praise.

CECILY DALY

MARCH 20

Perfection in Progress

Therefore let us go on toward perfection. Heb. 6:1, NRSV.

"Will you look at this?" Verla asked, distress resonating in soprano. Reaching for the crumpled piece of paper, she scanned the scribbles on display. A frown marred her face. This was a homework assignment her son intended to hand in to the teacher! Then the muscles in her face relaxed. A moment of insight. "What we have here is perfection in progress. The failures are crossed out; the first thoughts revised. And look here," she said, pointing to the holes on the paper. "My son tried so hard to erase his mistakes that the paper disappeared. But the answers are all correct. That's his bottom line."

Verla thought about it for a while. It made sense. To a point. "But does he have to hand it in like this? Can't he rewrite it? I wouldn't accept it myself. How can he expect his teacher to do so?"

"Be that as it may," she conceded, "priority setting, not error making, is the issue here. The lad had only a certain amount of time, and the assignment had to be completed. We expect him to be accurate, but we will have to accept that situations like this will occur—once in a while. From now on I shall have to concentrate on teaching him how to decide what comes first. Then I'll help him manage his time and energy accordingly. First things first."

I suspect that's how our heavenly Father intervened on Rahab's behalf and brought her to the veneration implicit in Hebrews 11:31. I know that is how He works on my behalf. I may try to scrub the memory of my sins away to no avail. The blood of Christ erases my faults, and God presents me with a new page. A new possibility for perfection.

When He was on earth, Jesus always viewed people from the perspective of their potential. He saw the latent ability of the woman at the well and conscripted her to evangelistic service. "Go tell others," He said. He did the same for the seemingly un-focused and spineless Peter when He renamed him "stone."

What divine perception! What a Saviour! Through Him perfection is more than a probability. It's a promise!

GLENDA-MAE GREENE

MARCH 21

Just Wait and See!

For the Lord himself will come down from heaven, with a loud command, with the voice of the archangel and with the trumpet call of God, and the dead in Christ will rise first. 1 Thess. 4:16, NIV.

The dawn chorus sounded like an orchestra above our heads as morning consciousness filtered through our sleepy bodies. The early sun was warming the canvas, and it felt wonderful to lie in our cozy sleeping bags and listen to the sounds of nature all around us. Nathan, our 4-year-old, woke up eager to explore another day. We were staying at a small church camp for young families on the grounds of an ancient convent in the heart of the English countryside. Around us were trees, fields of cows, beautiful grounds with a tiny church and a lake, and it felt a bit like heaven.

Still drowsy, I pointed Nathan in the direction of his clothes and tied his laces so that he could go out and play while I gathered my things for the shower. As I crossed the field I saw him looking intently at the ground and wondered what he'd found. He was always discovering interesting things. This time he had found a dead mole, a little blind creature that digs holes all over the place. He was sad because it was dead, and it looked so sweet with its little pointy nose and pink paws. I gave him a hug and a kiss and went on to the shower.

On my way back, Nathan was still there with another boy who was about 3. Both of them were still staring quietly at the little dead creature. Then Nathan said to his friend, "It's a mole, and it's dead. But just you wait and see what happens when Jesus comes!"

The dead mole seemed to entertain the two boys until breakfast time. Nathan was always hungry, so he decided to leave the mole for a few minutes. He left his friend behind, watching solemnly. Finally Timothy's mom called him for breakfast too, but he was reluctant to go. When she came to see what the matter was, Timothy turned to her and said, "But Mommy, Nathan told me to wait here and see what happens to the mole when Jesus comes, and I don't want to miss it!"

His mom finally persuaded him to leave the scene and eat some cereal, but that precious moment of our children's faith will stay with us forever, tucked like a treasure into our hearts.

We too long to see what happens when Jesus comes. We don't want to miss it, either!   KAREN HOLFORD

MARCH 22

Beauty Is Only Skin-deep

Charm is deceptive, and beauty is fleeting; but a woman who fears the Lord is to be praised. Prov. 31:30, NIV.

The media constantly reminds women of their need to remain slim, young, and beautiful. The manufacturers of makeup and skin creams all claim that their product will help prevent aging and make you look years younger. The days of the voluptuous woman are over, and we now have slender women taking their place in the world. The perfect woman is now portrayed as being a goddess dripping with charm and beauty. Her appearance can be perfect if she will do what the women's magazines tell her to do. The problem is that these products may help to reduce the aging of the skin and give an outward appearance of youth for only a few more years. The Word of God reminds us that beauty is fleeting.

When a woman reaches her 40s (and sometimes earlier), her age begins to show. Gray hair starts to appear, and unless she spends time and money on hair coloring, she looks older and may feel less beautiful. A man, on the other hand, takes on a handsome, mature glow at 40, despite the gray hair and facial lines.

It's unfair, but we women can choose to ignore the ravages of time. We can, by our lives and the indwelling Spirit of God, be more beautiful as the years go by. There is the saying "Older but wiser." I would like to change it to "Older but more beautiful. Older but more kind. Older but more patient. Older but more loving. Older but more generous, joyful, peaceful, and gentle" (adapted from Gal. 5:22).

The ointments and preparations of this world are only transitory, but the oil of the Holy Spirit protects, preserves, and enlivens us for eternity.

Let us never become careless in keeping our bodies attractive, but may we never be so obsessed with the external that we forget that meek and quiet Spirit. May our Father grant us today a full measure of His Spirit that will be a balm in Gilead.

"Your beauty should not come from outward adornment. . . . Instead, it should be that of your inner self, the unfading beauty of a gentle and quiet spirit, which is of great worth in God's sight" (1 Peter 3:3, 4).

EUNICE MASON

MARCH 23

Feeding Squirrels

Now to him who is able to do immeasurably more than all we ask or imagine, according to his power that is at work within us, to him be glory in the church and in Christ Jesus throughout all generations, for ever and ever! Amen. Eph. 3:20, NIV.

Hand-feeding squirrels is a cherished activity for me. It's incredibly rewarding after sitting quietly for a long time to have a chipmunk or squirrel climb on my palm, looking for nuts and seeds. The intense emotion I feel at succeeding to entice it to feed from my hand is augmented by the knowledge that the little creature is there by choice. It can—and does—leave whenever it wishes. However, at that moment it prefers to be with me. I've learned not to permit even one tiny finger movement while a timid creature is learning to trust me. (Once while holding a chipmunk in my hand I trembled ever so lightly, and it leaped from my hand three feet into the air, landed several feet away, and didn't return for 45 minutes!)

Though I have been tempted, I never keep one of these little creatures by force. Once a friend tried to and watched as the chipmunk ran to its hole—with a very naked tail. When he opened his fingers, he was holding a handful of chipmunk hair!

Squirrels have never asked me to bring them food, and they rarely even imagine that I might. The amount I bring, however, is immeasurable to them. I have power they cannot comprehend, and they often bring me "glory" by somehow "witnessing" to their fellow creatures of my presence and my bountiful offerings. At times I've had squirrels tickling my hands, ears, and toes and hunting in my pockets all at once, because of the excited chatter of the first one to arrive. What glorious fun!

The joy of it gives me a glimpse of the pleasure my eternal God feels as I climb into His hand to feed on His Word. His storehouse is limitless, and He's been ever so patiently waiting for me to come. He'll never force me, but what satisfaction He experiences each time I return.

"Heavenly Father, now that I've learned to trust You, may my Christian conversation glorify You. May my friends join me in feeding on the Bread of Life. You offer to help us find mustard seeds of faith in Your hand. May we learn that 'the eyes of all look to you, and you give them their food at the proper time. You open your hand and satisfy the desires of every living thing' (Ps. 145:15, NIV). Yes, 'my mouth will speak in praise of the Lord. Let every creature praise his holy name for ever and ever' (verse 21). Amen."

PAM BAUMGARTNER

MARCH 24

Filling Up the Tank

Sustain me according to Thy word, that I may live. Ps. 119:116, NASB.

_M_ama, it's a hummingbird!"

I quickly glanced out the kitchen window to see a female hummingbird at the feeder. She tried each plastic "flower," then flew away. That food had to be sour—it hadn't been changed in weeks. All summer we had looked for the little birds to come to our feeder, but had been disappointed. Now I made a fresh solution, rinsed the bottle, rehung it, and kept a watch from the window. It wasn't long before the little bird was back, taking long drinks of the sweet fluid. All week she returned about every 10 minutes to drink from the feeder.

As the boys and I talked about the hummingbird, I remembered what I knew about their habits. It was the end of the summer—almost time for them to make their yearly trek to warmer climates. It's not an easy trip. It involves thousands of miles, crosses the Gulf of Mexico, and ends in Central America. Before they embark on this dangerous trip, the little birds start guzzling food to "fill up their gas tank." They gain about half again their weight as they build reserves for their flight.

As a Christian I am also preparing for a trip that is long and dangerous. And how can I prepare for this journey? The same way the hummingbird does—by more frequent feeding. My food? The sweet, life-giving solution of God's Word.

"O Father, please remind me often of the hummingbird. I want to be ready to meet You and to be prepared for all that the journey will hold for me. Help me to make frequent feeding on Your Word a priority in my life.   LILLY TRYON

MARCH 25

Justin Ordinary, Faithful Mom

Her children arise and call her blessed; her husband also, and he praises her. Prov. 31:28, NIV.

My children have a delightful little book entitled *Justin Ordinary Squirrel*, by Shawn A. McMullen (1991, Standard Publishing Co.). It's the story of a little squirrel named Justin who is content just being an ordinary squirrel.

That's like me, I thought. *I'm Justin Ordinary Mom!* Growing up, I always wanted to be extraordinary, I guess, and even though I did some things well, I hadn't attained fame by the time I became a mom. I don't think there is anything more humbling than having a baby. This screaming, demanding little ball of nerves thinks the world revolves around her, and mom is her personal attendant and maid.

My dreams of becoming a CEO by age 30 vanished. I wasn't a well-known doctor or lawyer. I wasn't a research chemist or nuclear physicist. I wasn't an authority on architecture or travel or gardening. In fact, I wasn't an expert on anything. I listened to James Dobson and imagined being phoned someday: "Yes, Mrs. Halim, this is James Dobson. I believe you have a lot to contribute on parenting. Would you like to do a weeklong series with Mike Trout and me?" The dream faded fast when I realized the phone call was from my husband, wondering if lunch was ready.

I don't have the time or patience to become an authority on a certain subject. My grandiose idea of becoming a professional reupholsterer landed on the skids when we forgot to put all the cotton batting back on the kitchen chair seat bottoms before stapling on the new fabric. There are 546 staples per seat—I know. We had to pull them all out when the seat fell through the legs because it was too small.

I tried to sell Avon once. I was going to make big bucks and lead the district in sales. My mom was my best (and usually only) customer.

I was in my clinical year of medical technology, on my way to becoming a famous surgeon. I had maintained more than a 3.5 GPA through college, but I knew I was in trouble when I got a big fat F on my first test. The vision of a scalpel in my hand evaporated as I studied parasitology and had nightmares of worms and other unmentionables floating under microscope slides.

I haven't failed in all my attempts, of course, but I've had to come to the sometimes painful conclusion that I'm Justin Ordinary Woman. I may not be known outside my neighborhood or circle of friends. No one may be awed or fascinated by my knowledge or abilities, but I'm still a worthy person and of value to my Lord. I believe it was Chuck Swindoll who once said, "As parents, we are not called to be a success, but we are called to be faithful."

I may not have Focus on the Family asking me to write a book on parenting, but I can be faithful. Faithful means loving my kids when they're unlovable, turning their thoughts often to Jesus, praying for their salvation, sticking to my convictions when it is not the popular or politically correct thing to do, teaching my children about responsibility and cause and effect, being true to my husband, working to preserve freedom, and keeping a global vision.

Yes, I may be Justin Ordinary Mom, but I hope it can be said that I'm also Justin Ordinary, Faithful Mom. ANN MALONEY-HALIM

First appeared in *The Heart of the Home* 9, No. 2 (1994). Used with permission.

No Distractions Between

If from there you seek the Lord your God, you will find him if you look for him with all your heart and with all your soul. Deut. 4:29, NIV.

*I*t's lost. I must accept the fact." Those words with their ring of finality sprang directly from an aching heart.

The lost item happened to be a much-treasured cassette tape of memories dating back through some 40 years of family life. It had its beginning when our grandchildren ranged in age from 6 months to 6 years. On that tape was a poem I had written, naming each child and including a bit of their special activities. Grandpa had provided sound effects with his violin for the dog story we read for them. Those grandchildren are grown now with children of their own. At our latest family reunion we listened to that tape with fond recollections.

Another recorded memory had been a number by a mixed quartet in which Grandpa had sung a bass solo part. Grandpa passed away 10 years ago. Hearing his voice at the family reunion added still more preciousness to the cassette. Requests were made for copies of it.

"Oh, yes," I promised, "I'll make copies as soon as I return home." But time slipped by. When I could finally do that copying, the tape was nowhere to be found. Just in case it had been overlooked, I carefully went through my collection of tapes three times. The pockets in my suitcase received a second search. I emptied drawers. I removed cushions from overstuffed furniture. The entire house underwent a serious treasure hunt. As I frantically dashed about, I prayed, "Lord, You know where that tape is. Help me find it." But no help came.

At last I gave up. Heartsick over losing those memories, I sank to my knees before our wonderful God. "O Lord," I prayed, "if it is possible that tape is yet somewhere in this house, please, oh, please guide me to it."

At once a thought popped into my mind. I had used a small carry-on case that I had emptied and put away the same day I returned home from the reunion. No time was lost in retrieving that case. Sure enough, in an outside pocket was the tape!

The search ended, but not the priceless lesson gained from the experience. I realized that my first prayer for help from heaven had been more or less tossed heavenward while I anxiously engaged in searching. With love and kindness He had waited patiently for me to come to Him in total commitment, with no distractions. Then He could grant my request. Faithfully He fulfilled the promise of His Word: "Then shall ye call upon me, and ye shall go and pray unto me, and I will hearken unto you" (Jer. 29:12).   MABEL LATSHA

MARCH 27

God Answers Prayers

Great and marvellous are thy works, Lord God Almighty; just and true are thy ways, thou King of saints. Rev. 15:3.

My daughter, Kathy, decided she'd get the room ready for the baby, even though she wasn't due for another six weeks. She needed to move her waterbed to make room for a crib. First she drained the water from the bed so it could be moved, then started the water to fill it back up. The rubber mattress wasn't quite straight, but we thought it would straighten as it filled. It didn't. Kathy and I tried to tug on it to straighten it up. Oh! It was so heavy with the water in it!

That night our muscles ached, and the next day Kathy started to have a small water leakage. Her regular doctor was out, but another doctor said it was nothing to worry about. Several days went by, and I became very ill with coughing and a temperature of 105 degrees. Then about 10:00 p.m. Kathy went into labor. Since she was so early, I thought she might be having false labor. I would drag myself out of bed and check on her. Then when her pains subsided, I would crawl back into bed and pray that her pain would go away.

About 4:00 a.m. the pains got worse, and we called the doctor. He said it sounded like labor and to take her to the hospital emergency room. At that moment my temperature dropped to normal and my coughing stopped. In the car my daughter con-

121

fided that she had been praying the labor pains would stop. I told her I had been praying the same thing. What we didn't know was that the cord had been severed. Without the pain we would not have known something was happening, and the baby would have been born dead. Little Ashley Anne was born at 8:24 a.m.—4 pounds 11 ounces, good and healthy!

Often we think we know what is good for us and want things to go our own way when God has other plans for us that are much better. We need to remember always to pray "Thy will be done."

ANNE ELAINE NELSON

MARCH 28

Super Saviour

Think the same way that Christ Jesus thought. . . . He gave up everything and became a slave, when he became like one of us. Phil. 2:5-7, CEV.

I feel sorry for worms. They are helpful, good for gardens, and hard workers, but very dumb. When it rains, worms come out in droves to escape the soggy soil, only to face death from the sun, being trampled upon by larger creatures, or becoming food for a waiting bird.

When I was younger, I would play a game I later called "Saviour of the Worms." After a rain shower the driveway would be covered with worms. It was my job to save them. First I'd stand by the edge of the driveway and toss the worms near the grassy edge back into the grass, where they could get cover from the sun and birds. Growing weary of that, I'd move to the middle of the driveway to worms with the most critical need. Reasoning that those farthest from the edge had the poorest chance to make it back to the shade, I'd start pitching these middle-of-the-roaders back to safety. Then I'd throw the largest worms back. (They'd be the most helpful to the garden.) With tiring arms and an increasing sense of futility, I'd concentrate on saving the smallest. Surely they would have the longest life span and could be most beneficial to me in the long run.

With the sun shining down on me, satisfied that I had helped as many as I could (and annoyed by their helplessness), I would go find some shade and a cool drink. The remaining hundreds of worms heading for destruction would be left to their fate. What a poor saviour I was! The worms' salvation was based on their usefulness to me and the amount of energy and interest I had.

There is a Saviour, however, whose care and involvement in our plight is not based on His convenience or our usefulness, but only His great love. A line from one of my favorite hymns reads:

> Alas! and did my Saviour bleed?
> And did my Sovereign die?
> Would He devote that sacred head
> For such a worm as I?

Never once did I pray to become a worm, to become identified with the reason for their rush to death, to warn them of their danger, and perhaps to find a way of escape for them. Yet Jesus, who was equal with God, did not count His equality something to hold onto, but took on the form of a worm to do these things for us. He left all glory, eternity, joy, and light to come to a sin-darkened planet to teach us, love us, and stop our headlong plunge to death. That's a real Saviour. A Saviour of the worms.

WANDA DAVIS

MARCH 29

Growing Out of a Garment

Grow in grace, and in the knowledge of our Lord and Saviour Jesus Christ. 2 Peter 3:18.

On Oakwood Drive, where I usually walk early in the morning, I spotted a light, translucent object slowly rolling along the ground, while the gentle breeze blew it toward the sidewalk. I picked it up. It was a snakeskin, about 20 inches long. I took the piece of skin with me to show to my grandchildren later. As I continued on my walk, across the street from where I found the first one I found a 40-inch-long skin with the head portion attached. That completed the whole snakeskin, including the eyelids of the creature. These two pieces gave me better material for show and tell.

Why, just "out of the blue," did I find these two portions of a crawly creature in the midst of my walk, and in the desert with just a few dry weeds around? And why did the objects' color, although blending well with the ground, catch my attention? When I returned home, I carefully taped the two pieces of delicate skin together and mended a couple other spots to preserve the wholeness of the object. Then I measured the skin and found that it was almost five feet long.

I turned to the Bible to search for answers. I realized that without a Creator this creature would not exist, nor would it grow. The animal had outgrown its vesture and was ready for a change of garment. So it must be willing to shed its skin in order to change to more suitable apparel.

Paul encourages us to grow in our faith exceedingly, that charity in everyone may abound toward each other (1 Thess. 1:3). Peter admonishes us to lay aside all malice, all guile, hypocrisies, and envies, so that, like newborn babes, we may desire the sincere milk of the Word and realize the Lord's graciousness (1 Peter 2:1-3). Daily we must grow spiritually. "But grow in grace, and in the knowledge of our Lord and Saviour Jesus Christ" (2 Peter 3:18).

May we each outgrow our filthy garments of sin and inherit a robe of righteousness.　　　　　　　ESPERANZA AQUINO-MOPERA

MARCH 30

Little Things

Even the very hairs of your head are all numbered. Fear not therefore: ye are of more value than many sparrows. Luke 12:7.

A recent incident made me realize just how much the Lord cares about even the smallest details of our lives. I love to cook and entertain. But on this day I was really running behind schedule, and my guests were due shortly. In developing the menu I had decided to make rice and beans. Don't laugh—I'm originally from a country in which this is a basic dish. I know many who could make it with their eyes closed. So you'd think it would come naturally, but it doesn't.

I had asked my mother for the recipe and followed the directions carefully. However, as I opened the pot for some last-minute checking, I stared in disbelief at a sodden, gooey mess. "Oh, no!" I groaned as the doorbell rang. "This would be good—as rice pudding." But there was no time to ask Mom for troubleshooting advice, or even to think of something else to serve. So I closed my eyes and prayed over the pot.

"Lord, You said to ask and it would be given me. Well, please help me. I'm going to be so embarrassed with this mess. This is the first time these folks have been to our home, and what a disaster awaits them if You don't intervene. Please help me. I don't know what to do." I opened my eyes—and the gooey mess was still there. Halfheartedly I went off to meet my guests.

The time to serve dinner came around much too quickly for me. I decided to put the rice into a pretty serving bowl. It might be bad, but at least the presentation would be nice. Hopefully, the other items on my menu would leave little room for rice. As I spooned the rice into the dish, it looked much better than I thought it would. I sent up a silent thank-You.

One of my guests actually complimented me on my beans and rice!

"It's quite tasty," she said. "I can never get mine to this consistency. What did you do?"

"I prayed," I answered honestly. My guests laughed, but the Lord and I knew this had been no laughing matter.

Thank You, Lord, for responding to even my "nuisance prayers"—those little things that others may think are trivial. I know You care about whatever is important to me. MAXINE WILLIAMS ALLEN

Never Miss a Call

Be joyful always, pray at all times. 1 Thess. 5:16, 17, TEV.

*O*ne of the first things I did when I was laid off from work was to buy an answering machine. When I was working full-time, I felt the machine would have been a luxury item. My family and friends wouldn't call when they knew I was at work, and in case of an emergency, they had my work number. Now that I was looking for a job, I had to be available to potential employers at all times. Even a trip to the grocery store could mean a missed opportunity. An answering machine was no longer an unneeded expense, but an absolute necessity. With my trusty machine hooked up, I would never miss a call.

Keeping "hooked up" to God is even more important. When I let my daily worries and busy schedule interrupt my prayer life, I am apt to miss His voice. Before I purchased the answering machine I was in danger of missing calls. But even with the machine I have to remember that it can't record messages for me unless I remember to plug it into my phone and turn it on. It needs to tap into a larger power source in order to work.

In order to plug into our spiritual selves we must sometimes shut off our secular selves. We live in a world in which noise is a fact of life. The television, radio, neighbors, traffic—all combine to keep us from quiet communion with God. Only by staying in touch with God through prayer and daily devotions am I able to live the Christian life I desire. I cannot conceive of a life without daily prayer and the sweet communion I enjoy with my Master. I never want to miss a single call!   GINA LEE

Morning

See! The winter is past. . . . Flowers appear on the earth; . . . the cooing of doves is heard in our land. S. of Sol. 2:11, 12, NIV.

The stillness of the morning was profound. Not one little zephyr broke the spell. The sun shone in the cloudless dome above. With lifted heart I walked about, checking my tiny garden, admiring the trimmed lawn, being thankful.

Then something made me halt—the constant cry of the mourning dove. I had been listening to it ever since I came back to the farm. How illusive it was—but forever calling. I saw it now, sounding far away, but very near on the uppermost branches of a partly dead tree. How could I be sure?

Cautiously I moved closer to get a better look. Blackbirds, ever aware, set up a chatter at my approach, and the dove stopped calling. I watched, hoping she would call again, hoping some body movement would indicate that it was she. Her head turned this way and that way, toward the racket of the blackbirds. Her body shifted on her perch. I waited. Then, spreading her wings, she dipped away and out of sight.

Disappointed, I returned to the house to take up my favorite spot on the porch. I heard her again, more distant now, crying to the world her mournful, repetitious song. Why did she leave? I couldn't have reached her on her high perch. God has put within His wild creatures an awareness of their surroundings, the danger signals, and the flight-or-fight response.

We have it too—or did, until we became benumbed by the cacophony of our surroundings. The shocking becomes the ordinary, the ordinary the commonplace, the commonplace the mundane. And we, if not actually accepting, try to ignore.

Dear Lord, sharpen my senses not only to the beauty of the world around me, but to the ugly, the tragic, the needy, the helpless. Not that I might fly away and be safe, but that I might do whatever is within my power to effect some change. Thank You.
EVA ALICE COVEY

Spring Cleaning

Therefore keep watch, because you do not know on what day your Lord will come. . . . So you also must be ready, because the Son of Man will come at an hour when you do not expect him. Matt. 24:42-44, NIV.

*I*f most of you are like me, you don't look forward to getting started on spring house-cleaning. It is a big job, time-consuming and tiring, a task that is very easy to postpone as long as possible. But the day comes when you have to face up to the task. There are closets to be cleaned, decisions to be made about what to get rid of, and kitchen cupboards and messy bureau drawers to straighten. Makes one wonder how they get that way. By the time the curtains are taken down, the windows washed, the rugs cleaned, and all the little tasks we feel have to be done every spring are finished, we are all worn out and glad to have it over with.

Wouldn't we be better off to work at our spring cleaning on a day-by-day basis, keeping things neat and clean all the time, not having to worry about the cleanliness of our homes if someone comes unexpectedly? Aha! Unexpected company. That brings me up short. If I worry so much about my house being just right when company comes, what about that special Company that will be coming for a visit one day soon. Will my heart home be ready? Will I have cleaned all the clutter out of the nooks and crannies and have my heart ready to receive Him? There will be no time to prepare and get ready for Him if I don't work at it every day, spending time in prayer, confessing and repenting of all of my faults, and begging forgiveness. Only by spending time with Jesus ahead of time will I be ready to greet my precious Visitor. Lord, help me to be ready!   MARION E. KNOX

Simple Faith

I tell you the truth, wherever this gospel is preached throughout the world, what she has done will also be told, in memory of her. Matt. 26:13, NIV.

When this woman approached Jesus at the dinner table to anoint Him with perfume, she was not planning for the moment to be recorded in the annals of history to be retold again and again. She simply acted upon the impulse of a loving and grateful heart. And like her, we may never know the impact our loving gestures and acts of faith will have on another heart as we live out our daily routines.

While working as a social worker in a nursing home, I came to be very close to a resident named Christine. She was diagnosed with terminal cancer, and I had frequent talks with her. She reminisced about managing a boarding house in the 1940s and 1950s, and her eyes glowed when she recounted her European travels.

The most remarkable thing about Christine was her immutable faith in God. She recalled how she earnestly and patiently prayed that her husband would accept Jesus as his Saviour. Ten years later he did. She longed to have children, but as the years passed and her dream went unfulfilled, she put her trust in the Lord while she waited. Her dream was realized when she was asked to care for two abandoned infants whom she later adopted.

Again and again Christine shared stories of trials and difficulties through which her faith in God never wavered. As she sat in her wheelchair looking out the window, she stated that she was ready to face death because of her faith in God.

The stories she shared with me were accounts of a daily life lived in faith in God. Yet it impressed my heart so deeply that I was moved to put her story into words that a musician friend put to music. Now her story and song have been shared in numerous churches and schools. Though Christine has passed away, the example of her quiet faith continues to inspire others, just as the woman who anointed Jesus.

Live your life well today and show your faith in God in the

large and small details. You may never know until eternity how many hearts you have encouraged. KATHRYN GORDON

APRIL 4

The Peach Tree

I am the vine, you are the branches. He who abides in Me, and I in him, bears much fruit; for without Me you can do nothing. John 15:5, NKJV.

A few years ago in early spring, before all the birds returned from the South and the spring flowers awoke after a cold, long winter, rugged loggers were harvesting the timber on a farm near our home. As I passed the cove this crisp April morning, I noticed some beautiful pink blossoms among a stack of huge logs. Surprised, I stopped my car and went over to investigate what kind of pink flowers could be in bloom this early.

What I saw really amazed me. The pink flowers were from a small wild peach tree that lay on its side. The loggers had apparently cut the tree off just above the roots. I stood looking at the small tree, still blooming but cut off from the roots, and knew that it would soon die.

I sent a silent prayer up to heaven. *Lord, don't let me be cut off above the roots. You, Lord, are my roots. I want to stay connected to You so I can grow. Help me to fulfill the purpose in my life that You have planned for me.*

We must remain in Christ so we won't die and be burned like branches in the fire. Jesus says to remain with Him, bear fruit, obey His commands, and love each other as He has loved us.

ELEANOR OWEN

Cast the First Stone

He who is without sin among you, let him throw a stone at her first. John 8:7, NKJV.

The most acute sorrow I have experienced as a nurse was witnessing a parent losing a child, either by death or rejection. The anguish and pain cannot be expressed in words. There was the mother whose daughter had rejected her Christian upbringing. As I listened so many times to the breaking heart of that mother, my heart went out to her as well as to her child. The mother's words are still etched in my memory.

"What did we do wrong? What can we do now? Should we break off the relationship?"

My heart went out to her, but Jesus gave me the words to say "Forgive her. Don't lose that daughter-mother relationship you still have. Just love her." It would have been so much easier to tell her to run away from the pain and make a complete break, to just let the daughter go.

Is that not true of us as we deal with one another? When a friend does a wrong to us, it is easier to escape and never see that friend again than to try to heal the friendship. The cost of forgiving is powerful. As the forgiver I must accept the wrong. It is easier to pass on the wrong than to keep the friendship. It takes time and costs much to bring healing to a wounded heart. There are so very few people who forgive. Jesus is our example. He always stands ready to forgive us. He remains our faithful friend, no matter what wrong we have done that has hurt Him.

Remember the story of the woman who was brought to Jesus because His enemies wanted to test Him? Jesus just started writing their sins on the ground. The Pharisees saw what He was doing and left one by one. Jesus then told the woman that He did not condemn her—to go and sin no more. Is this not the lesson that each of us needs to learn about forgiveness? Has Jesus not set the perfect example of forgiveness? CAROLYN VOSS

Are You Listening?

"Come now, and let us reason together," says the Lord. Isa. 1:18, NKJV.

I stalked to bed in frustration and hurt. All week my husband, Tim, had been busy. Preparing for a test. Finishing his assignments. Working. But all that was finished. I thought that tonight we could finally spend some time together. To talk. *I've been patient all week,* I told myself. *Why can't he just give me a little bit of time tonight?* Instead he was listening to music with the headphones, unwinding from a stressful week. I wanted his attention. I wanted to spend time with him. I wanted to talk to him and have him *really* listen. I fought back tears of hurt as I pulled the covers over my head.

Then I thought about God. He wants to spend time with me. He wants to talk to me and have me really listen. But so often I'm busy doing other things. Good things. Important things. Perhaps I would skim through my Bible study time, not really "listening." Too often I would linger in bed "just a little bit longer," only to get up too late for my time with Him and end up rushing through my morning. How does He respond to my busyness and inattentiveness? He doesn't retreat and hide. He doesn't give up on me. He keeps trying to get my attention. To talk to me through a friend. To give me a glimpse of Him through nature. To speak to me through a song or my sons. Gently reminding me that He's there, waiting for me. Wanting to spend time with me.

Thank You, Lord, for never giving up on me. I can barely comprehend that You, the King of the universe, long to spend time with me, to have my total attention. Lord, help me to listen for Your voice. Help me to take the time to spend with You. Show me how to make You the priority of my life.   TAMI HORST

APRIL 7

Friends, Part 1: Rebuilding the Dam

If they fall, the one will lift up his fellow: but woe to him that is
alone when he falleth; for he hath not another to help him up.
Eccl. 4:10.

*M*any nature videos are downright violent, showing in
colorful closeup a vicious tiger chomping into the
neck of a hapless gazelle. So I was delighted to view a beaver
documentary, depicting these cuddly creatures chomping into
timber instead of the jugular vein of a smaller animal.

But what impressed me most about the entire video was its
emphasis on a beaver's sense of community. Did you know that
when a beaver's dam breaks, other beavers come from *miles*
around to repair the damage? Waddling over land, swimming in
streams, climbing over rocks and stumps, the helpful creatures
rush to the rescue. Instinctively they sense that a beaver's dam is
more than a home; it is its life. Consequently, it must be repaired.
And through some wonderful beaver "E-mail," the message radiates out: "Dam has broken. Come at once." And they come.

But woe to the beaver who is alone when its dam breaks and
has not another to help fix it. How rare are such friends—those
who come rushing over when your emotional, financial, or spiritual dam gives way. One survey found that 23 percent of people
queried said they had numerous acquaintances, but no close
friends. Not even one! Another poll revealed that if you can truth-
fully say you have three or four real friends, you are indeed rare!

But before you start lamenting about how few friends you
really have, startle yourself by asking how many people consider you a real friend, not just an acquaintance. In a psychology class at Andrews I missed a question that I have always
been glad I got wrong.

"True or false: The most important consideration in a marriage is finding the right mate."

Easy question! thought I. *True, of course.*

Wrong! The answer was *false.* "To be a true statement," the
teacher explained, "the question should have read 'The most important consideration in a marriage is *being* the right mate.'"

The beavers I watched on that nature video came from miles

around to help rebuild another beaver's dam; they came from *instinct*. The truth of the matter is that they probably couldn't help responding. But Jesus took the risk of giving us choice, not instinct, to govern our relationships. So be a true friend by *choice*. To paraphrase Scripture: "He who hath friends must show himself helpful, willing to expend self, as Jesus did for us all."

WILMA McCLARTY

APRIL 8

Friends, Part 2: Friendly Fire

If anyone causes one of these little ones who believe in me to sin, it would be better for him to have a large millstone hung around his neck and to be drowned in the depths of the sea. Matt. 18:6, NIV.

*H*arming a friend can be unintentional. The military has a euphemism for such an action: friendly fire. The history of the Civil War might have been altered had not friendly fire wounded Stonewall Jackson, injuring an arm that became infected and had to be amputated. Jackson died of complications soon thereafter. Yes, Lee needed Jackson at Gettysburg, but he had been killed by friendly fire.

More recently Americans were sickened at the news of those soldiers killed by friendly fire while fighting in Desert Storm. What an unnecessary tragedy to those unsuspecting GIs! What unbearable grief!

But tragic as military friendly fire is, intentionally harming a friend causes misery of another kind. What do you think pained Jesus more: His treatment at the hands of the Roman soldiers, or Peter's betrayal of his Lord three times? From the Romans He expected such, but from His confidant, His apostle, His friend, Peter? Never!

Have you ever been shot down by friendly fire, intentional or otherwise? Have you ever been the perpetrator of either kind? Most of us won't be involved in any military friendly fire, but unfortunately, too many professing Christians practice their own version of friendly fire, developing subtle ways to kill those we are supposed to befriend. We engage in friendly fire when we kill somebody's reputation, when we injure a relationship by gossiping, and when we wound someone's potential by rejection.

Jesus said it would be better for someone "to have a large millstone hung around his neck and to be drowned in the depths of the sea" than to injure a child of God. And *all* of God's children need the assurance that they will not be struck down by the "friendly fire" of fellow Christians. WILMA McCLARTY

In Living Color

I have set my rainbow in the clouds, and it will be the sign of the covenant between me and the earth. Gen. 9:13, NIV.

My 8-year-old daughter and I drove up to my aunt's home. From the outside everything looked normal. But I knew that what we would see on the inside would be hard to face. There had been a fire a few days before. As we walked through the ashes and broken glass, my daughter observed, "There is no color in the house." She was right. What had once been family portraits on flowered wallpaper was now charred frames on smutty walls. No color. No life.

When I was a child I faced some things that children should not have to. I survived by not letting myself feel the things that hurt too much. On the outside I seemed like a normal, happy child. On the inside I was numb. As I grew up I missed out on some very happy moments before I realized what was wrong. In my effort to block the pain and fear, I had lost the other feelings. I had no color inside.

Now since I've found my Saviour I no longer have anything to fear. I took His hand and walked through the fear, the pain, the anger, and then finally into forgiveness and a spectrum of joy such as I had never known before. He can give you the same color in your life, too.

Heavenly Father, thank You for giving us a life in living color. What a wonderful alternative to the grayness of just surviving!   TAMMY B. VICE

APRIL 10

Think High and Walk Tall

And we know that all things work together for good to them that love God, to them who are the called according to his purpose. Rom. 8:28.

"Think high and walk tall" is the inspiration I constantly heard from my parents as I grew from childhood into adolescence and even into my adulthood. They often encouraged me that no matter what the crisis (and there were many for an African-American female growing up in the 1940s, 1950s, and 1960s), the ability to maintain my balance and a proper perspective was the key to success.

I have been able to allow this philosophy to enshroud my life. That is, until May 1995, when my husband was diagnosed with sarcoma (a form of cancer). A multitude of "what if" questions played havoc on my mind. My usually organized, focused agendas seemed to evaporate. Daily routines required my every effort. How could life be so unkind? Why had God allowed this to happen? We were just approaching the time of our life that we had dreamed about. The children were now adults, grandchildren visited at the appropriate times, and we chose not to have pets of any kind. We were reaching the pinnacle of our lives!

I had to dig deep into the resources of my mind to find comfort. What immediately came into my mind was my mother's saying, "Think high and walk tall!" As I began to think in more spiritual terms, there seemed to be a burst of power, Holy Ghost power, that allowed me to look beyond the moment and focus on the blessings God had already bestowed upon us. I learned to cherish each day with my God-ordained mate. Finally I was at a point to accept whatever God allowed me to experience.

I realized it is true: when we stop looking at the problem and turn in faith to God, the source of good, the difficulty disappears and a new condition takes its place. I stopped focusing on the cancer and the fears of "what if" and replaced them with faith and a belief that God would work out even this to His good.

I began to let go and allow God to enrich my life by listening to His divine prompting. I maintained a weekly noon prayer service that proved to be a source of strength and encouragement from a dedicated and spiritual group of women at my church. I changed my outlook by replacing my difficulties with faith, the kind of faith that allows me to walk into the darkness with no foundation beneath my feet, realizing that God will make a foundation or He'll teach me to fly! It all started with my mom's edict: "Think high and walk tall."   ELLA TOLLIVER

APRIL 11

Wrestling My Monster

Praise be to the God and Father of our Lord Jesus Christ, the Father of compassion and the God of all comfort, who comforts us in all our troubles. 2 Cor. 1:3, 4, NIV.

Friends and family continually reach out to me in love, which I appreciate. Cards and letters often come just at the time I need them. Prayers buoy me up, keep me going. Some say they understand, though never having been through what I'm experiencing, they really can't. Others say nothing because they really don't know what to say.

Yes, I've been told I have terminal cancer. My doctor says there is no cure. It hurts to be confronted so bluntly, yet I know he's only trying to be honest.

After 11 years of fighting this monster, time is running out. It is sometimes difficult to come to grips with reality. I get confused somewhere in between thanking God for the miracle of the extra 11 years and begging Him for the miracle of a few years more. There are times I feel very lonely. I'm in a world apart from my healthy family and friends. They lay plans for the future, talk about good things to come. I start to join in their enthusiastic chatter, then grow silent when I realize that unless God intervenes I won't be there. My future is elsewhere. Drawn back into my own little sphere, I need comfort greater than even a loving husband can give.

But I've discovered there is comfort. I've found it in Matthew 26, Mark 14, and Luke 22—the story of Jesus facing death. Lonely, He could find little comfort in Peter, James, and John. But He did find it in prayer. Desperately He prayed for strength to face trial and death that were only hours away. At 33 He was too young to die. The responsibility resting on His shoulders was awesome. Three times He turned to His friends; three times they were unable to help. But He found comfort and He found strength on His knees, alone with His Father.

Now I find comfort in Christ. He understands the loneliness of getting ready for death. He's the only friend I have who's been there.

Whatever trials or tragedy you may face today, remember that through it all we can trust in Jesus. He understands. "So do not fear, for I am with you; do not be dismayed, for I am your God. I will strengthen you and help you; I will uphold you with my righteous right hand" (Isa. 41:10, NIV).   ELLEN BRESEE

APRIL 12

The Resurrection

I am the resurrection and the life: he that believeth in me, though he were dead, yet shall he live. John 11:25.

Many songs and poems have been written about Christ. The lyrics speak of the mystery of His birth, the beauty of His life, the power of His death, the glory of His resurrection, and the majesty of His return. There is a poem whose verses repeat the same theme: "The crown that He wore and the cross that He bore were His own." From Scripture I realize that Christ wore the crown of thorns for me, for you, for us. He carried that cross, hung on that cross, and ultimately died on that cross for my sins, for your sins, for our sins. He sacrificed His life because of the love He had for us.

Christ was never disobedient. He never sinned. Evil thoughts never entered His mind. But we have done all the wrong things. He lived an exemplary life for us to emulate. He died to show us what the results of sins would be. Therefore, I say that the crown He wore and the cross that He bore were mine, they were yours, they were ours. Hallelujah! What a Saviour!

I am so grateful that the cross was not the final scene. Thank God for the crowning act—the Resurrection. When Christ rose from the grave, this demonstrated the ultimate victory over Satan. Thus dying in Christ gives us the expectation of rising to eternal life. The glory of His resurrection gives us unlimited hope beyond the grave. Let us be ever mindful of the relationship we must have with Christ. We live because He lives. We can face tomorrow because He holds tomorrow. And if we are faithful, we will get home someday.   MARIE H. SEARD

APRIL 13

The Empty Tomb

Why seek ye the living among the dead? He is not here, but is risen. Luke 24:5, 6.

It's early Sunday morning. Flowers are everywhere in bloom
As women bearing spices make their way to Jesus' tomb.
Though wearied by their anguish, love entices them along
O'er lesser traveled pathways to avoid the waking throng.

Their gifts for His anointing, in His cold tomb they
    will lay,
And with each step they wonder who will roll the
    stone away.
Oh, sad humanity, take heart, for Gabriel is there!
He's moved the stone, and heaven's grandest message
    waits to share!

Now in full view, a light shines forth. The tomb is
    open wide!

"He is not here," the angel speaks, and bids them
    look inside.
"Your Lord is risen! Jesus lives!" What joyous words to hear!
No more their tears of sorrow! Gone at last their hope-
    less fear.

No need to leave their spices, for the tomb is empty now!
Too late to place their gifts of love beside that thorn-
    pierced brow.
With overflowing hearts, the women have no time to lose,
For they must bear to Christ's disciples Gabriel's good news!

But Mary had come first and left that Resurrection day,
And sobbing out her grief, returns, inquiring where He lay.
She sees His resting place from which there wafts a fra-
    grance sweet
Spilled from an alabaster flask once shattered o'er His feet!

Oh, could it be this tomb was thought too stately for
    her Lord?
She gladly will herself provide for Him whom she adored!
Her brother Lazarus' grave lies empty, by Christ's
    mighty power.
To place Him there would bring her solace in this
    darkest hour.

So blinded by her tears, she senses not in her despair
That He who once restored her brother stands beside
    her there.
He speaks her name. That is enough. No voice was e'er
    so sweet!
Joy floods the heart of Mary, and she falls at Jesus' feet.

Today, like Mary, hearts despairing, struggle in their grief,
And know not that Jesus waits with longing heart to
    bring relief.
But though His presence to our tear-dimmed eyes may
    seem obscure,
He lives to heal our broken hearts! His promises are sure!

Oh, anxious soul, with tenderness, your Saviour waits
    to spend

Some time with you—a moment or an hour—as your
    friend.
So pause to let Him fill your heart with peace and hope
    anew.
The Christ who spoke to Mary waits to speak, just now,
    to you.

LORRAINE HUDGINS

APRIL 14

Family Reunion

Happy are those who wash their robes clean and so have the
right to eat the fruit from the tree of life and to go through the
gates into the city. Rev. 22:14, TEV.

All my life I've been moving. The worst year for me was
when I was 10 years old. That year we moved five
times, and I was in five different schools. We moved from New
York to Miami, Florida, to Puerto Rico, back to New York, and
finally back to Miami.

I still remember the day it all began. I went to school as
usual, but when I got home that afternoon and opened the
door, the apartment looked different. At first glance I thought
Mom was moving the furniture around. Then as my eyes surveyed each room, I realized the apartment was strangely
empty—no furniture, no pictures on the walls, no curtains in
the windows. Against one wall in the living room were a few
boxes and Mom's luggage. Everything else was gone.

I was shocked. Mom said we were moving to Miami. She said
Dad had run an ad in the newspaper for the furniture and everything had been sold in the one day. Even my toys were gone.

You see, my brother's life had been threatened by a gang,
and my parents' reaction was to move away quietly, without anyone's knowing. The most devastating part of the experience for
me was that I wasn't even allowed to say goodbye to my teacher,
classmates, or friends.

My family continued to move every few years, and now that

I'm a pastor's wife, I look back and count the endless moves we have made in the ministry. Saying goodbye, leaving friends and loved ones behind, is never easy.

What a beautiful comfort God offers us in the knowledge that one day soon Jesus will come, and we'll celebrate a grand re-union day when we enter through the gates into the city of God. We'll never have to say goodbye again!

Make your plans to be there for the grand celebration and family reunion.

CELIA MEJIA CRUZ

APRIL 15

A New Reason for Living

The Lord liveth; and blessed be my rock; and let the God of my salvation be exalted. Ps. 18:46.

Worse than my struggle to keep from drowning in the angry waves and the raging whirlpool was my panic at knowing there was no logical reason God should save me. As I looked at my unconscious friend bobbing in the water, I knew I had no chance. I had no strength left to call out to the Lord, so I raised my eyes to heaven and in my heart said, *Forgive me, Lord, and let Thy will be done.* In that instant I felt something tugging at my neck. I knew I was being saved.

I woke up in the hospital. Friends and classmates from my college in Beirut, Lebanon, visited and told me about the mirac-ulous way I had been saved. An ambulance had stopped near the shore for ice cream. One of the drivers happened to look out over the water and saw a distant swimming cap bobbing in the waves. They quickly came to our aid and pulled my roommate, Maria, and me out of the whirlpool.

Maria was in better condition than I was. She had been un-conscious most of the time, so she had not inhaled much saltwa-ter. I was hospitalized for 10 days before my condition improved. The pain in my chest was excruciating, and no one knew what to do. I was unable to sit or lie down, so I stood most of the time. The doctors finally took an X-ray and discovered four mililiters of salt that had remained at the edges of my lungs after the water was removed. If the salt had not been discovered within 24 hours, it would have pierced my lungs and I would have died.

I had been saved twice from certain death. I began to realize how much I took life for granted. The more I experienced God's miracles in my life, the louder my soul witnessed, "The Lord liveth!"

Today I am a healthy mother of three children, but when I look back on this incident that occurred 23 years ago, I can't help remembering the words spoken by the college church pastor when he visited me in the hospital. "Georgette, God has a purpose for your life."

Living for Christ gives life purpose. Let us not take life for granted. Every breath we take is a gift from God that is not to be wasted.

GEORGETTE GINDI

APRIL 16

It's Time for a Miracle

When you pass through the waters, I will be with you; and through the rivers, they shall not overflow you. When you walk through the fire, you shall not be burned, nor shall the flame scorch you. For I am the Lord your God. Isa. 43:2, 3, NKJV.

When my niece and nephew were younger, they loved stories. They told us in no uncertain terms that they preferred "told" stories to the ones we offered to read to them. I indulged them with much-loved Bible stories in dramatic narrative and childhood tales of the antics of my brother—their father. Later we moved to stories of people they knew and places they had not yet heard of. When my repertoire began to dwindle, Christine suggested that we create a story of our own.

As we sat in the sunroom of their grandparents' home in Florida, Jonathan began a hair-raising saga of two young boys (suspiciously like himself) roaming the countryside. Christine offered her spine-chilling contributions. Alligators roamed free. A hurricane threatened. Electricity failed. The rains came. The rivers flooded. Trees crashed across the roads. Night was coming. It was getting darker.

Their own apprehension heightened their delight in the story they were weaving. Clearly they were fascinated with the idea of frightening themselves. As I was about to chime in with some twist to the story that would alleviate the palpable tension in the room, I heard Jonathan's mandate: "It's time for a miracle!"

I could not resist a smile. My grin widened when Christine reminded him that Jesus was with those boys. "They were just too scared to remember that His hand was on their shoulders all along." Then with typical older-sister sagacity she added, "Jesus will send a miracle if He knows those guys can't handle the scary stuff."

Wisdom from an 8-year-old's lips. We are in enemy territory. "Scary stuff" is inevitable, but God never gives us more than we can handle.

Not wanting our discussion to end, I talked to them about safety strategies. Finally I asked them for suggestions of how to resolve the lost boys' problem. Their answers were amazing— sometimes simple (never panic), other times expensive (a cellular phone in their backpacks), but always wonderful. Their parents had taught them well. Then Christine, sincerity sparkling from her gray-blue eyes, echoed the words of the song wafting across the room. "But I recommend Jesus."

I am constantly awed by one of God's special gifts to us: adorable, receptive God-trusting children. Thank You, heavenly Parent. I needed that.   GLENDA-MAE GREENE

APRIL 17

Those Who Trespass Against Us

If ye forgive not men their trespasses, neither will your Father forgive your trespasses. Matt. 6:15.

*F*orgive us our debts, as we forgive our debtors" (Matt. 6:18). "Forgive us our trespasses as we forgive those who trespass against us." For years I had used one or the other forms of the Lord's Prayer in the military chapels or in my local church, and it did not make any difference to me which was used. My only concern was remembering where I was so I would know which one was expected. That is, it made no difference, until Shannon was murdered.

Shannon was a dynamic young Christian woman who lived and worked nearby. Although she made quite an impact on the people in her church, I would probably never have had the privilege of knowing anything about her if it hadn't been for her senseless death and our contact through her father. I knew I wanted to go to the memorial service for her, not only out of respect to her family, but for myself too. When a young woman is cut down before her time, it affects each of us, and I wanted to be there.

It was a beautiful service of singing, sharing, laughing, and questioning why. "Why, Lord, when this young woman had so much to offer?" "Why, Lord, when she was using her gifts for You?" "Why, Lord, why?" Each speaker struggled with the question in his or her own way. And then the pastor asked all of us to stand, hold hands, and repeat the Lord's Prayer.

Suddenly I remembered something I had heard just the week before, something that had impressed me with a new import. I had been attending a women's meeting at which we had also been asked to repeat the Lord's Prayer. The group leader suggested that she liked to use the word "trespass" because so many women have been trespassed against. So many are in pain because someone had used their bodies without their permission or had trespassed against them in some other way. And now I knew the Lord understood. "Forgive us our trespasses as we forgive those who trespass against us." If we think of the most horrific crimes against anyone, especially women, we think of violations against flesh and blood. How does one forgive? How does one let go of the outrage, anger, and hurt?

The answer is found only through Jesus. Only through the power of the violation of Jesus' body and blood for us.

Thank You, Jesus, for setting us an example. Even without being asked, You forgave those who trespassed against You, who violated You, who cruelly invaded Your body with nails and a spear. Even as Shannon was violated and died, You were there.

It felt so wonderful to even say those words, to be able to begin overcoming the anger that comes at such a time. "Forgive us." Yes, and help us to forgive those who trespass against us. Help us to have Your mind and Your character so that we too may be able to say, "Father, forgive them, for they know not what they do."

ARDIS DICK STENBAKKEN

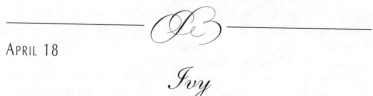

Ivy

Then he said to her, "Daughter, your faith has healed you. Go in peace." Luke 8:48, NIV.

I love ivy. It is such a fresh, green plant, creeping over life-less walls and dull bark. We have even stenciled ivy around our bedroom walls. Ivy always seems so full of life, even at those times when other plants seem to die back.

And there is another Ivy who is special to me, another Ivy who has clung tenaciously to life despite many serious medical challenges. We first met Ivy when we moved to a new church district. She always had a smile for us and an encouraging word, and often a little treat for the children. Although she was tiny, she was a spiritual giant, full of love and happiness and hope.

Then one day she became sick. In the hospital the doctors discovered that she was bleeding internally very heavily. She was given transfusion after transfusion, but nothing seemed to have any effect on the bleeding. Though she became weaker and weaker, she still had plenty of smiles for us.

One day she became so sick that she was sent away to a very large city hospital to be seen by a specialist. We decided to make the long journey to visit her there. As we entered her room, she seemed weaker and paler than ever. Her family hovered close by, and I wondered whether this would be the last time we would see Ivy. We held her hand and prayed with her, and as we prayed I suddenly had a picture of another lady with uncontrollable bleed-ing. Another lady with incredible faith and a quiet hope. A lady who knew she would be healed if she could only touch the hem of a garment, the garment of Jesus. *Dear Father,* I prayed silently. *Please brush the hem of Your garment over Ivy. We know that her healing is in Your hands, and You are the only one who can give her strength and life again.* Somehow we all felt more peaceful as we left that little room.

Within a day or two the bleeding subsided, her strength returned, and as I write this a few years later, she is still clinging fiercely to life. Scripture gives us strength for today and hope for tomorrow. — KAREN HOLFORD

He Touched Me

And Jesus came and touched them, and said, Arise, and be not afraid. Matt. 17:7.

Listening to the newscast this morning, I heard a reporter tell about an upcoming auction for the detailed belongings of the late Jacqueline Kennedy Onassis. The predicted prices were astounding! After describing some of her jewelry and personal things, along with their potential worth, the reporter said, "Anything that Jackie touched will be worth a fortune!" I was stunned. Just because she was famous, her items were worth millions?

Then I contemplated the worth of what Jesus "touched" with His blood on Calvary—souls since the beginning of time. He is a lot more famous, and when He touches us with His love and grace, no price can be put upon our worth! We are of immeasurable value.

There will be no auction needed to prove our worth. We already belong to the greatest kingdom there will ever be. We'll be going into the heavenly kingdom soon, where the mansions for you and me will outshine anything this old earth has even dreamed of, full of sparkling gems of real value, not from an auction, but from the Creator Himself.

Have you let the Master touch you today? — BESSIE LOBSIEN

God Spoke to Me This Morning

Give thanks to the Lord, for he is good; his love endures forever.
Ps. 106:1, NIV.

I was recovering from a bad case of the flu and feeling rather sorry for myself. The weather had been cold and dreary for several days, but now the sun had come out, and I retreated to our sunporch, where I have a nice, big recliner to curl up in and enjoy the lovely outdoors. As I sat there, a beautiful little purple finch landed on the bird feeder a few feet from my window, his bright, raspberry-colored head shining in the sunlight. I smiled as I looked at him, and God seemed to say to me, "See? I love you. I haven't forgotten you, and I have sent the little purple finch to tell you so."

As I looked again I noticed the lovely golden daffodils opening up. They looked so bright and cheerful against the lavender-blue blossoms and crisp green leaves of the vinca that covered the bank. And God spoke again and said, "See? I have even opened up the blossoms of the daffodils early to brighten your day and make you feel better, because I love you so!"

Then I looked in the direction of the back gardens, down by the grapevines, and there were mama and papa bluebird, preparing their home in the bluebird house my husband had readied for them. Bluebirds, my favorite bird, with their lovely deep-blue coloring reflecting the blue of the sky, had returned for the summer. And God spoke again. "See? I have sent the bluebirds, the robins, the daffodils, and the sprouting leaves of the maple tree in due season. Just as surely, My Son, Jesus, will return in due season to take you to the home He has prepared just for you. Watch and be ready, dear one."

I smiled again and thought of the many times in my life that I had neglected to spend time with God, and yet He shows His love to me every day without fail. I resolved that morning to spend more time with the one who never forgets, but goes on bestowing love and gifts upon me without measure.

Yes, God spoke to me this morning through the beautiful things around me, and I answered back. "Yes, Lord, I love You too, and I thank You for Your love and watchcare all these many years. And Lord, I will be waiting and watching and be ready, but please don't be too long, for I am weak and so weary of this old world of sin and sorrow." MARION E. KNOX

APRIL 21

God's Promises

I have set my rainbow in the clouds, and it will be the sign . . .
between me and the earth. Whenever . . . the rainbow appears
in the clouds, I will remember. Gen. 9:13, 14, NIV.

hunder rumbled in the distant clouds, just as it had the night before. But up until now, not one drop of rain had fallen. It was early morning, and the birds were singing their roundelay. Relishing this early chorus, I started for my morning walk down the lane. I thought I would try to go a little farther. Maybe soon I would be able to make it to the road and back.

On and on the thunder grumbled as the dark clouds moved westward. I could see white streaks that told me rain was falling somewhere. I went back up the lane and did a loop around the yard, as I always had since coming to the farm a couple weeks before. Then I sat and rested for a bit on the front steps, taking in the beauty, the fresh breeze, the still gentle sunshine. Far to the south came the raucous call of a flock of cranes. I wandered over to the edge of the yard, scanning the sky. There they came, a long skein, wings beating the air, calling encouragement to one another as they flew.

Above was the beginning of a rainbow. It grew, slowly, little by little, both sides creeping upward until they met in a beautiful arc in the storm clouds overhead. I could only echo the words of William Wordsworth: "My heart leaps up when I behold a rainbow in the sky." Drinking in the beauty of the blended colors, I thought, *What a splendid God we have to choose this way to assure the inhabitants of the earth that in spite of storm clouds, or perhaps because of them, He remembers!*

The winds of time, the storms of life, the clouds of grief may beat about us. But let us look up! Way up is the beautiful blended arc of God's promise of His love. The rainbow of promise. You can touch it from where you are right now!   EVA ALICE COVEY

Conquering Loneliness

Those who look to him are radiant; their faces are never covered with shame. Ps. 34:5, NIV.

I am a keen nature observer and enjoy relating it to my own life. Outside my church in Harare, Zimbabwe, there is a tree that observant worshipers can see through the glass-walled steeple of the church. There are times during spring and summer when the tree is full of lively green leaves, swaying gracefully in the breeze. I always think, during this time, about the loveliness of the tree and the joy it gives to the viewer.

There are times, however, when I notice the falling leaves of the tree. Then comes the winter, when all green leaves are gone, leaving us with only brown branches to see. And I think, *What a drab, ugly tree! Is it going to die?*

One cold winter day as I sat in a pew, I compared my life with that now-barren tree. My husband was traveling, my oldest daughter was in boarding school, and a close friend had died. I felt so lonely. I thought of myself as experiencing wintertime in my life. It is very hard to smile and share joy with the next person when you feel that way. But then I thought, *That brown, dry, leafless tree can still give beauty to the artist.*

In the midst of my loneliness I could still praise God. I could still give a smile to a little child, pat a friend's shoulder, and be a blessing to someone. Then I could forget myself and my loneliness. By associating with others I've helped myself. Didn't God say that those who will look to Him are radiant? We can continue looking to Jesus and be radiant in the midst of loneliness. When the hard winds of life blow on us, we can still sway gracefully for the Master Artist.   JEMIMA D. ORILLOSA

APRIL 23

He Went Before Them

The Lord went before them by day in a pillar of cloud, to lead them the way; and by night in a pillar of fire, to give them light. Ex. 13:21.

During my childhood, our only source of light at night was the kerosene lamp. At night it sat in the middle of the dining room table while we studied our school lessons. Sometimes it was necessary for Mama to take the lamp to another room for a few minutes while she searched for something. We children were ordered to stay seated until she returned. When she left the room, we were in utter darkness, afraid to move.

There were times when we were allowed to go with her. We carefully walked along behind Mama, clinging to her skirt as we walked lest we trip on something. Eerie shadows stretched behind and beside us as we strained to see where we were going in the dim light made by the kerosene lamp.

The Israelites, while moving from Egypt to the Promised Land, needed light at night so they could see where they were going. There were no highway signs, motels, service stations, or other accommodations along the route. God provided a visible guide for them. A pillar of cloud led them by day and a pillar of fire by night.

There were times when the cloud or pillar of fire stood still, indicating a period of rest in their tents for a few days or longer. The cloud denoted visible evidence of God's presence with them as they journeyed.

Along life's way we too face unknown paths, but if we keep our eyes focused on Christ, we can make it. When we followed Mama with the lamp, we had to keep our eyes on her and the light lest we stumbled, fell, and hurt ourselves.

Because God's "word is a lamp unto my feet, and a light unto my path" (Ps. 119:105), I am safe as long as I walk *in* the light. God's Word enlightens our understanding, and without it to guide us we stumble and grope in the darkness.

"The entrance of thy words giveth light" (verse 130). By ordering our steps in the light of His Word we are safe. Fortunately, we can't see around the corner of life's experiences,

but if we follow in the light provided in God's Word, we'll journey safely to the heavenly Canaan.   MABEL ROLLINS NORMAN

Like the Jasmine

Thanks be to God, who always leads us in triumphal procession
in Christ and through us spreads everywhere the fragrance of the
knowledge of him. For we are to God the aroma of Christ among
those who are being saved and those who are perishing. 2 Cor.
2:14, 15, NIV.

One of my coworkers, a lovely Indian woman, gives the
women she works with a gift of a fresh, white jasmine
blossom when they bloom in summer. As I write, a single blossom sits perched on my desk, permeating my whole office with
its heavenly scent. This morning, as Stella went from office to office sharing these fragrant blossoms, I thought how much the life
of the Christian should be like a jasmine blossom. I didn't plan to
write about it, but the blossom not only smells good; it brings a
spiritual lesson to my heart that I must share with you.

The single blossom is part of the whole plant, but even when
separated from the plant it continues to give off its unmatched
scent of sweet perfume. The blossom I have is pure white and
delicately formed, and its fragrance is constant. Stella braids
Jasmine into her hair, and when she walks through the halls she
leaves a trail of sweet-smelling perfume.

A few years ago Stella and I traveled to India, her native land
and the home of the jasmine plant. Together we walked the
streets of Bangalore and stopped to purchase fresh jasmine leis and
strands of jasmine for her hair. In the city the jasmine seller's carts
were laden with blossoms, and the slightest breeze carried their
sweet perfume throughout the market and along impoverished
streets. There is beauty wherever the jasmine introduces itself.

I want my life to be like the single jasmine blossom my friend
gave to me: able to retain my distinct fragrance when I must
stand alone, ready to spread the fragrance of the knowledge of

our Lord wherever I find myself, pure in character, and spreading the aroma of Christ wherever I go.

Thank you, Stella, for sharing God's love through a tiny part of His creation. My blossom keeps whispering His love to me.

ROSE OTIS

APRIL 25

I Can Help

He saw that there was no man, and wondered that there was no intercessor: therefore his arm brought salvation unto him; and his righteousness, it sustained him. Isa. 59:16.

My husband and I were planning a move from the North American far north to the far south. We could not make that decision, however, without finding out what it would mean to our two young daughters. So we took a fact-finding, are-we-going-to-like-this-place trip.

We took them to church. My younger daughter was charmed, for the first time giving me permission to leave her while I went to my own Bible class. My older daughter was enchanted with the program and her young classmates. My husband went to the university he was considering attending. It met his requirements. We took them to visit their grandmothers. Delight on all sides. I checked out the job market. Definite possibilities. One final prerequisite: school for my daughter. I prayed and hoped for a perfect match.

My daughter was invited to spend a morning in a classroom. Bright-eyed with excitement, she took a seat. The other children did exercises, answered questions, listened to stories. My daughter said nothing. Only her eyes showed her involvement. Finally, a 6-year-old sitting close by could stand it no longer. He could tell, it seemed, that she wanted to share in the synergy of the classroom. To him, her silence could only mean one thing: Spanish, not English, must be her mother tongue. Politely he tugged at the teacher's sleeve.

"Teacher, does she speak Spanish?" he asked quietly. "Let her talk. I can help. I'll translate."

155

I was moved by his thoughtfulness. His assumption about language was inaccurate—Takara just takes a while to check out her new environment, but when she feels comfortable, it's non-stop dialogue. However, his young mind was already on the way to understanding the principle of intercession. More important, he was practicing it.

Sensitive, Spirit-taught child wonder—a testimony to witness. This gracious youngster was prepared to curtail his own sharing to bring my daughter, a subdued stranger, into the circle of caring association.

Our investigative trip is now complete. The final decision affirmative, made easier because of one who cared enough to say "I can help."

Now imagine this scene. A celestial circle with a throne. Our Supreme Parent and ourselves. Consider the habitual sinner on the edge of the circle while our Elder Brother in the inner circle asks, "Father, let Me speak. I can help. I can translate. I've been there, and I speak the language."

Perhaps today I can invite someone into the circle of love.

JANET M. GREENE

APRIL 26

Following a Dream

God is our refuge and strength, an ever present help in trouble. Therefore we will not fear. Ps. 46:1, 2, NIV.

When I was a small child, my mother and I often went outside to listen to the doves cooing in the woodland near our home. We never saw them there, but they were ever present, and we loved them. They are a familiar sight in our yard—visiting the feeders, walking unafraid just beyond our reach, and constantly making their presence known by their soft, gentle calling.

Recently I heard the familiar sound of doves cooing outside my dining room window. My daughter and I went outside and found a very young-appearing little dove busily working on the narrow window ledge. Her mate arrived often, bearing materials which she incorporated into the rather sad little nest she was building. When I checked again later, I discovered that a wanton breeze had blown her precious creation away, leaving only a few strands of grass. Undaunted, she began all over, only to meet with disappointment again and again. However, she didn't become discouraged. The sounds of her cooing were a constant reminder that they were still working, still trying, and despite adversity, making a bit of progress.

We felt admiration for these small creatures who, against all odds, steadfastly pursued their dream. We wondered why they insisted upon this unlikely spot and have come to the conclusion that the ledge's location behind the sheltering branches of a large yew tree represents safety to them. Here they were protected from the crows who in the past had menaced their young, and from the lone hawk who had recently found our yard, with its abundance of birds, a very interesting place. Here was safety from the world's dangers, and although the task was difficult, they were determined to make their home there. How complimented we were that although they were aware of our presence they found us to be no threat.

Obviously, these dear little ones had not chosen the path of least resistance, and I found myself relating their struggles to the life of a dedicated Christian. On our journey toward heaven, Satan strews our pathway with difficulties, and problems confront us at every turn. Yet we know there is safety in staying close to our heavenly Father and that through life's trials He is always near. Like the little doves, we have not chosen the easy way, but it's the road home, and we travel it gladly.   HAZEL MALCOLM

APRIL 27

Try Me!

Bring the full amount of tithe to my Temple so that there will be
plenty of food in my house. Try me, and see if I will not open the
gates of heaven and pour out so many blessings on you, spiritual
as well as material, that you will not be able to number them all.
Mal. 3:10, Clear Word.

My mother was a single parent without a profession,
without child support, and with three young daughters to raise and educate. Factory work and cleaning offices and
homes were hard work, but these jobs provided her with the necessary finances. Keeping her daughters in church school was her
number-one priority. This meant hand-me-down clothes for all
and purchasing only absolute necessities.

The first fall as a single parent was especially difficult. The
church school teacher, learning of my mother's financial struggle,
decided to have the children in our one-room school bring in
food for a Thanksgiving basket. How surprised my mother was
when the teacher brought the Thanksgiving basket to *our* home.

My mother decided she would assess the value of the food
and pay tithe on this amount. When she shared her plan with her
sister, my aunt replied that my mother was too poor to tithe the
food and that the Lord didn't expect it of her. My mother dis-
agreed with my aunt's theology, and the next Sabbath her tithe
was in the offering plate.

A few days later our pastor came to our apartment. The
church had planned a food shower for us. The pastor's car was
filled with food. The Lord truly opened the "gates of heaven" for
us. His blessings continued to flow through the years. Mother
saw two of her daughters become educators and one become a
nurse. Her example in tithing and educating her girls in our
church schools has continued to be practiced even "unto the
third generation."   PATRICIA MULRANEY KOVALSKI

A Parent's Nightmare, Part 1

He who has begun a good work in you will complete it until the day of Jesus Christ. Phil. 1:6, NKJV.

I've read this scripture numerous times. However, the verse was only words until my husband, Ben, and I received a suicide letter from our daughter, Laura.

It was in January 1993. Ben was out of town (of course). The letter started out with a friendly tone, and then came the sentence "I want to commit suicide!" Within a few minutes my joy immediately changed into horror. "Where have we failed!" I cried out to God.

You see, the letter was about how depressed, lonely, and out of touch with reality she had been. She wrote: "I have no place to turn. . . . I think that I want to commit suicide, but I'm just not sure how to do it, because it may be too painful."

It was difficult for me to continue reading through the flood of tears. Laura explained more of the trauma she was experiencing. Because of a cross-country move (east to west), loss of all of her close friends, and lack of security, she was desperate from loneliness and was crying out for help. She had tried to "carry the burden alone" (as we all do), but life had become too heavy and overwhelming. So she wanted to end it all.

The last paragraph read: "Mom and Dad, I love you, and it isn't your fault!"

Have you ever received a letter like that? What do you do? Whom do *you* turn to? The sense of failure, embarrassment, guilt of "What if someone finds out?" rains down upon you with the force of thunder and flashing lightning. How could I ever talk about it? All these questions, feelings, and thoughts flooded through my mind—and still do.

Even as I write this my eyes are filled with tears as I relive the trauma we went through. The knowledge that God is so good through difficulties and trauma was the glue that held me together and gave me sanity for the rest of the story. He is the God with Super Glue who carries you through these situations. I couldn't hang on very tightly; the grip I had on Him was slippery. At that moment I gave Laura—mentally, physically, and spiritually—to the *real* Saviour.

That is when today's text became a promise to me. The rest
of the story tomorrow.   MARY MAXSON

A Parent's Nightmare, Part 2

I will sing of the mercies of the Lord forever; with my mouth will
I make known Your faithfulness to all generations. Ps. 89:1, NKJV.

Both Ben and I have been handling these types of situations for more than 20 years in our pastoral team ministry—but we were always on the "other side of the desk." We
have experienced years of counseling, but when it comes to your
own, what do you do?

It seemed like we were in a maze of wonder the following
four to six months. Our hands felt totally tied. I ached inside,
wanting to fix it, wanting to save Laura, wanting to redo whatever part we may have had in this. But we had to step back and
allow God to heal her and us. *Wow!* If that's not painful!

You see, some of us have this "Messiah complex" where we
have to fix everything that needs fixing. And the hard facts are—
we *can't*, because we are *not* the Messiah! We don't have power to
save! We don't have power to fix it! But how often we think we
can because "we are in the ministry, and that's our job." Only *Jesus*
has that power!

Those grueling months were spent in constant revelation of
ourselves and our family—self-examination. We had to allow
God to teach us what step to take moment by moment. When we
felt as though we couldn't see beyond our tears, somehow the
Lord brought a special, God-given person into Laura's life.
Recognition on our part of how we should restructure our
lifestyles was one life-changing need.

The Lord realizes that unless we go to Him for our answers,
we can self-destruct. But it sometimes takes experiences such as
this to get our attention. Through a series of prayers, total re-
liance on the Lord, and the services of a good Christian counselor for us both, we were able to work through all the issues. We

are different pastoral parents now. We aren't afraid to "speak out." Somehow some of us have the idea that because of our positions we shouldn't talk about our struggles or problems. God has brought many situations across our path so that we have been able to share with other parents who are struggling with their children. We can help because we *know*, because we have *experienced* the pain of a suffering, hurting child.

Laura packed her bags to attend college back East, across the country. What a fear was in my heart when I thought, *What will she do if she gets "low" again?* Then I had to remind myself that I wasn't the One who had "saved" her to begin with. It was my loving Saviour and Lord, who cares far more about her than I do. Oh, the doubtless love and compassion my dear Lord and Father has for us. How He longs for us to come to Him and to allow Him to hold us, to embrace us with His strong arms, His healing touch, His peaceful words of love, His life-giving, saving power and strength.

Laura had a rebirth experience during her year away from home! I constantly continue to release her to God. To go through the pain and then sit back and watch it happen—pleading for God to show us—is a freeing experience, but it is not without a struggle.

I've learned that God is a much greater, much more compassionate God than you or I can even begin to imagine. My devotional life has deepened. I now personally experience the love letters that Jesus writes to me. His promises, my prayer diary, sharing with others, have given me the opportunity of telling the story of Jesus. He is a real, *personal* God, alive, well, and still performing miracles for us and our children—only if we allow Him.

MARY MAXSON

This article is adapted by permission from the *Shepherdess International Journal* 13, No. 3 (third quarter 1996).

So Trust

I am the Lord thy God . . . which leadeth thee by the way that thou shouldest go. Isa. 48:17.

The shortest way may not be best to choose.
The smoothest road may not be safe to use.
So do not be surprised if God
May lead us over rougher sod;
May measure out the farther trail
Through chasms bleak or chilling gale;
Along the stony, narrow way
That steeper grows day after day.
But in His wisdom, God metes out the test
And joyfully, we find His way was best.

LORRAINE HUDGINS

Lessons From the Daffodils

Casting all your care upon him; for he careth for you. 1 Peter 5:7.

What excitement! My little ones came running into the house shouting, "Mommy, Mommy, come quick and see. It's finally spring. The daffodils are blossomed."

It had been a long, dreary winter that year in New England, and it seemed that spring had taken a detour around our part of the country. The sky preferred the color gray to blue, and the ground looked like a brownie with melted vanilla ice cream. How we longed for spring to *really* come—for the grass to be green and the flowers to bloom.

Oh, the brave little daffodils did push through the hard ground, but there wasn't any promise of the flowers opening their cheery blossoms until that day when it was finally sunny *and* warm—no March wind to chill the air, and no cold April showers.

This bed of daffodils brought enjoyment to each of us as it heralded the promise of warmer days ahead. The bright blossoms that nodded in the breeze cheered our hearts. Several times a day the children and I would go around the house to admire them. We learned wonderful lessons from those beautiful flowers that had survived the cold of winter.

You can imagine our dismay to awaken one morning in May to look outside and see it snowing—again. And snowing hard. The children quickly bundled up to go out and check on the flowers. They soon came back inside with sad faces.

"The daffodils are all bent down. They are covered with snow."

It looked as if the daffodils were dead. Being a typical New England day, however, it wasn't long before the snow stopped and the sun pushed the clouds away. The children bundled up once again to go out and play. They had hardly gotten outside before they were back in the house calling excitedly.

"Mommy, the daffodils are OK. They aren't broken after all."

They were right. The bright sunshine had melted the snow on the blossoms, and their bright, cheery petals were lifted up to the light.

As I admired the beautiful flowers, I seemed to see a parallel in my own life. The weight of responsibilities and cares, like the heavy snow, weighed me down almost to the breaking point at times. But the warmth of the Son was always there to lighten my load and uplift me when I turned to Him.　　ANITA L. JACOBS

MAY 2

Ivory Keys

Choose you this day whom ye will serve. Joshua 24:15.

My two little granddaughters came to visit me. They made their customary rounds of the house, pausing only briefly to examine the ceramic doll, recline on the lounger, and use the speaker phone. Then they gravitated to the piano.

The older one takes piano lessons, so we recognized her tune without difficulty when she manipulated the ivory keys. When the younger one joined in, however, our ears noted the difference.

Sitting beside the two small bodies, I set boundaries for their keyboarding exploration. The older girl got the octaves above middle C; the younger one the keys below that note. My strategy worked wonderfully—for about three minutes. And then we heard the distress call.

"Grandma!" the older one shouted. "She's playing on my side!"

"Sweetheart," I chided the younger virtuoso, "remember to stay on your side. If you want to play, you have to do it together. If you can't play together, then you can't play at all." Problem solved, I returned to the kitchen to fix supper.

A minute later I was surprised to see the little pink-clad cherub marching determinedly to another room. Then with the insight grandmothers are supposed to have developed once they attain that venerated status, I came to understand her line of reasoning. She had been given a choice, and she had made a decision and acted on the consequences. It wasn't the choice I would have preferred her to make, but I respected her decision, even though she was not yet 2.

God is the same way. He will not force us to choose His way, but lovingly bids us to follow Him. What choices are we making each day? May our choice be to serve the Lord, and Him only, for the rest of our lives. That decision will make God—and you—very happy.

CAROL JOY GREENE

MAY 3

God's Quick Answer

If we confess our sins, he is faithful and just and will forgive us our sins and purify us from all unrighteousness. 1 John 1:9, NIV.

For years I had been afraid to confess to cheating in two classes. I had always rationalized that in both cases I had known the right words and only forgotten them temporarily.

In the first incident I had been distracted by my classmate

drinking perfume during a science test, and had stopped to re-
prove him. Then I forgot the definition of gravity. But he had the
answer on his paper. A few days later I even boldly asked my
teacher why I got only 99 percent instead of 100 percent on the
test! I should have confessed then.

Six years later I copied a word from a fellow student. I should
have left it blank. I hadn't even liked the science teacher, but this
class was taught by one of my favorite teachers. She considered me
one of her best students and had praised my prompt and thorough
work before the class. Once I had mustered up enough courage to
go to her house to confess my deed, but upon arrival I discovered
another classmate there, so I talked about something else.

After two years of teaching, I was still carrying that load of
guilt! Soon I was to marry. My husband and I would be teaching
in another state. It seemed to be now or never. I decided to go to
my future mother-in-law to pray a very specific prayer with me.
I told her my problem, and we knelt there in the kitchen and
prayed, "Dear Lord, please put those two teachers in my way
when I go up to the college!"

I walked about three blocks to the corner of the building, arriving just as my science teacher walked out of the business office!
"Pardon me, professor," I began. "May I speak to you for a minute?"

He forgave me so graciously that my dislike for him vanished
immediately!

I walked to the main entrance, and out stepped the other
teacher! She seemed in a hurry, but I asked for a minute of her
time anyway. When I told her what I had done, she was shocked.
"Oh, Phyllis!" she exclaimed. Then she added, "Of course, I'll forgive you," and hurried on her way.

I was almost in tears. *She'll never love me again!* I thought. But she
did, and whenever I saw her, she was interested in my teaching.

This specific and speedy answer to my prayer was a great
blessing not only to me, but to others as well. While I was teaching English to theology students at East Brazil College, I told this
story during vespers one evening. Afterward one of my students
confessed to this same offense, for which I graciously forgave him.

There is never a problem too small or too large for our loving
Lord to solve. Take your guilt, your problems, your heartaches to
Him today, knowing that before we call He will answer.

PHYLLIS THOMPSON MACLAFFERTY

Music in My Soul

Be filled with the Spirit, . . . singing and making melody to the
Lord in your hearts. Eph. 5:18, 19, NRSV.

 here's music in my soul today," and it's there largely because my fifth- and sixth-grade teacher made hymn mem-
orization a part of our curriculum. I can't remember whether "We
Would See Jesus" or "Holy, Holy, Holy" was the first hymn I
learned, but many years later I still remember all the verses to
both of them.

One day many years removed from grade school, I was sitting in church beside a woman I admired. When we stood to
sing, I noticed that she didn't open her hymnal, so I offered her
mine. "Thanks," she whispered, "but I know this hymn."
Watching her sing from her heart, unencumbered by written
words, motivated me to start jotting down the words to hymns I
wanted to learn. I kept them with me in the car and at my bedside until I knew them.

"In my heart there rings a melody," and almost every morning I awaken with one running through my head. Sometimes
the melody stays with me all day, but most often it disappears
soon after I get up. Sometimes it's just what I need to give me
strength for the day, and I gather courage from it. Other days
it might be a popular "oldie," a tune from a TV commercial, or
even something silly. (I've been known to hum "Does Your
Chewing Gum Lose Its Flavor on the Bedpost Overnight?" for a
half day or more.) But that's OK—nostalgia and humor are part
of life too!

"All praise to Thee, who safe hast kept and hast refreshed me
whilst I slept," sung to the tune of Tallis' Canon, is my favorite
way to focus on God when I first open my eyes in the morning
and realize that it's another day and I'm alive. Likewise, I can't
think of a better way to fall asleep than with the words "All praise
to Thee, my God, this night, for all the blessings of the light" on
my lips. Singing, whether aloud or silently, is a wonderful part of
morning and evening worship, an element I miss when for some
reason it's not there.

"Holy, holy, is what the angels sing." I wonder if in the heavenly realms we'll remember any of the songs we've learned while inhabiting earth. Maybe "Amazing Grace" or the "Hallelujah Chorus"? If not, I suspect there will be better songs. The Song of Moses and the Lamb, for instance. Surely the God who gave us the gift of music will provide enough of it with which to praise Him throughout eternity. "Blessing and honor and power and glory be unto Him."

JOCELYN FAY

MAY 5

The Irritating Teddy Bear

Create in me a clean heart, O God; and renew a right spirit within me. Ps. 51:10.

Kenny was a chubby, adorable, ninth-grade teddy bear— irresistible to most of the girls in my English class. Moreover, he had a gift of entertaining everyone around him. Having taught college classes for years, where discipline was rarely a concern, I found this class of 30 wiggling, uninhibited freshmen to be a challenge from the first day. Kenny chose a seat on the front row, and the girls jostled one another to find seats near him.

Now, Kenny didn't appear to be malicious, just mischievous, and I tolerated his minor disturbances fairly well. But as the days went by, he didn't settle in to the serious business of learning, and he was quite effective in keeping everyone around him entertained, but untaught. I tried putting on a stern face while calling for order in the class, and things would settle down momentarily. Then Kenny would pop up with some comment, the girls would giggle, and I would react with threatening remarks.

Kenny was learning just how to "push my buttons," and the whole class was enjoying his skill. I was stewing a lot and enjoying teaching less, to the point where I dreaded that ringing bell signaling the beginning of class.

Kenny had gotten to me, and it was becoming quite obvious to both of us. I felt so defeated about my own reactions to this student. I'd been praying about him, asking God to inject him with some maturation compound. Then it dawned on me that maybe *I* needed a little of that maturation I was seeking for Kenny.

I sincerely prayed that God would change my feelings about him, that He would "create in me a clean heart . . . and renew a right spirit within me." In the short distance between my office and my classroom, an inner miracle took place. With no conscious effort to change my attitude, I saw Kenny in a new light. He became the lovable kid that he really was, not the intolerable thorn in my flesh who was spoiling my teaching days. Maybe I smiled more warmly at him, maybe I began laughing at his jokes, maybe the girls began to see me as a more tolerant human being. But somehow Kenny gradually found it less necessary to interrupt, and I discovered that learning could happen without my drill-sergeant attitude.

If there is someone in your life you are struggling to get along with—your spouse, a coworker, your mother-in-law, your boss—try praying that God will change *you* first, not the other individual. You just might find yourself enjoying that person— and your own life—a lot more.   MARGY ASHER GEMMELL

MAY 6

He Was Not There

He is not here; he has risen. . . . Then go quickly and tell his disciples. Matt. 28:6, 7, NIV.

We were a group of eight pastors, their wives, and a few Brazilian friends sojourning in the Holy Land in the summer of 1995. Among the biblical places we visited was the tomb of Joseph of Arimathea, where Christ had been laid in His death. There on a metal plaque are the words: "He is not here; He has risen." What a marvelous message!

When visiting other tombs, such as Muhammad's in Mecca, we saw the great difference. His body continues to lie there and is venerated because of that. But Christianity is different. It is alive. We did not go to the garden tomb to worship the mortal remains of a great prophet, but a risen Saviour.

We spent the entire morning in that garden, singing, praying, and reading passages that referred to Christ's life and death. "He is not here; He has risen." What blessed hope! The verse continues: "Then go quickly and tell his disciples."

This same responsibility is ours today. Angels plead with Christ because they would love to have this privilege, but it is not allowed. It is reserved for us. What a pity that not everyone is awake for such a message. Our Father gave us a task, and we rebelliously acquit ourselves of this duty. He is returning, and how slow we are to share His wonderful gospel.

May He enable us through the assistance of the Holy Spirit to do what the angel told the women: "Go quickly and tell." May God make us wise to hear the message and go out to proclaim the imminent return of Christ to all the nations.

ELITA MARLEM BALOGH COSTA

MAY 7

Beginning Again

If any of you lacks wisdom, he should ask God, who gives generously to all. James 1:5, NIV.

Going back to college at age 39 was a scary experience. My first thought was that I was too old to learn—my brain wouldn't function well enough for me to read, comprehend, retain, and recall all this information! *There's absolutely no way that I will ever be able to pull this off!* I worried.

Those first few weeks were ones of trepidation. Just keeping up with the assigned reading was a challenge. I found myself reading an entire passage, then wondering just what it was I had read. So then I would read it again, claiming the promise given in today's text. Finally I would understand the concept with which I was struggling.

As time passed, I found myself becoming accustomed to the schedule, and studying became easier. School became a wonderful new world to me. The more I studied and learned, the more I desired to learn. Learning required long hours of poring over textbooks and listening to (sometimes) boring lectures, mountains of paperwork, and long, tedious hours of research. But I became excited about learning.

Along with changing my career, I made the decision also to change my relationship with my heavenly Father. The more I've gotten to know my Saviour, the more excited I've become! I realize there is so much to learn about the Lord that I've only begun to scratch the surface. He is so patient with me in my weakness. His love for me astounds me! He proves that love to me in so many little ways. Even though there are many ways in which I still fail Him, He never gives up on me. I praise Him every day for His goodness to me. The more I learn about Him, the more I love Him.

Time has flown. The long-anticipated graduation day is just around the corner. Not only will I be graduating, but I will be graduating with honors. I give Him all the credit. God has kept His promises to me so many times. He has imparted His wisdom to me. I praise Him not only for the way that He has blessed me with my education, but most important, the way He has led me in my spiritual life. I can't wait—I have an eternity to learn about my heavenly Father! I can't wait for the learning experience of all learning experiences—to learn at the feet of Jesus.

CAROL BRACKETT

MAY 8

A Second Mom

My God will meet all your needs according to his glorious riches in Christ Jesus. Phil. 4:19, NIV.

Ever since I can remember, the thought of *not* having children never really occurred to me. In my late 20s, when I was seriously thinking of marriage, my husband-to-be and I talked about a family that would include no fewer than two to three children. We both frequently participated in, and enjoyed, activities involving children.

One day I was informed by my doctor that there could possibly be an infertility problem preventing me from bearing children. After several months of nuptial bliss, I became pregnant, but I was not able to carry the pregnancy to term. After several attempts at pregnancy, I was finally told by my obstetrician that I would not be able to carry a pregnancy to term. At that time I was in denial, because I felt I could be a mother as well as any other woman. I was, inappropriately, angry with God for missing out on the experience of a lifetime, an experience that I felt I very much deserved.

For some time I refused to attend baby showers, christenings, or any other activity associated with newborns. The pain of such activities was intense and made it more difficult for me to let go of the anger that pervaded my thoughts constantly.

Fortunately for me, children have always been an integral part of my adult life. A friend frequently asks me to provide child care for her 2-year-old. I found myself watching the development of this child, and although she is not my own, I cared for her as if she were mine.

I gradually became aware of the need to accept my situation and began to embrace children who needed a second mom. God has blessed me with three young women in my life who call me their second mom. What a wonderful feeling to be loved by them and their children. I will never know what it feels like to be a natural mom, but at this point it really doesn't matter to me. What *does* matter is that I am able to share in the nurturing of my spiritually adopted children. The pain of not being able to bear children of my own is no longer an issue and has dissipated entirely. My life has evolved into a spiritually extended family of many lovely people who include daughters, sons, nephews, nieces, and *now* grandchildren.

As an adult in my sixth decade of life I can truly say that I rejoice in God's promise to supply my every need abundantly, including my maternal need. Thank You, Lord, for the wonderful family You have given me. MARTHA HARDY-LEE

Love Letters From My Backyard

I have loved you with an everlasting love; I have drawn you with loving-kindness. Jer. 31:3, NIV.

*E*ven though I'm a horrible correspondent myself, I love getting letters. The advent of E-mail, and the persistence of a friend who flew across the country to show me how to use it, has improved my communication patterns. Somewhat. But it is not the same as the brilliantly humorous card a girlfriend would craft, or the affection-laden scrawl from that special someone.

One frosty evening as my trek to my mailbox garnered nothing but bills and notices addressed to "Current Resident," I groused to the star-splattered sky, "All I ask is one letter."

The next morning, curled up in an overstuffed rocker near the window overlooking my backyard, I found my first love letter. Three bright-red cardinals were perched on a small, snow-laden tree. I had never seen them so close. *God's love letter to me.* All those years I had been getting letters and never once picked them up. Now I see them everywhere. In every season . . .

In the spring,
>> the roses covering the thorns
>> the protective doe with her fawn in the distance
>> *His love embraces me.*

In the summer,
>> the ruby-throated hummingbird sipping nectar from the daylilies
>> the sweet succulence of ripe peaches plucked from the trees
>> *His love enchants me.*

In the fall,
>> the fruity fragrance of neighboring vineyards
>> brilliant chrysanthemums shouting His glory
>> *His love sustains me.*

In the winter,
>> blankets of snow encircling the pine trees
>> branches extended to help me navigate an icy path
>> *His love supports me.*

In people . . .

> the spontaneous toothless grin of my baby niece when
> > I cuddle her in a fond embrace
> the infectious chuckle of my 11-year-old neighbor as
> > she shares watermelon, green peppers, and her
> > brand of wisdom
> a gentle, unsolicited kiss from my 'tween-aged nephew
> *His loves exalts me.*

Year round, in His Word, "see how great a love the Father
has bestowed upon us, that we should be called children of God; and such we are" (1 John 3:1, NASB).
His love humbles me.

Thank You, loving Lord. Your love letters encircle my soul.
Open my eyes so I can see them. Open my heart so I can feel
them. Open my arms so I can share them.   GLENDA-MAE GREENE

MAY 10

My Mother's Love

I have loved you with an everlasting love. Jer. 31:3, NIV.

ime to go to bed!"
When Mother spoke in that tone, I knew I'd better
obey. Reluctantly I trudged upstairs and crawled under the covers.
I was not sleepy. I wanted to play. Suddenly I got a marvelous
idea. I threw back the covers, tiptoed across the room, and carefully opened the door to the hall. I could hear the radio. My father would be sitting in his big chair, listening to the news. I could
hear my mother in the kitchen, talking to someone on the phone.

I can do it! I told myself. *They will never know.* Slowly I tiptoed
down the stairs to the basement, where Frisky, my cocker spaniel,
was tending six puppies in a wooden box. Lifting out two puppies, I held them close and tiptoed back up the stairs. I paused a
moment at the hall doorway to listen. My father was still listening to the news; Mother was still talking on the phone. I crept up
the remaining flight of stairs as quietly as possible, closed my
bedroom door behind me, and put the puppies in bed with me.

What fun! Their tiny paws tickled as they climbed over my body. I giggled softly and rubbed their fat little bodies.

Just then I heard the thud of footsteps on the stairs. *Oh, no! That would be Mother, coming to say good night. What will I do?* I pushed the puppies to the foot of the bed, pulled the covers tight under my chin, and pretended to be asleep.

Mother opened the door and turned on the light. "What are you doing, Dorothy?" she asked.

"Sleeping, Mommy," I said with a yawn.

Just then the puppies started to squirm.

"What's going on down there?" Mother sounded suspicious.

"Nothing! It's just my toes." I wiggled them furiously under the covers.

Mother threw back the blankets, picked up the two puppies, and laughed. "Funny-looking toes," she said.

I thought, *Now I'm really going to get it! I've been bad, and Mommy will punish me for sure.* I closed my eyes to await my punishment.

Mother bent down and kissed me on both cheeks. "I love you, Dorothy. Good night. Go to sleep now; no more tricks!"

When she was gone, I sighed and snuggled deeper under the covers. *Mommy loves me, even though I was naughty,* I thought. *I have the best mommy in all the world.*

On this day I pause a moment to thank God for a mother who demonstrated God's gracious, forgiving, unconditional love. Sometimes after a difficult day when I have failed to be what God wants me to be, I sense God's kiss of forgiveness on my cheek and hear His words echoing across the years, "I love you, Dorothy."

I snuggle deeper under the covers and sigh with relief. *God loves me, even though I have sinned. What a wonderful God is mine!*

DOROTHY EATON WATTS

First Steps

I tell you the truth, unless you change and become like little children, you will never enter the kingdom of heaven. Matt. 18:3, NIV.

My daughter started walking at the age of 10 months, 3 weeks, and 1 day. That may seem inconsequential to those of you who have watched it numerous times in your own homes, or never witnessed this event at close range. But in our home God, Daddy, Mommy, and Kayla rejoiced.

How do I know God rejoiced with us? Because during this six-week process of watching Kayla catch her balance, God prompted my heart with a few lessons. First of all, I noticed that when Kayla walks, her brain is elsewhere and her feet stumble over everything in her path. At least that was my first impression. But as I watched her more closely, I noticed that her eyes were fixed on a faraway goal—across the room. And when she stumbled, it didn't even slow her down. She would move the object that had tripped her up or shift directions slightly to go around the object, but her eyes never left her goal.

I was humbled as God drove the lesson home to me. How often do I let the cares of the world distract me, change my course, stop me entirely from looking toward my goal?

The other thing that fascinated me as I watched her was her sheer determination. She got it in her head that she could walk one day, and she kept trying until she got it right. She would come toward me with reckless abandon and a big grin, falling down and getting up, again and again, until she had reached me, still wearing that smile.

How easily I give up, by comparison. I change goals, shift directions, decide it's not a possible task at all, forgetting that my God is the God of the impossible.

Something else is happening in our home: Kayla is starting to talk. Her communication comes out something like this: "Didum, ighty ba ba bear bear razzzzzzzzzzz." Gibberish to the common ear, but to Mommy it means, "Please hand me my bear. I would like to play with it." Kayla never doubts my ability to understand her, and we have the most interesting little "conversations."

I am thankful for a heavenly Father who not only understands my gibberish, but loves to listen to me and make sense out of my garbled communication. I need to learn to trust that God is listening and that He cares immensely about what I am trying to say to Him.

Dear Father, help me to focus myself on Your goals for my life. Prevent me from letting anything distract me from those goals. Teach me to communicate daily, trusting You to listen and understand. Daddy God, teach me to become like a little child.

SHONNA R. DALUSONG

MAY 12

Snake in the House!

Be self-controlled and alert. Your enemy the devil prowls around like a roaring lion looking for someone to devour. 1 Peter 5:8, NIV.

I opened the windows and let the fresh mountain breeze blow the drapes and tickle my nose. The daffodils were blooming, bees were humming, and birds were singing to their hearts' content. Clearly, it was a beautiful spring day in the mountains of southwestern Virginia.

All through the year my children helped with the household chores. I kept a chart on the refrigerator with the weekly rotation cycle of chores each one was expected to do, but spring cleaning was out of their league. It was time for a good cleaning job, and I felt I was the best qualified to do it. But with four young boys, a toddler daughter, and two dogs in the family, I was a bit slow getting around to it. However, I was determined to tackle it that Monday morning.

I decided to begin in the living room, since that was obviously the most visible room to everyone. I moved furniture along one wall at a time and vacuumed the furniture, walls, and drapes, and washed the sliding glass door that opened onto a front deck. I finally got to the last wall with a seven-foot couch sitting in front of it. As I moved the couch, I discovered a black snakeskin under it! My heart began pounding, and I was visibly shaken! I finally got my measuring tape and found it to be six feet long and seven inches wide. I was horrified as I thought of my children, and wondered how long that snake could have been inside the house. How was it possible for it to be there, perhaps all winter, and the dogs and children never be frightened by it or even see it?

I wish now I had kept the snakeskin to use as an illustration of how Satan works. He silently waits, undetected, for the right opportunity to strike out at us. If we are not in tune with heaven on a daily basis, we won't even notice that he is there.

Lord, keep me in tune with You today.   CELIA MEJIA CRUZ

MAY 13

Love Doesn't Give Up

Let us not get tired. Gal. 6:9, TLB.

After my mother died, it seemed as if my brother and I both questioned, in our own way, God's love and justice. My brother became distracted and didn't involve himself with the church. My first reaction was to "preach" him back into the church. Then I became angry and wanted to lecture him and show him his wrongdoing, as if I had none of my own. These approaches were of no effect. I felt bad, and my brother felt irritated.

Then I really met Jesus and became acquainted with His approach—consistent and steady, but always with love. Look at Him with the woman at the well. He could have embarrassed her; instead He offered her a gift. He gave her acceptance and forgiveness. He loved her; He didn't give up on her.

I began to live out my faith. I had to bite my tongue many times. I went on a kindness crusade, knowing that kindness unlocks human hearts. My brother and I began talking more about spiritual things, and he shared his inner feelings. I learned to listen and pray. I learned to love unconditionally and see hope and potential.

My brother attended alumni weekend with me recently at Oakwood College. When Pastor Doggette made his appeal, my brother was one of the first ones up! He is taking Bible studies now, and we are prayer partners.

Continue praying for your loved ones, remembering that silence and acceptance are sometimes the best gift to give. And hopefully you will begin to see that even the most hardened heart can be softened by a love that doesn't give up.

TERRIE E. RUFF

MAY 14

I Love You!

I have loved thee with an everlasting love: therefore with lovingkindness have I drawn thee. Jer. 31:3.

Deep in my inner heart I seem to hear
The Father's gentle whisper in my ear:
I love you more than you can ever know!
I've made so many things to tell you so,
And placed them everywhere your eyes may fall
So you'll discern My caring in them all.

The budding rose, bright pansies in the spring,
Tall oaks caressing songbirds as they sing,
The fruits and grains abundant in supply,
The bleating lamb, the beauteous butterfly,
Orion and its bright-red Betelgeuse,
A baby's smile, My promises profuse;

But grander things I have in store for you
Where pain is gone and everything's made new.
A home I have designed right near My throne—
A mansion you can call your very own!
Oh, I can hardly wait for you to be
Secure and safe at home, My child, with Me!

"I hear You, Lord!" Hot tears upon my cheek
Flow down in gratitude! I earnest seek
To know You better, learn to trust You more
Than ever I have trusted You before.

Take now my heart; I give it all to You.
O precious Father God, I love You too!

LORRAINE HUDGINS

MAY 15

911!

For the eyes of the Lord are on the righteous and his ears are attentive to their prayer. 1 Peter 3:12, NIV.

*H*er name was Greta, and she came from Sweden. She was a beautiful blue 1984 Volvo 240. After the shop got done with her and we had meticulously scrubbed the inside, installed new mats, and waxed the outside, she was a sight for sore eyes. Finally Kristina, our college senior, had a car so she and her sister could come home more often on the weekends. No more begging for rides! The girls were ecstatic—and their parents were a bit apprehensive about their driving on the congested freeways.

I will always remember that Monday in August. Our church school had just started, and during the worship hour we had a prayer for Kristina's safe return from Southern College, where she had gone to take her sister and assist with a college health fair. We didn't, however, pray for Greta, the car. When I got home from school, I found on the table a hastily scribbled note from my husband. "I've gone to Calhoun to get Kristina. She totaled her car, but she's OK."

The hours until Kristina and my husband arrived home were some of the longest in my life. I prayed and wondered and prayed some more. As the story unfolded, we learned that Kristina had been driving down the freeway in the left lane when all of a sudden she hit some sharp debris that punctured a tire. She lost control of the vehicle, hit the median, careened across three lanes of traffic, left the road, and rolled down an embankment, landing right side up. Fortunately, she was wearing her seat belt. She walked away from Greta with a minor cut to the head, shaken but otherwise unhurt. A trucker stopped to call 911. He told her he had barely missed hitting her. She informed him that she was a Christian and had prayed for protection.

That night as Kristina mourned the loss of Greta (we had only third-party coverage for the old car), we hugged her, realizing that life is irreplaceable and can be snatched away in a moment.

What a joy it is to know that our heavenly Father cares and sends His angels to watch over us, according to His promise. Only in heaven will we know of the many dangers from which He has saved us. Praise God for the ministry of angels!

KAARINA FORDHAM

MAY 16

Another Time, Another Place

I saw a new heaven and a new earth. Rev. 21:1.

One evening I grabbed a bowl of Gala apples, a comfy afghan, and a book my older daughter, Rhonda, had given me for Mother's Day and curled up on the sofa for a good read. The book, *Living a Beautiful Life: 500 Ways to Add Elegance, Order, Beauty and Joy to Every Day of One's Life*, appealed to me. For busy career women of the nineties, it is easy to compartmentalize one's obligations so completely that there is little space left over for beauty. Rhonda knew I'd enjoy the author's insights and suggestions as much as she had.

Now, it is not in my nature to have a place for everything and everything in its place. Still, I appreciated reading the author's suggestions for organizing one's mail, correspondence, and lingerie drawer. Being a more sensuous person, I liked her suggestion to cut up Christmas tree branches (after Christmas, of course) into hand-sized sprigs, store them in a basket (I can do that. I love baskets!), and place the basket by the fire. A few bunches tossed into the flames recall the joys of Christmases past.

If I want to reminisce about my vacation in Florida or California, the author suggests that I throw a few orange peels into the fire. The aroma of burning pinyon wood chips can transport me back to Santa Fe, New Mexico, for a few minutes.

H'mmm . . . What a pleasurable mind trip. Makes me homesick just thinking about other times and other places that I've enjoyed with those I love.

But my greatest longing is for another time and another place that I have never experienced, one that I cannot begin to enjoy even in my wildest imagination. I can't toss pinyon wood chips on the fire to appreciate the aroma of heaven, nor orange peels to inhale the sweet aroma of Paradise. Instead, I open the pages of a Book that teaches me how to truly live beautifully here and now, and in the land of eternal beauty.

I read, "I go to prepare a place for you . . . and there will be no night there . . . for the Lord giveth them light . . . and there will no wise enter into it anything that defileth, neither worketh abomination or maketh a lie" (adapted from John 14; Rev. 21; 22).

Ah, I can almost smell a sweet hint of peace, the air of tranquillity, the delicate fragrance of love, and the heady aroma of joy right here in my parlor. I'm feeling a touch of nostalgia for another time, another place. Come quickly, Lord Jesus!

KAY D. RIZZO

MAY 17

A Special Prayer

In the same way, the Spirit helps us in our weakness. We do not know what we ought to pray for, but the Spirit himself intercedes for us with groans that words cannot express. Rom. 8:26, NIV.

Today I found out that my 17-year-old nephew has been drinking alcohol for three years.

Today I found out my friend from college has AIDS.

Today I found out my friend's 2-year-old daughter has AIDS.

Today I listened to a doctor tell my colleague that the cancer had spread to her stomach and her left kidney.

Today I began a prayer that goes like this: Father, bless my nephew, my friend, my friend's baby, and my colleague. Show me how I can share Your love with those who are hurting. Father, place Your healing hands on those who are sick. Teach me how to praise You in the midst of trials. Use me to spread joy. Anchor me in Your Word. Gather me in the nave of Your will. And Father, I don't always know what to pray, so compel me always to pray a prayer of healing for the sick. Amen.

RAMONA L. HYMAN

MAY 18

Red Ink and Red Blood

But with the precious blood of Christ, as of a lamb without blemish and without spot. 1 Peter 1:19, NKJV.

I recall an English teacher I had many years ago when I was in high school. She was a wonderful teacher, and she told me something I've never forgotten. After choosing a research topic that met the teacher's approval and having obtained the necessary information to complete my report, I decided to write it in red ink so that it would not only sound good, but look good too. Another classmate had the same idea and wrote her assignment in red ink as well. My pride turned to dismay when the teacher lectured the two of us in front of the entire class that we should never, *ever* write in red—not even our names—especially in her class. I cannot recall the reason she gave, but I never did it again!

One thing I do recall and know with certainty from my Bible reading is that the color red is significant to me and others like me, who were born in sin and shaped in iniquity. Red is the color of blood—specifically, Christ's blood.

First John 1:7 tells us that "the blood of Jesus Christ his Son cleanseth us from all sin." As one songwriter puts it: "There is pow'r, pow'r, wonderworking pow'r in the precious blood of the Lamb." That Lamb hung on the cross many centuries ago, bowed His head, and died for our sins, never uttering one mumbling word. That Lamb is Christ Jesus. "He has made from one blood every nation of men to dwell on all the face of the earth" (Acts 17:26, NKJV).

On life's journey, when Satan's darts are hurled at me and the woes of life seem to destroy my hopes, I look to the cross, reflecting on the blood of Jesus shed there. For it is "in the cross of Christ I glory." Knowing that His precious blood on Calvary was shed for me gives me back my hope. That red blood will never, ever lose its power, either today or throughout eternity.

ANNIE B. BEST

MAY 19

The Hummingbird Feeder

And God created . . . every winged fowl after his kind: and God saw that it was good. Gen. 1:21.

This summer we put out a hummingbird feeder, and in a very short time we had some "well-paying" customers. Yes, we were truly well paid by watching these precious little birds partaking of the food that we had carefully prepared, hoping it would be just the right thing to feed and nourish them.

Our little guests are called anna's hummingbirds. The male has a very striking appearance. The beautiful red plumage on his forehead and throat makes him look like a tiny neon light when in the sun. He sings a real song. The female's green tail is broadly tipped with white, and she has a few red feathers. Such tiny wonders!

How, I wondered, could they possibly know that we had put that feeder up? Was there some kind of invisible signal emanating from it? Some secret ad that led them there? It was in a rather obscure place—yet they had found it!

What marvelously intelligent creatures God has made! How intricately their little bodies move as their tiny wings beat so fast the human eye can scarcely see them, moving them effortlessly backward, forward, up, or down. What mighty Engineer perfected this model? Truly, God's ways are past finding out. His mercies to us never fail. How can we ever doubt who set the world in space, spoke, and it was made?

Can we begin to comprehend how He keeps this vast universe going day after day? I get frustrated at times just trying to keep everyday happenings moving smoothly, but God keeps the hearts of all of us beating and the blood coursing through the veins. He keeps the streams flowing and sends the rain and snow that refresh the earth. Who set the stars in place? How very insignificant I feel when I look at the power of God. Yet as one of His created beings, I am entitled to all the benefits He so richly bestows. With humbleness and deep gratitude I say, "Thank You, God."

PAT MADSEN

God's Impressions

Your ears will hear a voice behind you, saying, "This is the way; walk in it." Isa. 30:21, NIV.

I was taking my lunch break at the hospital where I worked as a registered nurse and wandered into the gift shop. My eyes scanned the many glass shelves of lovely dolls, crystal items, figurines, and stuffed animals. My gaze stopped at my favorite display—the music boxes. *Ah, there's a new one,* I thought. I picked it up to get a closer look at its unusual shape and the delicate rosebuds painted on the lid. Carefully I wound the stem on the bottom and opened the lid to see what song would treat my ears. As it played the song "You Needed Me," my mind sang the words. Indeed, it was a very beautiful song, but it was of no particular significance to me. I closed the lid and replaced the box on the shelf. As I turned to leave, I felt compelled to take another look at the music box. Then I bought it without quite understanding why.

When I arrived home that evening, I carefully carried my purchase into the house. All the while I was thinking, *Why did I buy this?* There was no occasion for which I needed to purchase a gift. I placed it on the top shelf of the coat closet and forgot about it.

Several months later my husband and I received an invitation to an anniversary party. I had to work from 7:00 a.m. to 7:00 p.m. and would be unable to buy a gift before going to the party. My husband said, "We'll just have to go without one."

All day I kept trying to think of some little memento to take for a gift. Suddenly I remembered the lovely music box tucked away in the closet. When I arrived home, I carefully wrapped the music box in cream-colored, flowered paper and tied it with a deep pink bow. I proudly carried my gift to the party.

Since the happy couple was from out of town, we enjoyed catching up on all the news. We were favored with a short slide presentation of their wedding day and served delicious refreshments. When it was time to open the gifts, I tried not to stare as she untied the pink ribbon and removed the wrapping paper from my present.

As she opened the box, she exclaimed, "Oh, how pretty!" She held the box close to her ear. As she listened, tears welled up in her eyes and ran down her cheeks. "This was our favorite love song when we were dating," she explained. Both of them were visibly touched, and I felt privileged that I had been permitted to give a gift that brought them so much joy on this special occasion.

The next time you feel impressed to do something and don't understand why, take a risk! The Lord may be showing you a way to bring happiness, encouragement, or comfort to someone else.

ROSE NEFF SIKORA

MAY 21

Deliverance Assured

The Lord is faithful, who will establish you and guard you from the evil one. 2 Thess. 3:3, NKJV.

What a glorious morning to be enjoying the crystal-clear springs and pristine river in Silver Springs, Florida! The great blue herons, mallards, and American egrets were among the feathered population swimming, sunning, calling, or perching on low-hanging branches, waiting for breakfast to swim past. I sat in a rocking chair on the dock, reading a book and silently giving thanks to God for the privilege I had of living only a mile from such a beautiful place.

While reveling in the myriad of sights and sounds, I overheard a buzz of conversation. I was in just the right spot to watch a crew from *National Geographic* as they filmed alligators underwater. Employees from the wildlife section of the park had captured two six- or seven-foot alligators and brought them by boat to the filming site. This would allow a more controlled and safer environment. The boat containing the alligators—with mouths taped shut—and a crew of two glided into position. The underwater photographers—complete with wet suits, air tanks, and cameras—and the spotters slid into the water from the dock area.

Excitement mounted as a young woman cautiously removed the tape from the first gator's mouth just as he slipped into the water. Everything was going as planned. No problems. No danger. As the appreciative audience relaxed, the same process began with the second alligator. Then with lightning speed the reptile chomped down on the girl's forearm with his jagged teeth and refused to let go.

"He's got me!" she cried as the blood began to trickle down her arm. She remained in stoic silence while the rescue workers ran to her aid. After several minutes she cried out again, "I can't take this much longer!" Finally her arm was released in exchange for the life of the alligator.

The alligator's unexpected attack is something like Satan's reaction to our unguarded moments, our carelessness, or unrealized danger. We need to cry out, "He's got me! Lord, save me!" Our Saviour will. We have His promise. "When you pass through the waters, I will be with you; and through the rivers, they shall not overflow you. When you walk through the fire, you shall not be burned, nor shall the flame scorch you. For I am the Lord your God, . . . your Savior" (Isa. 43:2, 3, NKJV).

DOROTHY WAINWRIGHT CAREY

Life in a Fishbowl

Do you bring in a lamp to put it under a bowl or a bed? Instead, don't you put it on its stand? For whatever is hidden is meant to be disclosed, and whatever is concealed is meant to be brought out into the open. Mark 4:21, 22, NIV.

*N*ew missionaries on an island in Micronesia, we were outdoors in the village when I caught a movement out of the corner of my eye and glanced up from brushing my teeth. A teenage girl smiled shyly and continued to watch with interest as I finished.

Walking along a trail submersed in ankle-deep water, with Lisa and Rachel following behind like little ducklings, I could feel the eyes of a dozen people as they stopped what they were doing to watch us pass by.

And the eyes peering through the screens and around the doorway, intent on seeing just *how* an American chews her food.

Most days I'm able to do the necessary things and not be bothered by the constant stares of our friends and neighbors. But there are those days when I just feel like blowing my nose *without* anybody watching.

Being constantly watched has made me think about what Christ said about Christians: "Ye are the light of the world. A city that is set on an hill cannot be hid. . . . Let your light so shine before men, that they may see your good works, and glorify your Father which is in heaven" (Matt. 5:14-16).

It's one thing to be watched once in a while. It's quite another thing to be watched every waking moment—and into the night as well. Transparent lives . . . I know that is how we are all to live the Christian life. In fact, I've become more and more aware that the closer we get to the return of Jesus, the more our lives will be an open book for any and all to read. For isn't it God's purpose that people have something to choose from? We see wickedness and satanic influence all around us. Isn't it fair that God also demonstrates His goodness in and through the lives of His representatives? So join me, won't you, in being willing to be opened and read, in being available to Christ to demonstrate His way of life through us.

Live out Thy life within me,
O Jesus, King of kings!
Be Thou Thyself the answer
To all my questionings;
Live out Thy life within me,
In all things have Thy way!
I, the transparent medium
Thy glory to display.

TERESA KRUM

But Where Are the Oranges?

Casting all your care upon him; for he careth for you. 1 Peter 5:7.

Times were financially hard for our young family because of heavy debt and a job change. Some payments were past due, and our previously plentiful shopping days were dwindling down to purchasing just the bare necessities.

One morning at breakfast I set the last of our fresh fruit on the table, along with some other food. Our 3½-year-old son was asked to say the blessing, and in his prayer he asked the Lord to please send some oranges to eat. *Oranges?* At this time in our life they were considered a luxury item and wouldn't even appear on the grocery list.

During the noon meal that same day the phone rang. A doctor's wife asked, "Would you be interested in baby-sitting my three children while I go shopping this afternoon?" I replied that I would be glad to help her out. She then asked if there was anything she could get at the grocery store for me in payment for my services.

"Oh, no," I answered, "I don't need anything." I hated asking for food.

She laughed and asked again.

"Well, I suppose you could get some apples for us," I replied, choosing an inexpensive Michigan fruit.

With her shopping done, she arrived to pick up her children, but also brought in several grocery sacks and set them on the table. After she and the children were gone, my son and I proceeded to look excitedly through the bags. It was obvious she had bought us more than just apples! But when everything had been looked over, my son disappointedly asked, "But where are the oranges?" I said something about being thankful for what we had.

Our family attended prayer meeting that evening, and at the conclusion of the service a friend walked with me to our car and mentioned that her sister had just sent her a box of Florida oranges. There was no way her family of three could eat them all before they spoiled. "Could you use some?"

I was overwhelmed by the miracle that a caring God had performed in answer to our son's prayer.

Lord, please help us to remember all the many blessings You so wonderfully bestow upon us. How wonderful to know that You care about the seemingly little details of life. Help us to go on our way rejoicing because You are always there. Amen.

VALERIE HAMEL MORIKONE

MAY 24

Always Content

Not that I speak in regard to need, for I have learned in whatever state I am, to be content: I know how to be abased, and I know how to abound. Everywhere and in all things I have learned both to be full and to be hungry, both to abound and to suffer need. Phil. 4:11, 12, NKJV.

In the sixties I was a sophomore at a boarding school. It was an economic necessity that I work, so I applied for several campus positions. These positions were the usual: receptionist, office worker, or resident assistant. But I wasn't hired. The only positions available were in maintenance, the cafeteria, or the book bindery. Since I had held positions in the physical plant and cafeteria already, I reluctantly accepted a position in the book bindery.

My responsibility consisted of spending four hours a day covering wood and cardboard magazine holders with a special material. It was not the most challenging job one could hold, and frequently I was at the table alone. I remember grumbling about the injustices, complaining, and feeling disgruntled. However, somewhere in that experience a transformation occurred. God revealed to me the secret found in our text for today—Philippians 4:11, 12. It's the secret of contentment.

As a result of my transformation I began to hum and smile at work. I laughed more and soon was known as the canary. The hours at the job sped by. God had taught me a valuable lesson—contentment. I wish I could say that the lesson learned many years ago was one I never had to learn again, but I have struggled to make this lesson a rule of my life. Each time I have had to relearn this lesson, the results have been the same. Once I allow God to lead, I am content and find rest under the shelter of His wings.

The beautiful thing about the text is that it is followed by Philippians 4:13: "I can do all things through Christ who strengthens me" (NKJV).

Your life is complex—you can do all things through Christ.

You've had a recent loss, disappointment, tragedy, or difficulty—you can do all things through Christ.

You have financial difficulties or job-related stress—you can do all things through Christ.

God specializes in situations we view impossible, and He will do what no other one can do! He will answer your prayer for help in the way that is best for you from His all-saving, all-knowing vantage point. Yes, He can do all things. Praise God!

EDITH C. FRASER

MAY 25

Assurance of God's Love

O Lord, you have searched me and you know me. You know when I sit and when I rise; you perceive my thoughts from afar. . . . You hem me in—behind and before; you have laid your hand upon me. Ps. 139:1-5, NIV.

How wonderful to feel the assurance of our God, knowing that He created us and sustains us. He knows our needs and knows what goes on inside us. God's love is endless; it is a spring that never ceases to flow. Knowing the scope of His love makes us feel more secure. We can go through trials and hardships knowing He is going through them with us.

One day I was talking to a physiotherapist who lives near my house. She told me about the great anguish she suffered when she came home one morning to discover two armed burglars inside her house, stealing everything they could. Her children and maid were locked in the bathroom while the thieves ransacked the house, looking for jewels and money. The checkbook and credit cards were taken. At the time my friend didn't know if her family would all be killed or not, but she could feel God's voice giving her the ability to negotiate with the thieves so that they would leave her home without harming anyone. It took many days to restore order in the house, but the most important thing was that her family was spared.

A deep confidence in God's love and mercy is able to work miracles, for His hand is mighty and His love is powerful. His love brings comfort, cares for a small child, heals the sick, gives vision to the blind, makes the lame walk, and forgives the sinner. This love may be yours and mine through Jesus Christ. He is always available, no matter what the circumstances. We can be certain that God's answers to our prayers will never be too early or too late. He's always right on time. May you receive this day the complete assurance of God's love.   MEIBEL MELLO GUEDES

MAY 26

The Joy of a Child

Elisha summoned Gehazi and said, "Call the Shunammite." And he did. When she came, he said, "Take your son." She came in, fell at his feet and bowed to the ground. Then she took her son and went out. 2 Kings 4:36, 37, NIV.

If you will read the story in 2 Kings, you will discover that the Shunammite woman did not ask for a child, and when he died, in the bitterness of her loss, she reproached Elisha, saying, "Why did God give me a son and then take him away?"

It was not like this with me. When my fiancé and I were courting, we discussed the matter of children. It was not possible for me to have a child, but I very much wanted to adopt a daughter. However, he refused absolutely, not because he objected to adoption, but because he did not want fatherhood. His childhood had been somewhat unhappy, and he thought we would be better off without children.

After five years of failed persuasion, I turned to God, who needed only one month to change my husband's mind! Our little doll arrived very tiny, fragile, sober-faced, and with such a severe middle-ear infection that I was uncertain whether or not we could save her. But there was immediate, mutual adoration, and Sherri started growing like a weed.

Her inability to withstand infection demonstrated itself often in the first year of life with us. First it was amoebic dysentery, and then asthmatic attacks racked her little frame. My husband and I were working 14 to 18 hours daily, and it was difficult to miss sleep night after night with Sherri's struggle to breathe.

Finally the night came when I had tried everything to ease Sherri's breathing, but nothing seemed to help. Daddy, utterly exhausted, had fallen asleep across the bottom of the hospital bed. I sat propped against the head of the bed with my little daughter resting against my shoulder, since this position seemed to give maximum relief from the croupy spasms that racked her tiny chest. With tears streaming down my cheeks I pleaded silently, *OK, God, You win. Heal her if You want, or take her if You think best. I cannot struggle anymore.* I must have fallen asleep then, because suddenly I woke up as dawn peeped in the window. Sherri's breathing was so quiet that I thought it had ceased, and I woke my husband in panic. When the light was turned on, we saw that our little daughter was breathing normally and was as pink as a rose.

This was not the last attack, but never again did she come so close to death. Sherri has grown through the "terrible teens," and we have survived together her need to seek her biological roots. What a joy it was to hear her say, "Mommy, I now have my thinking straight and my priorities in order. You are the only mother I have or will ever need."

What joy it gives our heavenly Father when we have strayed from Him and we return to tell Him, "I have my priorities straight now. I know You are the only Father I shall ever have or ever want!" YVONNE (STOCKHAUSEN) BAZLIEL

Love

Love suffers long and is kind; . . . bears all things, believes all things, hopes all things. 1 Cor. 13:4-7, NKJV.

I won't ever forget him as he strolled into class.

"Well, I guess I have no choice," he said.

It was said that he was one of the most difficult students one could have. The teachers were all tired of him. His behavior didn't seem to be improving. Was he acting out a cry for attention, or did he just want to be bad? I believed it was the former.

Months have passed, and I have seen some positive changes. I must admit there were times I felt like giving up. However, despite his behavior, every day I told him that I loved him. Every day I prayed for strength and wisdom to deal with him. One day I told him that I prayed for him every morning. He smiled.

"Why do you do that?" he asked.

"Because I love you. I believe you have the potential to be a very good boy. You have a good brain, but you use it for the wrong things," I told him as I patted him on his shoulder. He smiled and shook his head. I wondered if anyone had ever told him that they loved him. I knew from the records that he came from an alcoholic and drug-abusive family.

Four months later I said to him, "Matthew, you are changing. No more do I have to put you in the time-out room or call for assistance to get you out of the classroom. What's happening?"

He smiled. "It's those prayers you say for me," he said.

I was surprised at his response. I didn't know he remembered what I had told him.

During my lunch break I reflected on my life. I was fortunate to have parents who cared for me, and even when I did things that were not pleasant, they never abandoned me. They still loved me. Then I thought about God and how He treats me, His child. I recalled the many times when I did or said something that must have really grieved His heart. I ask Him to forgive, and He forgives me. He treats me as though I have never done anything wrong. He never gives up on me. He is patient with me and keeps right on loving me. I am glad I serve a God like that. Aren't you?

Today, try to reach out to the child or the adult who seems

the most difficult to love. They are the ones who need our love the most. You'll be surprised how soon that person will reciprocate your love, and there will be a change in attitudes. I love the words of Dr. Martin Luther King, Jr.: "Love is the only force capable of transforming an enemy into a friend." It may take awhile, but you will see results.

ANDREA A. BUSSUE

MAY 28

Against All Human Logic

The foolishness of God is wiser than man's wisdom, and the weakness of God is stronger than man's strength. 1 Cor. 1:25, NIV.

*I*t was a hot afternoon during my junior year at Loma Linda University, and I had a deadline to get somewhere. As I was scurrying around my dorm room, trying to find my car keys, I was becoming increasingly frustrated that they were nowhere to be found. Heat, haste, and frustration can quickly join forces to work against us at the least welcome moments.

Finally, in desperation, I quickly knelt at my beside, knowing that God knew exactly where those keys were. Pleading with Him to give me a mental picture of the keys' location, I suddenly pictured a winter coat in my closet. For a moment I was tempted to argue the point—my car keys couldn't possibly be in a heavy winter coat when there was a "barn burner" heat wave going on outside. But given God's track record with me, I couldn't argue.

In faith, I jumped from my knees, flew over to the closet, and grabbed my coat pockets. There were my urgently needed keys! "O thank You, dear Lord, for answering my prayer!" I immediately said. "You were just waiting for me to get down on my knees and ask You to supply my every need, according to Your riches in Christ Jesus!"

Many times have come and gone when I've prayed for God to give me a mental picture of where an item is located, knowing that He knows where it is. He doesn't always answer the way I expect, but He's always on time!

That day, acting on His answer went against all human logic. And because of it that was the day my trust in God took a quantum leap!

JUDY COULSTON

MAY 29

The Nests

It is of the Lord's mercies that we are not consumed, because his compassions fail not. They are new every morning: great is thy faithfulness. Lam. 3:22, 23.

*L*ooking at an empty nest must surely be traumatic for a mother bird. Each summer a persistent little mother killdeer insists on honoring our church parking lot with her small cache of speckled eggs. Those tiny eggs blend so precisely with the large gravel of the drive and the parking lot that we seldom know when the nesting season arrives and passes. I remember at least two seasons when this has not been the case.

My heart has beat in sympathy with the frantic calls and desperate flutterings of the mother bird as church members walk too close to the sacred precinct of her nest. Seeing her distress, we move quickly away, knowing that she is pleading with us to hurry. We have even placed protective barriers around the nest. In this way tender hearts remove at least one of the dangers that threaten the precious lives so diligently guarded by the little mother.

In my own life I look at my almost-empty nest. I remember the years during which my children have given purpose to each day. I have found much joy and great challenge in allowing them, one by one, to outgrow the confines of my attentions. The nest has become too small. The emptiness could easily consume me. Like the mother killdeer, I too have spent time fluttering and frantically protecting what is precious to me. In the midst of what is both progress and loss, I find meaning in Jeremiah's victorious lament. God in His faithfulness does not forget our vulnerabilities, our limited vision. In compassion He places a hedge about what is precious to us. We can trust His attentions and rest in them day by day.

STELLA THOMPSON

God Is Our Pilot

I will praise you, O Lord, among the nations; I will sing of you among the peoples. For great is your love, reaching to the heavens; your faithfulness reaches to the skies. Ps. 57:9, 10, NIV.

The four of us—a pastor, a missionary pilot, a social worker, and I—had spent the day at an orphanage near Poptun, Guatemala. We planned to return to Guatemala City that afternoon in the same small plane we had flown in on during the morning.

By the time we said our goodbyes to the enthusiastic children and staff members at the orphanage, it was much later in the evening than we had planned. Darkness was rapidly descending upon us, so we hurried to the plane. We had been airborne only a few minutes when we encountered fog. At first it was patchy; then we entered areas covered with heavy fog. For a little while we flew on, looking silently out the plane windows.

Suddenly the pilot spoke. "We're heading back," he announced. "We'll have to spend the night. It just isn't safe to try to get to Guatemala City tonight."

I have thought many times about the wisdom of that pilot. He wasn't willing to take a chance with the lives entrusted to him as the guide of the little plane. I am very thankful he was a careful and conscientious man. That's the kind of pilot I want in charge when I travel!

There is great peace in knowing that God is our pilot. He always has our best interests in mind while taking us through our journey of life. He can be trusted! Place your life in God's hands today. His "faithfulness reaches to the skies."   SANDRA SIMANTON

MAY 31

Our Endings . . . God's Beginnings

He said to me, "My grace is sufficient for you, for my power is made perfect in weaknesses." Therefore I will boast all the more gladly about my weaknesses, so that Christ's power may rest on me. That is why, for Christ's sake, I delight in weaknesses, in insults, in hardships, in persecutions, in difficulties. For when I am weak, then I am strong." 2 Cor. 12:9, 10, NIV.

*I*t was the fall semester. I was a senior accounting major, looking forward to sitting for the certified public accounting (CPA) exam that following May and to graduation in June. For three years I had taken a full load of classes, but I'd never signed up for my foreign language requirement. In desperation I took my foreign language dilemma to the Lord in prayer. Under His direction I decided to take the course by correspondence. I knew I had time.

I was in the middle of my final semester when I remembered my foreign language requirement. I received a pink slip from the registrar's office stating that my grades for Spanish had to be submitted in three weeks or I would not graduate. I also knew that the CPA exam, which had a 27 percent national pass rate, was in two weeks. At the time I had two jobs, five other classes, and a boyfriend—all needing my undivided attention.

My responsibilities overwhelmed me so much that I could not sleep or eat. Some of my teachers gave up on me. But I knew God had not! We women oftentimes "bite off more than we can chew." We take on large amounts of responsibility that are nearly impossible to accomplish. When I reached this level in my experience, God was my only hope. I asked Him to touch my mind and increase my understanding, to anoint me with His Spirit. My boyfriend and friends also prayed for me. And God answered!

The Lord led me to 2 Corinthians 12:9 and 10. I accepted the realization that all I could do was *all* I could do. I simply began to do what I could, because God had promised to handle the rest. I trusted Him. God stepped in when I could do no more. My endings became His beginnings. I graduated on time, and today I am a certified public accountant. I am closer to God now than I have ever been. And that boyfriend who prayed for me is now my husband. God meets our needs when we come to the end of ourselves.

KEMBA MALENE ESMOND

Sounds of the Morning

The Lord himself shall descend from heaven with a shout, with the voice of the archangel, and with the trump of God: and the dead in Christ shall rise first: then we which are alive and remain shall be caught up together with them in the clouds, to meet the Lord in the air: and so shall we ever be with the Lord. 1 Thess. 4:16, 17.

I struggle to open my eyes. Across the room the red lights of my digital clock flash 5:00 a.m. Once out of bed with face washed and teeth brushed, I enter my special room for devotions. Since it's summertime, I raise the window to let in the fresh morning air. I am surprised to hear so many sounds that I hadn't even noticed before.

The sounds of the birds—not just one, but many. To my untrained ear they are just birdsongs, but there are many, all distinctly different. I've seen cardinals, sparrows, robins, starlings, mourning doves, and others I couldn't identify that must be part of the bird chorus I am now enjoying. Then there are the insect sounds, my neighbor's truck starting, the rhythmic sound of a jogger's feet, and the barking of the dog across the street.

As I kneel in front of the window for prayer and look up into the morning sky, I think of the sounds we will hear on that resurrection morning, when Jesus appears on that great white cloud. First we'll hear the clear, piercing sound of that great trumpet as Jesus calls His sleeping children to come out of their graves. We'll hear the rushing sound of angels as they fly to earth to assist their earthly charges who have fallen asleep in the hope of the resurrection. What a sound when tombs break open, earth cracks wide, and opening caskets no longer can hold their captives! What a sound when mothers and fathers cry out with tears of joy as an angel hands them their precious children that death had snatched from their arms! What a sound of joyous reunion as wives and husbands, friends and loved ones, are reunited! I'll hear my dad's voice calling my name as he awakes from his sleep, scarcely able to comprehend the change in circumstances since he closed his eyes in death.

And then we'll hear the loveliest sound of all—the melodious voice of King Jesus calling all His children, those resurrected and those who will never see death, to join Him in the air. "Come, children," He'll say. "It's time to go home."

I look forward to the sounds of that morning and the countless mornings after that in our heavenly home. With John the revelator I say, "Even so, come, Lord Jesus" (Rev. 22:20). I'm ready to go home.   NANCY CACHERO VASQUEZ

JUNE 2

Betrayed

Some friendships do not last, but some friends are more loyal than brothers. Prov. 18:24, TEV.

I was sitting in the college dorm parking lot with my best friend, whom I'll call Doreen. We had just come back from town. Normally Doreen was a fun person who kept me laughing, but tonight she was unusually quiet. I asked her what was wrong, but she just sat there.

"Whatever it is, you can tell me," I urged. "After all, we're best friends."

"You're not my best friend!" she shot back.

That hurt. "Well, we're friends, anyway," I countered.

"We're not any kind of friends," she argued.

That was only the beginning. For the next hour she told me that she disliked me and that we could never be friends, because I knew what she was really like.

Many years have passed since that night, and I still don't know what was going on with my friend. I know she had some emotional problems, but I never got an explanation for why she dropped me so abruptly after we had been so close. I had drifted away from friends before, but nothing compared to the betrayal I felt when Doreen sat next to me and told me she hated me.

It took a long time for those scars to heal, and it is difficult for me to make friends to this day. I had nowhere to take my sorrow but to the Lord. When I opened my heart to Him and told Him that I had been betrayed, the answer came back, "So was I."

So was I? Usually when you think of betrayal you think of Judas, but I remembered Peter. It was Peter who so painfully betrayed Jesus by denying that he even knew Him. Imagine the emotional pain Jesus felt—in addition to the physical anguish! Somehow Jesus found the strength to forgive this deepest of betrayals, and Peter continued preaching about Jesus until his death.

I forgave Doreen for what she did to me. For several weeks after the breakup of our friendship I attempted to reconcile with her, but I finally realized it was impossible and let go. But Jesus, who had known the worst possible betrayal, gave me the courage to go on. Because He has known such sorrow—because He has been there and understands—He is my greatest solace. Let Him be yours too.   GINA LEE

JUNE 3

An Angel in White

The angel of the Lord encamps around those who fear him, and delivers them. Ps. 34:7, RSV.

Mission appointments have taken us to live in homes of various sizes. Some have been spacious bungalows with verandas encircling the house. Others have been crowded tenements or crowded apartments with cluttered surroundings.

One of the latter was in Bombay, where my husband was the pastor of the English church. I disliked living in the city. Our two boys had no place to ride their tricycles. The only yard was the space around the steps leading to our first-floor apartment. And the only unoccupied space was the driveway leading to the mission moving van garage.

One Friday afternoon the two boys were playing outside. Our little girls were asleep, I was busy with housework, and my husband was out visiting. My preoccupation was rudely interrupted when Gordon, our second son, came running into the room. Slamming the door behind him, he screamed, "Mama, Mama, the car ran over my brother!"

Dashing out of the apartment, I saw that a crowd had gathered. My heart pounded, my legs trembled. Then, out of nowhere, my precious older boy appeared. He looked smaller than his size, and he was covered with automobile grease. He came straight to me, put his arms around my waist, and buried his face in my skirt. My arms tightened around him as I whispered, "Thank You, Lord."

I learned that three boys had jumped on the bumper of the van as the driver backed out of the driveway. The two older boys jumped off as the van neared the end of the driveway, but my son didn't. Instead, he fell off and the vehicle drove over him.

The driver was visibly shaken. He hadn't known that the boys had climbed onto the bumper. The crowd was still standing around when I asked Glenn how he got out from under the van. He said, "A man dressed in white pulled me out."

Wanting to thank the man, I asked Glenn to identify him. He looked around, then quietly said, "He's not here. He's gone."

We believe that it was an angel who rescued our son that Friday evening and brought him back to us. Praise God for angels that encamp around us and deliver us!   BIROL C. CHRISTO

JUNE 4

In His Time—God Delivers!

He shall call upon Me, and I will answer him; . . . I will deliver him and honor him. Ps. 91:15, NKJV.

*I*t was one of those hot, humid camp meeting days. Lunchtime had come and gone, and my family and I had settled into an afternoon meeting in the main auditorium. The tent was so hot! I struggled to concentrate on what the speaker was saying, but it did little good. His voice seemed to drone on and on. Then I noticed that two of the participants on the platform had fallen asleep! *If I could just quietly exit the meeting and find a cooler place,* I thought—but I knew there was no cooler place anywhere. So I resigned myself to the situation—I was stuck.

Then out of the blue, it seemed, I heard the speaker say, loud and clear, "If we will just look up and ask the Lord, He will *even* deliver us from the desire for alcohol." He continued his discourse, but I wasn't listening. I was *really* ready to leave now! I had been pleading with the Lord for more than 20 years to deliver me from the desire for alcoholic beverages, to no avail! After I was baptized, I had kept my vow never to touch alcohol again. But oh, how intense the craving had been all those years!

Now I was hearing that it was as simple as that—"Just look up and ask!" I sank back in my chair, let out a big sigh, and looked up. *Please take this craving away—only You know the struggle I've had,* I pleaded silently. I can't tell you the name of the speaker or what his talk was all about that day. All I know is that something incredible happened right after that prayer. The craving was gone. So final—so gone! I didn't notice the hot tent anymore; nothing else mattered. As we stood up to leave, I felt so different—a change had come about, and my heart couldn't stop singing praises to God!

Who can explain the workings of the Lord? How does He do it? There was no brush of angel wings—only a deep, *deep* sense of deliverance. Why does He heal some in an instant, while others must wait, as I did, or perhaps never be healed at all?

Only our Lord can read the peculiar circumstances of each life. My story goes back to when I was 4 years old, when my parents began giving me before-meal appetizers of beer. This was the custom of people of my ancestry. Even though we never attended any church, the difference between right and wrong was strongly taught in our home. However, alcohol was an acceptable custom. For the first 21 years of my life there were no restrictions on me as far as alcohol was concerned.

The cure that camp meeting day was permanent. Many times since, drinks have been served in restaurants practically under my nose. But nothing happens as they pass by. There is no response from within. The sight of drinks doesn't mean anything anymore. I have no feelings to desire—or even not to desire—them. They are just there. A fact of life in this world. So amazing!

How does one explain a miracle? Let me tell you, my friend, the deliverance was worth it all! If you are struggling with something evil, take heart. Trust Him to know the right time for you. Keep looking up. Stay on the Lord's side, and He will reward you mightily—*in His time!*   DIANE R. MUSTEN

JUNE 5

Lasting Impressions

Be imitators of God, therefore, as dearly loved children and live a life of love, just as Christ loved us and gave himself up for us. Eph. 5:1, 2, NIV.

I'm going to my twentieth high school reunion this year. Another 10 years have passed since I've seen most of my classmates, and we've gone through many different experiences during that time. I attended a large high school, and there were more than 400 in my graduating class. It's going to be a challenge to decipher who is a classmate and who is an overwhelmed spouse!

Thinking I'd better do a little review of names and faces before I go, I took out my old yearbooks and went back in time. It seems like only yesterday that we were walking the halls of Sentinel High, but a look in the mirror quickly brings me back to reality. I remember myself as a quiet wallflower who didn't attend many social events, so I don't expect many people to remember me. But as I read the personal notes penned in my yearbooks, and as I recalled the 10-year reunion, I began to realize that people I had forgotten had commented on our friendship and the fun we had had.

We tend to think that the things we say and do are our own business. If our words or actions touch someone else, it's no longer just our business. The problem is, we may not be aware of whom we have touched. Nowhere in the New Testament does it say that Jesus mumbled hurtful words or gave someone a dirty look. He didn't ignore the unpleasant, the filthy, or the sick and lame who came to see Him. He accepted the responsibility of being an example to others.

Someday soon we all will have an opportunity to attend a grand reunion. I know I want my loved ones to all be there, and

I can't wait to see my friends again. I hope that any of those who are there are not people I didn't treat kindly, or to whom I spoke harshly. Let's remember that even though we may be just one person among the many with whom someone may come in contact, a positive response to them may override many negative ones in their life, leading them to chose God's way and be a part of that grand reunion.

PATTY KNITTEL

JUNE 6

When We Know God Knows, the Peace Just Flows

Before they call I will answer; while they are still speaking I will hear. Isa. 65:24, NIV.

I flicked through the pattern book and found just the style I was looking for to sew a jumper I needed for work. I chose the fabric, the buttons, and the thread. As I wandered around the shop, I picked up a few small craft items I needed for a class I was teaching in my home. I was trying hard to be frugal.

We had moved—again—and it had been a major drain on our resources. Our new home had needed a new shower stall because one of the walls had rotted away. That had cost us far more than expected, but I had a new job, and I finally felt I could afford to spend a little bit on myself.

At home I opened up my bags and looked at the things I'd bought. I thought of the fun I'd have sewing new clothes, creating lovely things for my home, and sharing new ideas with my women's craft group. It was so nice to feel free from all the scrimping and saving of the past few months.

The phone rang. It was the personnel department of the hospital in which I worked.

"Are you sitting down?" the lady asked. "I hate to tell you this, but we have been overpaying you, and we think you owe us £500 to £600."

I was stunned. That was more than I earned in a month! How

could this have happened? She told me the finance office had wanted to stop paying me for a whole month to make up for the difference, but it was just before Christmas, and we had no savings at all. Finally she agreed that whatever I owed could be repaid over the next 12 months.

All the joy in my new things dissolved into concern about our financial predicament. I felt guilty about the few things I'd just bought. I sat and prayed that God would work everything out smoothly, and that we would be able to cope with an even smaller income. As I prayed, I felt enormously at peace. I sensed that God had gone ahead of me and had worked everything out already. There was nothing else for me to do. God was in control of the whole situation, and I could leave it with Him.

That was four months ago. It took the finance office an amazingly long time to work out my income. A couple weeks ago I finally received a letter of apology and a check for £20. When all the calculations were worked out, they owed *me* money instead!

Yes, God had worked it all out ahead of time, and He knew I didn't need to worry about a thing. He'd already fixed it and proved to me once again that "when we know God knows, the peace just flows." KAREN HOLFORD

JUNE 7

The Littlest Sand Dollar

Be ye therefore perfect, even as your Father which is in heaven is perfect. Matt. 5:48.

As I played a whimsical game of tag with the billowing surf of the incoming tide, I noticed a little sand dollar. *What a prize,* I thought. When I picked it up, I noticed what a beautifully perfect sand dollar it was. I've found a good many over the years, but never one this tiny, this perfect. A few minutes after my extraordinary find, a young man with a small boy in tow asked me if I'd like a sand dollar. He handed me a medium-sized one. It was also very perfect and beautiful. Then, as an afterthought, he gave me a very, very tiny one, perfect in its development, even though it had a long, long way to go before it would reach maximum maturity.

As I walked the beautiful beach, there were many other sand dollars. All had flaws—breaks or missing parts. I had no use for the imperfect ones, so I didn't collect them. What made one sand dollar valuable to me and another of no value at all? After all, they were all sand dollars. It was the perfection of the sand dollars, regardless of how large or small they were. The only ones of value were the perfect ones.

As I was pondering the thought that only the perfect ones were of value to me, I thought about our heavenly Father. Has He not given us the admonition to be perfect? Deuteronomy 18:13 tells us: "Thou shalt be perfect with the Lord thy God." Ephesians 4:13 says: "Unto a perfect [woman], unto the measure of the stature of the fullness of Christ." Job 8:20 says: "God will not cast away a perfect [woman]." I got a new perspective on the many Bible verses on how God wants perfection in those He died to redeem. It became very clear why God wants to make up His kingdom with perfect people. "Nevertheless we, according to his promise, look for new heavens and a new earth, wherein dwelleth righteousness" (2 Peter 3:13).   PAT MADSEN

JUNE 8

"Weatherproof" Faith

He replied, "You of little faith, why are you so afraid?" Then he got up and rebuked the winds and the waves, and it was completely calm. Matt. 8:26, NIV.

*B*angladesh, where we lived, the *Guinness Book of Records* cites as the worst-hit area for tornadoes, with the highest death toll. Here we had a life that seemed to my barely 10 years of existence one of endless fun, frolic, and friends, even during tornadoes. Until one afternoon.

A drizzle had turned into a pitter-patter of marble-sized hailstones. Back home in the Philippines, anything that resembled snow was an awesome phenomenon. I was instantly lured to run out and gather the "white ice cubes" with the other children. I was fascinated. Skipping over puddles under an umbrella, I had almost filled my loose T-shirt with the hailstones when the wind suddenly took a violent turn. In seconds I felt myself being sucked up from the ground and swept a few feet away. The hail was now the size of paperweights. The fierce wind tore at my umbrella and turned it inside out, but I foolishly held on to it as I was shaken wildly about like a rag doll. In panic I cried out a prayer for help. In no time I felt myself being pulled to safety by a friend who somehow managed to brave the winds and rescue me.

Meanwhile, inside the concrete walls of our house, the rooms became a hard-hat area. My otherwise brave and unshakable mother dropped to her knees amid the flying window glass, light fixtures, and books and prayed earnestly for her husband, who was coming in from a long trip, and her only daughter, who was out gathering hailstones.

Later, when the heavens glowed in their signature after-a-storm hue, we thanked the Lord for His overwhelming love. Dad had been in a bus that had overturned in a ditch at a crucial moment. No fewer than 10 people fell on top of him, and his trousers got torn in half. Yet he was barely scratched. And Mom was soon ready to help meet the demands of all-night surgery on the storm-injured patients who filled the hospital.

In the calm of the sunset, I learned that though the tornadoes of life may rage and trials strike painfully, these help toughen our trust in our Father. Our faith is kept steady by His reassurance in the heavens, like trees that remain firmly rooted despite strong winds. Temptations that beckon like harmless hail eventually turn into deadly weights of sin. How could I ever forget His promise to heed our call for help and pull us out of danger? In the darkness and forces of the tornado, I felt that those hands that guided me to safety belonged to an angel. And though we tend to hold on to false securities that only lead us farther away from the Rock, I pray that we will always believe that God is ever ready to lead us back into the shelter of His fold.

HANNAH A. GUERRERO

Going Home

Rejoice with me; I have found my lost sheep. Luke 15:6, NIV.

Ted stood at the gate of the preschool playground and watched his daughter, Sandra, climb to the top of the jungle gym, ignoring his presence. I waved across the playground to him, and he waved back as he slowly walked to the jungle gym and climbed up inside to where Sandra played with her friends.

"Let's go home," he suggested, holding out a hand.

She nodded solemnly, almost automatically, and slowly climbed down to the ground to her father. He reached over and took her hand, and together they walked across the playground toward the gate.

She looked up at her father, tentatively. "Dad, can I ride on your shoulders?"

Her question brought a broad smile to Ted's face. "Sure!" He bent down, swung her to his shoulders, and together they giggled as they "galloped" to the car, then went home together, both smiling.

Our heavenly Father waits at the corner of our playground, the earth, hoping with divine hope that we want to go home with Him. He wishes He could change circumstances in our life. Illness, starvation, accidents, wars, death, and separations were not part of His original plan. He will not force people to undo choices they have made, and He does not alter the results of those choices. He stands patiently, inviting, "Let's go home."

We wait a bit tentatively, afraid of our Father because the enemy has brought untrue accusations about a solemn Father-Judge who looks for reasons to make us ineligible to go to the home He has gone to prepare.

God waits until we realize, as our daughter did, that our heavenly Father is more than willing to carry us home on His shoulders as He did for the sheep in the parable. Let's choose to go home with Him.

CONNIE NOWLAN

One of Those Days

Whenever the rainbow appears in the clouds, I will see it and remember the everlasting covenant between God and all living creatures of every kind on the earth. Gen. 9:16, NIV.

I had heard the cliché many times: "It's been one of those days." This particular day qualified. It started with waking up and looking at my alarm clock, which indicated it was more than a half hour beyond the time I needed to get up for work. I had forgotten to set the alarm the night before. Fortunately, I managed to get it together and make it to work on time.

When I walked in the door, I was immediately informed that the computer system was down. As one would expect, trying to work without a computer was extremely difficult. For the rest of the day the computer continued to do things its own way, rather than how we needed it to. To add to the fun, it was pouring down rain, threatening to leak into our office. At least the roof held. To add to it all, my husband called to inform me my car had a cracked engine block and might not be repairable.

By the time the workday was over, I would say I was quite frazzled. As I left work, I noticed the sun was shining against the rain clouds. Walking toward my car, I saw a dazzling rainbow shining before me. How great God really is! How wonderful the promises He has given us! The rainbow is a reminder of one of His greatest commitments to us. It also gave me a wonderful experience after a crazy day.

Next time your day gives you a heavy rain, you may find a rainbow in the promise of God's watchcare and love.

CORINNE A. GURNEY

God's Tender Blindness

This is my commandment, That ye love one another, as I have loved you. John 15:12.

A special treat awaited me that comfortable summer afternoon—a little block of unscheduled time in the middle of the day. I took my Bible and sat on the lawn, leaning against the trunk of a young maple.

Turning to Psalms, I read, "Forever and ever I will sing . . ." Reading the Psalms had always been an uplifting experience. How could people concentrate on their own problems when reading David's exclamations of thanksgiving and praise? He had some tough times too. But he came through them knowing God as a constant and eternal Friend and Saviour.

"God," I prayed, "help me to sing Your praise forever and ever, including today."

"Forever and ever I will sing about the tender blindness of the Lord." *Tender blindness?* The term stopped me short! I did not remember reading in the Bible before about the tender blindness of the Lord. What could it mean? I looked into the azure sky, contemplating God's tender blindness. I thought God was omniscient, all-seeing. That nothing was hid from His view. To what is God blind?

He has "blotted out" our sins (Isa. 44:22). "As far as the east is from the west, so far hath he removed our transgressions from us" (Ps. 103:12). He has "cast all their sins into the depths of the sea" (Micah 7:19).

So that's it: God is blind to what He chooses not to see. He chooses not to see sins that are confessed. "Their sins and iniquities will I remember no more" (Heb. 10:17). Indeed, how tenderly He loves!

As a fluffy white cloud floated eastward across the broad sky, I praised God for His tender blindness toward me. Then He reminded me, "This is my commandment, that ye love one another, as I have loved you."

Just as I have sinned, so have my brothers and sisters. But just as God has loved me with tender blindness, so I must love them. "Is it really possible, God? Can humans possess and demonstrate that kind of love?"

The answer came immediately. "My grace is sufficient for thee: for my strength is made perfect in weakness" (2 Cor. 12:9). "I can do all things through Christ which strengtheneth me" (Phil. 4:13).

"Love through me, God," I prayed. "Forgive through me. Be blind through me."

I looked at the text again. "Forever and ever I will sing about the tender kindness of the Lord!" (Ps. 89:1, TLB).

Tender *kindness?* I had misread a word but understood clearly a part of the message of the text. Indeed, tender *blindness* is a part of God's tender *kindness*—a part I must emulate.

HELEN HEAVIRLAND

JUNE 12

Celebrating Summer

A time for every purpose under heaven. Eccl. 3:1, NKJV.

We pass from spring into summer, newborns grow into their youth and adulthood, plants deliver their bounties, and all is wonderful and correct in the time frame of God's world. Solomon, in his wisdom, proceeds to list the different times in an individual's life, including: a time to heal; a time to build; a time to weep; a time to laugh, dance, embrace; a time to gain, keep, or throw away; a time to sew; a time to speak or to keep silence; and a time to love.

Summer—the perfect time to embrace life to its fullest, to throw away the old dusty matters that have been clogging our lives. A time to breathe in the fresh air of changes and to grow into the full scope of womanhood.

During one three-month summer vacation from school, one of our children grew five inches in height, a growth pattern which is by far faster than the normal growth spurts children have. This meant a complete new wardrobe had to be provided for the child.

This is the season for spiritual growth. We too may have a growth spurt that is beyond the usual expectations. We too may have need of a complete new "wardrobe."

In our northern climes, we see plants grow with a rapidity that astonishes us. God has programmed the plants to grow quickly because the growing season is short. Women sometimes find it necessary to grow quickly. If we approach the challenge of growing with an attitude of openness and excitement, our lives will be fresh and full of the beauty of a plant that has grown quickly into its full potential.

The invitation has been given for us to use this season of our lives as a time to heal and build. It may mean that a few tears will need to be shed before healing can begin. As in surgery, pain is sometimes inflicted for the healing process to begin. As healing takes place, healthy tissue, healthy relationships, and healthy women replace that which was unhealthy.

Practicing the art of when to speak and when to keep silence will do much to promote the formation of fruit in our lives. Our sinful world presents us with times when keeping silent will bring forth fruit, and other times when we need to speak words of love and encouragement for fruit to form.

Summer is the time to emulate the fruit of God's bounty and let our words, "fitly spoken," be "like apples of gold in settings of silver" (Prov. 25:11, NKJV). Our lives will become filled with the opportunities to laugh, to embrace, and to walk a pathway that is filled with the dancing steps of our light hearts. Love permeates every corner of our lives and radiates to all with whom we come in contact. We will find that as we make Christ the key factor of the healing and growth patterns of our lives, we will have grown so much that we will need a new "wardrobe."

Summer's wardrobe is a colorful display of the colors of our lives. The blue of loyalty, the red of devotion, the white of purity, the pink of new love, the lavender of sweet fragrance, the green of new growth, and the purple of royalty will be our colors as women live this life-season for Christ.   EVELYN GLASS

First appeared in *Bouquets* 2, No. 3 (1991). Used with permission.

Baby Lessons

Assuredly, I say to you, unless you are converted and become as little children, you will by no means enter the kingdom of heaven. Matt. 18:3, NKJV.

My two adult daughters and I decided to take a four-day minivacation of sightseeing and shopping. Of course, in addition to my daughters, my precious little 16-month-old granddaughter, Megan, would be going along. She was the added bonus for her aunt and me.

On the first morning we decided to have breakfast at a scenic Danish restaurant. After we were seated, my attention fell on some of the other diners. In particular, I noticed a lonely-looking man sitting by himself at a nearby table, and down the way a young couple sat in their wheelchairs.

After a while the man's face broke into a big grin, and we heard him say, "You are going to be a politician, aren't you?" We realized he was looking in the direction of Megan, who was smiling and waving her diminutive hand at him from her high chair. Then she turned her face toward the pair in the wheelchairs, giving them the same kind of happiness treatment. They too began smiling and waving in amused response.

All through the day, as we pushed her stroller down the streets and in and out of quaint stores, Megan continued to use her special talent, usually picking out the people who seemed to need her own sweet brand of attention the most—those who looked a bit downhearted, or those who were disabled. Finally her aunt said, "God seems to have given Megan a special gift of love. How blessed she is."

What a lesson it was for me! Do I spend my days spreading happiness to those around me? Or am I too busy with the cares of this life to notice a stranger who needs a cheerful greeting? No wonder Jesus said, "Unless you . . . become as little children."

MILDRED WILLIAMS

A Father's Gift

A gift is as a precious stone in the eyes of him that hath it: withersoever it turneth, it prospereth. Prov. 17:8.

*S*everal years ago a close family member gave me the opportunity to select one of our father's Bibles. Several had been left in his home after he died. Now my brother lived there, and the choice was mine. The Bibles had been in a closet for more than 30 years, and I quickly decided to select the one that looked the "most used." It was a wise choice. Since that day I have enjoyed so much time leafing through the pages and reading, thinking, analyzing, and praying. It has been a very personal gift from Dad. I was thrilled to have this gift in my possession. The leather cover is worn, even frayed in several places. The inside pages are fragile; some are torn and yellow. I see his handwriting here and there; texts are checked and underlined. How I treasure this gift!

But there is more to my gift than what first met my eyes! Inside are all sorts of little messages, texts, poems, and clippings that warm me each time I search through my gift. These mementos were collected at least 35 years ago—perhaps even longer. On the back of one clipping I see grocery ads: "Pea soup, 6 cents a can; meat, 27 cents a pound!" Handwritten lists of texts outlining how to find a deeper spiritual life are included. The poems tug at my heart as I read about "The Little Secret Place of Prayer," "The Refiner's Fire," "Message to My Mother," and "If Jesus Came to Your House," to name just a few. There are bookmarks and postcards. Memories flood my being as I tenderly touch the pages.

I seldom spend time with this gift without the tears starting to come. My dad loved his Lord, and his vision for the future was the coming of Jesus, when all his family would be reunited. Our mother's life was cut short at age 50, and all five of us missed her so much. Dad worried about keeping the family intact. He spent a lot of time on his knees. Perhaps that explains one of the messages in my "gift," entitled "Five Rules for a Happy Life." There was no date or source on the clipping, but even after nearly 50 years the message is timeless:

"Psychologists have given many formulas for a happy life, but most agree on five basic qualities if a man or woman is to have a happy existence. To be truly happy, an adult must be:

"(1) capable of standing on his/her own feet, taking full responsibility for one's own actions;

"(2) careful to maintain a regard for other persons, regardless of their race or religion;

"(3) able to start work under one's own power and not be driven to do a task;

"(4) mindful of the fact that happiness comes only to those who have a purpose in life;

"(5) able to take good fortune with a gracious smile, and bad knocks on the chin."

Dad knew the value of this message—he left it for me in his well-worn Bible. Such a gift to treasure—*more* than precious stones!

ARLENE COMPTON

JUNE 15

Prayer Did It

Pray for one another. . . . The prayer of the righteous is powerful and effective. James 5:16, 17, NRSV.

I was not really looking forward to my trip to Africa. Oh, the people I meet and the stories I gather thrill my soul. But I knew it would be hot. And heat saps my strength. "Lord, You know I do not do well in heat. Please help me get through this trip," I prayed.

On the day I left for Africa my 18-year-old son left on a mission trip to Romania. As we said goodbye I promised him I would pray for him and challenged him to pray for me as well.

It was as hot as I thought it would be, and air-conditioning often was no more than a weak breeze filtering through an open window. But I was coping—far better than I thought I would. Often I thought of my son in Romania and prayed for him, for his physical strength as well as his spiritual growth. And when I heard that it was snowing in Bucharest, I added all the other young people to my prayer list. I marveled that he was battling snow while I was battling the heat!

Zaire was the hottest country on my itinerary, but by then I had become accustomed to the climate a bit. We wiped perspiration from our necks as we sat listening to testimonies of God's goodness and His leading in the lives of Christians. Our workdays often stretched to 15 hours, and our workplace could be a table in a stifling room without ventilation, or in a church courtyard with little shade and barely a breeze. Nights were not appreciably cooler.

When we finished our work in Zaire, one man commented, "It has been unusually hot during your visit here, but it didn't seem to bother you." I assured him that I had felt the heat, but that I also had felt God's hand cooling us.

I returned home with exciting stories to tell my children, and listened to my son's account of his trip to Romania. One day the school secretary told me, "You know, when we were in Romania we had worship every morning. And every morning Scott raised his hand to ask us to 'pray for my mom in Africa.' After a while, when he raised his hand, the other students chimed in, 'Pray for Scott's mom in Africa!'"

I told my son how God had answered his prayers for me. I hope it strengthened his faith. It surely strengthened mine.

Let someone know that you are praying for him or her today!

CHARLOTTE ISHKANIAN

JUNE 16

Bumps in the Night

The Lord will keep you from all harm—he will watch over your life; the Lord will watch over your coming and going both now and forevermore. Ps. 121:7, 8, NIV.

I thought I had it all planned out. It would be a 12-hour overnight flight that would arrive in San Francisco after breakfast. So I had decided to work on my cross-stitch and watch the TV reports until about 9:00 Hong Kong time. I would then sleep for about five hours, waking in time for breakfast. Although I still had another six-hour flight before I would be home, I hoped this plan would get me there relatively rested.

My plan worked well until it was time to try to sleep. Just as I got settled with my pillows and eye mask to keep out the light, the pilot began speaking over the public address system. There were reports of turbulence ahead; all passengers were to return to their seats, buckle their seat belts, return seats to upright positions, and put away and latch all tray tables. Prospects of a nice sleep were gone immediately. My seatmate, Celine, and I visited a while and read a bit, but nothing happened. I was beginning to get sleepy and was ready to try sleeping again when we hit the turbulence. We shook, rolled, and pitched. The overhead bins chattered and shook. The whole plane popped and creaked. We were truly sitting up straight now. My seatmate looked pale, and we were both white-knuckled. I prayed. She had shared with me earlier that she was not a Christian. I wondered now what she had to turn to for comfort.

Suddenly one of the flight attendants was talking on the speakers: "Sit down! Fasten your seat belts! This is not only for your safety, but for the safety of those around you!"

I wondered who would dare to be out of their seats, but thought maybe they were sick and trying to get to the lavatory. I know I was not tempted to stand up!

After what seemed an eternity, the air became smoother. The captain came on the speaker system again and said we could get up out of our seats and move around if we cared to. I was traveling with two friends, Liz and Shirley, who were seated in another section of the plane, so I decided to go see how they were doing. Both told me that they had been scared too, and that one of the attendants had said it was the roughest weather she had encountered in 38 years of flying. I was glad I didn't know that earlier!

Then Liz said something that really got me thinking. She said that although she was scared, two things comforted her: she knew that at least three people on the plane were praying, and since the pilot knew ahead of time about the storm he surely must have thought he could go through safely.

When we face any crisis or personal time of trouble, those are two good things to remember. Knowing friends are praying has tremendous comfort! Ask others to pray with and for you. It will help all of you. And Jesus, our Pilot, knows what is ahead. He knows what we can safely pass through and will keep and protect. A wonderful promise we can claim is Psalm 9:9, 10: "The Lord is a refuge for the oppressed, a stronghold in times of trouble. Those who know your name will trust in you, for you, Lord, have never forsaken those who seek you" (NIV).

ARDIS DICK STENBAKKEN

Birth Notes

He tends his flock like a shepherd: He gathers the lambs in his arms and carries them close to his heart; he gently leads those that have young. Isa. 40:11, NIV.

*A*ges and eons and lifetimes have passed in a few short days. You have given birth and have been reborn. You are not the same person and will not live the same life you did before. It is a bittersweet experience, and the letdowns, though expected, are sometimes denied or despised. We must learn to embrace them and feel them and let them "be" in order to heal. The passage into motherhood is new and varied with each child. While there is joy and expectation, yes, there is mourning, too, for what is left behind.

What you want and hope for and dream of is pushed a little farther back into that sometimes-dusty closet that mothers call "myself." Such a privilege and honor to guide the life of a child! But also what a sacrifice. To look in the trusting eyes of your babes and know that for many years—yes, even until they become parents themselves—they will probably not realize you are a separate, distinct person apart from being a mother, that your goals and dreams did not always include them, and that you are a woman, first and foremost, then a wife, and finally a mother. To them you are always and only a mother.

So let the mourning and gladness, excitement and sorrow, mix as you are formed into a new woman. You will be stronger in character, gentler in spirit, and more understanding in heart than ever before because of this passage. Children are unrelenting teachers and artisans, pushing us to the very limits of our souls' endurance. But without them we would never know who we really are, what we are really made of, and most of all, the depths of our capacity to love.

So sleep, baby, sleep. Wonder, new mother, wonder. Birth is beginnings and endings, and life will never, ever be the same again.

ANN MALONEY-HALIM

First appeared in *The Heart of the Home* 6, No. 6 (1991). Used with permission.

JUNE 18

Behold, I Stand at the Door

Behold, I stand at the door. Rev. 3:20.

It was the combined church and last-day-of-school picnic, and we sat alone at a table watching the children play.

"You know how much I want you to come back to church," Milly said, as she had so many times before. "But that is your decision to make. And as much as I want to see you in heaven, I have to respect your right to say no. That choice is yours." She glanced at the playing children, mine among them. "But if you don't come back, they don't have a choice." Her words, though spoken gently, cut into my heart. For a few minutes I couldn't say anything.

"I don't think that's a possibility." I blinked away the sudden rush of tears, feeling very keenly my isolation from the rest of the church "family." "You see how I am treated," I told her. "Most of them don't talk to me here. What makes you think they will in church?"

"It doesn't matter." Her love washed over me as she placed her hand warmly on mine. "I'll stand by the door and wait for you every week and sit with you until you feel welcome again."

That was a turning point in my life. In her unconditional love I saw Another who stood at the door. Another who refused to give up on me, in spite of myself. Another who had no condemnation, but gently and tenderly pleaded with me to come back. Another whose prayers ascended for me, who was willing to go to any length to save me.

Is there someone who needs you to encourage him or her to

return to Jesus? Ask God to give you the words to speak and to show you the right time to speak them. RENEE COPELAND

Prayer Power

The smoke of the incense rose with the prayers of the saints . . . before God. Rev. 8:4, RSV.

Elijah prayed for rain, and Solomon for wisdom sought.
The thief prayed for salvation; Jacob for a blessing fought.
King David pleaded for cleansing; Daniel prayed to understand,
And Moses prayed that he could go into the Promised Land.

Not always did God give each one precisely his request,
But wisely granted blessings that for them He knew were best.
And He who shut the lions' mouths is still the same today,
Supplying us our every need when we take time to pray.

Our Saviour spent whole nights in prayer for power to overcome,
And in His strength we flourish; as He was, we can become.
His nights of prayer brought days of strength, and finally on the cross
He won our ransom—at the risk of His eternal loss!

So grasp His outstretched hand, my friend. Though dark may grow the way,
His presence lights our path and gives direction when we pray.
Then like the glorious sunset, when we finally take our rest,
May heaven's beauty linger on, in lives that we have blessed.
LORRAINE HUDGINS

The Harvest

Do you not say, "Four months more and then the harvest"? I tell you, open your eyes and look at the fields! They are ripe for harvest. John 4:35, NIV.

here are few things more beautiful to the eye than a field of ripening grain gently swaying in response to a south May breeze. It is a peaceful, refreshing time. But it is also an earnest time of preparation for the day of the harvest.

In May this preparation begins. Headlights and batteries are changed. Chains and bearings are oiled for service. Sickles and shears are sharpened. Filters and cabs are cleaned. Belts and bolts are tightened. One by one, as their preparation is complete, the combines, trucks, tractors, and plows emerge and take their place to wait for the day of the harvest.

And then, one magic day in June, suddenly, unexpectedly, and with such fervor that the Super Bowl pales in comparison, the day of the harvest arrives! With the skill of a craftsperson, the huge mechanical monsters meticulously masticate the heads of wheat and separate the straw from the grass and weeds, and the precious heads of grain are sifted from the chaff. The cleaned, ripe grains of wheat are then placed in waiting trucks and quickly transported to safety. Following the harvest of the grain, the tractor and plow swiftly enter the field to do their work of destroying the grass, weeds, and chaff.

As I behold the fields of ripening grain all around our home, I thank God for giving us a time of preparation and the day of the harvest. But you and I must ask ourselves, Have we prepared for the day of the harvest? Has our love for Jesus resulted in a character change? Have we allowed the Holy Spirit to fit us for service? Do we pray and study God's Word daily? Has our faith in the righteousness of Jesus been strengthened?

Let's resolve to be among those who are transported to heaven—not among those who are left for destruction.

PATRICIA STOCK

Lead Me

I will lead the blind by ways they have not known, along unfamiliar paths I will guide them; I will turn the darkness into light before them and make the rough places smooth. These are the things I will do; I will not forsake them. Isa. 42:16, NIV.

We really had many other things to do, but at the insistence of our daughter (she even bought our plane tickets), my husband and I found ourselves taking part in a mission adventure in southern Mexico. We had lived in this part of Mexico for 15 years as our children were growing up, so it was like returning home after a long absence. Upon arrival we joined up with a small group who planned to help build a school auditorium in a remote Indian village.

The fact that there was no road to this village and that we would have to hike or ride mules the last eight miles didn't deter us, since this was a familiar experience from our past. We were told that the trail was mostly downhill anyway, and since this was not the rainy season, we didn't think there would be a problem.

We reached the trailhead later than planned, but decided to go ahead because the mules and our guides were ready and waiting for us. I didn't want to ride a mule—my former experience on muleback had not been pleasant. However, after struggling through knee-deep mud for a while (the dry season had been wetter than usual), I realized there was no other way I'd reach our destination. The sun had been shining as we started out, but soon the wind came up, and it started to rain hard. As the mule hopped over rocks and sloshed through mud, it was bad enough when I could see the steep trail ahead, but then it got dark. Out in the jungle there were no lights. The stars were obscured by the clouds, and it was pitch-black. I was almost petrified with fear, but the young Indian who led my mule wasn't slowed down by the darkness. Without the help of even a flashlight, he plodded along steadily, as he knew the trail well. After several hours of much prayer on my part to boost my sagging spirits, we reached a small village where we found refuge from the cold and rain.

This experience reminded me of how God guides through

rough times and difficult circumstances. Many times we can't see the way ahead, and problems seem insurmountable. If we remember that our Guide knows the way and that all we need to do is follow Him, He will "turn the darkness into light . . . and make the rough places smooth." And the most encouraging part is the promise "I will not forsake [you]."   BETTY J. ADAMS

JUNE 22

They're Home!

If I go and prepare a place for you, I will come again, and receive you unto myself; that where I am, there ye may be also. John 14:3.

The day I have been longing for is finally here. After months of seeing them off to school each morning, my two girls are home for the summer. I am aware that not everyone shares my sentiments about summer, but I love nothing more than having my children underfoot.

No, it's not always convenient—there are days when the entire living room turns into an Indian village, complete with life-size tents and tepees (is that my bedspread stretched across the room?), and days when mud balls line the back patio ("Mom, how many doughnuts would you like to buy?"). Forget the inconvenience. My kids are home!

Summertime means more chances to hug them, to read to them, to hear them chattering, and to know who they really are. It's true that I can reach them with a phone call when they are in school, but it's not the same. I like to look into their eyes when we talk. I find their presence energizing, and my perspective seems fresher when they are near.

I'm told that my heavenly Father feels the same way about me. There is a day for which He is longing, and He's as eager for that day as I was for this one. He can't wait to have me underfoot. It's a thought I find almost unbelievable—the King of the universe longing for *me?* I so often dwell on my own desire for heaven that I forget it is a day *He* anticipates as well. It's true that we can talk now, but once my schooling here is over, we will be able to look into each other's eyes when we talk. Think of it! Imagine it! Long for it!   RETTA MICHAELIS

My Heavenly Pilot

God is our refuge and strength, a very present help in trouble. Ps. 46:1.

*M*any times I have sat in testimony services and listened with some amusement as person after person (particularly the older folks) told of some harrowing near-death experience. However, my outlook has changed on this subject somewhat. When God in His mercy reaches down and rescues you, you cannot help but give Him thanks. For this reason, at a recent testimony service I found myself sharing a near-death experience with my partner.

It happened about a month before the service. I was traveling with several coworkers from Toronto, Ontario, to Orlando, Florida, for a company conference. When we changed planes in Cincinnati, Ohio, our group wasn't seated together. I was seated toward the back, next to an older couple I noticed right away were Christians.

As the plane started to taxi down the runway, I gazed out the window. Suddenly I saw huge orange and black flames coming out of the side of the plane and lashing out beneath the wing. In panic I grabbed my purse and attempted to get up, forgetting that I still had my seat belt fastened. Almost immediately the aisles were filled with terrified passengers, but there was nowhere to go, as the doors were locked. I felt that the plane would surely explode and my life would be over. I started to pray. I prayed that I would see my loved ones again in the earth made new.

Almost as suddenly as the flames had started, they stopped. Several large trucks appeared on the runway, and men started to inspect the plane. The pilot announced that for some reason too much fuel had gone to the hottest part of the engine, causing it to burst into flames. He soon announced that everything was satisfactory and that the flight would continue. Needless to say, he was flying with some very uneasy passengers. My seatmates, who were very kind to me, agreed that we needed to pray during the entire flight. It was good to have fellow Christians beside me. There was relief all around when the plane landed safely in Orlando. As we exited the plane I heard people all around me saying they would fly with this pilot anytime, but as I offered a prayer heavenward, I knew it was Pilot Jesus who had brought us through.

KAREN BIRKETT

JUNE 24

A Mountain Experience

I lift up my eyes to the hills—where does my help come from? My help comes from the Lord, the Maker of heaven and earth. Ps. 121:1, 2, NIV.

J am so fortunate, because every morning when I awake, the first scene that comes into my view, even before I get out of bed, is a beautiful mountain range that is a part of the Great Smoky Mountains in North Carolina. I never cease to appreciate the majesty of this scene. We live on top of one of these mountains and can look down and across the valley, then on to the foothills, and finally to the distant peaks. Each morning when I get up, I stand before this scene and realize I have an increasing need to sense the presence of God and the help He alone can give.

At times it seems that all I can see is the valley. The mountains are enshrouded by the clouds. Some mornings it is dark, and all I can see are the tiny lights in the valley and scattered on the hillsides. At other times the mist settles in the valley pockets and gives the appearance of vast lakes with mountain peaks jutting above the sea of fog. I watch intently as the mist passes away and the sun begins to shine. Some mornings everything seems just too beautiful. With the air fresh, the sun shining, the mountains clear, all seems right with the world.

I wonder if life is not like the scenes I view. The valley experience seems so intense that we feel we will never again see the mountain peaks. Can you see the little lights that indicate there is life even in darkness? Do you remember that the mist of trouble will dissipate and the sun will shine again? Do you breathe in the freshness of the Holy Spirit and bask in the Son of righteousness? Remember the mountain peaks when you can see only the valley, and view the beauty that is found in Christ.

JUNE E. LOOR

JUNE 25

There Is No Such Thing as Only

The Lord said to me, "Do not say, 'I am a youth,' because everywhere I send you, you shall go, and all that I command you, you shall speak." Jer. 1:7, NASB.

She was only a little girl, whisked away from her parents by a band of marauding warriors. Left alone to struggle with homesickness, fright, and the stench of leprosy in her new home, she could have heaped criticism on her new master's head. In a blaze of tears, she could have said to herself, "Serves him right! That's what happens when you abduct innocent children." But she didn't. She could have reasoned, "I'm just a girl. I'm too young, too new here." She didn't. Instead, she made a single health-restoring suggestion. "If only my master were with the prophet who is in Samaria! For he would heal him" (2 Kings 5:3, NKJV).

Two short sentences. Wistful, yet accurate. The pathos and the power of those words must have moved her mistress to action. After all the doctors, all the anguish, all the failed treatments, here it was. The diagnosis and the cure in one small voice.

The little servant girl could have left the telling to someone else. But she resolved to share the message of hope. With God's help. And the God of the universe saw the workings of faith in that little girl. She had no status, no special abilities, no money, or so it seemed. Yet God used her to lead the captain of a great army to exclaim, "Now I know that there is no God in all the world except in Israel" (2 Kings 5:15, NIV).

He was only one small boy bringing the lunch his mother

must have lovingly prepared to the Master's preach-in. When Andrew asked for his lunch, he could have said, "I'm too young to share, much less to starve. You adults know how long these meetings run. Plan ahead!" But he didn't. He could have suggested a compromise: "I'll just keep one loaf and a fish and give you the rest." He chose not to. Willingly he gave up his lunch basket. And here in Mark 6 we have the recipe for a miracle:

To five small barley loaves and two small fish, add one small boy with a big heart. Wrap it in the touch of the Master's hand. Yield: Lunch for 5,000 (15,000 when you count the families).

Sometimes when God performs miracles, He uses someone quiet enough and little enough to do great things for Him. With his lunch and Christ's touch, thousands of hungry worshipers were fed.

If You can use little children, Lord, please use me.

GLENDA-MAE GREENE

JUNE 26

Delivered in the Name of Jesus

The name of the Lord is a strong tower; The righteous run to it and are safe. Prov. 18:10, NKJV.

*T*hat beautiful, sunny day in the hills of Oakhurst, California, was an open invitation to go hiking. A friend and I set out on foot along a trail cut out of the side of a mountain, one side going nearly straight up, the other straight down. My friend had been enjoying the Bible studies I had been giving her recently, but it was apparent that she had no intention of making a serious commitment to Christ, despite all my earnest prayers.

The peace of the gorgeous scenery on our hike was suddenly shattered by the nearby horrendous growling and barking of a pack of ferocious wild dogs. Looking up, we were terrified to see the dogs rapidly descending toward us with "dinner" flashing from their wolflike eyes. We were frozen with fear. In a split second they were only 10 feet above us, and we had no escape. The very next leap and they would be upon us, tearing us to shreds.

In desperation I blurted out, "In the name of Jesus, not one inch closer!"

The dogs stopped dead in their tracks. This time the terror was on *their* faces. They immediately swung around and ran back up the steep mountainside.

After we caught our breath and regained our composure, my friend turned to me. She was still in shock and could only say, "Judy, I've seen your prayers answered before, but never anything this amazing!" We marveled at such a vivid demonstration of the power that is found in the name of Jesus.

That day we saw proof of how our extremity is God's opportunity. That experience of deliverance from imminent harm was the turning point regarding the Bible studies. My friend became deadly serious about studying the deeper truths of the Bible. I subsequently experienced the great joy of seeing her baptized into God's family of believers.

Looking back, I wouldn't change that hiking trip for anything. It was one of the most frightening experiences of my life, yet it brought thrilling results, teaching me that Christ meant it when He said that if we ask anything in His name, He will do it to the glory of His Father (John 15:16). Rehearse over and over in your mind that when crisis strikes, you will call on the name of Jesus, "a strong tower"!   JUDY COULSTON

JUNE 27

Stampede!

He will command his angels concerning you to guard you in all your ways. Ps. 91:11, NIV.

*I*t was a hot summer day and I was 2½ years old. At the time, our family was renting a farmhouse in southern Virginia. Some friends were visiting with my parents on the large porch that ran the length of the house, while my four brothers were in the barn taking care of the four horses. The cows were out in the field munching on grass when all of a sudden they got spooked and started to go crazy, trampling down the fence separating their field and our yard.

My mom, dad, and brothers immediately ran to try to get the cows under control. My dog, a weimaraner named Cinder, leaped off the porch, barking and nipping at the cows' legs, trying to round them up and get them out of the yard. Seeing all the commotion, I shuffled off the porch and grabbed a small stick and ran after the cows as fast as my little legs would carry me. I was like a child in the middle of a crazy mob. Across the yard my mother frantically yelled at me to get back on the porch. She couldn't get to me, because too many cows were in the way. I couldn't get back to the porch, because I was in the middle of the mad herd. Cinder was fiercely trying to protect me, forcing the cows to go around me.

We finally got the cows out of the yard and under control, and I was unharmed. I thank God for sending His angels to protect me. If they hadn't, I would have been trampled to death.

Eileen Cruz

June 28

He Who Is Able

Now to Him who is able to do exceedingly abundantly above all that we ask or think, according to the power that works in us, to Him be glory. Eph. 3:20, 21, NKJV.

*D*anny, a member of the youth group I pastored, had frequently been in our home for meals and social gatherings. At his request I had given his girlfriend Bible studies and had participated in her baptism. Later I attended their wedding in a distant city. After they were married, they established their home in another town.

Then we received notice from our landlord that in 30 days we were to vacate the house we had lived in for four years. Danny had bought it for his home and business site. To say we were let down would be putting it mildly. The place was ideal for us. How could Danny do this to us, in light of the close relationship we'd had?

We began searching for another rental property. Apartments were available in that congested Latin American city, but there were few houses. We looked in the newspaper. We asked realtors and friends. On Sundays we drove up and down streets, looking and asking. Time was running out. Our prayers became more intense, but it seemed as though an apartment on a busy thoroughfare was the only option.

One night I dreamed about an elegant house with a formal dining room that didn't need to be used for everyday meals. As I woke up I thought, *Alas! We'll never live in a house that pretty—at least not while we're in the mission field!* I continued to pray, "Lord, we need something quickly. Please, Lord!"

One day a friend told us that relatives had a house available. Within an hour I was in an elegant house that had a formal dining room. "We aren't diplomats," I explained. "We are missionaries on a limited budget." I made them a ridiculously low offer, considering the value of the split-level, nearly-new house with its lovely mahogany banisters and stairway and courtyard garden. But they assured me that my offer was good enough.

What a joy to live in that house! During the months that followed I often praised God for His gracious love that gives us above all that we ask or think. Never does He take away something without replacing it with something far better. How could I ever distrust Him?   FELICIA PHILLIPS

JUNE 29

Words Can Still Create New Worlds

By the word of the Lord were the heavens made, their starry host by the breath of his mouth. . . . For he spoke, and it came to be; he commanded, and it stood firm. Ps. 33:6-9, NIV.

*G*od's words are full of energy and power. As Christians most of us accept the biblical account of Creation. We believe that the heavens and the earth were created from nothing more than God's imagination and words.

But how about our words, human words? Do they have creative power?

When I was in college I studied theology, physical education, English, and education. On the side I did some writing. I wanted to study writing, but we had no journalism program. So I wrote stories for the student newspaper and did news releases for the college Public Relations Department. I wrote "sound and light" scripts on Bible themes for religious programs. I edited the school yearbook. While fun, these extracurriculars led nowhere.

Then my band director, Melvin Hill, took me aside. I was a passable trumpeter and played third chair, but what he talked to me about was writing things to read as a narration for our home and out-of-state concerts. "Do something creative," he said. "I know you can."

Mr. Hill's words were strong enough to create something. An idea. An opportunity. And lots of encouragement. I wrote "Psalms in College English" for one afternoon band program. I wrote commentary for concerts and alumni weekend. Some of it was serious, some of it was fluff. Still, the surge of energy I experienced from this opportunity might have all ended there.

But on the sunny May afternoon that I finished college, three people—a speech teacher, a midlevel administrator, and the academic dean—all said something to me in graduation line that caught my attention. Did they come looking for me? I doubt it. But in God's providence each happened to come my way. In three separate conversations they said virtually the same thing: "Do something with your writing. Don't give it up."

Their words had creative power in my life. Although I had been accepted into graduate school, when I learned later that summer of a distant private college that taught journalism, I took a bus across the country to enroll in every writing class it offered the next year.

I am grateful to all those along my life's way who have created new worlds of possibility for me by speaking words of insight and encouragement. Words still have creative power!

KIT WATTS

An Urgent Call

Today, if you hear his voice, do not harden your hearts. Heb. 4:7, NIV.

On Monday I usually visit an elderly woman who suffers from Parkinson's disease. We always talk about biblical truths. I sing for her and read the Bible. When I leave, she sleeps in peace, waiting eagerly for the next Monday.

One Monday I was deciding whether I should visit my friend or not. I had had a hard day and was too tired. I was planning to take a shower, eat dinner, read a while, and go to bed. However, I was impressed that I should go see my friend. A voice inside me said, *Go to Mrs. Clemencia's house! Don't delay!* The voice insisted many times that I should go, but I was not willing. I was too tired. But the impression remained so strong that I finally decided to go, in spite of my fatigue.

On the way over, I suddenly didn't feel tired anymore. Reaching her home, I called her name, but received no answer. Again I called, then heard her weak voice inside saying, "Hurry up, dear! I fell down and can't stand up!" The door was locked, and I couldn't get in. I got her spare key from my cousin and opened the door. She was kneeling down, sweating profusely from her failed attempts at reaching the bed. She told me she had been crying out for some time, but nobody had heard her pleas. Now I understood the insistent voice of the Holy Spirit.

Every day Jesus calls to us to study His Word, to pray, to meditate on His love. Have we answered His call? I don't know what would have happened to my friend if I had refused the impression of the Holy Spirit on my heart, but I do know what will happen to me if I silence that voice.

The voice of the Holy Spirit brings joy and salvation. Leave your activities for a moment this morning and listen to the voice of the Spirit as He impresses you.   JUCELINA MOURA DA SILVA

JULY 1

His Word Is Our Shield

With man this is impossible, but with God all things are possible. Matt. 19:26, NIV.

When I was in Brazil helping to establish women's ministries programs, two church leaders invited me to witness the results of such a program firsthand. I was forewarned that the church we were going to visit on the outskirts of Rio de Janeiro was situated in a crime-ridden area and that gangs and drug lords roamed the streets. I found myself wishing that our bright-red car were less obtrusive, because it drew attention as we made our way down the narrow, dimly lit streets. Young men stood in groups on street corners and in the street itself, almost defying us to enter their territory.

When we arrived at our destination, I took note that the neat chapel was bordered by a high iron fence. A padlock hung from the locked gate. Just as I was wondering how long we would have to wait for someone to open the gate, the door to the neighboring house opened and the pastor's young daughter ran to meet us with a key.

Inside the church I found straight-backed, wooden pews and windows of bars, rather than glass. I had never been in such an atmosphere before. My coworkers and I took a seat near the front of the vacant sanctuary and waited for the evening to unfold.

In a matter of minutes I heard female voices singing softly in the distance. I couldn't understand the Portuguese words, but the hymn tune was familiar. Soon a steady stream of people filed into the narrow rows, happy-faced children of God carrying Bibles and bringing their trophies with them.

The pastor welcomed us to the midweek service, then, for the sake of the guests, began to share the story of the phenomenon that was taking place in his congregation. The conference had wanted to close his church because the membership had dwindled. Because of the gangs, people were afraid to come out of their homes to attend meetings. The young pastor could not bear to give in to the criminal element in the streets, and so he bargained for a little time. Working quickly, he taught 30 women to share the gospel. He armed them with the Word of

God and prayed that a band of angels would accompany them on their journey into the unknown.

In a matter of three or four months these modern-day disciples had brought 100 souls to the Lord. A once-dying congregation now shook the rafters with their praises to God, and while thieves and pimps lurked in the shadows, God was praised. Knocking on doors behind which residents hid in fear, they found men and women who rejoiced at being discovered by someone bearing hope. They willingly gave their hearts to the Lord and rejoiced at the thought of fellowship with God's children.

One after another, these 30 women stood to share their experiences, and with tears flowing like a river down their faces, they invited their trophies to stand. Yes, tears fell and God was praised as these "Bible women" told how miraculously God had taken their fear away. They demonstrated how they carried their Bibles as shields over their hearts. And even the cruelest of the street people had not dared to defy God's Word or His messengers.

Never before, and not since, have I sat in a congregation of miracles. The Power of the Holy Spirit exuded, and I sensed that I was seated among mothers and grandmothers who had dared to live up to their destiny. I want to be like them, don't you?

ROSE OTIS

JULY 2

The Song of a Bird

Let me hear what God the Lord will speak, for he will speak peace to his people, to his faithful, to those who turn to him in their hearts. Ps. 85:8, NRSV.

He was just an animated bunch of gray-brown feathers, tiptoeing on the branch of a shrub. His head was thrown back and his tiny throat pulsed with the song he was tossing out on the spring breeze. Listening to the spring song of a Bewick's wren had long been one of the greatest pleasures of my life. Only this time I couldn't hear a thing. I could see the quivering throat and knew he was singing his tiny heart out, but not even one thin note sounded in my ears.

This was my introduction to the world of the hearing-impaired. Gradually the song sparrows dropped into silence, then I couldn't hear the "fee bee" of a chickadee. Finally even robins no longer sang in my world.

It's been about five years since I heard the chorus of my feathered friends at dawn on a May morning. Recently I purchased a hearing aid. One day while walking I heard the strangest sound. I stopped to listen, turned up the volume on my aid, and finally realized I was hearing a robin sing. No mechanical ear can accurately reproduce the sounds of nature, but that robin's song was a delight all the same.

Then last week I was in a store that sells all manner of supplies for bird feeders, as well as books for birders and tapes of bird songs. I tried to listen to several cassettes, but wasn't able to hear the songs. Then I came to one that I could hear, even in the confusion of a busy store. I bought that tape and put it on my stereo at home. I sat down, turned up the volume, and suddenly robin, thrush, and meadowlark songs filled the room, wrapping me in glorious sounds.

And I wept, overcome by the sheer beauty of melodies I had forgotten existed.

Fortunately, the most beautiful sound in the universe doesn't depend on ears that can hear. It requires only a listening heart to hear God gently whispering, "I love you." When you can no longer hear His voice, just ask Him to turn up the volume. He is always there. His love surrounds you and will sing in your heart.   BARBARA ROBERTS

JULY 3

Moving and Planting

They shall build houses, and inhabit them; and they shall plant vineyards, and eat the fruit of them. They shall not build, and another inhabit; they shall not plant, and another eat: . . . and mine elect shall long enjoy the work of their hands. Isa. 65:21, 22.

Before my husband and I were married in 1950, some lady friends of our family graciously asked if I had chosen crystal, china, and silver patterns, or if I would rather have more practical gifts. Knowing that our goal was to serve in the ministry, which would involve moving rather often, I preferred the more mundane but practical household items.

I was right about the moving. In the years of our marriage, we have lived in four states in everything from a small trailer to an apartment to small houses, big houses, old houses, new houses, and now our "retirement" home. We did start out in pastoral work, then moved on to youth work and educational work.

I have been blessed (or perhaps plagued) by having what some of my family call the "gardening gene," inherited, no doubt, from my grandmother, who was an avid gardener. As a result, we nearly always left behind flowers for the next occupants of our homes. Tulips, hyacinths, daffodils, roses, chrysanthemums, lilacs, iris, rhododendrons, lilies, forsythia, and gladiolus all grace our yard now, just as they did other homes we've lived in. I hope the ones who have followed us over the years have loved and cared for these flowers and shrubs as much as we did.

We too had the joy of finding flowers planted by previous occupants of the homes we moved into. In Atlanta we found, at the side of the house, three huge gardenia bushes whose perfume was a little foretaste of heaven! Other wonderful surprises included rose bushes, iris, peonies, and lilies of the valley.

Today as I planted gladiolus, columbine, candytuft, pansies, Shasta daisies, and a few other things, and pulled pesky weeds, I thought about the promise we have in Isaiah that in heaven we will not plant and another reap. There won't be weeds to pull, either. We will just enjoy the work of our hands, and everyone will have a "green thumb" there. I'm looking forward to that, aren't you?

MARY JANE GRAVES

JULY 4

And God Said Yes!

Pray for each other so that you may be healed. James 5:16, NIV.

*C*arefully carrying the cut-flower arrangement, I rode the elevator up to her room. The evening before, my sister of choice had been too groggy from the anesthetic to appreciate flowers; today would be different. I thought ahead. The surgeon had told her she'd probably be discharged in a couple days. But as I reached her bedside I knew something was dreadfully wrong. She was lying so still, gasping for each breath.

Quickly I went in search of the head nurse. Aspiration pneumonia, she explained. It had come on suddenly, and even with oxygen her saturation levels were dangerously low. One lung had collapsed, and the doctor would be in momentarily to insert chest tubes. I groaned. As if there weren't enough tubes already: Foley catheter, nasal oxygen, two IV lines, and a nasogastric tube.

Two days later her condition had decidedly worsened. The sounds of high-tech medical care were all around us. The chest-tube suction bubbled incessantly, the IV pumps clicked regularly, the oxygen hissed softly. The monitors whined, but the treatments weren't working. She was dying. No question about it.

I knew what prayer could accomplish, and I was praying for her almost constantly. But there must be something else to do. Of course! Why hadn't I thought of it before? The research about prayer! A group of postsurgical patients who were prayed for had experienced fewer complications and lower mortality rates than those in the control group. What's more, the patients in the study hadn't even known they were being prayed for. Imagine what might have happened if they had known . . .

"I'll be back later," I told her. "I'm going to make a few phone calls; I'm going to ask some women's ministries directors to start a prayer chain."

Her head nodded almost imperceptibly.

And they prayed, sisters in Christ all over the United States and Canada. There was no instantaneous healing, but it was miraculous nevertheless. Nearly three weeks later she was finally discharged—weak, unsteady, still gasping for breath, but alive. We had many wonderful conversations during the three months of convalescence she spent in our home. I recall one in particular.

It was the Fourth of July. We were sitting in the family room watching fireworks create their transient patterns against the night sky, although it was a bit strange to hear the sound about three seconds after the display. "I'll make a better chaplain because of this surgery," she said softly. "I know what it's like to walk through the valley of the shadow of death." The Good Shepherd had been with her and even now was helping her to climb the mountain on the other side of the valley. No doubt about it, she would be more empathetic.

This time God had said yes; there was still a work for her to do. And every one of the women who prayed for her would have a part in that work. There is power in prayer! ARLENE TAYLOR

JULY 5

Keeping Your Sparkle

Hitherto have ye asked nothing in my name: ask, and ye shall receive, that your joy may be full. John 16:24.

The other day my children and I were in a store that sold lots of buttons and bumper stickers with witty sayings. One said "Welcome to Wyoming. Don't forget to set your clock back 25 years." Another lamented "If I'd known grandchildren were so great, I would have had them first."

All of a sudden our son chuckled. "This is true!" I looked over his shoulder and read the bright-red words: "If Mama ain't happy—ain't nobody happy!"

I didn't know whether to take his comment as a rebuke or a compliment! But a few days later, when I was in the same store, I purchased the sticker and put it on the front of my refrigerator as a reminder that my home should be to my children the most pleasant place in the world, and that my presence should be its greatest attraction.

How Satan works to wear us down with worry and work, multiplying stress and pressures. It was a wonderful lift for me to read that it is for our own interest and that of our family when we save ourselves all unnecessary taxation and use every means at our command to preserve life, health, and the energies God has given us. We will need the vigor of all our faculties for our great work of raising our children. A portion of our time should be spent outdoors, in physical exercise, that we may be invigorated to do our work indoors with cheerfulness and thoroughness, being the light and blessing of our homes.

"OK!" I tell myself. "You must take time to keep your sparkle. It is a lot easier to be happy when you are physically fit. But even then Satan can tempt and annoy me with discouraging events."

The best cure I have found for those "unhappy" days is to ask Jesus for help and sing praises to Him.   GERITA LIEBELT

This first appeared in *The Heart of the Home* 7, No. 2 (1992). Used with permission.

JULY 6

The Bottom Line

He has told you, O mortal, what is good; and what does the Lord require of you but to do justice, and to love kindness, and to walk humbly with your God? Micah 6:8, NRSV.

Remember the parable of the sheep and the goats in Matthew 25? Jesus instructs the "goats" to depart and tells the "sheep" to come and inherit the kingdom of God. What's the difference between the two groups? Their motives and spirit? The sheep know their Master and truly love and want to serve Him.

One of my favorite authors asks, "Who has the heart? With whom are our thoughts? Of whom do we love to converse? Who has our warmest affections and our best energies? If we are Christ's, our thoughts are with Him, and our sweetest thoughts are of Him. All we have and are is consecrated to Him. We long to bear His image, breathe His spirit, do His will, and please Him in all things" (*Steps to Christ*, p. 58).

That's the bottom line of Christianity, isn't it? In the end everything boils down to serving and knowing Jesus through our relationship with Him. If everything rests on that relationship, shouldn't we be asking every day, "How can I build a better relationship with Jesus?" A relationship is a very personal thing, so each of us must seek God in her own way. But there are at least three very basic ways that will work for all of us: studying God's letter to us, talking with Him, and sharing what we have learned with other people. If we consistently spend time with Jesus, we will be able to "act justly and to love mercy and to walk humbly" with our God.

BRENDA FORBES DICKERSON

JULY 7

God-given Talents

Moses then called . . . every skillful one to whom the Lord had given skill, everyone whose heart was stirred to come to do the work. Ex. 36:2, NRSV.

*I*t is exciting to realize that our talents are actually gifts from God, our Creator. Sometimes we have talents we aren't aware of until we have an opportunity to exercise them.

Many years ago, when I was in grade school, my music teacher would push a piano from one classroom to the next. Certain students' talent for music was obvious at an early age. An art teacher had a room filled with intriguing supplies. I remember one student whose talent was so apparent and unequaled that despite his age he was called upon to do any artwork needed for special events at the school. It was obvious to the teachers which of their students, even when those students were in first grade, were going to do very well in certain subjects. As parents observe their young children they can determine what their unique talents might be.

Seven-year-old Heather noticed a pretty scene painted on something. She got very excited and said, "I think I can do that!" She disappeared into her room and was back in a few minutes with a good replica of what she had seen. I think she has found one of her talents.

Eight-year-old Larry asked to see the movie *Apollo 13* instead of a cartoon. He has shown a real interest in science.

Twenty-five years after leaving elementary school I met the student who excelled in art. He has a studio in Florida, where he produces beautiful paintings for the tourist trade. He was a straight-A student all through school. He could have been anything, but he chose to do what he loved most.

My late husband, who was an orthodontist, once said, "Don't tell anyone I said this, but I love my work so much that I'd do it for nothing!" Isn't that the ideal for every working man or woman? It is God's hope that you will discover the talents He has given to you to make your life fulfilling each day.

"I saw that there is nothing better than that all should enjoy their work, for that is their lot" (Eccl. 3:22, NRSV).

MARY C. EDMISTER

JULY 8

Stay True to His Word

I wait for the Lord, my soul waits, and in his word I put my hope.
Ps. 130:5, NIV.

*I*t was a brisk 15-minute walk from the hotel where my husband and I were staying to the train that would take us to meetings in Utrecht, Holland. My husband had left earlier, and I had decided to take the 9:35 a.m. train. I was looking forward to the walk since it was a lovely time of day and the path went by well-kept flower and vegetable gardens.

As I left the hotel I checked the train schedule and my watch once more. Yes, I had a half hour for the 15-minute walk, plenty of time to enjoy my surroundings. A few wispy clouds hung in the brilliant blue sky. Sheep grazed on a nearby hillside: What a peaceful sight!

Then I noticed a gentleman about 100 yards ahead of me. I recognized him as the university professor whom my husband had introduced me to a few days earlier. Suddenly the man sped up, then began to run, as though he were afraid he would miss the train. Should I be hurrying too? The beauty of my walk evaporated as I started worrying about missing the train. I opened my purse, checked the train schedule and my watch once more, and decided I had enough time. No need to hurry. I had time to enjoy the walk, fresh air, blue sky, and those lovely gardens.

The man had slowed to a walk again. But now I was unsure. Maybe my watch wasn't working right. If I were to miss the train, maybe I wouldn't be able to find my husband. *I really should hurry*, I thought. Now I was oblivious to the beauty of the gardens.

The man started running again. Yes, something had to be wrong with my watch. Or maybe there had been a change in the train schedule. What if he had more accurate information than I? After all, he was an important man. In either case I knew I had to hurry. I had to do what he was doing. Perhaps I should even run a bit.

I arrived at the station hot and breathless—the train was scheduled to arrive 14 minutes later. The schedule had not been changed. The time on my watch matched that on the station's clock. And there sat the professor on a bench, contentedly reading a book.

As I stood there disappointed, trying to regain my breath, some thoughts came to mind. Do I find myself doubting the signs of His soon coming? I need to enjoy the Christian life today and every day, resting secure in His Word and guidance. Because I am guided by God's Word and His Holy Spirit, I can enjoy the path to heaven. I don't need to be worried or upset by attitudes, ideas, or "new theologies" that suggest that unless I do as others do I won't be saved.

The train arrived. I returned the gentleman's cheery greeting. Now, instead of thinking that he had ruined my walk, I thanked God for this simple and beautiful lesson.   EUNICE PEVERINI

Hurting Hands

So he said to them, "Unless I see in His hands the print of the nails, and put my finger into the print of the nails . . . I will not believe." John 20:25, NKJV.

I know what it is to have painful hands. For years I suffered with carpal tunnel syndrome and the hurt that comes when hands swell from overuse and median nerves get severely pinched. Surgery to cut the bands of fibrous tissue that pressed on the nerves became a necessity, and I felt the burning, searing misery where the scalpel cut into my hands.

As I mended I thought about Christ's hands. I realized that what I went through, painful though it was, could not begin to compare with what He endured in His hands and feet when He was nailed to the cross. Those nails went all the way through Him. Throbbing, burning, aching—He felt it all!

My hands are now much improved. Yes, I have scars. But each time I look at them, they remind me of Christ's scars. I know that when Christ comes and we receive new bodies, my scars will go away. But His will be there throughout eternity.

When I think of the price He paid, I have mixed emotions— shame and consternation that I helped hurt Him that way, but gratitude for what He did for me. I'm thankful that He died to save us and that someday, thanks to Him, those who love Him can go to heaven and live in a new earth where there will be no more sorrow or pain (Rev. 21:4).

Lord, help us to remember that You were wounded for us. May we keep our hands in Your nail-scarred ones. Help us to bring others into those same hands.
BONNIE MOYERS

JULY 10

He Carried Me

Save me, O God; for the waters are come in unto my soul. Ps. 69:1.

When I first became a Christian, I felt as if I had "arrived." Not that I thought that from then on life would be smooth and without trouble. I just had no concept of the type of problems I would encounter in my Christian walk.

One of my greatest trials came when my health began to fail. Instead of being able to wake early to spend time in Bible study and prayer, I found that I couldn't wake up. And when I forced myself to get out of bed to read, I could neither concentrate nor remember what I'd read. Many times I would get down to pray and slowly doze off to sleep on my knees! My prayers for help seemed to go unanswered. What could I do? I knew that God was watching over me, even though outward appearances seemed to deny it.

It took a couple years before I learned that I was actually suffering from an illness. By this time my personal devotional life was nearly nonexistent. And a Christian without God's Word is like a soldier without a sword—fair game for the first adversary that comes along.

Why this happened to me, I don't know. Since my illness, it seems I have fallen too often in my Christian experience. Things that hadn't been a temptation for me earlier in my Christian walk now seemed like impossible hurdles. But I know that I have a Saviour who understands, who cares immeasurably, and who can "make a way to escape, that ye may be able to bear it" (1 Cor. 10:13).

Many times, like David in the Psalms, I have felt like I was sinking into a pit of mire from which there would be no escape. But the Lord has heard my cries for help. After being more careful with my health, I find it is starting to improve. Once again I can read and understand the Bible. And best of all, I remember it! I am finding that He is creating "in me a clean heart" and renewing "a right spirit within me" (Ps. 51:10). I am thankful that the Lord has been so patient and merciful with me.

Whatever your circumstances or challenges in life, you too can know that God understands and loves you. We have

242

an anchor for our souls, and that anchor is Jesus, our Lord
and Saviour.   CAROLINE ANDREW

Heaven: Who Wants to Go?

What is a man profited, if he shall gain the whole world, and lose
his own soul? Matt. 16:26.

While standing outside the office waiting for Lorna,
through the door drifted a mixture of voices in conversation.

"Lorna, do you want to go to heaven?" a baritone voice
questioned.

"Heaven? Why should I want to go there when I have everything I ever wanted now?" As she left the room Lorna muttered
half aloud, "What a strange question to ask somebody!"

Throughout the day the question and Lorna's answer nagged
me. "Why should I want to go to heaven?" Why should you—or
anyone else—want to go there?

Lorna is considered upper class and lives quite comfortably.
Apparently she has no desire to leave her accumulated wealth
and possessions. Lot and his family lived comfortably and enjoyed the association of others like themselves. When they
learned of the imminent destruction of Sodom, they did not hasten away. "The angels urged Lot, saying, 'Hurry! Take your wife
and your two daughters who are here, or you will be swept away
when the city is punished'" (Gen. 19:15, NIV).

When Lot and his family hesitated, the angels grasped them
by their hands and led them safely out of the city. "Do not go
back, but flee for your lives!" they urged.

Lot dallied, thereby giving his wife time to grieve for her
children and possessions. She looked back and lost her life.
Many, like Mrs. Lot, cling to their worldly possessions, families,
associates, and jobs, counting them more important than heaven.

No human eye can visualize the beauties of heaven. The
music of heaven surpasses any heard on earth by mortal ears. Our

earthly lives are fraught with heartaches, trials, pain, sadness, and disappointments. We struggle and sacrifice to acquire wealth, but another takes it away by theft or fraud. Burdens overwhelm, and we long for the peace and security that only heaven provides.

In that beautiful city none will live in alleyways, abandoned cars, or temporary shelters. The redeemed will build houses and inhabit them (Isa. 65:21-23). Utility companies will be nonexistent; there will be no need for candle or sun—for God is the light (Rev. 22:5).

Because the inhabitants will not experience pain or sickness, hospitals, doctors, and nurses will be unnecessary. The leaves of the tree of life are for the "healing of the nations" (verse 2). Undertakers will have buried their last dead, for there will be no more death. Earth's miseries will be ended, for the "eyes of the blind shall be opened, and the ears of the deaf shall be unstopped. Then shall the lame man leap as an hart, and the tongue of the dumb sing" (Isa. 35:5, 6). I want to go there, don't you?

MABEL ROLLINS NORMAN

JULY 12

And I Didn't Even Ask

The Lord God is a sun and shield; the Lord bestows favor and honor; no good thing does he withhold from those whose walk is blameless. Ps. 84:11, NIV.

I'm in charge of the budget and the bills at my house. My family simply states their needs, and I try to work with them. They remind me that I'm the one with the business degrees and turn deaf ears when I respond, "Business acumen and miracle-working are not mutually inclusive!"

Last year, with a new house, a new car, and a daughter who wanted to go to college 2,000 miles away, I had to be both creative and stringent. I rearranged our priorities. Tithes and offerings still came first. Postchurch luncheons for a dozen or more lonely college students were a must. Some things had to be scratched, but other items had to be added: long-distance phone calls, quarterly flights home during each break, the new wardrobe . . .

A few weeks ago my mortgage company sent me a refund check. I was sure they had made a mistake. But when I called, they assured me that the money was mine. I put it in a special account and refused to touch it.

As I was renewing the contract for my car insurance, I was struck by a thought. Perhaps I should use the same insurer for the house. The insurance agent promised to investigate the possibilities. A few days later he called back. He was delighted to inform me that I would save quite a bit if I did it the way I was proposing. The only drawback was that I had to submit a rather hefty down payment right away. Then he quoted the amount—the exact amount of my refund check!

The power of this small but very significant experience in my life reminded me that God is all-knowing. Even though I did not pray specifically for this particular problem, God had already provided the means for me to effect the change in my insurance coverage.

ELAINE HOILETTE

JULY 13

God's Flowers

I am the rose of Sharon, and the lily of the valleys. As the lily among thorns, so is my love among the daughters. S. of Sol. 2:1, 2.

I was once a shy, timid, fearful child, almost "afraid of my own shadow," as they say. Childhood traumas had much to do with that, though by nature I was born an introvert—scared to speak up, afraid to be seen, and petrified to get up front and do anything. I knew God loved me, but I didn't really love myself.

I can praise the Lord today, however, that He has blessed me in learning to overcome my past and to accept the challenges of each new day by reaching out in service to others. No, I haven't become an extrovert. I'm never the first to help out or accept leadership roles. But I do enjoy being up front once I get there. God has helped me give up being a drab, fragile, and drooping wallflower and blossom into a colorful and vibrant Iris (pun intended, since that's my name). As a result, I have accepted opportunities to be a member of numerous church boards and nominating committees and a leader and/or superintendent of various children and adult church activities and groups.

Blossoming didn't happen overnight. The seed was planted. A voice (the Holy Spirit, I'm sure) consistently whispered to me, "You are somebody!" I ignored the voice, not ready to believe it or act on it. The seed lay dormant, my talents and gifts unused. During the decades that followed I eventually began to feel like somebody. The bud began to blossom—tiny little blossoms that really didn't amount to much (to me, anyway) till one day I accepted Christ. I mean, *really* accepted Him. I was able to say sincerely, "Use me, Lord. Make me what You want me to be."

As I daily consecrate myself to Him, the blooms continue to mature. Many times over the years I've had to fight the urge to become a wallflower again. In God's miraculous strength alone I continue to have the potential to be a beautiful flower in life's vast garden of life, giving joy to others.

God wants each one of us to be a flower in His garden. A Lily. A Rose. A Daisy. A Violet. An Iris. Won't you allow the refreshing waters of His Holy Spirit and the wondrous light and warmth of God's Son to transform you into a fragrant, thriving blossom? Won't you accept His nourishment and grow to your full potential today?

Iris L. Stovall

JULY 14

The Bubble Gum Dream

The hour has come for you to wake up from your slumber, because our salvation is nearer now than when we first believed. Rom. 13:11, NIV.

I had a dream a few years ago, and it certainly wasn't my favorite. It didn't seem like a dream at the time. I thought I was really chewing gum—a wad of pink, juicy, sweet, sticky bubble gum. As I chewed, that wad of gum seemed to increase in size. It continued to swell until it became so large that I began to choke. I couldn't breathe. Forcing my fingers between my teeth, I pried my mouth open, grabbed the rubbery mass, and flung it away. Then I could breathe again! The bubble gum was all gone except for a minute bit that just seemed to be stuck in an indentation in one of my teeth. After what I had just been through, I wasn't going to worry about a tiny dab of bubble gum.

It seemed like only seconds later that the speck of gum began to grow. That piece began to choke me too. In sheer panic I again reached into my mouth, took hold of the glutinous goo, and threw it as far as I could. I was so glad to get rid of it! But I couldn't seem to get it all out. Another tiny piece was left behind, and I was terrified. I remembered what had happened the last two times, and I didn't want to suffer anymore. Alas, I did (in my dream, of course)! When the gum grew a third time, I thought for sure this last wad would kill me. Much to my relief, I woke up.

Thinking about the dream, I see a parallel between that bubble gum and sin. We start out with just a tiny bit of sin, then it seems to grow and keep on growing. We often don't notice it until it starts to become a problem. If we don't get rid of it, any piece that's left, no matter how small, can keep expanding until it chokes the eternal life right out of us.

The devil would like to keep us asleep so he can really gum up our lives. But the Lord wants us to awaken from our slumber before it's too late. He reminds us that He's the solution to every problem of sin, regardless of its size. He's on our side, and He knows exactly what to do. He invites us to ask for His help. There's no situation too sticky for Him to handle.

And that's no silly dream. That's for real.

MARCIA MOLLENKOPF

JULY 15

Words of Metaphor

I am the rose of Sharon, and the lily of the valleys. S. of Sol. 2:1.

I would have thought about 20, 30 possibly. But more than 140? Surely not! However, once again I learned from my students. The literature class was studying figurative language, so I'd given an assignment to find as many as 20 names Jesus was called besides Christ. One student stunned us all by bringing in more than 140 titles Jesus had been given in the Bible, metaphors chosen to help us understand the incomparable Christ.

Black ink on white paper—that's all words are, really. Weak mediums to describe the indescribable Saviour. The Bible writers must have been frustrated in trying to depict Him adequately. So they turned to a powerful word technique—the use of metaphors to help explain the varied dimensions of Jesus, with different authors selecting one or more facets of Christ to emphasize or one of His roles to accentuate. The result is that we now have in the Bible a mosaic of metaphors showing that Christ is indeed the man for all seasons, the man for all people.

To the builder, He is the Cornerstone.

To the scholar, He is the Great Teacher.

To the botanist, He is the Rose of Sharon.

To the shepherd, He is the Lamb of God.

To the troubled, He is the Great Counselor.

To the statesman, He is the Prince of peace.

To the grieving, He is the sympathetic Man of sorrows.

To those needing protection, He is a mother hen.

The psalmist released a rush of power images—six in one verse—so overcome was he with the majesty of Christ: "rock," "fortress," "deliverer," "buckler," "horn," and "high tower" (Ps. 18:2).

Not only did the Bible writers use metaphoric language when describing Christ; Jesus often referred to Himself in figurative speech.

For the historian: "I am Alpha and Omega, the beginning and the ending" (Rev. 1:8).

For the astronomer: "I am . . . the bright and morning star" (Rev. 22:16).

For the hungry: "I am the bread of life" (John 6:35).

For the blind: "I am the light of the world" (John 8:12).

And for *everyone*: "I am the way, the truth, and the life" (John 14:6).

No matter what the need, there is a dimension of Christ that speaks directly to it. Paul's words still comfort: "But my God shall supply all your need according to his riches in glory by Christ Jesus" (Phil. 4:19).   WILMA McCLARTY

JULY 16

All Joy?

Count it all joy when you fall into various trials. James 1:2, NKJV.

I must confess that I have been amused by a piece of advice given by James, one of the early Church Fathers: "Consider it pure joy, my brothers," he advises, "whenever you face trials" (James 1:2, NIV).

"Come on, James," I mocked. "You know that nobody, but *nobody*, considers trials to be pure joy!

"As for me personally," I piously boasted, "I will endure trials, I will suffer them patiently, but consider them 'all joy'? I don't think so, James!"

Then one day my lofty disbelief in that Scripture portion suffered a serious blow. I spoke to my friend Margaret and listened as she demonstrated the embodiment of this great philosophy of James' in magnificent reality. Unbelievable problems have bludgeoned this lady. I sometimes marvel that she is still sane. Her husband is an alcoholic. He had abused her physically until a police restraining order was necessary to protect her life. Her son, a drug addict, has been brought to trial for so many misdemeanors she has lost count. And on the day I encountered her she had everything going more "wrong" than usual.

"But," she concluded, "the army grubs are in my lawn, and I am so happy about that because I just don't have time to mow it. The grubs keep it trimmed!"

"But Margaret," I objected. "I am cursing those grubs because they make havoc of my lawn."

"Not mine," she laughed. "They save me mowing time!"

If that were not a James-type trial, I don't know what is. But Margaret hadn't finished her "pure joy" report. "You know, last week the teachers were on strike," she reminded me.

"Now, don't tell me there is any joy in that, Margaret." I knew that teachers forfeited their wages while they were on strike, and she needed her income with all her difficulties.

"Oh, you're wrong!" she laughed. "Paperwork has been piling up in my classroom, and I have been spending nights trying to get caught up. But now a welcome strike leaves the children at home, and I have whole, wonderful days to catch up on my work and reorganize my room that I have procrastinated doing for far too long. Oh, that teacher's strike was sheer joy!"

She misses one of her sons terribly because he is away in the Pacific. "But," she hastened to assure me, "it just makes me so happy that he is doing missionary service. I acknowledge the lonesome days, but rejoice in the work he is doing."

So I reflected deeply about this lady. Maybe James is right. Counting trials "all joy" might just unveil hidden blessings to the rest of us. Wise old Solomon seems to support the notion. He asserts that "a cheerful heart is a good medicine, but a crushed spirit dries up the bones" (Prov. 17:22, NIV).   EDNA HEISE

JULY 17

Calling Names

Do not fear, for I have redeemed you; I have called you by name, you are mine. Isa. 43:1, NRSV.

I have always had trouble sleeping through the night. When my children were babies, I would wake up just to make sure they were still breathing. When they got older, they grieved with me over my sleep-deprived nights. Not because they pitied my insomniac state, but because they knew I would use those wakeful hours to make lists of extra chores they could do! Even now, although they are grown and have families of their own, they make a great show of commiserating with their father on the probable expansion of his chore load when they hear of my sleepless nights.

Recently, though, I've learned of a special treatment. It is not intended to cure insomnia so much as to utilize those sleepless hours in an others-centered way. Now, instead of counting sheep, I talk to the Shepherd and pray for people by their names. Starting at the beginning of the alphabet, I pray for individuals in my circle of influence.

A . . . "Dear God, thank You for Annie's special friendship." B . . . "Bert's back needs Your attention." And so it continues until I fall asleep again.

Sometimes I remember where I left off and begin there. G . . . "Guide Glenda-mae in her work." Other times, I start in the middle and work backward. R . . . "Work with Richard and his family as they make plans for the future." I include the entire household, especially when I know them well. E . . . "Bless Eric in cold, sunny Saskatchewan, his wife, his daughter, his son, his in-laws . . ."

Intercessory prayer is a powerful phenomenon. Just the process of formulating the thoughts to shape the prayer brings me closer to the person. Sometimes when I mention that I had been praying for some individuals, I see a glow on their faces. Their response is heart-warming: "I feel better knowing that you prayed for me. Now I have more courage to face my challenges."

More important, prayer brings me closer to God. Talking to God gives me a clearer understanding of His goodness, His character, His omnipotence, His omnipresence. It brings me peace, and I fall asleep, knowing that He is in charge.

God knows each one of us by name. When we call each other by name as we pray, we are all blessed. Thank You, loving Lord, for the comfort of prayer.   CAROL JOY GREENE

JULY 18

Family Values

If you belong to Christ, then you are Abraham's seed, and heirs according to the promise. Gal. 3:29, NIV.

*I*t came as a great shock to me to learn that I was not, as I had always believed, middle class. In fact, I was not even working class. I was lower working class. The home in which I lived was a slum, and I came from a deprived background.

It took me a long time to come to terms with this revelation that shattered my delusions. In my childish naïveté I had equated cleanliness and godliness with class. I knew we were not well off, but we couldn't be poor—we had a cooked meal every evening. We went to church in our best clothes three times every week. I had seen my mother actually take the food from our table and give it to people who had nothing. We did not have hot water or a bathroom, but our home was clean and neat, so it couldn't be a slum, could it? My mother grew sweet peas in a tin bath in the yard.

As for being deprived, didn't our parents love us and look after us well? Weren't we allowed to bring our friends home any time, and wasn't it an accepted fact that our friends were automatically invited to share whatever meal we were having? Poor people didn't do that. Poor people were dirty and ragged. They didn't attend church and do their homework on time, and they didn't work hard, as my parents did.

When I went to my mother with my heartache, she opened my eyes to the dangers of trying to label communities or of trying to fit people into categories. She taught me never to be ashamed of my origins or my home, but to be proud of the warm welcome that was extended to all. She taught me that in God's sight all His children are equal, and that He expects us, regardless of how much or how little we have, to share with others. Far from having a deprived childhood, I realize now that I had the richest upbringing a child could have. My mother made our hearth a good anchor that has held me fast through many trials.

My mother did not subscribe to sectarianism, so we learned from an early age to appreciate and value other religions and other cultures. We learned the value of family life and the importance of a strong, joyful faith in God.

Looking back, I realize I was right all along. We were rich. Not in monetary terms, but in the values that matter: a loving family, faith in God, being a trustworthy friend, and sharing God's blessings with others. These are values that are needed even more now than they ever were. Pray with me that our homes will be a strong anchor for ourselves and for our children so that as children of the King we will share the benefits of our inheritance.

AUDREY BALDERSTONE

JULY 19

The Squirrel and Lacey

"I will now rise up," says the Lord; "I will place them in the safety for which they long." Ps. 12:5, NRSV.

Lacey sat on her haunches in the snow outside our window, looking up into the tree at a squirrel perched on the uppermost branches. The squirrel, twitching its tail and looking down at the dog, seemed to be wondering why Lacey was sitting and watching so intently. Lacey waited as quietly as she could, hoping the squirrel would come down near enough so she could give chase and have a little excitement in her life.

Soon friend squirrel was dashing along the treetops, trying to make believe he was leaving. Patiently Lacey waited, hoping the squirrel would let down its guard and venture onto the ground at the base of the tree. Instead, the squirrel went to some leftover seeds, still hanging on the tree from the past summer, and started to eat. By and by Lacey became weary of the wait and left to pursue other interests.

The squirrel chose to stay where it was safe, to stay where it could be sure it was in control of the situation. A wise choice. Lacey let her patience wear thin and gave up her vigil to go on to do something involving more action.

Far too often I am like Lacey. I tire of the wait. I want to have answers now, and I grow impatient. Since I was given more intelligence than a dog, it is time for me to grow into a more patient person. Like the squirrel, I watch the adversary waiting for an opportunity to chase me farther from the Lord. I will choose to stay safely in the arms of my Lord. It is the wise choice.

EVELYN GLASS

Skoro Ochen Skoro
(Soon and Very Soon)

Go and make disciples in all the nations, baptizing them into the
name of the Father and of the Son and of the Holy Spirit, and
then teach these new disciples to obey all the commands I have
given you; and be sure of this—that I am with you always, even
to the end of the world. Matt. 28:19, 20, TLB.

It all started with a simple request as I stood over the sink
washing dishes. "Lord, I want to speak and sing more for
You." A few months later I was on my way to Novokutnetsk,
Russia, as the singing evangelist and chorister for an evangelistic
series (To Russia With Love). As our small plane landed in the
Siberian region of Russia, I felt the rush of heat and fear. After
spending four hours on a plane with no air-conditioning, ripped
carpet, peeling paneling, rusty toilets, and flies, I was in no hurry
to fly with this airline again any time soon.

The environment was primitive. The people seemed to have
only the bare necessities. How was I to serve in a country such as
this? I thought I was prepared to do without the modern
American conveniences, but certainly nothing like this. Squat
holes served as toilets, and toilet paper was unknown. And the
poverty. How could I make a difference when I could barely relate to their experience? I couldn't speak the language, and for
many I was the first Black person they had ever seen! All I could
see were barriers. But God saw opportunities.

Friendships began to develop; people attended the meetings
and accepted Christ. By the end of our time there, more than 50
people were baptized and a new church was formed. What many
of the Russian people lacked in material possessions they made
up for in spirit. They were so willing to give their last if it made
us happy. The many things we took for granted they thought
were beautiful, such as having a new Bible for the first time. One
of my most touching moments after singing was when a woman
told me my voice was from God! God still uses ordinary people
to do extraordinary things. Don't wait for some future opportunity to serve; do what you can with what you have.

I cried when it was time to leave. I was taking away far more than I had given. Even though there were tears, I realized that one day we will be united in the clouds of glory. "Skoro Ochen Skoro."

TERRIE E. RUFF

All That Baggage

Provide purses for yourselves that will not wear out, a treasure in heaven that will not be exhausted, where no thief comes near and no moth destroys. For where your treasure is, there your heart will be also. Luke 12:33, 34, NIV.

My job this past year has taken me on a number of airplane trips. And two times the airline has misplaced my luggage. The first time my hanging bag didn't arrive with me. The agent told me it could be in Houston, Texas. Or Kansas City. Or Milwaukee. Or Cleveland. After three days it turned up and was delivered to me.

The next time my large suitcase didn't show up when I flew into Seattle, Washington, for a youth leaders' seminar. The airline sent out a tracer and assured me that most people get their luggage back within 24 hours. (I knew better.) Fortunately, I was staying at my sister's house, so we headed home and went to bed. That was Thursday night. By Friday afternoon, still no suitcase. We went to the mall, where I bought some pumps and pantyhose to go with my church dress.

The suitcase didn't show up Saturday. Or Sunday. Or Monday.

I flew back home, and after two months I gave up ever seeing my belongings again. The airline must have given up too, because they sent me a check.

But I learned a few lessons. (I'm wondering if God *really* thinks I need to learn them since this has happened to me twice in one year!) Anyway, here they are:

1. **Almost everything is replaceable.** By the end of my luggageless weekend I had bought another pair of jeans, suede dress shoes, tennis shoes, a peach sweater, a jacket, and all kinds of

other things I liked just as well as the items I had packed. Some I liked even better. The stores are full of stuff.

2. We need other people, and they need us. That first night my sister got out a nightgown for me to borrow. The next day she loaned me a clean pair of underwear and a T-shirt and jacket. I needed help, and she came through. Next time someone might need *my* help.

3. You can get by with very little. I had the clothes on my body, some stores, and a little help. And I got along fine. Maybe I don't need to pack so much next time.

And maybe I shouldn't depend on my stuff. Like the Bible says, material objects rip and shrink and go out of style. But His Word and love last forever. LORI PECKHAM

Rebirth

He saved us, not because of righteous things we had done, but because of his mercy. He saved us through the washing of rebirth and renewal by the Holy Spirit. Titus 3:5, NIV.

When he was small, my son was fascinated with hunting. His adventures ranged from chasing butterflies and squirrels to catching insects. Later on he crafted traps to catch stray cats and dogs. As he reached adolescence, his interest in hunting included more advanced equipment. A BB gun was to die for; however, no amount of persuasive tactics was convincing enough for me to satisfy this want. As time progressed, so did this enthusiasm. Finally, when I realized he was being consumed by this obsession, I decided to intervene on behalf of nature.

One day after observing his target practice with makeshift artillery, I simply sat him down on the backyard steps for a heart-to-heart. "Son," I told him, "do you realize that God wants us to be happy, even though sin is all around us? He has given us His promise that He will still be our God, even if we don't do what He wants us to do. And to remind us that He is always with us, He gave us nature, and the beautiful creatures serve as a reminder of

His loving-kindness. When we hurt God's creatures, we hurt God."

I wondered if my words had fallen on deaf ears, but there seemed to be sincerity in his "OK, Mommy" response. Some time after that we acquired a large herd of dairy goats. Dairy goats require a lot of care and attention, so this became a family project. Each family member shared in the responsibility of caring for and feeding the animals. My son carried out his duties willingly, but without much discussion. Later on that year we experienced our first kidding season. It was then that I knew God had revealed to my son the greatness of His love through nature.

When my son saw the first kid being born, he doubled over in speechless astonishment. As the wobbly, wet kid rose to his feet, my son let out a loud "Wow!" His face shone with amazed wonder. From that day he was transformed from the hunter to a good shepherd.

Just as the reality of birth caused a boy to see the value of life, rebirth as a Christian points us to the nature of a loving and remarkable God. SONIA PAUL

JULY 23

God's Forgiveness Is Complete

Wherefore I say unto thee, Her sins, which are many, are forgiven. Luke 7:47.

*M*ary of Bethany invited ridicule when she washed Jesus' feet at a Pharisee's dinner party. Her presence there was loathsome enough, but touching the Master was the limit! Having experienced the Father's forgiveness, however, she could place her love for Him above her reputation.

There is much to learn from Mary. She refused to allow Satan to tempt her into believing that her sins were too heinous for God to pardon. She "loved much" because she was forgiven much. The party's host, Simon the Pharisee, did not fully understand God's promises of forgiveness and cleansing. In our human relations we tend to offer forgiveness based on degree. As such, God's vindication appears too simple—too simple to exonerate the drug user, prostitute, or cheat. The good news is that God's forgiveness is complete!

Each believer can rest in the knowledge that "if we confess our sins, he is faithful and just and will forgive us our sins and purify us from all unrighteousness" (1 John 1:9, NIV). Only if our hearts become obdurate and we spurn the influence of the Holy Spirit will God withhold forgiveness (Matt. 12:31). However, when God's Spirit leads us to repentance, our Judge and Advocate forgives and treats us as if we had never done wrong.

In Isaiah 43:25 and Jeremiah 31:34 God promises to forget our sins. We can have a new beginning with Him. The challenge for us is to chew on His promises, digest them, and allow them to nourish our guilt-ridden souls. Only then can we enjoy the peace that accompanies God's absolution.   MARIA G. McCLEAN

Living Waters

If you are thirsty, come and drink water! If you don't have any money, come, eat what you want! Isa. 55:1, CEV.

*F*or weeks the heat had been oppressive. Farmers in our small corner of England complained that the lack of rain was affecting the crops; lawns degenerated into patches of brown, and trees showed signs of distress. Vegetable gardens yielded little or nothing, and soft fruits shriveled on the vine.

Occasionally dark clouds would cover the area, then quickly vanish before the onslaught of a pitiless sun, together with all hopes for refreshing showers. Fortunately, my husband had earlier installed two rain barrels in the garden to catch rain from the gutters. From these we watered our flowers and indoor plants. But now they were almost empty.

One Wednesday afternoon was even more sultry than usual, and occasional rumbles of thunder in the distance raised our hopes again. I even washed the windows, then the car, hoping to entice more moisture from the skies! Later that evening, on our way to prayer meeting, we were treated to a wonderful display of *son et lumiere*, as lightning flashed across the skies, accompanied by crashing thunder. The deluge began suddenly, turning dusty country roads into miniature lakes. Then it stopped as quickly as it had begun.

The following morning all the bathroom tap would yield was a tiny trickle of water. A call to the water company confirmed our worst fears: the entire village was without water. No reason was given, but it was assumed that lightning had damaged the equipment. We might be without water for hours.

We checked our water barrels. The five-minute miracle the previous evening had filled them both to overflowing, giving us plenty for our immediate use. In desperate need of some water, a neighbor peered over the fence.

"Help yourself to what's in our barrels," I told her.

"Oh, could I?" she gasped, gratefully accepting my offer. "I'll go get my bucket!"

Another neighbor appeared, needing water to wash up before going to work. I invited her to use the rain barrels. "There's enough for all of us," I said. I was so excited to help and wanted to rush down the street, calling everybody to help themselves to our water supply.

Now, imagine neighbors coming over and asking if we have the Living Water, of which Jesus said, "No one who drinks the water I give will ever be thirsty again. The water I give is like a flowing fountain that gives eternal life" (John 4:13, CEV).

Do our neighbors know we have a supply of Living Water and are willing to share it? Are we willing to lead them to the heavenly supply? Commit yourself to pray for your neighbors who are thirsting for the Living Water. One day they just might ask you for a drink.   EDNA MAY OLSEN

The Airport Samaritan

The King shall answer and say unto them, Verily I say unto you, Inasmuch as ye have done it unto one of the least of these my brethren, ye have done it unto me." Matt. 25:40.

*I*t was a muggy summer afternoon as Patricia, Denise, and I, returning from a conference in New Orleans, disembarked in Chicago. We desperately needed to make the final connection to the small airport close to home. Our previous flight had been delayed by more than two hours, but the steward suggested that if we hurried we might make that last connection. We opted for speed. We had to make this flight. One hour later would mean that we would miss that special Friday night vesper program in our church.

Rushing to the gate, we were appalled to hear "I'm sorry. The plane just took off. We couldn't wait, because there is a storm threatening in the area. We have no later flights, but there is another airline. They may have space on their next flight."

Intent on getting to my destination, I ignored the crowd of distraught people milling around and raced toward the terminal. Then I noticed something. Denise and Patricia were not with me. I would not leave without them. My eyes scanned the crowd. Finally I spotted them talking to someone. Resigned, I retraced my steps. They had been comforting a bedraggled teenage mother and her baby son, crawling fretfully nearby. Reaching the group, I heard part of her tearful tale. The young woman had never flown before and did not know how to handle this crisis. Her mother would be waiting pointlessly at the airport. Her boyfriend had no phone. She had very little money. Fatigue seemed to seep through her pores.

Without a moment's hesitation, Patricia came to the rescue. "We're going to find a way to that airport, be it plane, bus, or car. You can come with us."

The sun came out in the young woman's blue eyes. She was now among friends. Her problems were solved. Leaving the baby with us, she went to freshen up. It didn't matter that the baby's diaper needed changing, or that his crawl on the well-trodden floor had left him grimy. Patricia picked up that precious bundle, cradled him on her lap, and sang to him. He smiled. Our hearts melted.

When the young mother returned, Patricia and Denise gathered up all her paraphernalia—baby carriage, car seat, tote bags—and trudged through miles of airport corridor to our new destination.

Following behind the tired but goal-directed little group, I could not help marveling at the turn of events. Pharisee-like, I had been rushing to go to a religious service, while my friends paused to live that religion, to reach out and help their neighbor.

I don't know if that young woman still remembers my friends' intentional act of loving kindness. I suspect she does. What I do know is that what they did for my "sister" made a difference in my life.   GLENDA-MAE GREENE

JULY 26

Superwoman

The poor you have with you always, but Me you do not have always. John 12:8, NKJV.

*I*t was one of those days; you know the kind. My 3-year-old daughter, Lauren, had just uprooted my lemon tree with her sand shovel and was standing in my kitchen covered from head to toe in potting soil. My 3-month-old daughter, Taylor, was letting me know in no uncertain terms that it was time for her to eat, and my dachshund, Kasey, was wildly barking at the man cutting my lawn out front. I needed a break!

Cradling Taylor in one arm, I pushed Kasey into the bedroom with my foot, and pulled the door closed with my free hand. (I sometimes wonder why God chose to give the octopus eight arms, while moms got only two!) Now, how could I bathe Lauren, nurse Taylor, and get my break all at the same time? That's when I heard the sprinklers go on out back. I grabbed my Bible and headed outside. While Lauren ran through the sprinklers, Taylor nursed, and I prayed.

Lord, it's been a busy, busy day. Yet somehow in the middle of all that's going on with raising two little girls, I sometimes get this overwhelming feel-

ing that I should be doing more—more for my church, more for my community. . . . Just plain more!

I picked up my Bible and opened it to the story of Mary pouring the perfume on Jesus' feet. Judas condemned Mary, saying the perfume could have been sold and the money used to help the poor. As much as I didn't like the idea of agreeing with Judas, I thought to myself, *He's right. That money could have been used to help the poor.* Then I read Jesus' reply: "The poor you will always have with you. . . . But you will not always have me" (Mark 14:7, NIV).

I stopped reading and looked up at Lauren running through the sprinkler. The sun was shining on her long brown hair, and her green eyes sparkled with excitement. She squealed and laughed as only a little girl can do. Could it be possible that this was the same little girl who only a short while ago was lying in my arms as Taylor did now? I gazed down at Taylor, now fast asleep, her chubby little body completely relaxed as her lips let out a contented sigh. Where was the tiny newborn we had proudly brought home from the hospital only three short months ago?

Yes, Lord, I can always find more to do, and it would be important, just as important as helping the poor of Jesus' day. But the fact is that my little girls will not always be with me. Help me to make the most out of the short time they are at home. Thank You, Lord, for the privilege of motherhood; even when it is one of those days!

STACEY KENNEDY

JULY 27

Hands of a Rescuer

They pierced My hands and My feet. Ps. 22:16, NKJV.

I read a story once about a little girl who was trapped in a fire-engulfed house. The neighbors all tried to save her as she cried from the upstairs window. When the onlookers found out that the fire company was not going to arrive in time, a stranger took a ladder, climbed up, and disappeared inside the house. He soon reappeared with the child, climbed down the ladder, and delivered her to the waiting crowd. Then he disappeared.

Later it was discovered that this child was an orphan with no surviving relatives to claim her. So the townspeople met to determine who would take care of her. Several volunteered, from a teacher to the richest man in town. During this meeting a man limped in. He held up his badly scarred hands. The little girl joyfully ran to him and hugged him, saying, "This is the man who rescued me!" The man's burned hands showed just how much he loved this little girl, and he was awarded custody of her.

My Rescuer came to search for me when this earth was at its darkest. He stretched out His hands to save me from the fires of hell. And those hands of His, as well as His feet, were scarred in the process. There is no doubt—He wants to adopt me, an orphan of sin, into His holy family and take me home.

When He comes, I will run to Him with joy and gladness, just as that little girl did. And I can say to Him, my wondrous Rescuer, "Amen! Blessing and glory and wisdom, thanksgiving and honor and power and might, be to our God forever and ever. Amen" (Rev. 7:12, NKJV). MARGUERITE THYGESON

JULY 28

Payback

You reap whatever you sow. Gal. 6:7, NRSV.

Recently our family celebrated my older sister's completion of requirements for a doctoral degree. And our younger sister has since begun completing the requirements for a Doctor of Philosophy degree as well. They do the classwork, and I, their middle sister, hold them up in prayer.

I thoroughly enjoy our weekly telephone exchanges that concern academic challenges. Often their perceptions of their progress cause panic to set in. As the semester becomes more intense, I ask God to pay them back for all their hard work and earnest efforts. Because He's faithful, and they are as well, my prayers are answered.

After the recent graduation, I couldn't resist writing a "payback" note to my sister's department chairperson. Since writing the note, I've been thinking about the law of "payback." "You reap whatever you sow." Is the attitude of revenge (payback for evil) learned or inherent? For example, when Elisha the prophet was called "bald head" by mischievous youngsters, note his response in 2 Kings 2:24. And to the contrary, are some people just "naturally" prone to do good to others? Perhaps there's a doctoral candidate out there who would like to accept the challenge of researching this thought-provoking topic.

As I was saying, I took it upon myself to write the note to Dr. Glen. Donna had mentioned him again and again. He had apparently been supportive throughout all her academic hurdles. I wanted to affirm his well-deserved kindness. What would I give that could express my sincere thanks? I could think of no monetary gift that would match the level of support he'd offered.

Aha! I thought. My "payback" would be my prayers. I would petition the God of the universe and request that all of this man's temporal and spiritual affairs be managed by an intelligence of God's own choosing. I'd ask for supernatural blessing of health and good familial and professional relations above all that he, Dr. Glen, could ask or think. My ultimate request was that God would "shine on him and give him peace."

"This is the confidence we have in approaching God" (1 John 5:14). I know God will "pay back" exactly as I've asked, for He is faithful.   LYNN MARIE DAVIS

JULY 29

God's Comfort

As one whom his mother comforts, So I will comfort you. Isa. 66:13, NKJV.

*M*y mother had suffered a malignant brain tumor. Her usual eloquence had been reduced to one-syllable words in sometimes garbled statements. After having experienced what seemed like a miraculous recovery, she slipped into a coma. My family and I lived 1,200 miles away. Yet God provided money from outside our limited budget for several trips west to be able to help and comfort my parents.

264

One Friday noon the clothes from the last trip were in the washer. Bread was in the oven, and dinner was bubbling on the stove when Daddy called to say, "Mama is gone."

"Oh, Daddy," I cried. "I still hoped for a miracle. We'll get there as soon as possible."

As we got into the car about midnight, I asked my husband if he had gotten some tapes for me to listen to when I took my turn driving. "Yes, yes," he answered. "Let's just get out of here." He drove several hours while the boys slept. There was no way to relax my mind or to court sleep. Finally he announced, "You'll have to drive for a while."

I fumbled in the dark for the tapes. To my surprise, my husband had brought tapes that I had searched for many times to no avail. They were a series from camp meeting that I had misplaced a year before while teaching. Each time I drove during that long night I listened to another tape. Nearing home, I was afraid I would break down in front of my dad, who we feared could have a fatal heart attack any time.

During the last sermon on the tapes the minister asked for testimonies from those who had a keen sense of the reality of the resurrection. Several spoke; then I was electrified to hear my mother's voice. She told of her thrill that my husband would be ordained to the ministry that weekend. She told how they had stopped at her parents' grave on the way to camp meeting to see the recently erected marker. She spoke of the joy that would be hers on the resurrection morning when an angel would bring her little sister to her mother's arms.

Tears streamed down my face. Hearing my mother's testimony was as consoling as if an angel had told me that I would see her again. God had hidden those tapes from me with the knowledge that my mother's voice had been recorded there, saving them for this precise moment. I drove on through the night with tears of grateful reassurance streaming down my face, treasuring this private, sacred moment. The Lord Himself had comforted me.

Friends, don't let anything keep you from being ready on the resurrection day when Jesus comes to reunite us once again with our loved ones.   FELICIA PHILLIPS

The Promise

Do not cast away your confidence, which has great reward. For you have need of endurance, so that after you have done the will of God, you may receive the promise. Heb. 10:35, 36, NKJV.

The church administrative offices where I work are located on a strip of highway nestled among the foothills of the Koolaus, a mountain range that divides the east and west sides of the island of Oahu. An early-morning ride along this strip of highway can be a very uplifting, albeit humbling, experience as one's eyes feast on the glories of nature in all its majestic splendor. Sun-dappled treetops in varying shades of green; dew-kissed flowers in riotous colors, unfurling their petals and fragrance to the warmth of the sun; and the cacophony of songbirds singing their hearts out in praise to their Maker bring me peace and tranquillity whenever anxious thoughts threaten to overwhelm me. It is here that I seek my Maker's promises whenever the world seems to start closing in on me.

I'd had a particularly busy day, one that had helped to keep my anxious thoughts at bay. But now, as things were beginning to wind down, I could feel once more the same anxious thoughts beginning to invade the calmness of my world. As I pondered the many things that contributed to my anxieties, I felt impressed to seek the Lord's promises. I had flashbacks of many answered prayers, and as I ran up the stairwell to seek the Lord in the solitude of prayer, I felt my troubled thoughts begin to dissipate.

In a quiet corner near a picture window that afforded me a beautiful view of the mountainside, I laid my burdens upon the Lord and claimed His promises once more. I also asked Him for a sign—a sign that would allow me to feel His presence and know that I was enveloped in His arms of love. In the stillness of the moment I opened my eyes to see not one but two of God's precious promises in the arch of a double rainbow, displaying all the vivid hues in a kaleidoscope of color that took my breath away. Somewhere in the background the beautiful strains of the song "Leaning on the Everlasting Arms" came through soft and clear. I knew I was not alone. Today there would be only one set of footprints in the sand, because the Lord was carrying me in His arms of love.   NORMA C. GALIZA

Oh, Dear, What to Wear?

After this I looked and there before me was a great multitude that no one could count, from every nation, tribe, people and language, standing before the throne and in front of the Lamb. They were wearing white robes and were holding palm branches in their hands. Rev. 7:9, NIV.

I'm sure you have heard the joke of how Eve turned to Adam and said, "I have nothing to wear!" Men love to joke about women and their clothes. And clothes are important to women. Our clothes tell much about us, and buying, washing, ironing, and mending clothes take up many hours of our time. And some women are more clothes-conscious than others.

We lived in Honolulu when Imelda Marcos was forced from her home and came to live in Hawaii. To show her new status, she made a point by wearing the same green dress to every function; it became a big joke in the local media. And of course there is Princess Di. Some wish they could dress like her.

But have you ever thought about how important clothes are in the Bible? When something pivotal happens in many Bible stories, there is a change of clothes. Adam and Eve are the first example. With sin came a change of clothes. The fact that Adam and Eve were naked seems to have been the first tangible evidence of the change sin had brought.

The story of Joseph is full of changes of clothes. His fancy coat that caused the problem with his brothers was taken from him, dipped in blood, and given to their father after Joseph was sold into slavery. Potiphar's wife took Joseph's coat when she accused him of assaulting her. When he left prison to go before the king, he changed his clothes. I imagine that one reason the brothers did not recognize Joseph was because of his royal Egyptian clothes. And when he revealed who he was and sent for his father, he sent along changes of clothes.

Esther changed her clothes to go before King Xerxes. And when Elijah's ministry was passed to Elisha, the exchange of the cloak symbolized the event. You will remember that when the prodigal son came home in tatters, his father placed his own robe around him to cover his shame.

When they took Jesus to trial, they dressed Him in a purple robe and mocked Him. That someone would gamble for Jesus' clothes was foretold in the Psalms, and they crucified Him with no clothes at all, the ultimate sign of humiliation. He was willing to die with no clothes that we might be clothed in robes of righteousness. Jesus has promised that when we get to heaven, He will provide a white robe for anyone who wants one, forever to replace the beautiful "clothes" that Adam and Eve lost.

As you prepare for the day ahead, what will you wear? Our earthly clothes are important, but the robe Jesus offers you and me is the most important item of dress we can consider this day.

ARDIS DICK STENBAKKEN

AUGUST 1

Providential Circumstances

You are the God who performs miracles. Ps. 77:14, NIV.

It had been a particularly difficult move to a new location. Two days after our arrival, I was thankful for my husband's suggestion to leave packing boxes and go with him to tour our new surroundings. As we drove into the nearest town, a billboard attracted our attention. A gigantic sign instructed us to "call 911."

"Good thing to know," I mused. As we drove along, I practiced our address aloud over and over—the house number had five digits, and the street name was also a number. I was sure I would never keep all those numbers straight!

Ten miles down the road we planned our next stop. However, we turned one street too soon and found ourselves at the emergency entrance of the hospital. *Well,* I thought, *there is 911, and I know where a hospital is located—not that I have ever used either.*

The rest of the afternoon seemed to be a maze of unknown roads and countryside.

The next day the main item on our agenda was hooking up the washer and dryer. While my husband worked in the laundry room, I tuned in the local Christian radio station. The music sounded as if it were on slow speed and groaning. When I turned off the radio, I realized the sound I was hearing was coming from the laundry room. As I walked in, I saw my husband on the floor with a gash on his head. His eyes were open, but fixed in a stare. He was barely breathing.

Suddenly the billboard flashed through my mind. *Call 911!* As the person asked our address, I was able to relay perfectly all those numbers. Once the ambulance arrived, it was decided that my husband needed to be transported to the hospital. As they attempted to lift him into the ambulance, the two female EMTs realized his weight was more than they could lift. Fortunately, a man driving by in a truck stopped and offered to help.

"Just follow us!" they shouted, speeding away, leaving me in their dust.

As I got into my car, I knew exactly which way to turn onto the highway, what road to take, and where to find the hospital's emergency entrance. I never saw the ambulance ahead of me.

After anxious hours, my husband was released. Days later we learned he had received an electrical shock from the washer plug. As it was a small community in which everyone knew everyone, I tried to find out who the man was who had helped the EMTs. No one had ever seen anyone of that description or that type of truck in the area. Did all the previous day's events just happen? Surely there is a God who does perform miracles, a God who sends His angels in time of need.
LAURA HARTMANN

Needing to Belong

He gives the lonely a home to live in and sets the prisoners free. But the rebellious remain lonely and stay imprisoned within themselves. Ps. 68:6, Clear Word.

My heart skipped a beat as I heard the familiar voice on the other end of the telephone. "It's over," Jan said. "We won!" Emotions surged and tears flooded my eyes as the caseworker explained that the judicial decision that would determine the destiny of our two foster daughters had at last been issued. The appellate court hearing had been held two weeks before, and the prayers of God's people throughout the United States had ascended to heaven on behalf of two teenage girls with an uncertain future. Jan had told us it could be as many as three months before the decision would be rendered, but in His mercy God had given it to us in 14 days. We had won! Praise God, we had won!

These delightful young women would now remain in a Christian family, pursue a Christian education, live in safety, and become my daughters—adopted by my husband and me.

Immediately the girls wanted to call those who had been a part of the prayer chain and tell them the good news. The first call enthusiastically went to their former caseworker, who had worked for three years on their behalf. As I slipped away to give them privacy, I heard our 13-year-old share, "Now I'm finally going to belong to somebody!"

In the still of the night I lay still and contemplated her words. How could I, one who had always been loved and cherished, understand the soul's aching need to belong? How could I come close to comprehending my daughter's pain and grasping the significance of a wistfully hoped-for future?

Then I remembered that I hadn't always belonged. My Father adopted me, too. I was lost, scared, and confused. In mercy He enshrouded me with love. He gave me knowledge so I could grow. He taught me how to trust and helped me to feel safe within His family. My Father worked tirelessly to undo the damage caused by sin's abuse, and then He claimed me as one of His own.

We won, Lord! We *all* won!

JOAN BOVA

Sing a Song, Take a Bath

Let us draw near with a true heart in full assurance of faith, having our hearts sprinkled from an evil conscience and our bodies washed with pure water. Heb. 10:22, NKJV.

He was barely 2 years old, but he had been carefully taught to be quiet during church services. Could I, his mother, expect him not to be excited and full of questions as he witnessed his first baptism by immersion? No, I couldn't. However, the questions failed to come. He watched intently as several individuals were baptized. After each baptism the congregation sang hymns. I decided he must be too young to attach any particular importance to the service. I should have known better!

It was not until the drive home that he reached over and turned my face toward his (to be certain he had my full attention) and solemnly said, "Mom, sing a song, take a bath, sing a song, take a bath."

I wondered if my baby had a better grasp on the baptismal ceremony than many adults. While he could not understand all the ramifications of the service, he did seem to understand, to some degree, that the candidates had been cleansed.

From time to time we allow Satan to make us feel guilty over sins that have long ago been washed away—permanently. May we remember that we "sang a song and took a bath." We have been forgiven and cleansed from all unrighteousness (1 John 1:9). Praise God!   DOROTHY WAINWRIGHT CAREY

Your Creator Will Be Your Husband

Your Creator will be your "husband." The Lord Almighty is his name; he is your Redeemer, the Holy One of Israel, the God of all the earth. Isa. 54:5, TLB.

*S*ell our little "Pine Perch" that my husband and I built ourselves in the Ozarks? The house was surrounded by trees—pines, dogwood, and red bud. And I mustn't forget the handsome wildlife specimens—cardinals, pileated woodpeckers, a nest of scarlet tanagers.

No, I didn't want to sell, but after my husband died suddenly, I was soon many thousands of miles away, teaching theology students English at Northeast Brazil College. The people who were staying in our Ozark home often did not keep up our little refuge. I'd have to sell it. "Dear God," I prayed, "You promised to be my husband. Please sell our place at the right time, with the right terms and price, and to the right people!"

A realtor, a member in the church we'd built at the county seat, agreed to arrange for the sale. I wrote asking him to advertise in the weekly county paper. My son and son-in-law would have only one week to help me sell my household things, pack up, and bid it all goodbye.

When I arrived at my son's home in the United States, I called the real estate agent to see that my request had been handled. He had done nothing! I urged him to attend to it immediately, as we would be arriving the next week to sell and move. As we drove to the entrance of my property, the agent was just driving up. He had not yet advertised the sale. He suggested I take advantage of a free advertising opportunity on the radio.

Several people came. Some bought household goods. Some wanted to buy the property, but had no cash. Soon the week passed, but still the place hadn't sold. We had to leave and were just doing the last loading when a car drove up. Another agent had been looking over the place and asked me a few questions about the property. When he asked for my lowest figure, I reduced it by the amount of the commission. We agreed to handle the deed and his check through the bank by mail, since we couldn't do business on Sunday. After about an hour's delay we were on our way. We reached eastern Arkansas just after a tornado had passed through the town where we stopped to get gas.

Not only had the property been sold, but the delay had prevented us from experiencing the tornado. Truly my Creator was my husband. He answered my prayer to sell my home at the right time, for the right amount and terms, and to the right person. Praise the Lord! He is faithful! — PHYLLIS MACLAFFERTY

AUGUST 5

Loneliness, a New Disease

A merry heart doeth good like a medicine. Prov. 17:22.

We were shocked as we watched the local evening news that ran a story from one of the nearby suburbs. The police had found a 73-year-old woman dead in her house. The horrifying fact was that she had been dead for *four years*, and no one had missed her! The neighbors all had excuses. They hadn't seen her around and thought she must be in the hospital.

"Yes, I cut her lawn when I did mine, and that was not a problem," said the man next door. He added, "No, I never talked to her; she didn't seem to want to talk to anyone."

Although her two brothers lived across town, there had been some sort of family falling out.

This story is hard to believe, but the cold facts were given to us. Do we know our neighbors? Do we wave and smile or make some sort of contact? Would you miss your neighbor if something happened to him or her? Sadder yet would be if they wouldn't miss us. This is a world of busy people and fractured families, and probably many of us think we have time to do only our important duties.

A few years ago my friend Sarah was dying of cancer, and her family stayed with her at the hospital around the clock. They asked if I could take an evening, and I answered, "Gladly." But it was with trepidation that I went into her room, where the lights were dim. I kept her comfortable and knew, somehow, that she sensed it was I. The important thing was she did not want to be alone at this time. She died with her family present a couple nights later. I will never forget that darkened room in which Sarah was so sick. Inside me also gnaws the thought, *I don't want to die alone.*

I don't want to live alone, either. I want a smile from the clerk and a hello from the neighbor, and I want to return those greetings. I want to do whatever I can to make this world a place of friendliness and sunshine.   DESSA WEISZ HARDIN

AUGUST 6

This Plane Ain't Goin' Nowhere!

We can make our plans, but the final outcome is in God's hands. Prov. 16:1, TLB.

*F*astening my seat belt on the DC-10, I hummed a few bars of "When It's Springtime in the Rockies." My husband and I were headed for a four-day conference in Aspen, Colorado, and I was giddy with anticipation. In addition to meetings, outings were planned for white-water rafting, back-country hiking, and a Jeep ride to abandoned gold mines.

The various thumps and bumps of preflight testing were in process. Out the window I could see the last of the baggage being loaded and the fuel truck backing away from the plane. Lights went off and on in the cabin, then off again. Soon the pilot's soothing voice informed us the electrical system wasn't performing optimally, but that the mechanics were working on it. No problem. We wouldn't have too late a start.

A half hour went by, and the pilot came on with the disquieting word that the electrical system seemed to be OK for a while, then it would short out again. He'd get back to us after more fine-tuning had been done. A man two seats over got up with his briefcase, told the flight attendant he didn't feel good about this plane, and exited.

After we'd been on the plane for an hour and a half, we got the news that a switch was being replaced and would then need to be tested, entailing another hour's delay. We were free to deboard with our ticket stubs. I sent up a prayer for a positive outcome as we filed out of the stuffy plane into the cooler terminal amid exasperated grumbling. Some folk queued up at the counter to check on other flights to Denver. We sat down for the wait. What a great arena for people-watching!

A teenage boy returned from the McDonald's concession with a fragrant brown bag and happily sat inhaling French fries, two cheeseburgers, a large Coke, and a soft pretzel. An elderly man lay down across three seats and fell fast asleep. Readers pulled best-sellers and magazines out of hand luggage, and a mother of twin toddlers chased them up and down the aisle. A well-dressed woman with a distinctive Cajun accent intoned loudly, "This plane ain't goin' nowhere," as she wheeled her designer luggage down to the shuttle bus area. Business heads bristled with cellular phones, canceling appointments and making arrangements for a late arrival.

Another hour went by with several status updates—still checking. Finally, after five hours in the airport, we were told Flight 501 would not be taking off that night. A wave of relief washed over me. Who would really want to be 29,000 feet over Kansas City and have the electrical system turn off? True, the key meeting my husband needed to attend was at 8:00 a.m. the next day, and he was not going to make it. We might as well stay home now. We'd gambled on the plane's being fixed in time and had lost. On the other hand, we had a "gift" of four unscheduled days handed to us. Retrieving our carry-on luggage, we headed to the parking lot.

In five hours of close proximity to scores of strangers, we'd viewed a myriad of reactions to stress. Some angrily blamed the airline for the delay. Others slept through it, engaged in a quiet pursuit, or chatted with seatmates. Creative persistence marked those who tried to find other flights or handled their business by phone. Seasoned travelers philosophically accepted this as part of air travel.

This slice of life highlighted the wisdom of making plans and checking our options, then placing them in God's hands and accepting the outcome. CAROLE BRECKENRIDGE

A Little More to the Left!

Trust in the Lord with all your heart and lean not on your own understanding; in all your ways acknowledge him, and he will make your paths straight. Prov. 3:5, 6, NIV.

We've all had times when we just weren't getting through to someone, whether it was our children, a salesperson, or our spouse. I like to think I am a good communicator, but my husband wouldn't have agreed one particular Friday afternoon last summer.

We had recently purchased a tent trailer and were taking it on our first weekend outing. We chose a campground at nearby Mount Hood, but we got a late start and arrived just before sundown. We were all eager to get camp set up, but first things first! By default, I jumped out to direct my husband in backing the trailer into the space. He rolled down the window to receive my instructions and started to back up.

Now, if you have never backed up a trailer, you have missed out on one of the biggest challenges a human (or the spouse) can endure! I had done it, so of course I knew just what my husband needed to do! But he was doing just the opposite of what I was telling him, and the trailer was simply not ending up where we both wanted it. Eventually our new campground neighbors became aware that our tailer wasn't cooperating and that we were not happy with each other.

Finally my husband called me over in desperation and explained that he didn't know if my pointing one way meant I wanted him to turn the steering wheel that way, or if I expected the trailer to go that way. Well, once we cleared up *that* little detail it was amazing how quickly the trailer was in place! I think I even heard a silent cheer go up from our neighbors.

Sometimes we know that our communication with God isn't real clear and our lives just aren't lining up right. That's when we need to call a time-out and ask God what He means for us to do. There may be no question Who we want giving the directions in our lives; we just need to ask for clarification now and then and listen more closely for His directions.   PATTY KNITTEL

The God of Elijah

If you believe, you will receive whatever you ask for in prayer.
Matt. 21:22, NIV.

Bagdal is a village in Karnataka, India. The people are simple, uneducated farmers. They depend on monsoon rain for cultivation. Unfortunately, the monsoon failed for three consecutive years. Famine struck, and the people became desperate.

One morning a preacher visited the village and presented a sermon. In his message he pointed out that Elijah had prayed earnestly for rain and that God answered his sincere prayer. This Bible story moved the heart of the children and the youth. After the meeting they met together and decided to pray for rain.

That afternoon the young people, ranging in age from 6 to 20, went to a hill nearby to plead with God on their knees. They were going to remain there with closed eyes until He answered them. The sun sank in the west and darkness set in. There was no sign of hope, but no sign of giving up, either. The young people continued their pleas. At about 8:30 p.m. they felt raindrops. In a few minutes the heavens let loose with a torrential downpour. Their plea turned to glee. Their petitions turned to words of gratitude.

With clothes drenched and hearts thankful, they returned to the village praising God. The parents and villagers welcomed them with joy, their faith in the God of Elijah strengthened. "The Lord heard Elijah's cry" (1 Kings 17:22, NIV). Be assured that the same God will hear your cry as well.   HEPZIBAH KORE

Going Home

> I go to prepare a place for you. And if I go and prepare a place for you, I will come again, and receive you unto myself; that where I am, there ye may be also. John 14:2, 3.

Our little plane took off at the first blush of morn. The cool, green mist of the early hour and the rising sun just beginning to shine across the city created a beautiful scene. The lakes sparkled as the cool water lapped the shores. Around the city more lakes spread out for miles. It was easy to see why Minneapolis is called the "City of Lakes." The morning haze indicated a hot, sticky, August day was in the making. It was good to enjoy the beauty of the early morning coolness.

Flying across the rural Minnesota countryside, I saw the roads crossing and crisscrossing, stitching an ever-changing intricate design like beautiful patchwork quilts. Sometimes it was a very orderly "block quilt," and other times a "crazy quilt." But always a panorama of soothing greens, with the blues of the lakes blending in. Here and there was a block of golden ripening grain, accented by the farm buildings with their white walls and dark-colored roofs.

At times the scene was veiled by low-floating clouds, fluffy and light, like wisps of cotton floating in the atmosphere. Little villages where families live and play and work and study were still asleep. The trees gave a perception of depth and even more shades of green, some in large patches, some just around the buildings and in the yards.

There I was, flying home—to my husband. His is the life of one who loves the land. He has fought the elements and won. He has been able to give our family a deep love and commitment to the land and our home. Going home! How wonderful!

My thoughts now turned to that great homeward trip yet to come. How wonderful it will be to meet my Saviour! To bask in His love and enjoy the home He has prepared for us will be the best! Come soon, Lord Jesus.

EVELYN GLASS

The Peace of God

The peace of God, which transcends all understanding, will guard your hearts and your minds in Christ Jesus. Phil. 4:7, NIV.

As I write, Australia's ex-service personnel and many others are celebrating the fiftieth anniversary of VP Day—Victory in the Pacific, the end of World War II. The beginning of peace, or so it was hoped. An unfounded hope, as it has turned out. But of course the absence of war is in itself no guarantee of peace. One's peace may be threatened by many things apart from war, such as escalating crime and violence, illness, work pressures, and conflict in the home or even in the church.

It took me some time to realize, however, that looking for peace is not the way to find it, that real peace does not depend on the existence of a favorable set of circumstances. Real peace is a gift. Said Jesus, "Peace I leave with you; my peace I give you. I do not give to you as the world gives. Do not let your hearts be troubled and do not be afraid" (John 14:27, NIV).

Such not-of-this-world peace is the only explanation for the tranquillity of mind that could allow Christ to sleep in a storm-tossed boat (Mark 4:38), or Peter to sleep in prison on the eve of his trial and probable execution (Acts 12:6), or Paul and Silas to sing while bound in the stocks (Acts 16:24, 25).

As I look out on an anguished, strife-torn world, even from the comparative safety of a country like Australia, I find it easy to be filled with dread. There is so much war and hatred. So much suffering. But how precious it is to be able to grasp Christ's promise. "I have told you these things, so that in me you may have peace. In this world you will have trouble. But take heart! I have overcome the world" (John 16:33, NIV).

JENNIFER M. BALDWIN

August 11

The Angel's Surprise

You have put gladness in my heart. Ps. 4:7, NKJV.

*Y*ou'll be leaving Thailand in about a week. Let's get up early Sunday and have one more morning of birding at Khao Yai National Park," our friends suggested.

"Great idea!" I said. "Takes an hour to get there, and we could be out in the jungle with our binoculars just as it gets light. Maybe we could add several new species to our life list."

So a van load of us faculty member nature lovers left Mission College long before dawn. We spent a delightful morning in the cool mountains, listening to the birdsongs, finding old bird friends from previous birding trips, and spotting several we had never seen before. By midmorning the temperature began to rise and the birds became less active.

"Time to head back to the college," our driver announced. "Guess the birds and wild animals here in the park are resting in the shade. The van's air conditioner would feel pretty good right now."

Driving slowly on the curving mountain roads, we saw several signs pointing to elephant salt licks, each littered with fresh elephant droppings. At another curve we were surprised to see a sign in English: "Beware, elephant crossing!"

"That must be to impress the tourists," my husband commented.

"Since we'll probably never be in Thailand again, wouldn't it be great to see at least one elephant on our last visit to Khao Yai?" I commented.

Moments later the car ahead stopped quickly and motioned for us to stop. And then it happened. . . . From the dense jungle a huge trunk appeared on the roadside, then another, and another. We grabbed our cameras and watched breathlessly. A mother elephant, followed by her baby, stopped. She looked at the two cars, flapped her ears, held out her trunk, and trumpeted loudly, as if to say, "Don't come near my baby or you'll be sorry!"

The herd (we counted 12) seemed in no hurry to cross the road. Several stopped to eat by the roadside. For several exciting minutes we watched them before they disappeared into the jungle on the other side of the road. Listening, we could hear them

280

breaking down shrubs and trees as they cleared a path and ate their fill.

You know what I think? I think God wanted to give us a surprise farewell gift, so He sent His angels to guide that herd to that very spot, at that very time, just so we could have the thrill of seeing those magnificent animals. Like a loving Father, He delights in making His children happy. I am sure that God is smiling at the joy and gladness He has put into our hearts, and that He is waiting for you today. — EILEEN LANTRY

AUGUST 12

Lord, Send Me

So then, men ought to regard us as servants of Christ and as those entrusted with the secret things of God. 1 Cor. 4:1, NIV.

As I sat cradling the little boy in my arms during church service today, I was reminded that when Jesus calls us to do a duty, He doesn't ask for our résumé or past job experience to justify doing His duty. He just puts a duty before us and expects us to follow through with it.

About two weeks ago my phone rang. I was asked by the church choir director if a deaconess could be present in the mothers' room during church service; a little boy was disrupting everyone there. My immediate thought was Where is the mother or father? The next day the pastor called to ask the same thing. After hanging up, I asked myself, Why me? I have no experience with little children; I don't even have any of my own. So I talked to a friend who is a grandmother, and we agreed that it wasn't up to deaconesses to monitor someone else's children. But I told the pastor I'd give it some thought and see if someone might be willing.

I pondered the problem, and at the next church service I went into the mothers' room to check on the situation. The little boy was there, being disruptive just as they had said he was. The man who brought him to church wasn't even his father, I learned. But when the little guy came near me, I talked to him and in a few minutes got him to sit on my lap. In almost no time he was fast asleep. Who doesn't love a sleeping child?

It happened again today. There he was, saying loud "Hallelujahs" and not wanting to be quiet. But who wants to silence a 3-year-old child who is praising God? He warded off my good intentions by sitting in the wooden rocking chair and repulsing every overture I made toward him. Finally, when he left the rocking chair, I sat down in it, and the next time he went by I just picked him up, put him on my lap, and started singing "Jesus Loves Me" very quietly to him. He stared back at me. After about 10 verses he fell asleep again.

Who says Jesus needs experienced people to do His will? Or people who can sing on key? Or who are experts at handling children? I don't know how long my luck will hold out, but Jesus, if You want me to do something, tell me, and with Your help I'll do it. You know my capabilities and will not give me more than I can bear.   GWEN LEE

AUGUST 13

Left at Church

Be on guard! Be alert! You do not know when that time will come. Mark 13:33, NIV.

The year was 1971. My husband was going to college full-time, and we were the church custodians. We had two little boys of our own, a 1-year-old and a 3-year-old, and four foster children, ranging in age from 19 months to 4 years of age.

Every Thursday was church cleaning day. We would pack our van with a picnic lunch, diapers, toys, blankets, and changes of clothes for the children, and spend the day at the church. I would clean the sections of the church that were closest to the nursery so I could keep an eye on the children as they played and took their two naps. My husband cleaned the church annex and the rest of the church building. The last room we would clean was the nursery.

Since we had so many little children, we developed a system

of counting them every time we loaded them into the van to be sure they were all there. The older children would help with the seat belts for the younger ones.

One Thursday as we were finishing packing things up to go home, one of our foster boys, 4-year-old Charlie, was sitting behind the nursery room door putting his sneakers on and tying them. I called to the children to be sure they were all getting in the van before locking the nursery door on my way out of the church. Once we were all in the van we said a prayer, asking God to send His angels to keep us safe as we traveled home. After traveling one block, I realized we had not counted the children yet. I called over my shoulder to the children to start counting. "One, two, three, four, five . . . I quickly turned and counted for myself. Charlie was missing!

My mind and heart raced as we turned around and retraced the mile we had traveled. Was Charlie safe? Was he walking down the road, crying? Had someone picked him up? We scanned each yard as we passed by to see if Charlie was there. When we got to the church, I remembered seeing him behind the door in the nursery. I ran to the nursery, calling his name. He looked up and smiled. He had finally gotten his shoes tied! He had been so preoccupied with his shoes that he hadn't even realized he had been left behind! I was so happy and relieved to see him that I scooped him up and held him close as I cried, thanking the Lord.

As I recall the incident, I think of how Satan tries to keep us so wrapped up in our own projects, however good they may be, that we don't even realize that we have shut Jesus out from a close, personal relationship with us.

I pray that we will each have an intimate relationship with Jesus and be ready for the trip to our heavenly home.

CELIA MEJIA CRUZ

Voles!

Catch for us the foxes, the little foxes that ruin the vineyards, our vineyards that are in bloom. S. of Sol. 2:15, NIV.

A year ago I didn't know how much pleasure I would get out of my garden. I had never really had a garden of my own to putter around in. And so when I started landscaping our garden, trying to transform a big mound of earth sprouting all kinds of weeds into a little paradise on earth, I was entering new territory.

The lawn started growing quite nicely, and I planted bushes and flowers. What a difference it made! And then one morning as I looked at my lawn to assess its progress, I saw two long earth mounds crisscrossing my new lawn! My husband thought that must be the work of a vole. I remembered that the vole does not like strong smells, so I stuffed garlic in the burrows and closed the holes. The next morning the entrances were once more open and the garlic had been thrown out! Well, why not try a bit more garlic? But after a few days I got tired of this game.

We went to a shop and asked what we could do to get rid of our voles. The salesclerk asked us if we wanted to kill them or just chase them off our property. We decided not to kill them. Our kids would not have liked that. So we got a tin of a foul-smelling granulate that would develop gas when put in the burrows. Every time I found an open burrow I would put in a spoonful of the granulate and close the hole. But after a while I realized it would have been better to kill them after all. There were holes around all my bushes, and I could just imagine the voles feasting on the roots of my precious plants!

In the fall I found out about *Fritillaria imperialis*. This beautiful flower has a bulb with a smell voles can't stand. I planted a couple of these bulbs and hoped for the best. Whether it was the cold winter or these flowers, I haven't seen any signs of voles this year.

My battle against the voles taught me that if I don't pay immediate and energetic attention to little things, little sins, they will become so much more difficult to get rid of. It's like small, harmless-looking habits that will grow and multiply until the struggle against them becomes almost overpowering. I was helpless until I found the natural antidote, God's provision against voles in the flower He had created. God has power to help us in our battle with sin, too, if we ask Him to do so.

HANNELE OTTSCHOFSKI

AUGUST 15

"Oops! Goofed Again!"

When he, the Spirit of Truth, is come, he will guide you into all truth. John 16:13.

*O*uch! You'd think after all the times I've stuck my feet in my mouth I'd be as nimble as an Olympic gold medalist. Unfortunately, my spirit muscles hurt from the stretch.

A few years back I overheard two women who were around my age, discussing the possibility of returning to college to complete their degrees. The woman named Leanne told how her sister had so wanted to graduate with a degree in elementary education, but hadn't had the opportunity to do so.

Being an enthusiastic late college graduate, 10 years after the fact, I interrupted. "If your sister really wants to complete her degree she should check into the adult programs available at . . ." and proceeded to tell the two women about the terrific program at my alma mater. I rattled on, unaware of the horror growing in the women's eyes, until Leanne touched my sleeve. "My sister's dead. She died two years ago."

Oops! Talk about feeling embarrassed! I apologized profusely, but by the looks on their faces, I'm not sure they were listening.

Mistakes. We all make them. And we're not alone. Studies show that the average person makes one bad choice in every five. Remember, I said *average.* Sometimes I believe my average is higher than average. Like the time I slipped out of my high-heeled shoes to get into the driver's seat, drove to my next stop, then realized my shoes were still sitting in the bank's parking lot, 45 miles away. Or the time I inserted my library card into the ATM (they are the same color), then rushed inside the bank to complain that my card wouldn't work, only to be told that I was trying to use the wrong card. Or like the time I bought what I thought was a ready-made pumpkin pie for Thanksgiving dinner. When I removed it from the refrigerator to serve it, the raw pumpkin sloshed all over the counter, leaving nothing but a soggy pastry shell in the pan.

Recently I saw an advertisement for a book entitled *How to Do Everything Right.* I thought, *That's what I need.* Then I remembered I already had a Book in my library that contains all the answers to living—the Holy Bible. When it comes to the important choices, ones that will impact my eternity, I don't want to make even one mistake. That's why I turn to the Book that not only contains the answers to my questions but also tells me how to be forgiven when I mess up anyway. My salvation is too important; eternity is too near. My wisest choice is to leave nothing to chance. I depend on God's Word, through the power of the Holy Spirit, to lead me into all truth. KAY D. RIZZO

AUGUST 16

The Flat That Foiled a Fire

In every thing give thanks: for this is the will of God in Christ Jesus concerning you. 1 Thess. 5:18.

*O*ur remodeling project was almost done! For two years my husband and I had worked on remodeling our kitchen and adding a family room to our century-old house. Every day we came home from our full-time jobs and sanded, painted, cleaned, and did all the things we expected to do—and many we didn't. We also tried to give quality time to our four children. The stress had taken its toll on our marriage and my health.

For about a year I had been suffering from migraine headaches. When I was finally referred to a neurologist for help, it took almost a month to get an appointment. I looked forward to my appointment and to the relief that I hoped the doctor would give me. I wondered if it could possibly be stress. My marriage was at an all-time low, I was depressed, and at times I wondered if I could make it through another day.

August 16 finally arrived. I rose early to get the kids fed and dressed. With my 7-year-old helping, we had just enough time to tidy up the kitchen before we left. I couldn't help looking at the kitchen and admiring the work my husband and I had done. The custom-made cherry cupboards were gorgeous. Home-canned fruit lined the top of the cupboards, adding to the country atmosphere. It looked and felt homey.

"Well, girls, let's get in the van, and don't forget to buckle your seat belts." The girls obeyed immediately. They loved to go to town. As we approached the van my heart fell to my feet. The tire was flat! I was shocked, because I had just driven the car the night before, and it was fine then. I had never had any indication that the tire was faulty. I indulged in self-pity and wondered what else could go wrong. The girls went out to play on the swing set, and I went back into the house. As I was going in, the text in 1 Thessalonians 5:18 came to my mind. "In all things give thanks." I am ashamed to admit that I said aloud in a rather sarcastic tone, "Yeah, thanks for the flat tire!"

I was sitting at the end of the counter feeling sorry for myself, looking straight ahead at the appliance garage. It appeared to have something very sticky all over it. I got up and wondered what the kids had gotten all over the cupboards this time. When I ran my hand across the mess, it felt hot. I opened the door and discovered that the toaster had been on when it was put away. It had malfunctioned and didn't turn off. My electric can opener had melted, and the sticky-looking stuff on the cupboards was the finish bubbling up. If I had gone to my doctor's appointment, my house would have burned down.

Then I truly did give thanks for my flat tire! I asked for forgiveness for not trusting and for being sarcastic when the Lord gently brought the text to my mind. I learned a valuable lesson that day. I play this story over and over in my mind and marvel at how good the Lord is. He demonstrated His love for me in a way I will never forget.

Oh, and by the way, after I put air in the tire it never went flat again.

SUSAN BERRIDGE

AUGUST 17

Of Palaces and Preparations

I saw the Holy City, the new Jerusalem, coming down out of
heaven from God, prepared as a bride beautifully dressed for her
husband. . . . It shone with the glory of God, and its brilliance
was like that of a very precious jewel, like a jasper, clear as crystal. Rev. 21:2-11, NIV.

*W*e ran down the gangplank, catching the last boat out
to the island. Then we had to almost run the mile to the
palace, getting there just as the last tour was ready to disappear
through the giant doors. When we handed our tickets to the
guide, she informed us that our tickets were only for the boat and
did not include the palace, as we had thought. After all the effort
to get there, Linda and I were not about to miss going through
Herrenchiemsee, the Bavarian palace built by King Ludwig II. So
we paid the extra 14 marks and joined the tour. We knew by then
that the tour guide would be speaking German, but at least we
would be able to see the interior, even if we weren't always sure
just how the room was used or any details on the execution of the
architecture or the decor.

Herrenchiemsee was built on the same plan as Versailles in
France, but perhaps even more elaborate. The opulence was astounding. The marble grand staircase, the heavy brocade drapery,
the hand-woven upholstery, the painted and even three-dimen-
sional ceilings, the carving, the inlaid parquet floors—there was
too much to comprehend. We stood looking into a room almost
entirely furnished and decorated with Meissen china, from the
chandelier to the table, from the fruit and bowl to the fireplace
mantel. What wasn't priceless china was carved and gilded.

Linda shuddered, "This would drive me crazy!"

I quickly assured her that if she lived there she would not
have to do the dusting, but she explained that it was just too or-
nate, too gaudy. She would feel overwhelmed. Later, as we made
our way back to the boat, we discussed what we had seen. I remarked, "Just think what heaven will be like with all the gold and
jewels." I could immediately see the look of horror on Linda's
face, so I continued quickly, "Of course, with a much better dec-
orator with superior taste!"

Let your imagination soar. The things God has planned for us will be exquisite beyond belief, and planned just for our personal comfort. Although building Herrenchiemsee drained the royal coffers, Ludwig II lived in his incredible palace for only one week. We will enjoy heaven for eternity. What a heritage, what an inheritance, as daughters of a king! "They will build houses and dwell in them; they will plant vineyards and eat their fruit. No longer will they build houses and others live in them, or plant and others eat" (Isa. 65:21, 22, NIV). For someone who has been moving every couple years during her entire life, that is an incredible promise!

Thinking about heaven makes me think about preparations. I certainly do not want the stress of running up to the pearly gate, hoping I can slip through the crack at the tail end of time like I did at Herrenchiemsee! Prior planning and preparation certainly would add to the pleasure of the trip! The promises of the Bible are for now, as well as the future. I want to enjoy both.

ARDIS DICK STENBAKKEN

AUGUST 18

God's Gems

Many, O Lord my God, are thy wonderful works which thou hast done, and thy thoughts which are to us-ward: they cannot be reckoned up in order unto thee: if I would declare and speak of them, they are more than can be numbered. Ps. 40:5.

Many years ago I woke up feeling really down in the dumps, for no apparent reason. I just could not seem to shake that depressive mood; however, I forced myself to crawl out of bed. I thought I should at least make an effort to attend church, whether I felt like it or not.

As I moped around the house, making sure each of my four daughters was dressed, my 11-year-old stopped me near the stairs. "Mama, you gotta see this!"

What now? I groaned in silent objection at the thought of her usual childish games. "Not now, Dana," I answered.

"Ah, Ma, c'mon," she coaxed, taking my hand.

Teeth clenched behind tightened lips, I followed her to the door and stopped, spellbound. On the porch, tiny raindrops clung to the roof. As they caught bits of sun, they each shot streams of light, shimmering like delicate jewels—emeralds, pearls, and rubies. The dark cold that had surrounded me lifted, leaving warm joy in its place. I smiled, thankful for my special gift.

I know now as I did then, God has many wondrous ways to lift our spirits and make us aware of His love for us. Without a doubt, I am rich in the broadest sense. You see, I will never forget the morning God gave me gems on my front porch.

ETHEL FOOTMAN SMOTHERS

AUGUST 19

Living Water

But whosoever drinketh of the water that I shall give him shall never thirst; but the water that I shall give him shall be in him a well of water springing up into everlasting life. John 4:14.

Recently I had the privilege of touring Egypt and the Arab Emirate of Dubai. My first glimpse of the desert from the window of the plane was mind-boggling. This vast expanse of barren wasteland with rolling sand dunes seemed endless. Then suddenly, in the middle of nowhere, would be a spot of green—an oasis with visible signs of life.

While the plane afforded a panoramic view of the desert, it was cruising down the Nile for four days that gave us a close-up view of life in the desert. As far as the waters of the Nile reached and could be carried by irrigation, the fields abounded with life: majestic coconut and date palms, lush fields of grain, fruit trees, and animals. Where the supply of water ended abruptly, the desert began again and stretched out as far as the eye could see.

In the wealthy state of Dubai—the shopper's paradise, where gold, fuel, and electronic goods are cheap—the most sought after and expensive commodity is water. While we were there, they were experiencing freak weather in the form of seven days of continuous rain, something unheard of in the desert. With the absence of drains and gutters, the streets became rivers. It was obvious the residents were having a field day!

How much we take water for granted, and how all life is dependent on it. My thoughts turned to the water of life. Our spiritual lives are barren and sterile, like the desert, until we drink of that living water. Jeremiah 17:7 and 8 reminds us: "Blessed is the man that trusteth in the Lord, and whose hope the Lord is. For he shall be as a tree planted by the waters, and that spreadeth out her roots by the river, and shall not see when heat cometh, but her leaf shall be green."

The water of life has such far-reaching effects, for not only does it make us strong spiritually, but our fruitfulness and productivity enable us to reach out and witness to others. It is a sobering thought that millions of precious souls do not know about the water of life, nor do they know its Source. We must lead them to it. There are not many things in life that are free. Let's tell them about the living water, freely available to all. Before we can do this, however, we need to drink long and deep ourselves, just like the camels in the desert.

We need never fear drought in our spiritual lives, because God has promised us living water in abundance. All we have to do is ask for it and use it for the purpose for which it is given. The well will never run dry!   FRANCES CHARLES

AUGUST 20

Our Direct Line

Don't worry about anything; instead, pray about everything; tell God your needs and don't forget to thank him for his answers. If you do this you will experience God's peace, which is far more wonderful than the human mind can understand. His peace will keep your thoughts and your hearts quiet and at rest as you trust in Christ Jesus. Phil. 4:6, 7, TLB.

We were living in Medellin, Colombia, where our daily life involved a lot of precautions and danger plans. One such measure was a "phone chain" at the school where I worked that was to pass on important information if a dangerous situation were to arise. The system allowed the principal to make three quick phone calls that would start the chain of calls to reach several hundred employees.

One morning as I prepared to leave for school, the phone rang. "David, our librarian, has been kidnapped by guerrillas!" announced Andy, my phone chain connection. "School is canceled until further notice, and we are advised not to go out in the streets."

Over the next several days of David's ordeal, I received many more calls through the phone chain. While I stayed in the relative safety of my home, I often wondered when the phone would ring with more news. I wondered how and where David was. Being the newest employee of the school and the last person on the phone chain, I also wondered if the news was still accurate by the time it reached me through a long series of phone calls. When would more news come? There was nothing to do but wait.

After several days of prayer and waiting, a call finally came to say that David had been released and was recovering in a hospital. As I prayed for David during those days of his captivity, I praised God that I had a direct line to Him. There is no "phone chain" to speak to my heavenly Father. There is no wait to communicate with Him. I need not worry if my message is getting through accurately. Wherever I am, whatever I am doing during the day, I can talk to my God.

Today as you go about your tasks, take a moment to say a prayer. He is waiting for you to contact Him. Enjoy the blessings of your direct line to God!   SANDRA SIMANTON

AUGUST 21

Video Camera Surprises

Nothing is secret, that shall not be made manifest; neither any thing hid, that shall not be known and come abroad. Luke 8:17.

I often like to use my video camera. I especially like to videotape nature scenes. The beautiful creations that God has blessed us with are always a sight to behold. Each sunset or sunrise, every budding flower, any tiny ant or butterfly, leaves an indelible impression on my mind. Viewing the tape a week—or even a year—later still brings the same refreshing joy and awe and rejuvenates me again and again.

I also enjoy videotaping people. At family reunions or church events I am usually the one most likely to be capturing the precious moments. Of course, the camera is rolling for the special highlights in the lives of my friends and family, too.

People always want to look good for the camera. Many have to get into "character," put on fake faces, pose, or act the clown when they know the camera is rolling. Some hide their faces, turn their backs to the camera, or walk away when they see me setting up to catch them in action. It is especially rewarding when I luck upon a spectacular scene now and then, when the people have no idea I'm videotaping, and they are their natural selves. At times like these there are no pretenses. There are no secrets. Nothing is hidden away, either. The camera tells the truth, the whole truth, and nothing but the truth. I think scenes like these are the most fun for me because they are a lot like the simplicity I find in the nature scenes. I've gotten lots of "people" video treasures over the years and enjoy watching these tapes too.

I wonder, does God enjoy watching the videotapes He views of each one of His children? Does He see actors, fake faces, Christians posed only for those who are watching, or folks who act like clowns? Does He see people who are their natural selves? If so, is the footage showing someone worldly, or someone Christlike? I personally know that as I reflect on a few of the videotapes God has of me, I shudder to think what He is thinking or feeling. If only I could rewind and let Him retake the scenes. How are you feeling about your videotapes?

IRIS L. STOVALL

God's Time

Give ear to my words, O Lord, consider my meditation. Ps. 5:1, NKJV.

I'm a sanguine, usually cheerful and outgoing, but I'm not a "morning" person. The mind is alert, just not eager to communicate. Ah, but in the evening, after a busy day, dusk wraps its soft arms around me and whispers peace. I lift up my eyes to hills touched with a soft glow from the recent sunset and praise my Maker for His boundless blessings. I enjoy the twilight, dreading the hour when I must turn on a light inside the house. My children, even when they were small, realized how special this time was to me.

Last evening I was sitting at my window, looking out over the back lawn. It was almost dark; only shadows were distinguishable. From beneath a bush cautiously stepped a little rabbit. Not willing to come out earlier into the glaring light that would have exposed it to its enemies, now it seemed fearless, making its way from one inviting clump of grass to another.

I, too, am like the little rabbit, enjoying the sanctuary that dusk offers. It is then that I especially like to talk with my Saviour, telling Him of my weaknesses, and feeling His protective arms around me. He is there, waiting to commune with me, for He loves me with an everlasting love. As the old song says, "He walks with me, and He talks with me, and He tells me I am His own."

I understand that some of you are morning people. Maybe that is the best time for you to spend some quiet time with the Lord. Lord, may we always spend the hour with You when we can feel Your presence most near.   ANN VAN ARSDELL HAYWARD

Just Enough Money

What things soever ye desire, when ye pray, believe that ye receive them, and ye shall have them. Mark 11:24.

I owned a 1978 Dodge Aspen. Its appearance showed signs of much wear. The car rattled and squeaked when it rolled over bumps and pitted surfaces in the road. People on the street could hear it jangle as I drove by. Occasionally heads would turn to see where the noise was coming from. My vehicle stuck out like a sore thumb next to the newer cars that sped past me on the freeway. But I swallowed my pride and reminded myself that this Army green "dinosaur" had been reliable, and I owned it, free and clear.

One morning I heard a new rattle and could faintly smell exhaust fumes. *It's the muffler,* I told myself. I wondered where I was going to get the money to fix it. Weeks passed as the rattle grew louder, revealing the urgency of getting it repaired. I had an idea: I would bring my problem to the Lord, asking Him to provide a solution.

So before taking the car to the garage, I prayed, "My heavenly Father, please provide a way so I won't have to spend a lot of money on the car to get it fixed. You know this is my only means of transportation. Thank You for Your answer to this prayer. In Jesus' name, amen."

As the car was put on the lift so the mechanic could inspect the muffler, he tapped it a few times in different places. "Here's the problem, ma'am—this piece right here."

I moved closer to get a better look and asked him how much it would cost, remembering my prayer request to God and the fact I had only $25 with me.

The mechanic looked in his catalog of car parts to determine the cost. As he was flipping through the book, he stopped occasionally to thumb down a page. With raised eyebrows and a hint of surprise in his voice he replied, "I can't find it in this book."

I thought to myself, *Without money or a spare part the car can't be repaired.* My heart sank into discouragement.

"Tell you what. For $20 cash I can fit a piece of metal where the old part is worn," he said.

God had answered my prayer! We may think we can come to

our Father only for the big things in life that perplex us because He is not concerned with the smaller details in our lives. Or perhaps we don't want to admit our dependency on Him for the "little things" because we feel we should be able to handle them ourselves. We are His children. Sometimes it takes the little prayers to show us there is no limit to God's love.

JAMISEN MATTHEWS

AUGUST 24

Tug of Worm

Look at the birds of the air: they neither sow nor reap nor gather into barns, and yet your heavenly Father feeds them. Matt. 6:26, RSV.

*I*t happened early on a June morning at a South Dakota campground while I was sitting in my RV reading and having breakfast. Out the window I noticed two birds flitting about on the weedy lawn, one bringing food to the other. It would stuff the beak of the younger one, then run away and find another morsel and bring it back. Finally it ran across the two-rut road and returned with a sizable worm in its beak. It tried stuffing the worm in the beak of the younger bird, but it wouldn't go in. It tried again. Finally the younger bird got ahold of the end of the worm, and they stretched it out between them for a couple seconds until the mother let go. The youngster gulped two or three times and the worm disappeared down its gullet.

What a sight to see! My camcorder was lying on the floor of my RV, but I had been too fascinated to think about filming the whole event. I thought about how God provides food for His creatures, ensuring that they are amply cared for. And what a dedicated mother that bird was! The little bird was almost as large as she was but still accepted food from her.

The birds of the field, does not God care for even them? I was buoyed up the whole day, thinking about how God cares for the birds and His other creatures. Because He made human beings only a little lower than the angels and so much higher than the beasts and birds of the field, I can be sure He will always care for us. Our privilege is to love Him and not to disappoint Him by doing something contrary to His will. He loved us enough to give His only Son so that we, unworthy as we are, might live in His presence for eternity. What a God!　GWEN LEE

AUGUST 25

The Garage Door

All have sinned, and come short of the glory of God. Rom. 3:23.

*M*att, my golden retriever, nudged my hand and whined. I scratched his ears as I continued watching the evening news. Matt ran a few paces and whined a little louder, then came back and nudged me again. I scratched his chest. Matt gave a sharp bark and ran a few paces. I got up, thinking he wanted out. Instead, he led me to the garage and whined again and sniffed at the door.

When I opened it, gasoline fumes stung my eyes and nostrils. Adrenaline pumped into my system. This was an emergency! Gas was leaking! If it came in contact with the pilot light from the water heater nearby, the house could explode!

I've got to get some fresh air in here! I reasoned, pushing the garage door opener button beside me. I sniffed around the two cars. The fumes seemed to be strongest near the red Suzuki hatchback. I jumped into the car and started the engine. (Foolish, I know! The adrenaline rush had bypassed my brain and set my muscles in action.) I put it into reverse and backed out. There was a loud crunching sound, so I jammed on the brakes. In my panic I hadn't noticed that the hatchback was up, and it caught on the garage door, derailing the door. The hatchback had been scrunched into the top of the car, doing more than $1,000 worth of damage.

I tried closing the garage door. It wouldn't budge. I was dripping sweat, and my muscles ached from trying to close that door, when the phone rang. It was my husband, Ron. I blurted out my tale of woe. "I guess I'll have to sleep in the car all night to guard the house," I told him.

"Don't be foolish!" Ron said. "Call someone."

I tried a friend. The answering machine was on. I tried another friend. He left company to rush right over and help. In no time he had the garage door back on track and the house was safe.

"Someone was watching over you tonight," Dale said. "You should never have started that motor!"

"I know what you're thinking," I replied. "Just like a woman driver! I know it was stupid, but I wasn't thinking."

"Don't think you have a monopoly on doing stupid things!" Dale laughed. "I've done my share of them too."

I felt better. It was good to know I didn't stand alone in the stupidity department. When I come to think of it, we are all in the same boat, aren't we? We all make mistakes. We all do foolish things, and we all sin. We are all in need of the blood of Jesus and the help that only He can give. It's good to be reminded of that once in awhile. —DOROTHY EATON WATTS

AUGUST 26

Be Sober and Watchful!

Be sober, be watchful. Your adversary the devil prowls around like a roaring lion, seeking some one to devour. 1 Peter 5:8, RSV.

One morning as I got up and went to the kitchen to prepare our breakfast, I couldn't open the outside door. The key didn't want to turn. It seemed to be stuck. I tried two or three times to turn it, but it resisted, and I was afraid I would break it, so I stopped turning.

Then all of a sudden an idea flashed in my mind. Maybe the door wasn't locked! I put my hand on the latch, pressed, and realized that it wasn't! I shivered as I thought how we had put ourselves in danger that night. We might have been robbed! We might have been killed! However, we had slept peacefully, believing we were secure!

When I got over my shock, I rushed to the living room door. Twice locked. With the key and a padlock. What nonsense to lock one door twice and leave another unlocked in a double-entrance apartment!

How often do we act so foolishly with our spiritual doors? We lock the living room door of our spiritual apartment twice. Carefully we select what we watch on TV. Meticulously we choose appropriate music to listen to. Systematically we read good books only. But what about the kitchen door? Are we careful about what we eat and drink? Are we temperate in our work, rest, and exercise? The kitchen door of our spiritual apartment is unlocked, and we think we are safe. No! with a capital N! We are in a great danger! The enemy is laughing at our foolishness! Imperceptibly he can benumb our mind and weaken our body. Smoothly and slowly he can cut our communication with God! Peril is close to us if we don't take care to lock *all* our spiritual doors.

May we always ask our heavenly Father to send His angels and His Holy Spirit to help us keep our doors locked. May we always be sober and watchful so that the "roaring lion" can never find one of them open.   JEANNE D'HARIMALALA RASOANINDRAINY

AUGUST 27

The Aftershock

Fearfulness hath surprised the hypocrites. Isa. 33:14.

The Northridge earthquake of 1994 that occurred just north of Los Angeles was one of the most devastating calamities in California history. It happened before dawn, when almost everybody was asleep. The big quake lasted only a few seconds, but there were numerous small aftershocks reported.

My 2½-year-old grandson, Brandon, was awakened by the quake. Frightened, he ran to his parents' room. Although their home in Loma Linda was about 70 miles away from the epicenter of the earthquake, they felt the jolt to their one-story house.

My youngest son, Jon, was attending Northridge University. I tried to reach him by phone, but there was no response. I called the university officials. They could not tell me if he was safe. I tried the police officers. They could not tell me where he was, either. The last call I placed was to the Red Cross center. My anxiety heightened when they could not find him. My eldest son, Bo, tried unsuccessfully to locate Jon also.

Radio reports indicated the death tolls were escalating. Bodies were found in the midst of the rubble of collapsed buildings near where Jon was living. Damages were inestimable, and the results were shocking.

Two days after the search for Jon began, Bo called to let me know that Jon had just called him. The telephone lines were finally open. The first thing Jon said was "I need a good bath. I have been transferred from one shelter to another three times, and there were no means of communication." I was finally able to breathe easily after I heard Jon was alive.

"Fearfulness and trembling are come upon me, and horror hath overwhelmed me" (Ps. 55:5). "My heart panted, fearfulness affrighted me: the night of my pleasure hath he turned into fear" (Isa. 21:4). "Fearfulness hath surprised the hypocrites" (Isa. 33:14). "Why are ye fearful, O ye of little faith?" (Matt. 8:26). "And [Jesus] said unto the sea, Peace, be still. . . . And there was a great calm" (Mark 4:39).

When the quake was over, my grandson said, "I think the monster is dead now."

Is there any monster within ourselves endangering our life or causing us fear of the unknown? Is our faith in God sleeping? In my busy hours of the day I occasionally lose track of my connection with God, and only a jolt will wake me up to the reality of the world's condition. God is trying to wake us up through all the unusual happenings. May the last-day events find us ever ready to meet with Jesus. ESPERANZA AQUINO-MOPERA

Just the Facts, Ma'am

How do you know, O wife, whether you will save your husband?
1 Cor. 7:16, NKJV.

*D*o you struggle because of an unbelieving spouse? Or perhaps you know someone who does. It is a very personal struggle, agonizing to the very depths of one's soul. Bonding with one's spouse begins while saying those precious wedding vows to love and cherish . . . for better or worse . . . till death do us part.

Sorrowfully, I spent much time on my knees, pleading with God for my husband's salvation. Upon hearing the word "divorce" come out of my husband's mouth, I thought our marriage looked as though it would not endure. Many times upon returning home after church, I found my husband inebriated and full of venom directed at me and my new lifestyle. I discovered the Psalms during those days of intense loneliness. I didn't know if the marriage would survive, and I needed assurance of God's provision for my emotional needs. He repeatedly led me to passages in Isaiah. His personal message to me was that He would nurture me and support me in place of my earthly husband. He was my "spiritual husband."

To turn a long, painful story into one of triumph, let me tell you that Jesus heard my petitions for my husband's soul. My husband was baptized in December 1993. That day he sang a song he composed. (He has been composing and singing ever since.)

Take heart, sister, if you too experience this loneliness. Be comforted in the sure *fact* that Jesus *does see* your tears, and although God does not force His will on anyone, He *will do* all He can to woo your husband or other loved ones from the one who would deny them their eternal inheritance.

Remember, you married a "possibility," and God will empower you to be a living example of His grace and love.

LAURA LEE SWANEY

Gifts

It's because of God's grace that we are saved through faith and not because of any goodness in us or any works on our part. It is a gift from God. Eph. 2:8, Clear Word.

*G*ifts. I like to receive them, and I find pleasure in giving them. The joy of giving is even more pleasurable when the gift is given for no specific occasion. Generally we receive gifts from people who love us. Some folks like to give but find it difficult to receive. Gifts can come in any form.

A few months ago when I purchased my bread machine, I was the recipient of one year's supply of yeast—12 coupons. I was most grateful, because yeast can be expensive. However, every time I went to the health food store to purchase yeast, I forgot to take my coupons. When I finally remembered, I took three months' worth of coupons with me. When I took my groceries to the checkout counter, I gave the coupons to the cashier and said, "They are free." He took them and scrutinized them for three minutes. He couldn't believe that they were free. When I thought he was satisfied and would begin bagging my groceries, he showed them to the other cashier. I couldn't believe it! I have never tried to manufacture my own coupons. Couldn't he see they were as authentic as could be? Finally he smiled and said, "You are right. They are free." Wow! What a discovery!

Salvation is a *free* gift. The Bible says it, and it is so. Yet so often in our disbelief we try to be good and perform jobs that would help us to earn our way into heaven. It seems too good to be true that eternal life is ours because of God's grace. Sometimes we even get into theological debates about salvation when it plainly states that it is a gift from God. All we have to do is believe it, because God says it, and He cannot lie. We do not deserve it, but it is given to us. Ask God to help you to believe what He says and accept His *free* gift of salvation today.

ANDREA A. BUSSUE

Can the World See Jesus in Me?

The Lord is faithful to all his promises and loving toward all he has made. The Lord upholds all those who fall and lifts up all who are bowed down. Ps. 145:13, 14, NIV.

The morning events were not that unusual for a mother with small children at home. The puppy had chewed one of the children's favorite toys and then proceeded to deliver a puppy "present" right in the middle of the living room floor. The orange juice had been spilled at the table. The telephone rang— a dear church member needed to relay her concerns to my pastor-husband. The painters arrived. Older brother smuggled a ball to the breakfast table and threw it for the puppy to catch, causing more chaos. Little brother announced he was finished with breakfast and jumped down from his chair too quickly, bumping the table and splashing more juice before he finally ended up on the floor with a scraped knee.

Those of you who have experienced the early years of parenting understand what I am describing. I have found that a few quiet moments spent alone in prayer and study at the beginning of my day give me an extra ounce of patience, stamina, and wisdom to face one potential disaster after another. Today's text promises that "the Lord is faithful to all his promises and loving toward all he has made. The Lord upholds all those who fall and lifts up all who are bowed down."

As I picked up little brother and carried him to the "nurse's station," I carried with me the extra compassion bestowed upon me by Someone who cares very much to help me with this awesome job. I washed the scrape, applied antibiotic ointment, put on a Big Bird bandage, and gave the little guy a kiss. With innocent eyes he looked up at me and asked, "Are you Jesus?"

I was taken back by his statement and tried very quickly to think about how I would answer it in a way that would make sense to a 3-year-old. I was struck once again with the realization that my actions, attitudes, demeanor, and responses are constantly being monitored by my little ones. We can read our children stories about Jesus, but we are the ones who will impress upon their hearts who Jesus really is. In terms he could understand we talked about Mommy's desire to be Jesus' girl, and if Jesus is in my heart, others will see Jesus in me.

DIANE J. THURBER

Hidden Blessings

The Lord will open the heavens, the storehouse of his bounty, to send rain on your land in season and to bless all the work of your hands. You will lend to many nations but will borrow from none. Deut. 28:12, NIV.

Directing the production of a promotional video for my school had been lots of fun, hard work, and had taken long hours. It was one thing to decide how to appeal to the market, to map out the script and decide on the visuals to complement it, and quite another to sit in the studio with the professional photographer and cut relentlessly, choosing only the best shots for my purpose.

I had chosen the short music "sting" for a slot and wanted to have a fast-paced sequence on the basketball court, culminating in a goal being scored. If you have ever tried to produce a film you will understand that even your best players sometimes shoot wide of the basket when that camera is following their every move. Out of 13 tries, the boys managed only two goals. And what I wanted was for one of those shots to miraculously display the name of the school on the ball as it passed through the hoop.

Methodically we watched each frame. The first goal showed the brand name of the ball magnificently. It would have been perfect if we wanted to promote the ball. We tried again. The photographer thought our chances were negligible, but I was determined. Frame by frame we inched the film through—and then there it was! The ball hung in midair, halfway through the hoop, with the school name aesthetically placed and easy to read. We froze that frame to fit the music we were laying over. It was a moment of sheer exhilaration in the studio.

The photographer said, "So your God came up with the goods!"

"He's got hidden blessings for us if we only freeze frames in our lives," I replied.

Words Meant for Me

I will both lay me down in peace, and sleep: for thou, Lord, only makest me dwell in safety. Ps. 4:8.

With mixed emotions I packed the bag for my scheduled hospital appointment. Ever since two doctors had verified my need for major surgery, I had looked forward to having the surgery with few if any misgivings until earlier that day. Being a private person, I discussed my intended plans with no one. But that afternoon someone entered the office where I worked and, without knowing the details, shattered my confidence by suggesting that my doctor might have erred in his decision, and that I should seek a *third* opinion.

Surgery was scheduled for 7:00 the following morning, a Thursday. After work, in preparation for the event, I read my Bible and prayed. While packing my bag, I struggled to think positive thoughts. The door opened, and my husband entered with the day's mail. A magazine lying on top immediately caught my attention. Printed across the bottom of the *Adventist Review* were heaven-inspired, timely words meant just for me. "I will both lay me down in peace, and sleep: for thou, Lord, only makest me dwell in safety." Who but God would know I needed His assurance at that very moment? Those words spoke directly to my heart and soothed my fears. I tucked the magazine into my bag to take along with me.

That night I read the verse again and again until I'd committed it to memory. While waiting for sleep, added comfort came through song: "Teach me not to rely on what others do, but to wait in time for an answer from You." God sent His assurance on the cover of the magazine just when I needed it most.

It is God who guides the hands of surgeons. He gives them wisdom, skill, and knowledge. He cares about you and about me.

More than 25 years later I'm here praising His name, living testimony of His greatness.

"I laid me down and slept; I awaked; for the Lord sustained me" (Ps. 3:5).

MABEL ROLLINS NORMAN

SEPTEMBER 2

Seeing Double

Love never gives up; and its faith, hope, and patience never fail.
1 Cor. 13:7, TEV.

Sometime between the ages of 12 and 15 I remember deciding to plant an iris garden. The iris rhizomes, the stones to border the garden, and the labor (my own) were free. There have been many gardening adventures since then. One thing is always true: the dreams fuel the work, and the dreams are more beautiful than reality.

That doesn't mean the gardens have been failures. It just means that sometimes bugs or mildew gets into the flowers, or a color combination isn't right. A few plants die. Some plants that were supposed to be 10 inches tall become giants and hide shorter flowers, making the flower bed look like an unarranged choir.

But dreams help me here, too, because my mind fills in the missing plants, moves the flowers around, and fixes the clashing colors. I see a double picture, the dream as well as the real flower bed. Then the next year I plant again and use what I learned the previous year to bring dream and reality closer together.

While pondering this phenomenon one day, I wondered, *Does God see double too, when He looks at us?* He easily sees our sinful motives and the sins we love. He sees us not only as we are but also as we appear in His dreams for us. Though we let God down every day, He loves us still. He doesn't give up on us. As long as we want Him to help us, He will continue to bring His dreams for us and our reality closer together until they merge into one clear picture.

ALBERTA HACK

Unwrapping the Gift

Every good gift and every perfect gift is from above, and cometh down from the Father of lights, with whom is no variableness, neither shadow of turning. James 1:17.

The deadline was fast approaching. Why was I dragging my feet? The opportunity to share my God-given talent and contribute to a wonderful blessing for women worldwide was about to pass me by. So far each women's devotional book had been a tremendous and uplifting experience. Was it possible that I could add to that spiritual gift?

I had written many short stories, poems, and words of encouragement before, so the writing part came naturally. I had even gotten up enough nerve to share those writings with my church family. However, when it came to sharing my thoughts with the world, I was not a risk taker. The women who had contributed to the previous books had penned such beautiful, heartfelt words. Could I do the same?

What if no one liked my writing style? What if no one shared the same interest in my talent as I did? Was I kidding myself, or did I really have a gift to share? Wait! Was I being selfish? Had not the time come for me to stop hiding my gift under the proverbial "basket"? Oh, yes! I had to let my light shine so others could see Christ. If that meant writing, then I had to write.

I knew the gift was there; God had given it to me. Who was I not to share my gift? Then again, who was I to share my gift? Then I thought to myself, *If my gift has truly come from God, then how can I fail?* God would never give a gift to someone for failure. The Scriptures recorded it, so it had to be true. "Every good gift and every perfect gift is from above." If my stepping out in faith with my gift from God would give someone else the courage to do the same, then let it be so.   TONYA L. BROWN

Light That Shines in Darkness

Dear friends, do not be surprised at the painful trial you are suffering, as though something strange were happening to you. But rejoice that you participate in the sufferings of Christ, so that you may be overjoyed when his glory is revealed. 1 Peter 4:12, 13, NIV.

It is said that one of the famous Brussels silk shops of years ago had a room reserved exclusively for the making of lace with the finest and most delicate designs. Surprisingly, and contrary to what you would expect, the weaving room was completely dark—except for a weak little ray of light that found its way through a tiny crack high up in the ceiling. The ray of light illuminated only the part of the pattern that was being woven; the weaver herself worked in absolute darkness. It was in this way that the best designs were done, the most beautiful and delicate lace produced.

How like life! How many times in the weaving of the pattern that makes up our existence have we found ourselves surrounded by the most profound and gloomy darkness! Job knew what it was to live in such darkness. When God permitted Satan to try him, he was discouraged to the point of exclaiming, "May the day of my birth perish. . . . Why did I not perish at birth, and die as I came from the womb?" (Job 3:3-11, NIV).

In Job's story, however, we're let in on the drama that was unfolding secretly behind the curtains. We're informed that Satan's goal was to separate Job from God. And of course Job's story is in the Bible precisely to warn us that this is Satan's most fervent desire for us as well. Despite all his trials, Job was at last able to say, "Though he slay me, yet will I trust in him" (Job 13:15). His experience drew him closer to God—and so should ours.

We hear God in the tranquillity of our daily life. But it's in conflict and adversity that we come to see Him face-to-face. The Lord permits our faith to be tried so that someday we can shine as brightly as the stars in the sky. In fact, we can't fully know the fulfillment of the marvelous promises found in God's Word until we face the situations those promises were given to meet. We can't fully comprehend the promises for protection in perilous times when we need no protection. We can't claim the promises of comfort for the sick while we enjoy perfect health. We can't understand the promises for the aged while we have strong arms, warm blood, and brave hearts.

Don't become anxious, then, even if you can't find any beauty or meaning to your existence. Don't become discouraged, even if the direction your life has taken troubles you, and you can't understand why God has allowed you to face the hard times that have come. Remember that when you trust in God, everything you experience develops character. Just as fire is the test of gold, so adversity is the test of a strong and victorious woman. Knowing that, you can be happy, however adverse your circumstances.

So let us, like Job, lean our arms awhile on the windowsill of heaven and gaze upon the Lord. Then with that vision in our hearts, let us meet the trials of our days with strength. Let us resolve to gather that which the dry wind of vicissitudes has scattered, even if it's just the broken pieces of our existence. However dark our paths, if we'll place the pattern of our lives under the full light of God, we will discover, with the passing of time, that the most exciting and wonderful work was done during those darkest hours.

O Lord, how like You to give me what I need instead of what I ask for. Thank You for always providing the best for me and for helping me see that all things come to me through Your hand. Amen. OLGA VALDIVIA

SEPTEMBER 5

New Clothes

He has clothed me with garments of salvation and arrayed me in a robe of righteousness. Isa. 61:10, NIV.

I quickly grew to be a tall child, as evidenced by fading school photographs and memories of visiting aunts exclaiming, "Haven't you grown!" As the eldest in the family, I had no hand-me-down clothes from a big sister. Each growth spurt meant alterations to existing garments, but there was only so much that could be done. So when there was a dire need for a new dress, the family budget was stretched to accommodate me.

Mom and I would take a trip to town to choose material and a pattern. I was encouraged to choose a design that was modest

("remember, you're a Christian young woman!"), not too complicated (I was being trained to sew), and not requiring many yards of
costly fabric. Then we would look at the materials. How I loved the
bolts of cloth and their smell! I looked at the colors. Mom's fingers
tested for "crushability." Was it of a quality that would last? Choices
were made, including buttons and thread, then home we went.

I found unwrapping the parcels almost as exciting as buying
them. Then Mom would spread the material on the table, decide
on the pattern layout, and start cutting. While she sewed, I
watched with fascination as the dress took on the appearance of
the illustration. Eventually we came to the point I hated—the fitting. Stripping down to my underwear, I would stretch my arms
above my head and Mom would slip the pinned garment on my
body. The pins always scratched. The more I wriggled and complained, the more they dug into me. The pins around the sleeves
were absolute agony!

"Stand still!" my mother urged. "Just pretend you're Princess
Elizabeth. She's taught to stand still."

When my mother was satisfied, the seam would be stitched.
I would then stand on the kitchen table while she leveled the
hemline, after which I was put to work sewing a neat hem.

I'm so thankful that Jesus has offered me a ready-made de-
signer-label gown. He knew just what I needed, and I didn't have
to endure scratchy pins for a fitting. All I had to do was hold out
my hands, and He slipped His garment of salvation over my
head. I'll never outgrow it, and the design is always fashionable.
I'm forever clothed in His righteousness.

JAN CLARKE

Did Jesus Chuckle Too?

Jesus said, "Let the little children come to me, and do not hinder
them, for the kingdom of heaven belongs to such as these." Matt.
19:14, NIV.

The family had gathered in the living room of our home to
view a video featuring the story of the good Samaritan. Our

three grandchildren sat patiently through the long introduction until finally the story began. The room was quiet except for the narrator's voice until Jesus came onto the scene. Our 3-year-old grandchild jumped up and began pointing at Jesus on the television screen. "That's Jesus," he shouted with obvious delight. "He's the one who lives in my stomach. Right, Mommy?" he said, pointing at his own small tummy.

"Yes, sweetheart, that's a picture of Jesus. But Jesus lives in your heart, not in your stomach. Remember?"

"Oh, yes. He lives in my heart, and I live in His heart too," he said with all the conviction a 3-year-old could muster.

The rest of us tried to stifle our giggles. His older brother and sister looked around the room at the adults who were struggling to keep straight faces, but Eric was right. Jesus lives in us and tells us that we are on His mind and in His heart, too. I like to think that Jesus had a good chuckle over Eric's wrong choice of organs, and then rejoiced that one to whom "the kingdom of heaven belongs" wanted Jesus to live in him.

Come into my heart today, Lord Jesus, and into my mind, and yes—even into my stomach. For You have created my body to be a temple of the living God, and the God of my life must live in all of me.

ROSE OTIS

SEPTEMBER 7

Feeling Lost

He hath said, I will never leave thee, nor forsake thee. Heb. 13:5.

I want my mommy," I softly whimpered, then wailed repeatedly, "I want my mommy!" I remember sitting on the floor, feeling terribly lost and confused in that big department store. All I could do was cry. I was about 4 years old. With me in tow, my mother had taken the rare opportunity to go shopping for a new dress for herself. She had been browsing, and I had tagged along, keeping close to her side, reassuring myself that she was still there by holding her hand or patting her soft lamb's wool coat.

Little ones daydream, and I must not have been paying close attention when she told me she was going into the dressing room to try something on. She gave me instructions where to sit and wait. Then she was gone. When my reverie ended, I looked around to find my mother, but she wasn't anywhere. I'd forgotten the instructions. And I had no clue as to where she could have gone. At first I was confused. But it wasn't long before my fear of being lost overcame me, and I panicked. That's when the tears began. I didn't know who was lost—my mother or I—but we were apart, and I was afraid. My dilemma didn't last long. My mother soon emerged from the dressing room wearing a beautiful dress. She came to me, comforted me, and reassured me that I was not lost.

I can laugh now, realizing that children forget so easily and live in the immediate present. Parents can no more forget their children than they can forget to breathe. But children don't know that. When our parents are out of sight, we instantly feel forgotten.

How like my relationship with my heavenly Parent. He has given me instructions to wait for Him. He has told me where to be. He has even said He's coming back soon. But I daydream sometimes, occupying myself with my own pleasures. I don't hear His instructions. I don't obey. Then I feel alone and suddenly need Him. But I've forgotten where He is. In my lost state I begin to cry. I am afraid. I am confused. I don't know where to go. He returns to me when I seek Him. When I read His Word. When I cry to Him in prayer. Really, He never actually leaves me. At all times I am protected by unseen angels. And His Spirit goes wherever I go. It is only when I stray that He is out of my sight.

But just like my mother, who returned to comfort me and take me where she was, my Father is sending His Son, dressed in royal splendor, to come for me and take me where He is. And oh, how I long for Him to come for this lost child!

ELIZABETH DARBY WATSON

A Circle of Quiet

And my people shall dwell in a peaceable habitation, and in sure
dwellings, and in quiet resting places. Isa. 32:18.

*H*ow I long for a quiet resting place!" I complained to the
Lord one Wednesday morning as I bustled around the
house helping my husband pack for a weekend trip. "This would
be the perfect weekend for a solitary retreat into nature," I continued. "The weather forecast is for gorgeous weather. Ron won't
be here. I'd love to withdraw from people for a while to enjoy
long hours of stillness with You, Lord. I need that after busy
weeks of mixing with people in seminars and retreats."

But as much as I wanted to escape, I could not. As a member
of our conference women's ministries committee I would be helping to run a weekend retreat for survivors of childhood sexual
abuse. I could see no way to escape the intense encounters with
people in pain. But so urgent was my own need for quietness that
I wrote in my journal, *Show me, Lord, how to bless those around me and
to be an encouragement to other committee members, and still to find time to be
renewed myself by the warmth and beauty of spring and time alone with You!*

Two books I had packed for the weekend retreat were a reflection of my need for quietness—*Meditations on a Rose Garden*, by
Carolyn Huffman, and *A Circle of Quiet*, by Madeleine L'Engle. I
didn't expect to have a moment to read them, mind you, but at
least they were a symbolic representation of my need, and it felt
good to include them.

Then the unexpected happened! The one who usually managed the lodge office could not be there. I was given the job of
sitting inside the glassed-in cubicle to answer phone calls and
deal with requests for information. It was the perfect assignment
for my mood of isolation. People flowed around that cubicle, an
occasional person needed to locate someone, and once in a while
the phone rang. But I had long periods of feeling enclosed in a
cocoon of stillness.

During the weekend I was able to finish both books. I wrote
several pages in my spiritual journal. And by the end of the weekend I felt renewed, refreshed, and thankful for God's gracious
provision for my own circle of quiet. I wrote, *Lord, You are con-*

stantly surprising me, doing what I never even imagined! What a joyous surprise to be given the opportunity for quiet and removal from the center of things by having to sit by the phone. What a wonderful blessing and refuge for me, and most certainly an answer to Wednesday's prayer!

DOROTHY EATON WATTS

Legacy

Jesus told him, "I am the Way—yes, and the Truth and the Life. No one can get to the Father except by means of me." John 14:6, TLB.

*I*n high school I participated as a line judge for track events. One event that always amazed me was the 400-meter relay. Four sprinters from each school represented would each run a leg of this race. The surprising thing about this event was that even the team with the fastest sprinters would not necessarily excel at this event. The key reason would be the passing of the "baton," a cylindrical, hollow 12-inch tube that weighed only a few ounces. If this special tube wasn't passed successfully, using one of three special techniques within a specified distance, or worse yet, if it was dropped, it would spell disaster for the entire team. Every participant's efforts depended solely on the vital passing of this tube and doing it absolutely perfectly and quickly. Constant practicing of these various techniques would be the only manner in which the movement would become second nature, a natural motion.

Recently my husband's mother celebrated 80 years of life. All of her children participated in honoring her with an open house, displaying her "legacy" of 80 years of life through pictures, numerous quilts, crafts, and handiworks, plus another love—gardening. However, most important were the children, grandchildren, great-grandchildren, and numerous friends who came to celebrate with her. What then was her true "legacy"? Was it the things she had made with her hands, or the deeds those same hands had accomplished through those she loved?

We too have been given a "legacy." Our Father God gave to

us, His children, the gift of His Son, Jesus Christ. And Jesus accepted the task His Father willed for Him in Gethsemane by cooperating with His Father and dying on the cross. He had His loving hands pierced for our deeds. All of this allows us to call Him our Saviour.

Are we sharing our legacy with others? What about our children? Have they been properly trained in the techniques necessary for running their race in this world so their deeds reflect a natural motion? Are they ready and able to take their handoff of the baton when it comes time to pass it to them? Or will the baton be dropped and spell disaster? And what race will they be running? Have we imparted the truth and light to them through examples in our own lives? through the deeds of our own hands? Have we given to them the knowledge necessary to run the race?

May we all take a moment this new day the Lord has so graciously given to us to focus on the greatest Gift we have been given, our true "legacy," the Way, the Truth, and the Life—Jesus Christ.

DIANA PITTENGER

SEPTEMBER 10

I Heard God's Voice

Thine ears shall hear a word behind thee, saying, This is the way, walk ye in it, when ye turn to the right hand, and when ye turn to the left. Isa. 30:21.

I was in charge of the women's wing of the large mission hospital on Muhammad Ali Jinnah Road, Karachi, Pakistan. My assistant, equally qualified and experienced, did her own surgery lists and clinics. We consulted together only over interesting or difficult cases. I was therefore surprised when the message interrupted my busy morning clinic.

"Please come to surgery immediately; lady doctor needs you."

After explaining to the waiting patients that I would return directly, I rushed to the surgery. Booted, gowned, and masked, I entered—and was faced with an enormous problem. The doctor had embarked on what she thought would be the simple removal of a large ovarian cyst and found herself with a malignant tumor, adhering to everything in the abdominal cavity. Wisdom would have indicated a rapid withdrawal without attempting anything more, but she had pressed on and now found herself in a position from which she could neither advance nor retreat.

I knew she would move from being surgeon to assistant the instant I was ready; however, I didn't know what to do in the situation either. But I was in charge of the unit, and if the patient died on the table it would be my responsibility. Moving to the adjacent scrub room, I started scrubbing my hands and arms and praying silently in anguish. *Lord, You see that I don't know what to do! Show me! Help me!* Suddenly I distinctly heard a voice in my left ear. It said, "Increase the incision maximally, pack the liver away, and start removing the tumor from the back, toward the colon. I know that is unusual and dangerous, but you will find a safe plane of cleavage in which you can work. Eventually there will be huge blood vessels that are supplying the tumor; you know how to deal with them. Then replace the mass, and attack it from in front. It will not be easy; just go slowly. I am with you and the patient will not die on the table." The voice ceased. I knew who had spoken. There was no one else beside me in the room.

Gowned and gloved, I went to the operating table, and, as expected, the doctor moved aside and took up the position as assistant surgeon. No shaking knees, no trembling hands were mine. Had I not been told what to do? After an hour the huge mass had been removed and all hemorrhage had been controlled.

"Could you manage the closure now, since I still have a clinic waiting?" I asked my colleague.

"Oh, yes, and thank you so much," she said.

It was impossible to explain my experience; I could hardly believe it myself. Never again has God permitted me to hear His voice, although He has spoken through my fingers in surgical gloves many times. After this experience I knew that "before they call I will answer; while they are still speaking I will hear" (Isa. 65:24, NIV).

Yvonne (Stockhausen) Bazliel

What Can Mortals Do to Me?

With the Lord on my side I do not fear. What can mortals do to me? Ps. 118:6, NRSV.

My two children and I were on our way to the grocery store that winter evening, when we passed two Middle Eastern men selling area rugs. I excitedly rushed over to see the carpets, because I wanted to get a couple nice rugs for our new house. The salesmen promised me that the rugs were authentic woolen rugs. I told them that I trusted them and wanted them to be honest with me. They vowed they were telling the truth.

Finally, after two hours of looking at rugs and negotiating, we came to an agreement on a pretty blue floral 8' x 11' rug and a gray five-foot runner, both for $350. They wanted me to pay in cash. Quickly. I told them I didn't have that much cash with me. Then, without knowing whether the merchandise was really worth the price or what company these men represented, and without even getting a name or business card, I went ahead and wrote out a check for $350 and gave it to them. They immediately loaded the rugs into my car and disappeared into the darkness.

By the time we got to the grocery store my children were bored and irritated with me for spending so much time on those rugs. They were in no mood to spend any more time grocery shopping. So my daughter and I divided the list, and each went our separate ways. After a few minutes my daughter appeared with the two carpet men. They had come to the store to look for me.

"What do you want?" I questioned.

"We feel guilty for taking this money from you, because those are not woolen rugs. We do not want to lie to you, so please, just give us $200 for both rugs." They handed back my check.

I was in total shock and couldn't believe they would be so honest as even to return my check. Then I recovered my bargaining mood and offered to pay $150. They smiled and accepted my new check.

That experience greatly strengthened my faith. I know my God is looking out for me. I had no way of returning those rugs or getting my money back. But my heavenly Father touched their hearts and revealed to them that I am His child and that they should not cheat me.

A few days later I saw an identical rug in a carpet store for $150. And I had gotten a rug and a runner for that price. I can wholeheartedly say, "With the Lord on my side I do not fear. What can mortals do to me?"

STELLA THOMAS

A Missed Concert

It is not good to have zeal without knowledge, nor to be hasty and miss the way. Prov. 19:2, NIV.

I got a newsletter from my Christian book club with a list of concerts to be held in the next few months. Hella Heizmann, one of my favorite Christian singers, was scheduled to hold a concert in Schömberg. That was just fine, as it was only about 15 miles away. Of course I would go there. I phoned the contact number to find out about the location and time. The man on the phone asked where we would be coming from and then said, "You are coming from so far away." We thought he had a funny notion of what "far" is.

So I drove to the town on the specified night and started looking for the kurhaus (main building in a spa) where the concert was to be held. Not one single poster was in sight in the whole town. That was a bit funny. I asked a few passersby where the kurhaus was. But there was no kurhaus, either! They directed me to the municipal hall, but that was deserted.

Finally one woman said, "Maybe you mean Schömberg in the Black Forest. That's about 60 miles from here. That's a spa, and there is a kurhaus there."

Well, I had to laugh at my stupidity. I didn't know that there was more than one Schömberg, and as the zip code started with a seven, I was sure it was in our region. I hadn't looked it up in the book. I had relied on my limited knowledge and experience.

As I drove home with my daughter, I started wondering if I was as superficial in more important matters as well. I had to think of what Jesus said to His disciples concerning the time shortly before His second coming. "For false Christs and false prophets will appear and perform great signs and miracles *to deceive even the elect—if that were possible*. See, I have told you ahead of time" (Matt. 24:24, 25, NIV).

Had I looked up the zip code, I would not have been deceived into going to a wrong place. God has given us His Book so that we can look up things and be sure. But if we don't bother to find out, we will surely be deceived. And we'd better take time to find out about things now so that we are not guided by our limited and superficial knowledge and experience, as I was.

Besides, if I had really listened to what the man on the phone at the contact number said, I would have realized that I was thinking of some other place than he was. But I was so wrapped up in my own expectations that the bell didn't ring. I didn't understand what he was really saying. Similarly, if we pray to God and don't listen to what He has to say to us with open ears, we probably will not understand His message. We expect a certain kind of answer and don't realize that God is answering in a better or different way.

At least I learned a lesson from my experience and decided to be more careful the next time. But if we are deceived in more important matters, there will be no next time. So let's take time today to find out what God has to say to us through His Word and in prayer.　　　　　　　　　　　　　　HANNELE OTTSCHOFSKI

SEPTEMBER 13

Midnight Meditation

I will make an everlasting covenant with them, that I will not turn away from doing them good; but I will put My fear in their hearts so that they will not depart from Me. Jer. 32:40, NKJV.

I awoke, alert, at 2:07 this morning. I seemed to hear a car. Sure enough, when I went to the window, there was a car beside the "road closed" barricade. I suspected young vandals with spray paint or sign-stealing intentions. Instead, the car rolled slowly around the barricade, and a spotlight beamed from the driver's window, slowly arcing back and forth across Penrod's storefront. At the bridge construction site the car pulled up and stopped. The occupant got out, checked the site with his bright light, then walked down to check that all was secure at Borcher's Outfitters. Eventually the police officer returned to his car, rolled back past our house, and continued on his rounds. What a secure feeling it gave me to know someone was out there through the night for the security of our little town. Many of us think of police officers as enforcers of the law, punishers of wrongdoing. (Ever gotten a speeding ticket?) But they are there for our protection, even while we sleep.

God keeps the night watch for us in this dark world of sin. He's guarding us, watching and caring continually, though most of the world's population are asleep to the fact. His role, like the police officer's, is often misunderstood. When I meditate on God's protecting mode, I come to realize that the "speeding tickets" He issues along the highway of life are not arbitrary and malicious. His role as law enforcer is an outgrowth of His greater role as our protector. Those seemingly harsh judgments are often a call to slow our rush to destruction, to come back within the boundaries of safety. They too are an aspect of God's merciful protection.

Today I'll thank God that as my protector He's keeping the night watch *and* the traffic beat for me.

KATHLEEN STEARMAN PFLUGRAD

SEPTEMBER 14

Wee Little Help

For of such is the kingdom of heaven. Matt. 19:14.

At 21 months old Malick puts his dirty diapers in the trash can, closes the cabinet, and puts his toys in the room when I ask him to. Most of all, he likes to help me vacuum and dust the furniture. I cut a piece of cloth for him, and we are both ready to work. I always congratulate him for trying, for his perseverance, and for his obedience. I appreciate his "wee help." I could do the job by myself, but we are building tomorrow today.

In the same way our heavenly Father can spread the good news of salvation without our help. He is mighty enough to finish it in the twinkling of an eye, but it thrills His heart to see His children try, to see us persevere in our little human efforts, to see us obey His command. The blessing falls right back on us. In the same way Malick is developing a helpful spirit, we, as we obey our heavenly Father, will develop qualities and a character that will allow us to live in His presence and enjoy heaven. He is preparing us for tomorrow.

We should then put all our effort, our time, and our money into building His kingdom, into snatching souls from the devil's snares. We should be willing to make sacrifices to hasten His return. God loves us and longs to have us reach the full stature of a mature Christian. He knows our individual limits and capabilities.

Give Him your very best; be excited about doing something for the Creator of the universe, for the One who has done, and still continues to do, so much for you. Remember, He can do the job faster and better without you, but it makes it special when you participate. ANNIE SOUARE-NDIAYE

SEPTEMBER 15

Two Proud Parents

In the beginning was the Word, and the Word was with God, and the Word was God. . . . Through him all things were made; without him nothing was made that has been made. John 1:1-3, NIV.

I sat on the balcony, feeling the cool evening breeze across my face. My young son was curled up on the bed, sleeping soundly. I gazed over the beach to the black ocean that met the even darker sky. The lights of the boats in the sea seemed to reflect the stars overhead. A full moon appeared over the water, lighting a path across the waves and up the sand. It lit up the enormous dragon the boys had sculpted from the damp sand. There she sat, a full four feet in diameter, with her tail curled around and tucked under her chin, holding three large sand eggs in her embrace. A few feet away was the huge sand castle they had built for her to guard. The tide would be coming in soon, and both would probably be gone by morning.

A couple walking hand in hand down the beach suddenly came upon the reposing dragon and her magnificent castle. Their voices drifted to my balcony on the night air.

"Look at this!"

"Isn't it awesome?"

"Wow! Someone even took the time to put on sand spots and draw eyelashes."

"She looks so protective of those eggs."

"And look at the castle!"

"Yeah, it's big enough that a couple kids could have sat in the middle to build it!"

"That's probably what they did."

"Take a look at the detail on the castle! Whoever made this sure must love medieval stuff!"

"I wish I knew who sculpted this stuff. These are great!"

Their voices trailed off as they moved on down the beach, but their interest attracted other night strollers who came to admire the sand sculptures. The sculptures *were* magnificent! I felt I would just burst with pride as they admired and appreciated the artwork. I wanted to hang over the balcony and shout, "My son made that! Isn't he great?"

Father, do You ever feel like that? I sit here admiring the rolling surf with the jumping dolphins and sleepy seagulls now resting in the moonlight on the water like little sea ducks. I am covered by a cloudless canopy of soft blackness and gently twinkling stars, and I wonder, do You ever want to lean down and shout, "My Son made that! Isn't He great?"   SALLY PIERSON DILLON

SEPTEMBER 16

Magic Words

I know that through your prayers and the help given by the Spirit of Jesus Christ, what has happened to me will turn out for my deliverance. Phil. 1:19, NIV.

My husband died slowly from emphysema over a seven-year period. His last three years were a nightmare. Our world shrank to the length of a 40-foot oxygen tube that had become his lifeline 24 hours a day. As his disease progressed, he became more angry and bitter, until all words of tenderness and appreciation vanished. Only words of complaint and criticism were left. Even though I knew that it was the illness speaking and not the man I had married 30 years before, a steady diet of harsh words and faultfinding destroyed my self-worth.

Being around people has always been an important aspect of my life. It was fun to be needed and involved. Becoming a widow left a terrible void in my life, but I felt that the chances of any kind of new relationship would be small. Besides, I was sure that the scars from my last few years of married life were all over my body, and that on my forehead was stamped "Damaged Goods." So I told the Lord that while it was probably best that I remain alone, I would need lots of help to deal with the loneliness.

Then a gentleman friend came along who assured me that he saw no scars or damaged goods. He told me I was easy to love, and suddenly the hurt was gone.

The parallel between human love and the love of Jesus is easy to see, except that God's love is everlasting and unconditional. How wonderful to know He knew me before I was born and knew what my name would be. He knows the number of hairs on my head and thinks about me constantly. He knows my thoughts, dreams, and heartaches and tenderly cares for me through them all.

The words "I love you" immediately change a relationship once they are spoken and received. Not only do we see each other in a different light; our attitude toward our heavenly Father changes as well.

Thank You, Lord, for loving me so much. I love You too.

SHEILA BIRKENSTOCK SANDERS

Shelter in a Garbage Bag

In the day of my trouble I will call to you, for you will answer me. Ps. 86:7, NIV.

We live in a very quiet suburb of Oahu, about 17 miles away from Honolulu, where I work and my daughter, Jennifer, attends high school. Because of the distance and because of the heavy traffic that congests the routes to Honolulu, weekday life in the suburbs begins at 4:30 in the morning. Alarms go off, and the little town of Waipahu becomes ablaze with lights.

On this particular morning we had awakened a few minutes later than usual and knew we'd never make our 5:45 bus if we didn't speed up on our early-morning rituals. At 5:30, fully dressed and ready to go, we stepped out and made a dash for the bus stop about two blocks away. Then it happened! Just as we sat down to await the bus, we felt the first drops of rain. Since we were both nursing the beginnings of a cold, we quickly looked around for shelter. To our dismay, we found that the large tree nearby had been chopped of its thick, overhanging branches the day before, so we found ourselves in wide open space. Along the sidewalk was a shoulder-high concrete wall that ran the perimeter of the block and enclosed an apartment complex that housed the elderly. Beyond that, all was quiet and dark, with no signs of life whatsoever.

At this point, Jenny, in the innocence of youth, quickly closed her eyes in prayer, and after a minute or so looked up into the heavens and very calmly but emphatically said out loud, "Hey, Lord, remember me, Your faithful subject?" Her outburst took me so much by surprise that I quickly turned to see if anyone was looking, then proceeded to admonish her about talking to God in such a way. To me it seemed rude and irreverent, but to her it was a matter of "talking to God as to a friend." Her response displayed so much confidence in her heavenly Father. However, I felt compelled to warn her that she might be in for a slight disappointment.

"Look around you," I said. "What kind of help or shelter could you possibly expect at this time of the morning?" As if to prove my point, the rain began its aggressive assault, and we knew that in just minutes we would be soaked to the skin.

Suddenly, from just beyond the wall, a deep voice, gentle in tone, said, "Here, use this." From an outstretched arm reaching over the wall came a big dark-green trash bag, large enough to keep us from getting sopping wet. We were so stunned and at a loss for words that for a few seconds Jenny and I could only look at each other. After recovering from our astonishment, we both turned to say thank you to our kind benefactor. The area was completely empty of all signs of life.

Jenny stepped into the bus with all the confidence of the very young, knowing that even in what seems to be an impossible situation, the Lord hears the cries of those who call on Him. I learned a valuable lesson that morning—no matter what the circumstances may be, nothing is impossible with God. Jesus once said, "Unless you . . . become like little children . . ." (Matt. 18:3, NIV). I pray that our confidence and trust in the Lord will not falter, but will be as that of little children.　　NORMA C. GALIZA

SEPTEMBER 18

Why Me?

Why then have You brought me out of the womb? Oh, that I had perished and no eye had seen me! I would have been as though I had not been. Job 10:18, 19, NKJV.

Why me, God? Why did it happen to me?" How many times have we asked that question when struck by misfortune? It's a question we can't answer. We don't know the reason. But in a different context I ask myself almost daily, "Why me?"

Yesterday as I stepped outside to prune a rosebush, I heard the squeal of the neighbor's children frolicking in their pool. From the street came the sound of buzzing lawn mowers and the distant hum of traffic. I thought of bright-eyed Elizabeth, a young girl who works nearby. How she would love to hear these sounds! But Elizabeth is totally deaf. Why was I granted the gift of hearing and not her? Why me?

The family in the corner house backed their car out of their garage. They were off to church. Again I wondered why I was so lucky to live in this prosperous, free country, where law-abiding citizens can come and go as they please. I couldn't choose the country of my birth. Why was I so fortunate? Why me?

I stopped to retrieve a fallen rosebud, and I noticed a bee hovering nearby. I watched a pair of cheeky mynahs pecking their way across the lawn, as a brilliant butterfly fluttered over my garden. I thought of Mrs. Clark on the next street and the millions like her who have never seen flowers and bees and birds. Why do I have the gift of sight while they don't? Why me?

I went into the kitchen to prepare lunch. What would we eat today? I looked into cupboards stocked with all kinds of canned and packaged food. I opened a refrigerator that guarded all types of perishables. I sighed as I thought about the many developing countries in which tens of millions of people don't know where their next meal is coming from—or whether they will ever eat again. What have I done that I should deserve a full stomach, and not they? Why me?

Night brought with it a sudden weather change. Wind whistled around our small house, and rain poured onto the tiled roof. As I snuggled in my warm bed, I thought of the hordes of people made homeless by war, disaster, and poverty. Why should I have shelter? Why me?

I don't know the answer to these questions any more than I know the answer to the questions people ask when sickness, accidents, or some other misfortune overtakes them. Only God knows the answers. Perhaps we would feel better if we spent less time griping and more time being grateful.

"In every thing give thanks: for this is the will of God in Christ Jesus concerning you" (1 Thess. 5:18).   GOLDIE DOWN

SEPTEMBER 19

Is He Rich!

My God shall supply all your need according to His riches in glory by Christ Jesus. Phil. 4:19, NKJV.

Sometime before I went to college, I joined a singing group in Egypt called the Praise Team. I learned much about the real power of praise. One of the songs we used to sing was "Philippians 4:19."

Toward the end of my final year of college in Lebanon, the president called me to his office and told me I had to pay a final payment of approximately $600 before graduation. I didn't have a penny. I thought I had worked and earned enough for that year, but evidently not. I couldn't even call or send a message to my parents about this, because I knew they couldn't afford to pay anything. I didn't tell anyone.

When I left the president's office, I headed for a quiet place. Alone with God, I started struggling in prayer, with tears. I cried, "I sing that You will supply all my needs according to Your riches in glory. If these words are only words, I can't sing them anymore. I have to experience Your promise."

That very moment the Holy Spirit led me to start praising the Lord and thanking Him for His many great characteristics. I sang, proclaiming His love, mercy, richness, wisdom, and above all His Fatherhood.

Meanwhile, in my home country my father had passed away. My mother, knowing how very close I was to my father, requested that my family not inform me of this until after graduation. She was afraid the news would affect my ability to complete my studies successfully. Not knowing about my father's death, but guided by the Holy Spirit, I was praising God for His Fatherhood. I went to my room feeling such a peace and joy inside.

Three days later I received a letter from a friend of mine. I opened it, and to my shock, I found $600! It was just too good to be true! I ran to my room, knelt down, and with joyful tears thanked my heavenly Father. I praised Him and promised to proclaim His wonderful love to all those around me and to mean sincerely every praise I sing, pray, or say about Him.

When I arrived home, I received that awful news of my father's death, but I was greatly lifted up and surrounded by my heavenly Father's love. The Scriptures are true. I continue to praise Him, because I have a Father who never dies.

SARAH BOULES GOUDAH

Woman on the Plane

A faithful witness will not lie, but a false witness speaks lies.
Prov. 14:5, NASB.

*I*n the mid-1980s I experienced a return and recommitment to God. As I made time with Him a priority and an integral part of my daily life, interesting things started to happen.

I was flying from California to my childhood home in Dallas, Texas, to visit my parents for a few days. Before boarding the plane I told God that I was willing to be a witness for Him if He made me aware of anyone needing my help. This would be a departure from my normal mode of reading or doing needlepoint to occupy my time during flights. I relish these few hours of quiet time in my busy life. But I was willing! As my story continues, you will see the Lord didn't infringe on my time without permission.

As I took my assigned seat, I briefly noticed I was sitting beside a young woman, so I smiled and took out my needlepoint. For a few minutes we were typical airline seatmates, each lost in thought during the takeoff and safety announcements. Then a lovely, soft voice caught my attention as my seatmate asked about my needlepoint project. Within a few minutes we were sharing our mutual love of Texas and its friendly residents. She was returning from visiting her parents in California and while there had met an old high school boyfriend. Their encounter had been one of excitement and had aroused old emotions of love and attraction. She was planning to continue seeing this old boyfriend and was considering leaving her husband for this renewed "old" relationship. She and her husband were the parents of two children, a son about 6 and a daughter about 4 years old.

For the next two hours we were in deep discussion, and I found myself telling her about how sacred marriage is to God and that adultery is a serious issue. I'm not sure of the exact content of our entire discussion, but I am aware that words just seemed to flow. I was not condemning her, but felt sincere compassion and concern for the life predicament she was in.

As the announcement came to fasten our seat belts for landing, she smiled and looked at me. "I've never met anyone like you," she said. "Are you an angel?"

As I caught my breath, I assured her that I was not, but that God had done wondrous things in my life and marriage and that I would pray for her. When we deplaned and walked to the luggage area, there stood a handsome young man with two beautiful children. She walked up, kissed him, and then looked at me, smiled, and waved goodbye.

I still get goose bumps when I remember the thrill of giving God permission to witness through me that day. If I had tried to lecture her, it would have been an awful failure, I'm sure. I like to believe she saw the grace of God in me. I still take reading and needlepoint on long flights and haven't had anyone ask me lately if I'm an angel, but who knows! Life is exciting with God as my copilot.   JANIS CLARK VANCE

SEPTEMBER 21

In His Time—God Helps Us to Be Healed!

To everything there is a season, a time for every purpose under heaven . . . and a time to heal. Eccl. 3:1-3, NKJV.

I halfheartedly accepted an invitation to attend a lecture by a visiting well-known physician. The subject matter sounded interesting. Although I felt tired after a busy day at the office, I let my friend persuade me to go with her.

The lecture proved to be fascinating—healing with natural remedies. When the subject of the treatment of beestings came up, my mind wandered back to the last time I'd been stung. I winced, thinking of the very large yellow jacket that had become entrapped in the sandal on my 5-year-old foot, and I momentarily relived the pain and terror I had felt that day so long ago. I then thought of my much-adored, 6-foot-tall uncle, who had tenderly bent down and covered my poor throbbing foot with cool, wet sand from the lake.

As my mind focused again on the lecturer, I thought, *Well, I certainly don't need to hear this now; I've lived all these years, gone on count-*

less family outings, and have never been stung since! I sank back in my chair, not quite as alert as I'd been previously, thinking, *Oh, well, it won't hurt me to listen anyway*. At the end of the evening I decided to purchase a container of powdered charcoal the doctor recommended for beestings "because it is good for other purposes too."

The next day was a holiday. As I was walking around in the backyard, I noticed that new growth on top of a long hedge had gotten quite out of hand. I decided to get out the electric trimmer and just skim off the tops of the wild growth until the hedge could be trimmed properly. I started at one end of the hedge with the noisy shears. After I had skimmed along for several feet, suddenly a swarm of hornets flew out at me from a large nest that was well concealed within the hedge. Five of them fastened themselves to my abdomen. I couldn't brush them away, because they were stinging me! The pain was excruciating!

As soon as I realized what was happening, my mind immediately registered "charcoal poultices for insect stings"! I threw the trimmer to one side, ran into the house, and quickly found the new can of charcoal I had purchased the night before. The directions were so clear in my mind: make a paste of water and charcoal, enclose it in gauze pads, and tape one on each sting. Total relief from pain came within minutes. Just to make sure, I left the poultices in place for the remainder of the night.

The next morning I was so amazed, for where there had been much swelling, only a tiny red mark remained at each sting site. My thoughts turned to our Lord, and I was even more amazed. Who else would have known that I would need that information *the very next day*? And after decades of not being stung!

God provides for us in a thousand ways, even without our knowing. God's timing is the best timing, isn't it? Wonderful Friend, Counselor, Saviour!   DIANE R. MUSTEN

I'll Never Go There Again!

A soft answer turneth away wrath: but grievous words stir up anger. Prov. 15:1.

When my late husband, Warren, and I were married in 1948, we lived just a few blocks from my maternal grandmother. She and I had always beem close, and I enjoyed visiting her almost daily.

I don't recall what caused it, but one particular day Grandma and I had a falling out. I went home, fairly stamping all the way, a scowl on my face and my hands clenched.

"I'll never go *there* again! *Never!*" I blurted as I entered our little cottage.

Startled, Warren asked for an explanation. After I gave him a detailed description, he gently took my hand and led me to the sofa. Always the soft-voiced one, he suggested that we sit down. Picking up our Bible, he turned to today's scripture. After he had read it, we knelt for prayer.

"I'll be back in a little while, honey!" I exclaimed as we arose. Then I, who just moments before had declared "I'll never go *there* again," was on my way to make amends.

After an apology on my part and a few hugs, I told Grandma about the Bible verse and our prayer. She asked me to find the verse in her Bible and leave it open at that page. I know I will always remember how I felt as I walked back to Grandma's house that day. I walked briskly, a smile on my face, and my arms swinging at my sides. But the best part was the feeling that my angel was walking beside me, *holding my hand!*

PATSY MURDOCK MEEKER

Unwrinkled

That he might present it to himself a glorious church, not having spot, or wrinkle, or any such thing; but that it should be holy and without blemish. Eph. 5:27.

*I*roning is not my favorite pastime! When I was quite young, a family we knew lost their home late one day to fire. In my mind one of the most tragic parts of the loss was the fact that the mother had spent hours that day ironing, and those newly ironed clothes were burned up!

What a relief it was when permanent press came on the market. I still remember a pair of dress pants we got for our older son, who even as a preadolescent was very particular about his clothes. It was a proud moment for me when he looked at those trousers after they came from the dryer and said, "Mom, I just can't believe you didn't iron them." Now that a lot of the old polyester is out and cotton is back in, the iron is pressed (pardon the pun) into duty more often than it has been for years. Too bad!

There was a time when teen-age girls ironed their long hair to make it straight. I never had that problem—mine was naturally straight, and it never got long enough to iron! People need ironing too, and sometimes the iron gets hot enough to be uncomfortable. We could call it being put into the furnace of affliction, or being chastened, and we don't like it! Hebrews 12:11 says that "no chastening for the present seemeth to be joyous, but grievous: nevertheless afterward it yieldeth the peaceable fruit of righteousness unto them which are exercised thereby." One author put it this way: "This is our washing and ironing time—the time when we are to cleanse our robes of character in the blood of the Lamb" (Ellen G. White, in *General Conference Bulletin*, 1903, p. 89).

A few years ago the motto of our school's gymnastic team was "whatever it takes." I'd like for that to be my motto too, even if it includes being pressed into service and having the wrinkles ironed out.

MARY JANE GRAVES

Diamonds Are Forever

This is love: not that we loved God, but that he loved us and sent his Son as an atoning sacrifice for our sins. 1 John 4:10, NIV.

I enjoy growing African violets. They don't require much care, nor do they occupy much space. They're easy to propagate, and the blooms last for a number of days. I have a few on the windowsill in my office. Every morning I turn them one quarter so they will grow perfectly round as they reach for the sunlight coming through the window. (My dream is to cover every windowsill in the office with African violets of every hue and color!) Tending them is very relaxing.

One morning a beautiful pink African violet caught the morning sunlight and transformed itself into an exquisite diamond-studded beauty. Curious, I looked at the others and noticed that every single flower was sprinkled with diamond dust!

A thousand years ago the Creator of the African violet said of another of His creations, the lily, that even the wisest man in all his glory was not arrayed like one of these. "'God is love' is written on every opening bud" (*Steps to Christ*, p. 10). Some say it with flowers, and some say it with diamonds, but when God says it with exquisite, diamond-dusted African violets of countless delicate hues, day in and day out, what kind of love is that?

We too can possess a tranquil beauty as we daily reach for the Son of righteousness, whose love shines on us.

HEPHZI OHAL

Sowing Seed

Sow your seed in the morning, and at evening let not your hands be idle, for you do not know which will succeed, whether this or that, or whether both will do equally well. Eccl. 11:6, NIV.

*P*am, you attract trouble for yourself," a friend's husband commented to me one day. He knew of my many "projects," and when he drove into our yard he discovered a 15-year-old mother cleaning it in exchange for food for herself and her family.

I smiled at his comment. But I wondered if he was right. Is my help a drop in the bucket of need? pointless? only trouble? It often seemed so. Among other examples, I remember a group of five siblings, led by Laura, their 12-year-old sister, who used to come three times a week to do this same job. I'd tried to interest them in Jesus, but they had no appetite for *Your Story Hour* tapes or for attending weekly Bible school. They came to work for me for several months, rowdy, disobedient little ones, who tried to take my children's toys home with them. They never seemed satisfied with what we gave them. They picked more than their fair share of citrus fruit from our trees and did not want to work when the fruit was gone. It seemed that no good came from my efforts with them.

Maybe my friend was right, I mused, but I just can't turn this young mother away. Not only does her child depend on her; she's also caring for her dying mother and two little brothers.

A few weeks later I attended the mission's harvest baptism at a nearby lake. Imagine my surprise to see Laura being baptized! I'd sown seed and someone else had watered it. Another time my daughter, Gabi, shared clothes with children attending a small state school not far from the school where she studies. Before we distributed the items, we prayed for the children who would receive them, especially asking for their salvation. As we passed out the clothing, children pushed, shoved, insisted on more, and generally made things difficult. Was it worth it? I wondered.

Among the clothes was a little black dress with a perky plaid jacket that Gabi had often worn to church. That dress became the key to seeing our prayer answered. About a year later a little girl came to church wearing that very dress. Each time we saw the little girl, Gabi and I felt a warm glow inside.

"Let us not become weary in doing good, for at the proper time we will reap a harvest if we do not give up" (Gal. 6:9, NIV).

PAM BAUMGARTNER

SEPTEMBER 26

Influencing an Unbelieving Spouse

For the unbelieving husband is consecrated through his wife, and the unbelieving wife is consecrated through her husband. 1 Cor. 7:14, RSV.

I saw the apostle Paul's inspired statement confirmed in my family during my childhood and youth. My mother had been a Christian for only two years when I was born. She embraced Bible truths and began attending church with her four daughters. My father did not share her beliefs, going instead to nightclubs and bars where he sang and drank, often returning home drunk.

Many times I saw Mother in the upstairs window waiting for my father to return so that she could remove his shoes when he fell into bed. The next morning we would find him with potato slices on his forehead, trying to cure his hangover. Not a word of disapproval or murmuring left my mother's lips, but I can remember the hymns she hummed while cooking at the stove.

Two additional children were born, and the six of us went to church with her to listen to the Bible stories. We sang during the worship times at home. Father, however, watched at a distance as his children grew under the wise guidance of a Christian mother.

Many dawns my father awoke to find my mother kneeling at his bedside. Her knees became calloused from the long periods of prayer. The Holy Spirit was silently operating, and after 18 years of humble witness, she saw her husband being transformed into a dedicated and active Christian.

Today my father continues singing, but his voice is lifted in praise to Jesus. He knows that his past mistakes have been forgiven, and through the patience and perseverance of his wife he can see that the love of the Saviour is worth much more than everything the world can offer.

The temptation is to be intolerant with an unbelieving spouse and think that our prayers are in vain! But Paul continues, "Wife, how do you know whether you will save your husband? Husband, how do you know whether you will save your wife?" (1 Cor. 7:16, RSV). Certainly God yearns to grant wisdom and patience to those who are married to unbelievers.

Let's plead for discernment, for the ability to allow the Holy Spirit to freely operate in our homes, and for the commitment to continue praying for our beloved unbelievers.

THALITA REGINA GARCIA DA SILVA

SEPTEMBER 27

Not by Might

Then he answered and spake unto me, saying, This is the word of the Lord unto Zerubbabel, saying, Not by might, nor by power, but by my spirit, saith the Lord of hosts. Zech. 4:6.

As a body builder, I have seen my physical strength increase over the years. The more weight I use, the stronger I get. But I realize that no matter how strong I get, I can't do anything without Christ. He is my physical and mental strength.

The Lord knows how we humans are: our tendency is to rely on our own strength. I have found in my life that relying upon myself is a scary thing. It is like building a house on sand. Nevertheless, I still find myself doing it, because I don't have faith to rely on the Lord, even though He has always come through for me in the past.

Several Bible characters experienced this same thing. Samson was probably the strongest man ever documented. Because of his lack of faith, he lost his physical strength. When Joshua was about to take over Jericho, he did not do it by physical means. He followed the Lord's instructions by marching around the city, and the walls came tumbling down.

When Jesus was on the earth, many of His followers felt that His kingdom would have to be established by overthrowing the Roman government. Jesus showed them that His methods are completely different. Before Saul became Paul, he thought he was doing the Lord's work by cleaning up the Christian community. He would annihilate anyone who got in the Lord's way, as he saw fit. But Paul did not realize which side of the fence he was on. When the Lord convicted him of his misguided behavior, he became a soldier for Christ. Because of Paul, many have discovered the Lord.

The stories may be different, but their moral is the same. We cannot do it on our own. The Lord is there to carry us through the good and the bad times. We just need to lean on Him.

MARY M. J. WAGONER-JACOBS

SEPTEMBER 28

In Need of a Saviour

Do not hold against us the sins of the fathers; may your mercy come quickly to meet us, for we are in desperate need. Ps. 79:8, NIV.

Recently I observed my granddaughter as she played. I watched as she crawled through the house, exploring every corner. Picking up objects from the floor, she quickly stuffed them into her mouth before her mother could reach her. It was as though she knew it was wrong to put them in her mouth, but the temptation to resist was just too great for her. I was amazed at the sharpness of her vision. Although the carpet was shag, she was still able to spot a string or button. Without the watchful eye of her mother, she could have swallowed something dangerous and choked.

This reminded me of our own human nature. We always seem to search out the things that are not good for us. It starts when we are born. Being the offspring of Adam and Eve, we have a tendency to sin. The Bible states we are born in sin and shaped in iniquity (Ps. 51:5). That's why we need a Saviour—one who is pure and sinless to direct our paths.

Just as my granddaughter's parents must protect her from the small objects that attract her, Jesus protects us from the small sins to which we are often attracted, things we are quick to see but slow to realize are detrimental to our walk with God.

It is because of His eagerness to come to our rescue that we are kept from the harm and dangers Satan places in our way. We do not always recognize that our very lives are often at stake. We can be grateful for a loving God who cared enough to send His Son to save us from sin. "For God so loved the world that he gave his one and only Son, that whoever believes in him shall not perish but have eternal life" (John 3:16, NIV).   JESSIE BEARD

Change of Plans

Commit your way to the Lord; trust in him and he will do this. Ps. 37:5, NIV.

*S*tanding in the bookstore, I tried to decide which books were correct for which classes. I was in my second semester at Sonoma State University. I looked up to see Phillis, a friend from one of my previous classes, and Beverly, whom I recognized from my research class, but did not know. We took a few minutes to catch up on our vacations, grades from last semester, and what classes we had enrolled in for the coming semester. When I mentioned that I would be taking the second half of research, Beverly spoke up. "I'm in that class too," she said, "only they denied my research proposal at the last minute, and now I don't have a project."

I stared in disbelief. "I'm working on my project alone and could really use some help in collecting data, doing fieldwork, and compiling statistics," I blurted out. Quickly I sketched the project to see if it would be interesting to her. Within 24 hours we had cleared our proposal to work together with the two instructors of the class and were on our way!

However, God had just begun to reveal His wonderful plans for us. People come from all over the San Francisco Bay area to attend Sonoma State University. Beverly lived only 20 minutes from me, making it possible for us to meet without much difficulty. We discovered we were the same age, had children just one year apart, were of the same religious background, had attended private schools, and knew many people in common. We had even been at the same private college at the same time for our undergraduate work! Consequently we became very good friends and remain so today. God had a plan for us in what we thought was a chance meeting at the bookstore. "'For I know the plans I have for you,' declares the Lord, 'plans to prosper you and not to harm you, plans to give you hope and a future'" (Jer. 29:11, NIV).

Oh, by the way, our research project was a success, and we received an A!   CAREL CLAY

SEPTEMBER 30

The Child Within Us

Assuredly, I say to you, whoever does not receive the kingdom of God as a little child will by no means enter it. Mark 10:15, NKJV.

Some friends and I were conversing the other day and swapping "kid stories." It never ceases to amaze me how great and strong the faith of our little ones can be. To them, God can do anything. And of course He really can. These little ones pray with the faith to move mountains, never doubting that God hears their prayers and answers every one of them—or does He? Children notice things we tend to be too busy for, such as bumblebees and snowflakes. Kids also love everybody in the whole world. And they love Jesus, too. Nothing is more precious than to hear the voices of these little ones praising the One they love best.

When Jesus was asked who was the greatest in the kingdom of God, He took a little child, set him in the middle of everyone, and told them that unless they were converted and became like that little one, they wouldn't inherit the kingdom at all.

It seems to me that while I was busy "growing up," I lost something along the way. I learned to think too much and pray too little. I learned to worry too much and trust too little. I learned to doubt too much and believe too little. I learned to complain too much and praise too little. I learned to be critical and forgot how to love. I lost my childlike faith.

Oh, how the Lord must love it when we adults take every little—and big—problem to Him. And whether the prayer is for us or for someone else, we know where the Source of our help is. And when something hurts, we do not hesitate to run into our Father's open arms and let Him lovingly wipe away our tears. How special it must be to Him when we stop and thank the Creator for making a flower or a butterfly! And when we feel like letting loose and praising Him at the top of our lungs, that's OK too.

Oh, Lord, restore to me that childlike faith You so delight in!

LYNDA MAE RICHARDSON

Talking About God

Those who feared the Lord talked with each other, and the Lord listened and heard. A scroll of remembrance was written in his presence concerning those who feared the Lord and honored his name. "They will be mine," says the Lord Almighty, "in the day when I make up my treasured possession." Mal. 3:16, 17, NIV.

I talked with Terrie, and she said to tell you hi," I told Steve, passing on greetings from our mutual friend. I was planning to stay with Terrie while I was at a conference in Tennessee, so we were touching bases frequently to coordinate dates and flight schedule.

That was last fall. After the conference we both got pretty busy with work and hadn't called each other much. Recently Steve passed me in the hall at work and told me he had talked with Terrie. The first time he mentioned it, I thought, *Great! I'm glad they're keeping in contact.* But after the second and third time in just a couple weeks, I started feeling as though I was missing out. *I* wanted to talk with my friend *too.* So I called her, and we had a wonderful time chatting together. It's so important to make time for friendships.

In today's text Malachi commends those who talk with each other about the Lord. The more we talk about God with each other, the more it creates a longing to keep in contact with Him.

If Steve had not told me that he'd talked with Terrie, she wouldn't have been in the forefront of my mind. And the more he talked about her, the more it made me long to talk with her too.

When I heard Becky Tirabassi talk at a women's retreat about the hour she spends in prayer each day, it encouraged me to be more faithful in my prayer life. When I share with people how I make memories with God in my devotional time, it encourages them to be intimate with Him too.

As we talk about God and our relationship with Him, it can be a powerful encouragement to others in their walk with God. We all have our ups and downs. But when we hear someone else talk about how good God is, about a special promise they found in the Scriptures, or about an answer to prayer, it can revive our faltering spirits.

So many times we put ourselves in spiritual solitary confinement. We're communing with God but not sharing the blessing with others. Often we can be at church and talk about religious things, yet not share the spiritual experience we have with God. There is a big difference between religion and spirituality.

Let's not be shy about sharing how God is working in our lives. It may be just the thing a sister needs to hear to encourage her in her relationship with God. In fact, God thinks it's so important when we speak with each other about Him that He stops to listen. And on top of that, He records our name in a book of remembrance. And He says these wonderful words recorded in Malachi 3:17: "'They will be mine,' says the Lord Almighty, 'in the day when I make up my treasured possession.'"

You love Him—so talk about Him.   HEIDE FORD

OCTOBER 2

Gratitude in Retrospect

Were not all ten cleansed? Where are the other nine? Luke 17:17, NIV.

I love family reunions, especially when they include children. Last Christmas my brothers and their families joined me at our parents' Florida home for a special gathering. Delighting in the workings of the minds of my nieces and nephew, I took advantage of every opportunity to listen to their reasoning.

One morning, when all the children were doing their own thing in various corners of the family room, my 5-year-old niece and I got involved in a deep discussion about Luke's account of the healing of the 10 lepers. Takara wanted to understand the disease. Were the lepers' sores in any way related to leopards' spots? I wanted to discover how well she understood the principle of subtraction, and how clearly she would apply the gratitude factor to this story.

Using men from her cousin's Lego set, I described the agony of the 10 sick men and Jesus' healing compassion. Then, picking up a single Lego piece, I told her that only one came back to say thanks. "Now," I said, my schoolteacher genes surfacing irresistibly as I rearranged the pieces into the two categories, "if only one came back, how many forgot to say thank You?"

She shot the right answer back. Matter-of-factly she added, "I would never forget to say thank You. How could they forget?"

Searching for an appropriate answer, I noticed her baby sister, not quite 2, starting toward us. Deliberately lifting two additional Lego men from the set her cousin had been carefully putting together, she toddled over to our corner.

"Thank you," she said, placing the pieces beside the lone "grateful" piece. Then smiling sweetly, she moved back to assist her cousin.

Her older sister's quizzical expression reflected my surprise. Cousin Jonathan, who usually gets incensed when people disturb his set, seemed untroubled as his eyes tracked the location of his choice pieces. Baby Brianna too was unconcerned, or so it appeared to us all. A thank-you needed to be said. Nobody was doing it. So she did. Case closed. That the omission was 2,000 years old (104,000 Sabbaths) was beyond her, and therefore irrelevant.

I wish I knew if that was a coincidence, or if that really was how her young mind worked. Some coincidences are, in actuality, miracles in which God chooses to remain anonymous. What I do know is that Brianna's action was a miraculous reminder to me of how pointless grousing about sins of omission can be.

If we can, when we can, we ought to get in there and rectify the glaring problem, then get on with life. If our heavenly Brother, Christ, was treated as we deserve so that we could be treated as He deserves (see *The Desire of Ages*, p. 25), surely we can follow suit on behalf of our brothers and sisters.

Children have such a beguiling way of helping us see things from a different perspective. No wonder Jesus loved to have them around.   GLENDA-MAE GREENE

Broken Umbrella

Truly I tell you, just as you did it to one of the least of these who are members of my family, you did it to me. Matt. 25:40, NRSV.

He came to the college campus chapel every Tuesday morning at 10:45, dressed in ill-fitting clothes. He wore thick glasses held together with brown tape and carried a tattered Bible in his hand. Sometimes he parked his old rusty bike right in the foyer. He never entered the sanctuary. Instead, he pulled a folding chair close by the door and sat there listening to the speaker. I too always sat in the foyer, monitoring students walking in and out of chapel. The first few times I saw him, I asked him to join the others, but he always declined. So the two of us sat across the foyer from each other, listening quietly. He didn't seem to be the kind of person who indulged in small talk, so I kept my thoughts to myself, but secretly wondered about this stranger.

One rainy Tuesday he came to chapel holding an old umbrella. Right after chapel I was busy with students and didn't see him leave. Back at my office and immersed in work, I saw our student worker, Ann, walk in, soaking wet. "You know that man who always comes to chapel?" she said. "I just gave him my umbrella." She told me how she saw the man walking out of the building holding on to an old, broken umbrella, trying desperately to keep dry. She was so moved by the sight that she followed him and offered the umbrella. He appeared reluctant to take it at first, but Ann assured him that she didn't need it.

I was touched, yet ashamed, after hearing her story. Here was a young woman who saw someone in need and did something to help. Ann didn't think that what she did was a "big deal," but she is wrong. I am sure the man appreciated her thoughtful act. Furthermore, she showed me that while it is good to be compassionate and to feel sorry for someone, it takes a little more effort to *do* something about the situation.

The man stopped coming after that, and I still wonder why. I wished again that I had done something for him, or spoken to him when I had the chance. Jesus said that what we do for His brothers and sisters we have done for Him. He gave me the opportunity to make a difference in someone's life and I failed. I pray that I will not fail again.

As we go throughout our day, let's seek out the "least of these who are members of [His] family" and let our compassion move us to action.

APPY NIYO BENGGON

OCTOBER 4

Island Hopping

It's not good to have enthusiasm without knowledge; being hasty only gets you into trouble. Prov. 19:2, Clear Word.

After attending meetings in Manila, my son Don and I had a few days left for "island hopping." Our plan was to see five cities in the Philippines before we returned to California. We were to go to Palawan that day on the 8:55 plane. We needed to be at the airport at least 30 minutes before departure. It usually takes only 15 minutes to get there by taxi from my brother's house.

We were standing by the road at 7:00, watching for our ride. It was Wednesday, and the traffic was exceptionally heavy that day because people were assembling in Baslarean. We didn't know it was Redemptorist Church Day and also Commercia Day, at which time anything goes. For all these reasons traffic was congested, and commuting was very slow.

After 15 minutes had passed, we realized we couldn't get a ride from the spot where we were waiting, so we walked several blocks to where there might be a better chance of catching a ride. We stopped a taxi. The driver agreed to take us if we paid six times the usual fare. We accepted, hoping to catch our flight. But the traffic was too slow. In spite of our anxiousness to get there, we had no control over the situation. When we reached the air-port, the driver dropped us off in front of the domestic terminal. We didn't know there were two departure terminals. In we walked with all our heavy luggage on our shoulders, only to discover that we needed to board at Terminal II. Hurriedly we dragged our luggage to the proper terminal, but when we got there, the doors of the aircraft were already closed. The plane was taking off. It was too late. We had been left behind.

We went back to the house to change our plans. The next plane to Puerto Princesa didn't depart for 24 hours. Besides the delay and all the other inconveniences, we had been reduced to standby passengers.

Today's text says, "It's not good to have enthusiasm without knowledge; being hasty only gets you into trouble." Ecclesiastes 7:14 admonishes that "when things go right, be glad and thank God. When things go wrong, go to God for help. You never know what will go right and what will go wrong" (Clear Word).

Life on this earth includes disappointments, but thanks to God's grace none of us needs to accept standby passenger status on our heavenly journey. — ESPERANZA AQUINO-MOPERA

OCTOBER 5

Of Empty Tanks and Lifestyles

I can do all things through Christ which strengtheneth me. Phil. 4:13.

*I*t is amazing how habits can get in the way of living. I have acquired a habit that has brought my life to a literal halt. Fortunately for me, this habit has been kept in control for the most part.

Have you experienced the embarrassment of sitting on the side of the freeway somewhere, hoping for some help? For some reason the car doesn't wait until the next exit to stall or until after you have arrived at some important meeting. Have you ever driven a car whose gas gauge read "empty"?

I know all the excuses: "I was in a hurry," "My spouse uses this car," or "I don't understand. I just filled it up." Time goes by so fast when you are in a hurry, and yet it appears to crawl when you sit in a car that has an empty gas tank.

I should know. Three times I've been at the mercy of others as I waited for gas. On one occasion I had to walk a distance in high heels in a foot of snow. (So much for arriving at an evening meeting looking dignified.) On another occasion I sat with a colleague in my car and waited until the local police came to our assistance. And my most current experience with an empty tank was during an evening trip home.

It had been a long day of meetings and travel. As the car jerked and sputtered to a stop, I had a familiar sinking feeling. While I sat and watched the sun set behind the mountains, all I could do was think. My busy lifestyle had not afforded me that privilege for some time. I began to realize that I'd been running on empty in some other areas of my life. Exercise was not a high priority. Running low on good health practices was bound to put a stop to my spinning lifestyle. And what about my daily spiritual time to renew and charge up for a new day of demands? I guess I was functioning on a "low tank" of spiritual strength as well.

Looking back, I'm thankful that it took a minor inconvenience to make me take notice of the other "gauges" in my life.

JILL HINES RICHARDS

OCTOBER 6

An Antidote for Weariness

The Lord is the everlasting God. . . . He gives strength to the weary and increases the power of the weak. Isa. 40:28, 29, NIV.

The trials of life seem to come in clusters. At least that has been my experience during the past three years or so. In this time I have found myself supporting a sister through her husband's illness and death from cancer. At the same time I cared for a parent undergoing major surgery and helped to care for a frail grandparent. I was coping with a painful schism in my church congregation, coming to terms with personal health problems, plus juggling a busy workload and the normal demands of life in the 1990s. I also found that facing life emotionally drained and chronically short of sleep is a challenge in itself. Many times I have been near to weeping with a weariness that encompassed body, mind, and spirit.

One day as I was wondering why, with everything else I had on my plate, I had agreed to prepare a devotional message for my coworkers, and how I would find the energy and inspiration to do so, I came across a chapter entitled "An Antidote for Weariness" in Charles Swindoll's book *Encourage Me.* Needless to say, it caught my attention! Quoted in that chapter was a familiar Bible passage that suddenly took on an extra dimension of meaning. Did God know how I would be feeling in the mid-1990s when He inspired Isaiah to write those words all those millennia before?

"Do you not know? Have you not heard? The Lord is the everlasting God, the Creator of the ends of the earth. He will not grow tired or weary, and his understanding no one can fathom. He gives strength to the weary and increases the power of the weak. Even youths grow tired and weary, and young men stumble and fall; but those who hope in the Lord will renew their strength. They will soar on wings like eagles; they will run and not grow weary, they will walk and not be faint" (Isa. 40:28-31, NIV).

The Lord never grows weary! Who better to sustain exhausted humans? And author Swindoll also brought me a new thought: God doesn't simply dispense strength and encouragement as a pharmacist might fill a prescription. He doesn't promise us something to *take* to help us cope with our weariness. Instead, He promises us *Himself.*

Spending some quiet time with God gives Him the opportunity to exchange my fatigue and discouragement for His rest and peace. What a blessing! And how marvelous to receive a personal invitation from Jesus: "Come to me, all you who are weary and burdened, and I will give you rest. Take my yoke upon you and learn from me, for I am gentle and humble in heart, and you will find rest for your souls" (Matt. 11:28, 29, NIV).　　　JENNIFER M. BALDWIN

What Would You Do?

You will again obey the Lord and follow all his commands I am giving you today. Then the Lord your God will make you most prosperous in all the work of your hands. Deut. 30:8, 9, NIV.

*M*om, if you were me, what would you do?"
I sigh as my 4-year-old asks an oft-repeated question. He is beginning to make choices and decisions, yet I must admit that at times I'm annoyed with this inquiry. What difference does it make whether he wears the red shirt or the blue one? buys gum or a toy with his new dollar bill? stays home with Mom or runs an errand with Dad? I just want him to hurry up and make the decision!

Yet his cautiousness has taught me a lesson. God wants me to have that same attitude, that same carefulness, in my daily decisions, to ask of my heavenly Father, "What would You do?" How different would my choices be if prefaced by that question!

Which activities would You plan for me to do today, God? What words would You say to my discouraged friend? How would You discipline my children, yet not break their fragile spirits? Whom would You visit or call on or write to? How would You respond to my coworker who has treated me so unfairly?

What effect would questions like these have on my Christian life? Sometimes my indecisive son isn't happy with my answers. At times he even does the opposite of "what I would do." I have to admit that I do the same with my heavenly Father. I ask Him for wisdom and direction, yet often I already know what I want to do—and don't even wait for His answer. And, yes, at times I have opted for my way over His.

LILLY TRYON

What Is a Christian?

If you suffer as a Christian, for living a life of kindness and compassion, don't feel ashamed, but praise God for it. 1 Peter 4:16, Clear Word.

Traveling from a weekend trip spent in the 1996 Olympic City, Atlanta, Georgia, I saw a billboard sign that proclaimed in very large letters: WHAT IS A CHRISTIAN? For miles afterward I looked for the answer, but saw none. So I began to formulate my own.

If a Christian is Christlike, then one is:

> **C**aring
> **H**appy
> **R**espectable
> **I**ndustrious
> **S**incere
> **T**olerant
> **I**nspiring
> **A**miable
> **N**eighborly

There are many superlatives that can be used to describe a Christian. It doesn't matter which ones we use as long as we remember that we are followers of Christ. And that means we will try every day to pattern our lives after His life, doing what He would do in any unpleasant situation in which we may find ourselves. We will be more sensitive to those in need. We will share another's burdens. We will be less eager to judge and more willing to forgive when we take Jesus as our example. In answer to the question What is a Christian? E. C. McKenzie puts it this way:

> A Christian is a mind through which Christ thinks,
> a heart through which Christ loves,
> a voice through which Christ speaks, and
> a hand through which Christ helps.

Had I remembered that Christ is always near to help, com-

fort, and cheer, looking for the answer would not have been necessary. *Lord, let me be a mind, heart, voice, and hand that You can use today.*
MARIE H. SEARD

The Black Bag

God has not given us a spirit of fear, but of power and of love
and of a sound mind. 2 Tim. 1:7, NKJV.

As I walked across a corner of my yard, I noticed that one
of my cats was frozen in place, her large yellow eyes staring in total fear. Following her paralyzed gaze, I realized she was
scared of the large black garbage bag I was carrying in my hand,
puffed to fullness by a slight breeze. When I got closer to where
she stood, Kitty gathered all her cat strength, tore her eyes off of
that dreadful black bag, and disappeared into what she considered
to be the safety of a nearby bush. Not once during the terrible ordeal did she look up to see who was in control of the "enemy."

I chuckled at my cat's dilemma, then my thoughts turned to
my reactions to what are sometimes unavoidable situations I am
called to face. Satan delights in carrying problems, disappointments, and heartaches in our direction. He puffs them out by un-
favorable circumstances, and we are paralyzed by fear, with our
focus centered on what is, or could be, happening. How easy it
is during those times to fail to look beyond Satan's black bags to
find the face of our blessed Jesus. To realize that although it may
appear He has forsaken us, He is the one who has promised to be
with us always. Although we may not understand the reason in
this present world, He is the one who sets the boundaries over
which Satan cannot pass. He even provides the precious "bush of
safety"—prayer—where we can hide for a while. *Thank You, dear
Jesus, for the lesson of the black bag.*
MILDRED C. WILLIAMS

An Instrument of Hope

I . . . will make the Valley of Achor a door of hope. Hosea 2:15, NIV.

*S*he was telling me about the fall festival. We laughed together at a picture of her costume. Autumn leaves of every shape and hue covered her little frame as if they had just paused for a moment while drifting by on the breeze. "That must have been great fun to wear, Melissa," I said.

"Oh, it was," she agreed readily, and in the same breath added, "Why do you travel so much?"

"I have something to show you, Melissa," I said. Going over to my as-yet-unpacked suitcase, I extracted a scrap of paper. It had been left on top of the overhead projector during my last seminar. Written in faded pencil on the back of a grocery store register tape, three sentences stared up at us:

"God sent you here just for me. The information you've shared has changed my life. Thanks for being an instrument.— No longer hopeless."

"I love being an instrument, Melissa," I explained. "That's why I travel. There's always someone who needs exactly what I have to share. Often I don't get to meet that person, but a note of appreciation makes it all worthwhile."

"Instrument?" The tone of her voice indicated she wasn't sure that was a compliment. She went to fetch the dictionary and soon read aloud its definition: "A means whereby something is done."

By way of further explanation I shared with her remembered fragments from the prayer of Francis of Assisi: "Lord, make me an instrument of Your peace. Where there is hatred, let me sow love; . . . where there is despair, hope."

A companionable silence was broken by a typical Melissa-type question. "Is everyone an instrument?"

"Everyone *can* be," I replied. "It's a choice."

Another silence. Then, with a cautious wistfulness in her voice: "Even someone my age?"

"Absolutely," I replied. "We can be an instrument at any age. We just need to stay alert to God's opportunities."

Her face lit up. Something momentous was obviously being evaluated internally.

A car horn sounded. Melissa's ride home had arrived. On the front porch I hugged her goodbye and waved to her parents. Just as the car door slammed shut, an exclamation of resolve drifted back on the evening air. "Guess what? I'm going to be an instrument!" I could just imagine the conversation in the car on their way home!

Later that evening I mused over Melissa's choice of words. She could have said, "I'd like to be an instrument" or "I'm going to try to be an instrument." She could have even said, "I wish I could be an instrument." But she said, "I'm *going* to be an instrument." What an admirable example! Once again, "a little child shall lead."

ARLENE TAYLOR

OCTOBER 11

The Missing Ingredient

But the fruit of the Spirit is love, joy, peace, longsuffering, kindness, goodness, faithfulness, gentleness, self-control. Against such there is no law. Gal 5:22, 23, NKJV.

The characteristics mentioned in today's text are the result of our loving relationship with God. They can be compared to the different ingredients necessary in producing a delectable cake. Sometimes we may cut the sugar or the shortening to make it less fattening or substitute one spice for another, but we cannot make a good cake if we remove something entirely from the list of ingredients.

Many years ago we were living in Bangkok, Thailand. One Friday afternoon I came home from teaching school and assembled all the ingredients needed for an applesauce cake, as I was expecting company for lunch after church the next day. No matter how busy I was, these meals were always special. I never knew who would visit the church, and I wanted to be ready all the time.

Now, walnuts and applesauce are very expensive in Bangkok, so I couldn't afford to mess this up! I knew the applesauce cake would top the lunch menu of tofu roast, scalloped potatoes, dinner rolls, broccoli, and tossed salad. The cake baked beautifully. I watched the oven window very closely and was elated to see the cake rise almost to the brim of the pan. I could smell the aroma of the cake permeating the house and could almost hear the compliments of my husband and guests.

At last it was time to take the cake from the oven. But horrors! As soon as I put the pan on the counter, the cake fell flat! I reviewed the ingredients, certain I had included them all. I cut a little slice to taste. It was awful! It had no sugar! What a waste of time and money. Even the cats and our German shepherd wouldn't touch it.

That experience taught me a sobering lesson: I need to have all the characteristics of the fruit of the Spirit in my life—not just one of them—to make me whole. *Lord, mold me and endow me with these beautiful traits from day to day. Develop in me a lovely character, patterned after Your likeness.*   OFELIA PANGAN

OCTOBER 12

And When She Was Bad . . .

We love because he first loved us. 1 John 4:19, NIV.

*T*here was a little girl who had a little curl right in the middle of her forehead;/When she was good she was very, very good, but when she was bad she was horrid."

For years I believed that nursery rhyme was about me. If you were to change the gender of the verse, it could also apply to my nephew, Andrew. Andrew was a precocious bundle of 6-year-old energy when I visited him recently. Pulling him onto my lap, I wrapped him in a big bear hug and said, "Andrew, you are so precious to me!"

Turning to me solemnly, he answered, "You haven't seen me when I'm bad."

Andrew, not knowing he was a child after my own heart, was worried that I wouldn't think he was as wonderful after seeing him misbehave. Poor Andrew! I can relate to that feeling! Shortly after this experience Andrew came and stayed with me for 10 days while his parents were traveling. Once he figured out that I thought he was precious, even when he had been naughty, he seemed to relax and have more fun. His naughty episodes became less and less frequent as we became buddies and enjoyed each other's company.

How much like Andrew I am! Fortunately there is Jesus, my friend who has seen me when I'm bad and loves me anyway! What a wonderful, secure feeling to revel in His unconditional love. And just like Andrew, I find that my behavior naturally improves around Someone who loves me, no matter what!

SALLY PIERSON DILLON

OCTOBER 13

An Unexpected Answer

We know that in everything God works for good with those who love him, who are called according to his purpose. Rom. 8:28, RSV.

A dog may be a man's best friend, but a computer is surely not a woman's! From the time I purchased my laptop computer I really learned the meaning of the word "stress." One afternoon I fought the usual battle of finding material that I had previously entered. As always, I went to God for help.

"Lord, why won't You *do* something?" I cried out.

Silence.

"Lord, I am *desperate!*"

Quietness.

I tried logic. "Lord, I spent two afternoons entering articles needed for the creative writing booklet. There is no time to retype them. The girls will be home from school soon. I want to spend time with them. Help me!"

This time I heard the response loud and clear. *Do not retype the articles. Leave the computer problem with Me.*

I felt angry with God. That was not the response I had hoped for. I tried everything I could think of to relocate the missing articles. I scrutinized every page in my textbooks that dealt with disappearing documents. I phoned a professional (who was not in). I tried all of my previous ploys to find my material. I even phoned a friend who has the same computer program. Nothing worked. I felt annoyed at God's uncooperative spirit. To be honest, I was fuming. My life was so busy that I could not afford to lose those articles. And everyone who was brave enough to venture into the kitchen as I prepared supper heard about my frustration as pots and pans were banged from one place to another. I had had it with my computer and its program. I was constantly losing work, only to locate it after a series of prayers. That is why I was so confused at God's apparent refusal to come to my rescue. He had bailed me out so many times before. Why not this time?

I found out why later that evening. The teacher in my writing class explained that I had missed the deadline for the book. It had occurred three weeks earlier. Later I shared my misery of the missing manuscripts with a member of my class. I explained that I had tried to find a college course that taught how to use my computer software, but had been unsuccessful. Although I had accumulated three textbooks on the program, I still felt confused. Tina, a secretary who knows my program well, agreed to come and teach me how to operate the system. Tina has been fantastic and has taught my illogical brain to deal with the logics of a machine.

Now, several months later, Tina is hungry for a closer relationship with God and is searching for a church that answers her questions. She comes regularly as I teach her what the Bible says.

When God says no to our requests, it is usually to say yes to something better!   MARY BARRETT

"Righted" by Human Kindness

"Here is the king's spear," David answered. "Let one of your young men come over and get it. The Lord rewards every [man or woman] for [his or her] righteousness and faithfulness." 1 Sam. 26:22, 23, NIV.

*I*t had been a good first day of our European trip. We had slept in until 11:00 a.m. (3:00 a.m. our time), had lunch with friends, and toured the historical town of Colchester, England, with its wonderful castle. My nephew, Arthur, was delighted to try on an ancient knight's helmet and coat of mail. After a long tromp around the castle and grounds, we were just sitting down to what looked like a wonderful West Indian meal when the mood exploded.

"Aunt Sheri, I've lost my money belt!" Arthur cried out.

A frantic search around the restaurant and several phone calls left Arthur without much of an appetite. During our entire meal we searched our memories for where the pouch could have been lost or stolen. The waiters helped us search the area, and some of the other diners commiserated with us. Having been a desperate American tourist before, robbed of all money and thousands of miles from home, I knew the helpless feeling. I also knew several days of our vacation could be tied up in replacing a passport, plane and train tickets, and hundreds of dollars' worth of traveler's checks. After a hurried dinner we spent a couple hours retracing our steps, ending up at the police station. We were disappointed that no money belt had been found.

As we turned to leave, a young woman entered and said, "I may have your money belt. Can you describe the contents?"

Not even a dollar was missing! What a relief! A stranger had reported finding the belt on the castle grounds, so we figured the belt had been loosened by the ancient coat of mail Arthur had tried on. That young woman walked 30 minutes across town to turn it in at the police station. Suspecting we had been wronged, we discovered we had been blessed.

How we loved the people of Colchester after that! One kind, thoughtful act flavored our opinion of all the townsfolk. Our entire vacation was brightened by this human kindness.

Today I want to pass this kindness on.   SHARI CHAMBERLAIN

Don't Panic!

Be careful—watch out for attacks from Satan, your great enemy. He prowls around like a hungry, roaring lion, looking for some victim to tear apart. Stand firm when he attacks. Trust the Lord; and remember that other Christians all around the world are going through these sufferings too. 1 Peter 5:8, 9, TLB.

Hagar the Horrible crouched in front of the aquarium. Every muscle was tense; his tail lashed, his whiskers twitched, and the pupils of his golden eyes were enormously dilated.

"Hagar, leave the fish alone!" I shouted. Whenever the big orange cat was bored or wanted attention—either food or a rub around the ears—he threatened the fish. Inside the aquarium the fish were safe. They had protection, warmth, and food. Their glass home had only one small opening through which they were fed. They usually ignored the cat unless he patted the glass; then they hid in the water plants.

But one night one of the fish became frantic, swimming rapidly around in circles. Suddenly it leaped out of the water and out of the aquarium through the opening. It flew through the air before crashing to the floor, thrashing about in a lethal environment in which it could not breathe and in which it was extremely vulnerable to the large orange enemy who was temporarily too startled to pounce.

While the cat waited hopefully for a repeat performance, the rescued fish spent hours on the floor of the aquarium, gulping. It was safe again after being panicked into leaving its only place of safety.

Lord, don't let me be panicked into leaving You, for only with You am I truly safe. GWEN PASCOE

God Really Does Care

Teach me your way, O Lord; lead me in a straight path. Ps. 27:11, NIV.

As a commuter on public railway transportation, I have lots of time to read. Actually, about three hours a day! My friends think I'm crazy, but while they are creeping along in the heavy traffic having their stress jag for the day, I am relaxing with a good book or magazine, or chatting with my seatmate.

About four years ago I decided to achieve one of my lifelong goals of reading all the books I have by one of my favorite prolific religious authors. Not just a paragraph here and there, but really reading from page 1 all the way to the end of each book. With red pen and ruler in hand, each morning I spend a portion of my "riding" time reading one of her books. Most of the time I get so interested that it involves my time in the evening too. When I finish a book, I put the day's date on the inside cover. That way I know that I have read that particular book completely—from cover to cover.

Recently my husband and I realized we needed to update some of our legal documents. In doing this, we discovered that we had a legal problem that was quite serious. We worried about it constantly for days. One morning before daylight we hurriedly left the house to catch the commuter train. As I was going out the door, I realized I didn't have a book to read. I had just completed one and was ready to start another. So I dashed back into the house and ran to the bookcase without turning on a light and reached for a book. Since we were a little late, any one would do! But the book I grabbed was stuck and wouldn't come off the shelf. So I reached for another one, but it was stuck too! What was going on? With one last effort I grabbed another book, and as it came off the shelf I threw it into my carryall.

After getting on the train and settling down, I pulled the book out of my case and discovered I had picked up *The Ministry of Healing*. *Oh*, I thought, *I've read this already*. I opened the book and checked the flyleaf: March 1992. *I read this book from cover to cover more than four years ago*. As I held up the book, I noticed a purple paper clip calling for my attention like a neon sign. Curiously I turned to see what I had marked—a *whole* chapter entitled "Help in Daily Living." What really got my attention, though, is what I had written at the top of the page: "When discouraged, read this chapter."

In rereading the chapter I found such gems as "The fact that we are called upon to endure trial shows that the Lord Jesus sees in us something precious which He desires to develop" (p. 471). "Our heavenly Father has a thousand ways to provide for us of which we know nothing" (p. 481). "The continual worry is wearing out the life forces. Our Lord desires them to lay aside this yoke of bondage" (*ibid.*).

Then it hit me—the books hadn't been stuck! The Lord knew I needed to read this particular chapter. He knew more than four years ago that today I would especially need these words of encouragement. He had a message ready and waiting for me.

Yes, God really does care!   BETTY BROOKS

OCTOBER 17

Traveling Home Together

I will come again, and receive you unto myself; that where I am, there ye may be also. John 14:3.

I've traveled to Mount Rushmore. I've observed Niagara Falls,
The works of Michelangelo, and Rijksmuseum walls;
Westminster Abbey, gondolas of Venice, and the Rhine,
The Arc de Triomphe, Petra, and Masada's steep incline.

I've scanned Alaska's glaciers; breathed refreshing Swiss Alps air;
Seen tulip fields of Amsterdam; the Kremlin and Red Square;
The Sistine Chapel, old Vienna, Cliffs of Dover white,
Rome's Colosseum, and the brilliant Eiffel Tower at night.

I've thrilled to Chopin's music; viewed the gold Dome of
    the Rock,
The grand Cathedral of St. Basil, Big Ben's mighty clock,
The Lipizzaner horses as they train; the Western Wall,
Gethsemane, Mount of Olives, Jesus' tomb—I've loved
    it all!

But I have toured the Appian Way and seen the catacombs;
The cruel concentration camps; the breaking up of homes;
Tornadoes and starvation; violent ravages of war;
Calamities and anguished hearts! I want to see no more!

I long to see this earth made new, where there will not
    be room
For arsenal or missile, firearms, or silent tomb;
For hospices or prisons; for gas chambers or police.
I choose to see a happier land—a land of joy and peace!

For all the sights this old world boasts fade in obscurity
When I reflect upon the wonders God has planned for me.
The marvelous Taj Mahal is but a shanty when compared
With mansions that my precious Lord has lovingly pre-
    pared.

Somewhere beyond earth's darkness there's a bright and
    glorious place
Where Lipizzaner horses o'er God's holy hills might race;
Where we may gather Eden's blossoms; drink from foun-
    tains pure;
And through God's giant forests stroll, forevermore
    secure.

I think there must be emerald-studded paths where we
    can greet
The patriarchs of ages who traverse the golden street;
Or sit with friends upon the slopes where lions romp
    with deer,
And realize that in this place there's no such thing as fear.

I want to hear our Saviour tell the "half that's not been
    told,"
Then beg Him to repeat it, for it never will grow old!

To see my Father bending from His sapphire throne
  of grace,
And hear Him say "I love you!"—watch the smile light up
  His face.

This world is growing dark! So dark! The mountains rise
  so steep,
And cherished ones who've loved us lie in dusty beds
  asleep.
Our Lord is eager to return. Oh, He can hardly wait!
He's lonely for His children, so why do we hesitate?

Let's make our reservation now. Just waiting is our Guide
Beyond Orion's corridor, to take us safe inside!
So come and travel with me, for our King of kings has
  planned
Our most exciting trip of all—to heaven's glorious land!

LORRAINE HUDGINS

OCTOBER 18

How Many Hairs on Our Heads?

Are not two sparrows sold for a copper coin? And not one of them
falls to the ground apart from your Father's will. But the very hairs
of your head are all numbered. Do not fear therefore; you are of
more value than many sparrows. Matt. 10:29-31, NKJV.

No doubt about it, I was having a bad hair day. My hair
was as contrary as the damp, cold weather, and it
wanted to stick out in all directions. In desperation I finally covered most of my unruly locks with a denim cap and hurried off to
my college classes. While driving to class, I thought of today's
text: "But the very hairs of your head are all numbered."

How many hairs do we have on our heads? The answer came
from an article entitled "Answers to Everyday Mysteries" in the
March 1996 issue of *Reader's Digest*. Redheads have about 90,000;
blonds have about 140,000; brunets are somewhere in between.

It also stated that most people shed 50 to 100 hairs daily.

How did the scientists do their figuring and come up with those numbers? To try to count every hair that even one person has on his or her head would take a long time—unless the person was nearly bald! Perhaps they marked off one square inch of human scalp, counted the hairs it contained, estimated the total number of square inches of hair-covered scalp, and then multiplied the number of inches by the number of hairs that were in the first inch that was parted, blocked off, and counted. But the answers would still be approximate.

Imagine! A God who loves and cares about us so much that He takes an interest in even the tiniest details of our lives! I'm sure He sympathizes with us on bad hair days, especially on days when nothing else is going that great either. I like knowing that we mean that much to God. Don't you?   BONNIE MOYERS

OCTOBER 19

Role Model

Even so hath the Lord ordained that they which preach the gospel should live of the gospel. 1 Cor. 9:14.

Recently I volunteered to take over temporary leadership of the earliteen class at my church. The earliteens were without a leader, and knowing the importance of dynamic leadership for this challenging age group, I excitedly (and fearfully) prepared myself. As I began thinking and planning, nostalgic memories of role models from my childhood church swept over me.

Aunt Hila. Uncle James. Little Mommy. The Gouldbournes. Sister McBride. The Martins. Sister Ogburn. Sister Howard Eachone, a special role model. Their guidance, acceptance, and love had carried me through difficult preteen and teen years. They all contributed to my spiritual and emotional growth, molding my mind, scolding when necessary, and holding my hand to lead me to the Saviour. They sponsored hundreds of activities for the young people: family home entertainment, skating, youth group, Pathfinders, Vacation Bible School, nature walks, fashion shows, breakfasts, dinners, and lots more! And in every activity they gave their time and talents in teaching God's way in their own unique ways. They preached the gospel, and they lived the gospel. And they did it with a warmth and love far beyond human comprehension.

I realize that now and thank God many days for the sacrifices they made. I pray that those of us who have committed ourselves to working with children, no matter what their ages, take seriously our roles to mold their impressionable young minds in the image of Christ. Each day will be an opportunity for us to demonstrate Christ's love to a young person. For me it means helping out in the earliteen class, whether it be for two months or two years. For you it may mean being a children's superintendent, assisting in Vacation Bible School, or conducting a story hour at your church. But each of us is called to live the gospel and to live it appropriately, so that all our youth see Christ in us.

God, I pray today that I will have the personal connection with You that will enable me to be the role model I should be for our young people. May I ever set the best example that will help each one of them to know and love Jesus, their perfect role model. Amen. IRIS L. STOVALL

OCTOBER 20

The Gift of Reading

We have different gifts, according to the grace given us. Rom. 12:6, NIV.

God has given me the gift of reading," Mujing suddenly announced. The soft yellow of her blouse brought out the depths of her chocolate bronze complexion.

We had been talking about gifts God has given us to use for Him. Mujing was known as a capable lay preacher and women's leader in her African village. Her home village had no school, she explained, and according to their heathen customs she married very young.

"When no children came, my husband's family told him to divorce me because I was a sorceress. He refused. We paid many chickens to a powerful witch doctor, but he couldn't help. Then my husband developed leprosy and I fell sick." She told how everyone warned them against going to a missionary doctor, but since no one else could help, they went to the mission hospital. "I got well. I had children. That lifted my curse in the eyes of the family, but in those days we had to stay at the hospital's leper village for my husband's treatment."

Mujing told about becoming a Christian and about the reading classes the missionaries organized for the women. "They were in Swahili," she said. "I didn't speak Swahili, but I went. Although I learned that for certain marks I should say certain words, I did not understand the sense of what I was saying. Then they gave me a Bible in my own language. I was so happy—until I realized I could not read it.

"I began praying. I promised God that if He would help me to read and understand, I would share what I learned with others. One night in a dream I saw an open Bible, and I read and understood the words in it. When I awakened, it was still night. I lit my fire and got my Bible. I looked and looked until I found the page I had seen in my dream, and I was able to read it!"

Night after night she had similar dreams. The Bible would always be open to a different page. In each dream she read and understood, then she would awaken, light her fire, get her Bible, find the page, and read. The dreams continued until she could open her Bible to any page and read.

"Did you also learn how to write?" someone asked.

She seemed surprised at the question. "I asked only for the gift of reading," she replied. "And as you see, I have kept my promise. I teach what God has shown me in the Bible to the other women who cannot read." CORRINE VANDERWERFF

My Backup Disk

I will put my trust in him. Heb. 2:13, NIV.

Computers continue to reshape our world today. Not only are they used in businesses; they are also becoming a prominent tool of education. I have enjoyed the convenience of my personal computer at school; it has made research, writing, and organizing materials much easier. But I haven't always found computing easy and have had many one-sided arguments with the monitor and experienced other frustrations when trying to communicate with my hard drive.

One of the first things I had to do after setting up my computer was to make backup disks for all the programs on the hard drive. I didn't enjoy the hour I spent running the disk image program and inserting floppy disk after floppy disk. However, a few months later I came to value the time spent.

I had messed up a program while trying to figure out how to perform certain functions. After many confrontations with the program, I inserted the backup disk and reinstalled the program. Everything ran smoothly once again.

In some ways God is like our hard drive. We study and learn to depend on Him as our daily source of power. As we spend time getting to know Him, we create a backup disk to serve in the unfortunate instances when we mess up our systems. By turning to Him and reinstalling the program the way He planned, we find that He reboots our system, and we are able to continue to work for Him.   HEIDI MICHELLE EHLERT

OCTOBER 22

I Will Guide Thee

I will guide thee with mine eye. Ps. 32:8.

*D*riving through a heavy snowstorm can be tense and frightening. One winter I had my share of such experiences. On one occasion the blinding snow had reduced visibility to about two feet. I could barely see the vehicle ahead of me, but I could see the tracks it made. I followed in those tracks and reached my destination without incident. On another occasion I was just in time to drive behind two huge plows as they cleared the highway.

In our text today we are reminded that the Lord, our ever-present guide, can be trusted to keep the highways of life clear, or make tracks for us when "snowstorms" obscure our vision. With confidence we can follow the Way, the Light. He is familiar with each route we travel. When, in His wisdom, He chooses not to remove the piles of snow, He guides us safely along another path.

It is also comforting to know that no storm surprises Him. He is seated at the wheel of the plow before the first flake of snow falls to the ground. When the snow is so heavy that we can hardly see ahead, the Father invites us to follow Him anyway.

We can join David in this prayer: "For thou art my rock and my fortress; therefore for thy name's sake lead me, and guide me" (Ps. 31:3). God's response is "I am the Lord thy God . . . which leadeth thee by the way that thou shouldest go" (Isa. 48:17).

MARIA G. McCLEAN

Train Up a Child

My son, do not forget my teaching, but keep my commands in your heart, for they will prolong your life many years and bring you prosperity. Prov. 3:1, 2, NIV.

He was leaving. The growing collection of personal effects packed and placed by the door mutely attested to that fact. The past few days had been a flurry of checklists, shopping, cleaning, and sorting. Old things, comfortable and familiar, were carefully chosen to mingle with the new and untried. Hopefully they would mellow together to make a "home away from home." Yes, he was leaving.

As I contemplated our 15-year-old son/mother relationship, I was hoping that he would grasp from it some tried-and-true values that would follow him, stabilizing his journey into the unknown. I wondered what choices he would make, what priorities he would establish as he traveled the path toward his own maturing uniqueness.

I clung to the belief that no matter how fallible we human parents are, the God to whom I had dedicated myself and my children would always be there as the ultimate parent. I had to remind myself that this same God also provided me with a role model of letting go, as well as the assurance that we are loved and accepted as individuals, even if our choices stray from His ideal plan for our lives. His all-encompassing love provides a climate in which it is always safe to return.

Almost on his way out the door, my son handed me a small collection of stories and poems. Alone at home, I read them carefully. They were characteristically imaginative, thought-provoking, orderly, and reinforced the fact that he did have a personal relationship with God. I was encouraged that he had chosen to include God in his life, in his future. I read:

> From the endless depths of space,
> To the highest mountain peak,
> O'er the rolling hills of green,
> Past the clouds that hide and seek.

Across the salty marshes
That descend into the sea,
Through the narrow, craggy canyons,
Wonders made for you and me.

Of all the shining stars
That God in the heavens flung,
The most impressive feat of all,
Is that on the cross He hung.

Nature's monuments above us stand,
And the mighty river flows,
But God's most wondrous gift He gave
Is that from the tomb He rose.

What comforting words to a parent! My heart overflowed
with gratitude. *Lord, may I always remember that even though I may be
older, You are still my future. Help me to cherish Your most wondrous gift, even
as my son cherishes it.*
DEBBY GRAY WILMOT

OCTOBER 24

The Big Picture

Now we see through a glass, darkly; but then face to face: now
I know in part; but then shall I know even as also I am known.
1 Cor. 13:12.

While waiting for our food to be served in a restaurant,
my 11-year-old daughter pointed to a picture on the wall
beside our table and asked, "What's going on in that picture?"

I couldn't give her an immediate answer. It took more than a
casual glance to figure it out. This picture had to be studied. It
was a painting of a woman on a rickety old cart loaded with
crates of chickens. She was traveling down a stretch of road at
the exact moment that a foxhunt was crossing that same road.
There were the usual horses bearing men of ample proportions
and swarms of hunting dogs. Seemingly hundreds of them! And
those mixed-up dogs were after the woman's chickens! Barking

furiously, they jumped up at the cart, sending the chickens into a cackling frenzy. All the commotion spooked the donkey that was pulling the cart, and the woman was desperately trying to bring him to a stop.

Her frustration at the men on the horses was obvious. There they sat in their saddles, some of them laughing. Why didn't they call off their dogs? What kind of dogs were these, anyway? Didn't they know the difference between a fox and a chicken?

What the poor woman could not see was that the sly fox had jumped onto her wagon and was perched directly behind her on the top of the crates of chickens. Had she been able to see what was behind her, she would have been able to understand the dogs' behavior and the men's laughter.

Funny situation. But only funny to those who could see the whole picture. A bit like life. So often when unpleasant or even tragic things happen, our inability to see the big picture keeps us frustrated and unable to understand why. Sometimes we even become angry at God. Why doesn't He do something? It does help to know that our blind spot is temporary. A day is coming when we will be able to see fully, because our vantage point will have changed dramatically. In the meantime, it helps to know that we are safe in the hands of the only One who sees the whole picture now!

RETTA MICHAELIS

OCTOBER 25

A Gift of Thanks

Each of you must bring a gift in proportion to the way the Lord your God has blessed you. Deut. 16:17, NIV.

From the address on the envelope I knew the letter came from Robert. What did he want or need this time? I didn't want to read the letter just then, so I put it aside, hoping to lose it among the papers on my desk. But somehow that envelope kept resurfacing.

We first met Robert on a trip out in the Zaire bush. He had come to the house where we lived on the morning we were to return home to Lubumbashi, asking if we had any leftover soap we could leave him. No, we had carefully calculated what we needed on this trip and had nothing left. He asked if we could send him some trousers. Just looking at his trousers told us he truly needed a few pairs.

Months later he wrote that he needed some soap and salt. Couldn't he just buy these from the local market? I had carefully calculated what we would need until we could order more supplies, soap and salt included. The local salt he would find would be coarse rock salt, but that was what he was used to. I used white, fine, iodized, imported salt. Well, maybe something different would make him happy, even if it was just salt. We sent him some soap and salt.

Now this letter. Hours later, bracing myself for another request, I opened it. Conscience demanded that I at least read it. Most of the contents expressed thanks for the items received. After signing his name, Robert added, "I have nothing to send you to express my thanks except a small bunch of bananas." That touched my heart. Robert, in his need, did not have to send any bananas. He could have eaten them or sold them to buy what he needed. My conscience hurt because I had misjudged him. Thoughts flooded my mind. I was rebuked by his efforts to express his thanks, not just with words, but with a gift.

In proportion to blessings I received, was I as willing to show God, not just tell Him, my gratitude? He never told me He had carefully calculated what I should receive. He poured His blessings abundantly beyond the basic needs of life. Even this small bunch of bananas was one of His blessings—food not only for the stomach, but more for thought.   BIENVISA LADION NEBRES

OCTOBER 26

How Do You Start Your Day?

In the morning, O Lord, you hear my voice; in the morning I lay my requests before you and wait in expectation. Ps. 5:3, NIV.

A huge television tower overlooks the capital city of Alma-Ata, Kazakhstan. High, snowcapped mountains bordering China provide the backdrop. Because of Alma-Ata's location, many of its people and buildings retain a Chinese influence. The Muslim religion is strong, but so is no religion at all, as the result of years of Soviet atheism.

As the warmer breezes of perestroika were just starting to blow into the valley where Alma-Ata lies, Harold and Rose Otis met with some of the pastors of that part of the Soviet Union. They gathered in one of the mountain meadows near the TV tower for cooler air and privacy. There Pastor Otis presented the pastors with a copy of a book on the life of Christ. They were thrilled to see and hold pictures of Jesus in the beautifully printed book—it was a concrete sign of new religious freedom. They had despaired of its ever happening. Then Pastor Otis pointed to the TV tower and said, "Someday, not too long from now, the gospel will even be heard from that tower." Many in the small group thought that was really stretching the possibilities—it would never happen in their lifetime.

But now, just a few years later, I was in Alma-Ata with Rose Otis to conduct women's ministries seminars, and no one in government cared particularly why we had come or what we were doing at the church. Religious freedom had come.

On the second morning the coordinators informed us that someone from the TV station was coming and wanted an interview. We were not certain what type of questions or even what topics might come up. An attractive young Asian woman conducted the interview; she was the host for the principal morning show in Alma-Ata. She began by asking questions about women, the challenges they face, and what we thought the solutions were. While the interview was going on, I could not help thinking of that TV tower overlooking Alma-Ata, and that this Christian message was going to be broadcast all over this heavily populated valley.

As the interview wound down, the interviewer turned to Mrs. Otis and asked, "How do you start your day?"

Mrs. Otis explained that the first thing she likes to do each morning is to spend time talking to God, her heavenly Father. She likes to dedicate herself to Him for the day and to ask for His guidance. She said she also likes to spend some time reading her Bible and getting her mind ready to face the challenges of the day. The TV host smiled and thanked us very much for the interview, and the photographer turned off the camera. Then the host turned to us, almost bursting with joy. "You answered that last question just exactly the way I wanted you to! So many

people say they do their exercises or walk their dog or something else first in the morning. But you answered exactly right! People here need to hear that."
ARDIS DICK STENBAKKEN

OCTOBER 27

My $10 Leather Coat

Your Father knows the things you have need of before you ask Him. Matt. 6:8, NKJV.

The crisp October days were a few days away. Weighing heavily on my mind was my need for a winter coat. I usually made all of the clothing for our family of seven children, including coats. Mine presented a problem, because good-quality fabric would cost about $75—more than our limited budget could afford. I would have to be content with my old faded coat that unmistakably showed its age.

One Friday afternoon after work I stood waiting my turn to pay a bill at the cashier's counter in a store. I glanced around and saw a rack filled with coats. I went closer and found one in my size and decided to place it on layaway. At the counter I asked, "How much is this vinyl coat?"

"Vinyl?" the clerk mocked. "This is pure leather and usually sells for $100, but it's marked down to $10."

"Why is it so cheap?" I asked.

She pointed to a three-corner tear in the right sleeve. "I know how to mend leather," I told her. I paid for the coat and left the store.

On the way to my car I met Susie, a friend with whom I shared my good news. She asked me to go back and show her where the coats were. She had been in there earlier but hadn't seen them. I put the coat in my car and returned to the store with Susie, who had decided to buy a coat for her daughter. We looked everywhere, but no racks with coats were in sight. Susie asked the floor manager where the leather coats with the reduced prices were.

"Those coats are for our Saturday sidewalk sale and were not supposed to be sold today," he snapped.

When I got home I showed the coat to my family. I explained that God knew I needed a coat badly. He knew also that I wouldn't be in the mall on Saturday, so He arranged for me to get the coat on Friday.

Through the years people have occasionally asked, "How can a family of your size make ends meet working for the church?" It was no secret then, nor is it now. God provides for our needs with celestial blessings—such as the $10 leather coat.

We serve an awesome God! "My God shall supply all your need according to his riches in glory by Christ Jesus" (Phil 4:19). This verse reassures me that God cares about our needs and has unique and timely ways of supplying them.　　　MABEL ROLLINS NORMAN

OCTOBER 28

Hospitality Plus

Jesus answered and said unto her, Martha, Martha, thou art careful and troubled about many things: but one thing is needful: and Mary hath chosen that good part, which shall not be taken away from her. Luke 10:41, 42.

*A*re you ready for dessert?"

As a teacher I received many invitations to dine in students' homes. On this particular occasion the family and I had been served warm corn bread and gravy for the first course, with water to drink. The host then brought on another platter of corn bread and a pitcher of syrup for dessert. I had received the best she could provide.

Because of the selfless love with which this simple meal was served, I relished every bite and was satisfied. My eyes had been opened. This wasn't a teacher's-coming-to-dinner spread, but rather a you're-one-of-the-family feast. Although elegant dining is delightful, I discovered the purest pleasure at a plainly set table.

How often do we neglect offering hospitality because we don't have a banquet of gourmet food to serve our guests? One doesn't have to kill the fatted calf in order to be a gracious host. Like Martha, we often become so engrossed in preparing the meal that we forget the guest. Being hospitable means showing friendliness, kindness, and solicitude toward guests.

I'm encouraged by the lesson of hospitality that Jesus taught when He fed the 5,000. He did not use His divine power to seethe a kid, roast a calf, or broil a lamb. He did not supply cakes, grapes, pomegranates, dates, raisins, and almonds. Instead He multiplied the daily humble fare of fisherfolk—barley loaves and fishes—to feed the hungry crowd.

Our resources may be scanty, our service plain, but it is the warm welcome we extend to our guests that is appreciated more than the most elaborate meal. It would be better for us to be less busy with preparing or thinking we must have a Martha Stewart table setting before we invite guests to our home or welcome a visitor passing through town. A simple meal of soup and crackers, chili on a bun, fruit and toast, waffles and applesauce, or popcorn and juice can be most gratifying.

The greatest need of our guest, as with Jesus in Mary and Martha's home, may be a listening ear or an encouraging word, rather than food. Perhaps a walk to a park or a leisurely drive in the country is the only refreshment needed.

Lord, help me to accept the challenge to provide genuine Christian hospitality.
EDITH FITCH

OCTOBER 29

Time

My times are in thy hand. Ps. 31:15.

*M*any people like it. Many people hate it. I am among the haters of daylight saving time. What does it save? After all, it takes just as much electricity to have lights on in the morning as it does at night. I once read about a woman who was happy that her plants would get an extra hour of sunshine every day! Haters compare it to cutting one end off a blanket and sewing it to the other end. When our children were small, it made it doubly hard to get them to bed on time. Now it's hard to get *myself* to bed on time!

My husband's grandfather had a different reason for his problem with DST—he was sure it was the fulfillment of the prophecy in Daniel 7:25 that someone in authority would "think to change times and laws," so he flatly refused to change the time on his watch or clocks. The trouble was that he could never remember whether his time was earlier or later. As a result, he would arrive at church or other appointments either an hour early or an hour late!

When I was in the eighth grade, my teacher had a habit, annoying to her students, of constantly reminding us that "there is a time for all things," but it never seemed to be the time to do whatever it was that we wanted to do at the moment. Many years later, when my husband and I were on the staff of a boarding high school, we had our weekly turn of supervising the evening recreation period before sending the students to their dormitories for study hall and bed. When that time came, one of our coworkers would call out, "Time to *goooooo!*" Some of the students even came up with a rap routine for a talent program, using Art's "time to *goooooo!*" line. He was a good sport and joined them in the fun.

There are many mentions of time in the Bible, but perhaps the ones we should consider most seriously are those dealing with the time of the end of this world. Romans 13:11 says that "now it is high time to awake out of sleep: for now is our salvation nearer than when we believed." In 1 Thessalonians 4:16 we are told that "the Lord himself shall descend from heaven with a shout, with the voice of the archangel." Maybe those voices will be saying, "Time to *goooooo!*"   MARY JANE GRAVES

OCTOBER 30

Our Focus

Withhold not good from them to whom it is due, when it is in the power of thine hand to do it. Prov. 3:27.

I stared in horror at the plant my coworker was holding, smiling at her accomplishment. My once-beautiful plant that had draped its green-and-white-fingered leaves above and down my rich golden oak cabinet now reached for the ceiling with pathetic, skinny branches.

"Trimmed!" I screeched. "It's *murdered!*" I remembered a time when I gave permission to my gardener to trim my adored fig tree, only to discover later that it no longer looked like a fig tree. Fortunately, it did recover. True, my coworker hadn't trimmed this plant like I would have, but she had volunteered to water and trim my office plants while I worked to finish a deadline. I had given her permission. Now as I looked beyond the injured plant, I realized that all my plants looked trimmer and prettier as they nestled on top of the oak credenza. Ninety percent of her work had turned out beautifully.

"Thanks," I said, "for all the other trimming and watering you did. They look nice."

I thought of the many times I've done good work, for the most part, but people have noticed the 1 percent that was a mistake or didn't turn out right. So often we fail to comment on the majority that is good, what turned out great, or what we like, and focus on the mistake, the part that went wrong. We completely ignore what went right. We withhold the good—the praise—when it is due.

In our speeches for the Toastmaster's Club we notice and comment on what the speakers do right and help them have confidence, as well as directing and guiding them to improve.

After my friend and I had resolved our first tiff, we sat down and mentioned things we liked about each other and things we had in common. Then we mentioned our differences. We had 20 items in common and only five differences. Looking at it from this angle strengthened our friendship.

The plant sits on my credenza with its skinny little leaves reaching for the ceiling, rather than copiously draping toward the floor, but I still have hope that it will regain its former beauty. It serves as a reminder to me to focus on what is right and good, and not just on what goes wrong.   EDNA MAYE GALLINGTON

OCTOBER 31

Will Your Relationship Hold?

In my distress I cried unto the Lord, and he heard me. Ps. 120:1.

While Job and his wife led a comfortable life, a debate was going on in heaven. Satan felt provoked by God's praising Job to his face. His cynical answer, "Would Job worship You for nothing?" made at least two things very clear. First, Satan believed humans to be incurably selfish, even in their relationship with God. And second, he was not only convinced of Job's self-ishness, but also that God protected Job and favored him, re-gardless of what really went on in his heart. When Satan left the heavenly courts, he had God's permission to prove his points.

Suddenly calamity after calamity fell on Job. When the mes-sengers had told their terrible news, Job tore his clothes, shaved his head, and worshiped God. He had been brought up to believe that all he possessed was not his own; it had come to him from God, and he could possess it only as God permitted. Job put that lesson into practice.

But what about Mrs. Job? Did she not go through the same ex-perience as her husband? Did she not lose all her children, her ser-vants, her position in society, her friends—everything except her husband, who was covered with boils and who smelled so bad that it was difficult for her to be around him? She certainly did! But at the time of her loss her reaction was different from her husband's.

As long as everything went well, Mrs. Job enjoyed a good re-lationship with God. She had raised 10 children and taught them well. When things started to go bad, it looks as though her faith disappeared as quickly as her possessions. At that moment, stripped of almost everything she treasured in life, she could see no reason to continue her relationship with God. Nothing could be gained from it. She walked down to the rubbish heap, where her husband sat scraping his sores with a piece of pottery.

"You are still as faithful as ever, aren't you? Why don't you curse God and die?"

The test for Job and Mrs. Job was the same, but their reac-tion to the testing was different. Why? Job stood the test because of his close relationship with God. The relationship, however, did not begin when all the troubles overwhelmed Job. On the contrary, that was the time for the relationship to stand its test. Their friendship had grown through all the good years. By now there was so much trust and love on both sides that God could use their friendship as an example for the whole world. Mrs. Job had failed to build up this kind of a relationship, and in the time of trouble her incomplete faith did not sustain her faith in God.

The story of Job and his wife gives us an opportunity to stop and consider our own relationship with God. Do we worship God because we love Him, or for what He can do for us? Could Satan rightly accuse us of worshiping God to gain the blessings we receive, or to ensure God's protection over ourselves and our families? Yesterday is in the past; tomorrow is still in the future; but today is ours. Ours to seek a relationship with God that is strong enough to say "Even if He slays me, still I will trust in Him."

BIRTHE KENDEL

NOVEMBER 1

Stinkin' Cat

I have called you by your name; you are Mine. . . . Since you were precious in My sight, you have been honored, and I have loved you. Isa. 43:1-4, NKJV.

She was a scraggly-looking thing. Her fur was tangled. She was tiny and could barely meow. But I loved her instantly. I had always wanted a cat, but my husband hadn't. We had a dog, a parakeet, hermit crabs, and tadpoles, but never a cat—until she followed us home one day.

We had set out on our regular walk around the country block where we lived. We had just begun when we heard her weak "meow." She began following us along the road. Afraid that she would get hurt, I finally picked her up and carried her. She seemed frightened but glad. At home we gave her some milk. She didn't seem to know how to drink, but she soon learned. As we played with her, we discovered she had fleas. Hundreds of them. She spent the night outside, crying pitifully. The next day we doused her with flea spray and checked the neighborhood to see whom she belonged to, secretly hoping that no one would claim her. No one did. She was ours.

Tim named her "Stinkin' Cat." I didn't like the name, but it stuck. She grew into a beautiful young cat. Long gray hair. Beautiful long whiskers. Elegant ears. And a sweet personality. She's terribly curious and very friendly. She doesn't meow well, but she purrs contentedly.

From the beginning she knew that she was mine. She'd curl up on my lap every time I sat down, and follow me all over the house. She "helps" me change sheets and sleeps with me on evenings when Tim is gone. I knew that God sent her to me, giving me such a sweet little cat. Even Tim has learned to love her.

She reminds me a lot of me. Scraggly with sin. Tangled by bad habits. Not knowing what I need or how to pray. Yet God loved me instantly, from the moment I was conceived. He washed me in the blood of Jesus. Fed me by His Word and fellowship with others. Taught me to pray and to know Him. He longed for my company more than I longed for a cat. He's shown me the pleasure in curling up in His presence. He saw past the sin, the bad habits, wrong motives, terrible attitudes, and selfishness, and saw someone special. And He's growing me into that person. I am His. And so are you. Precious to Him. Loved.

O Father, thank You for seeing something special in each of us. For looking past our scraggliness, for seeing the beauty underneath, and for working to bring that beauty out. Thank You for loving us and for making us Yours.

TAMI HORST

Green-Thumb Lessons

They are like trees planted by streams of water, which yield their fruit in its season, and their leaves do not wither. In all that they do, they prosper. Ps. 1:3, NRSV.

Although my thumb is not green, I enjoy keeping houseplants. Nothing exotic, just real hardy, the type that withstand a drought when I forget to water them! After moving from the East Coast to the Northwest, I decided to try my hand at growing a ficus plant. I had often seen beautiful specimens of this tall indoor plant with their lower limbs braided to give them the appearance of a trunk of a small tree.

My prized plant went in a semibright corner near the couch. No doubt it would be happy there, with plenty of room to grow and with light from the window nearby. But alas! My little ficus was not the least bit happy, and its attitude showed. Instead of growing shiny, new, vibrant-green leaves, my ficus started to shed leaves by the handful. I tried to water it less—and then more—but nothing seemed to stop the cascade of leaves.

In desperation I consulted with a florist who had a similar plant in her shop. She explained that ficus plants have some of the worst "attitudes." If you move or prune a ficus, be prepared for a real tantrum of leaves. By this time I was quite attached to my ficus, despite its attitude. Sacrificing some important space, I put it by the only low, southern-exposure window in the house. It continued to protest for a week or two, then recovered and is now doing nicely.

Above this moody flora I have a hanging pot of faithful philodendron. Despite my occasional forgetfulness, "good ol' Phil" is alive without a weekly drink. Furthermore, when a pruning is in order, my philodendron responds wonderfully, growing fuller, sporting an abundance of shiny, new, green leaves. I can't help comparing my two corner plants. I admire them for their graceful lines and the vibrance they bring to the room. If I had my choice as to which one I would be, no doubt I would want to be the faithful philodendron, consistent, content, and always producing. But deep in my self-reflection I know there are times I am like my ficus plant, fighting a move, complaining about my location, and putting up a grand fight when it comes to the "pruning" times in my life.

As I contemplate repotting my ficus, I am asking the Lord to make me a "living plant" with a converted attitude. When the Master Gardener plants me beside the river of life, I want to be ready.   JILL HINES RICHARDS

God's Promises

When they had come into the house, they saw the young Child with Mary His mother, and fell down and worshiped Him. And when they had opened their treasures, they presented gifts to Him: gold, frankincense, and myrrh. Matt. 2:11, NKJV.

One night I woke up shortly after midnight. I couldn't sleep; I was so worried about our teenagers. It seemed that all of the values and principles we had tried to instill in them were going down the drain. My one great heart's desire was for my children to love Jesus and be saved.

As I picked up my Bible to seek God's help, I prayed, as I usually did, before reading it. "Lord, You know what You need to teach me. You know my needs and the needs of my family better than I do. Please, speak to me through Your Word. I am thanking You ahead of time because I know You never let me down. I ask these things in Jesus' precious name."

Matthew was the book I chose to read. As I was reading chapter 2, verse 11 stood out. But instead of writing it down in my notebook, I continued to read to the end of the chapter, thinking that there must be some other verse God wanted to speak to me about that night. I couldn't see how that one related to my worries.

I reread chapter 2. It was still verse 11 that impressed me as having great importance to me at this time. While I was wondering what that significance could possibly be, God's still small voice spoke. Not audibly, but there was no mistaking it.

He said, *Write it in your notebook.* While I was writing, still wondering why this particular verse was so important, He spoke again. *What is your most precious treasure?*

I answered, "My family—my husband and my children."

Give them to Me. I will save them!

Oh, what a burden rolled off my shoulders! There have been many ups and downs spiritually, but every time I start to doubt, He brings this promise to my mind. He is not finished yet. Praise God that I can claim the promise in Philippians 1:6: "Being confident of this very thing, that He who has begun a good work in you will complete it until the day of Jesus Christ" (NKJV).

VIRGINIA DART-COLLINS

As Gold Is Tried

Yea, though I walk through the valley of the shadow of death, I will fear no evil: for thou art with me; thy rod and thy staff they comfort me. Ps. 23:4.

I had been working in the yard with my family that hot September day. I went inside, utterly exhausted. Everyone else decided to go straight to bed, but I wanted to freshen up before going to sleep. After washing up, I sat down on the side of the tub, feeling dizzy.

Suddenly the entire room burst into flames, igniting my clothes. I screamed, awaking the rest of the family. It felt as though I was engulfed in a giant blowtorch, and there was no escape. My family shouted to me to come out of the bathroom. The flames were too intense for them to come in after me. But I had gone into shock and could not move. However, in the next moment I was outside the blazing room. There was no way I could have possibly done this on my own. I know God sent His angel to lead me out of the fire.

My clothes had burned off, so I grabbed a sheet from the couch to cover myself and ran outside, crying for help. Seconds after all of us got outside, the fire reached the main gas line, and our home exploded like an atomic bomb.

Thankfully, all of my family escaped. I, however, clung tenuously to life, but God continued to show His miracle-working power. During my recuperation I learned that God really does walk beside us, especially during our trials. Indeed, we have nothing to fear, even when we walk "through the valley of the shadow of death," for He is with us, ever ready to comfort us in our time of need. JANICE M. CARVER

NOVEMBER 5

The Train Ride

Watch ye therefore: for ye know not when the master of the house cometh. Mark 13:35.

I joined the long line of people at King's Cross station in London for my trip north to the city of York, where I was to meet my sister and friends. I was amazed at these English people—they queue up so properly, and your place in line is assured. I began to worry about getting a seat on the train as the line of people stretched round and round the station. I was assured, "Never fear; there is room for you if you have a ticket."

Suddenly we all walked in a very orderly way onto the train. I put my heavy bag above my seat. This was my first trip to the north, and I showed my nervousness. When the conductor came by, I asked him the time of arrival in York. He was happy to help me and dug around in his pockets and came up with a piece of paper with scribbling on it.

"I have it right here," he said. "It is 13:36."

Not being used to the 24-hour system, I asked, "Is that 1:36?"

"Yes, ma'am," he assured me and left with a big smile.

I relaxed and watched the beautiful English landscape go by as we rushed north. At 1:30 I stood up and pulled my bag down and stood by my seat for a few minutes. No one else seemed to be preparing to depart. I didn't know how long the train would stop at York, and I must be sure to get off. So I walked clumsily with my bag through the car to the door. Restlessly I watched the minutes pass. Now it was 1:36. What was happening? Was no one else getting off at York? At last a young mother with her child joined me. "When do we arrive in York?" I asked her.

She looked at her watch and replied, "We are scheduled for York at 2:03."

The conductor had given me the wrong time, but what did it matter? I was now ready. I was even at the door. A few minutes later we pulled into the station, and the first person I saw was my sister.

Now we stand at the very gates of heaven. We wait. Are we in the queue? Do we have tickets? Are we on the train and ready at the door? These matters must be taken care of today. When

the train pulls into the station of heaven, the first person we see
will be Jesus. DESSA WEISZ HARDIN

NOVEMBER 6

His Nearness

Out of the depths I cry to you, O Lord; O Lord, hear my voice.
Let your ears be attentive to my cry for mercy. Ps. 130:1, 2, NIV.

*F*ive o'clock on a chilly morning is altogether too early for
a retired person to "arise and shine." But I had awakened
early, questioning, "What have I accomplished for good during
the many years of my life?" Only my failures and shortcomings
came to mind. A guilt complex deepened my feelings of complete
unworthiness before God. Pray I should, but pray I could not.

In desperation I turned on the cassette player at my bedside.
A voice was reading the Psalms, beginning with Psalm 117. The
reader continued on and on, but not one word broke through to
dispel my gloom. I promised myself, "I will listen through Psalm
130, then I will 'arise,' even though the shine part will definitely
fall flat. I had no particular reason for specifying Psalm 130. It
was just a convenient number I chose offhand. Or was it?

It quickly became evident that the choice had been
prompted by a loving and concerned heavenly Father. The words
of Psalm 130:3 provided the reminder I needed. "If You, Lord,
should mark iniquities, O Lord, who could stand?" (NKJV).

My spirits rose. I was not an isolated case. The entire human
race has sinned and fallen short of the glory of God. However,
this deplorable condition is gloriously set right by the truth in
the next verse. "But there is forgiveness with You, that You may
be feared" (verse 4, NKJV).

Still more comforting assurance flooded from verse 7:
"With the Lord there is mercy, and with Him is abundant redemption" (NKJV).

*O Lord, help us, Your earthly daughters, to be constantly aware of Your
nearness as You lovingly hold out to us the promises of forgiveness and abundant redemption. Amen.* MABEL LATSHA

384

Never Again

At that time I will gather you; at that time I will bring you home.
Zeph. 3:20, NIV.

*A*rmed with a tablet and pencil, I worked my way through the house, writing down everything that had to be cleaned, repaired, or replaced before our holiday company arrived. I love making lists and get a lot of satisfaction out of a clean, orderly house, so I was in my element. Clean blades on ceiling fans. Replace torn bathroom curtain. And the list went on. I put myself on a schedule, happily crossing off each task as it was finished.

Because I work full-time, thorough housecleaning is one of the luxuries I've had to give up. But I was determined to do everything possible to make our home ready for my son's return from college and the visit of my daughter and a friend from overseas.

"Why are you doing this?" my never-see-clutter husband asked more than once.

"Because I want to," I answered. "Because I enjoy getting ready."

Tompaul would arrive home first. We were at the airport long before the plane was due, but it didn't come. The flight had been canceled. Nothing to do but head home and wait. Our son called from a different airport late that night. Overjoyed, we jumped into the car and headed out in the fog toward the city. It was midnight when we finally reached the airport, but when we saw his lanky frame standing by the curb, it was worth every moment of anxiety.

Our daughter and her friend arrived a week later. It seemed forever as we stood scanning the river of faces that came through the passport checkpoint, but at last I saw them. Weary. Smiling. They'd be here two whole weeks. There would be time to fix all the foods she couldn't get overseas. Time to talk, to catch up on their world. Time to get reacquainted.

Two weeks passed in a heartbeat. On a rainy, foggy morning two weeks after he arrived, we put Tompaul on a plane to fly across the continent. I cried. I always do. It's such a long trip, three time zones away.

A blizzard closed the airports the day our daughter and her friend planned to leave, so they had to stay another week.

Happiness! But the days flew past, and no matter how many times I do it, saying goodbye never gets easier.

It's easy to draw a parallel between my getting ready for my children to come home and God preparing heaven for His children. The anticipation I felt. The joy in planning special things for them. The happy countdown of days until we were together.

But there are vast differences. And the one that appeals to this mother the most is that when God brings His children home, He won't ever say goodbye again.

And neither will we. PENNY ESTES WHEELER

Kodak Moments

Let us make humankind in our image, according to our likeness. Gen. 1:26, NRSV.

*I*n my mind's eye a Kodak moment is a snapshot of priceless moments held in one's heart. We take the photograph to capture and preserve the visual image of pets, plant life, places, or people involved in pleasurable or painstaking pursuits.

There are no live plants, pets, or children here at my abode. At times it makes for a rather lifeless environment. Perhaps you are familiar with the peaceful, yet sometimes piercing, silence. Mothers of young children and teenagers caution me to treasure these moments. It's not that they don't adore their "crumb snatchers," it's just that their quiet moments are so few.

Are you going through a difficult adjustment now that you are alone most of the time? Do you miss warm, busy bodies passing through the corridors of your dwelling? If you relate for whatever reason, read on.

Just now it occurs to me that God understands yet another human dilemma. He knows exactly what it's like to walk through Eden's acres and acres of landscape, only to be reminded of a 6,000-year vacancy. There's been no Adam to announce, "Eve! I'm home." No Eve to sing morning love songs to Adam as God listens in.

Thankfully, God has a super VHS video. With just a thought He can replay Kodak moments from 6,000 years ago. Won't that be something for us to be able, one day soon, to replay or rethink precious Kodak moments enjoyed here? I wonder how it will be.

Ours is not to spend hours wondering about that, I suppose. Ours is to be "camera-ready," here and now. Ready to reflect His image at all times, so that should we replay these moments in the hereafter, we will be pleased to see we were God's Son's spitting image. Made in the image of God, just as we were originally supposed to be.   LYNN MARIE DAVIS

NOVEMBER 9

Just Imagine . . .

In My Father's house are many mansions; if it were not so, I would have told you. I go to prepare a place for you. John 14:2, NKJV.

After repeating this verse together and discussing ideas about what heaven might be like, I asked the junior Bible study class to tell what they would like to have for their own heavenly home.

Immediately a girl responded, "My home should be square." She explained that that shape would allow her to have an open space in the center in which she could plant a garden. She wanted to see her garden from every room in her house. What would she plant in her garden? Roses! Roses of all colors, but mostly pink ones.

One boy wasn't too particular about the house. He wanted many trees to surround his home. They could be tall trees and short trees—dark-green leaves or light-green leaves. Some would have flowers. He hoped colorful birds would visit his trees to find food and build nests. He did want trees.

"My house," another girl explained, "will have many windows. And they will be big windows. I won't need any drapes, 'cause in heaven there won't be prowlers." It wasn't to have shutters, either, because in heaven there would be no destructive wind, snow, or rain storms to require closing them for protection.

The importance of many big windows was so light could enter and completely permeate her home. "And," she added, "that light won't be too dim or too bright, or too hot, either. It will be gentle and comforting." Them she reached the pivotal point: "That light, you know, will come right from God Himself!"

Light from God! Indeed! John explains that the city will be illuminated by the glory of God, and the Lamb is its light (Rev. 21:23). Rose gardens, abundant trees, homes filled with heavenly light . . . What aspects of heaven appeal to your imagination? Consider what would become of our constant frustrations, worries, and disappointments if each day we imagined the wonders of heaven, if each day we envisioned new and more glorious vistas, yet being aware that "eye has not seen, nor ear heard, nor have entered into the heart of man the things which God has prepared for those who love Him" (1 Cor. 2:9, NKJV).

LOIS E. JOHANNES

NOVEMBER 10

Prison Gates Open

> They [Peter and the angel] passed the first and second guards and came to the iron gate leading to the city. It opened for them by itself, and they went through it. Acts 12:10, NIV.

Hilkka was on her way to see the prison director. It was wartime. Her husband had been sentenced to a year in prison for refusing to carry arms, although he was willing to serve his country in any other way necessary. As she approached the massive iron gate in the prison wall, she breathed a prayer, asking God to help her. She thought of the Bible account of Peter being released from prison. She knew God could open prison doors. In the large iron gate that was opened only for heavy transport vehicles there was a little door that could be opened from the inside. In this little door was a tiny window that would be opened by the guard upon the ringing of a bell.

Suddenly the large gate swung open. Hilkka looked around to see if a truck was coming, but could see nothing. A nice-looking guard in uniform signaled for her to enter the courtyard of the prison. She walked in and was soon met by an angry guard coming from the building.

"Where did you come from?" he asked.

"The big gate was opened," answered Hilkka.

The guard looked astonished and asked, "What do you want?" Upon being told that she had an appointment with the prison director, he permitted her to enter the main building, where her husband was at that moment washing the walls of the long corridor. Hilkka got the documents she had come to pick up and was also allowed to spend a half hour with her husband, who badly needed encouragement.

This is a story I loved to hear as a child. Nobody can shake my faith in the ministry of the angels. How can I be so sure? Because Hilkka is my mother. The guard was sure the gate had been kept closed. My mother saw the gate open, just as it did in Peter's experience, with the difference that she wanted to *enter* the prison! God is able to help us if we come to Him in humble prayer.

HANNELE OTTSCHOFSKI

NOVEMBER 11

Lasting Footprints

I tell you, on the day of judgment you will have to give an account for every careless word you utter. Matt. 12:36, NRSV.

On our forays to Arizona to catch some winter sun, I enjoy walking out in the desert. I have a distinctive design on the bottom of my walking shoes, so my footprints really stand out in the sand. If I happen to walk back over the same route, I can make it look like my right foot was going forward and my left was going backward. The footprints are often there for a long time, until some other prints or the wind obliterates them.

Just as I leave an impression of footprints in the sand, some of the words we speak can leave an impression on those whose paths we cross. When I hear someone quoting something I've said or something I've done, I often wonder if it will turn out to be something I wish I hadn't said, something that should have remained unspoken or undone.

Scripture tells us that at Jesus' trial, He often gave no answer at all. He knew that His words and the meaning would only be misconstrued, so He remained silent. "And he answered him to never a word: insomuch that the governor marvelled greatly" (Matt. 27:14).

Words can come back to haunt us. Unkind actions, as well as opportunities we have lost in blessing others, are all sad footprints to leave behind. In Romans 14:12 we are told, "Each of us will be accountable to God" (NRSV). When our life's work is ended, let us leave behind a legacy of positive footprints. When we stand to give an account of ourselves, we will be thankful we left impressions that were helpful to those around us. PAT MADSEN

NOVEMBER 12

God Uses Broken Things

He healeth the broken in heart, and bindeth up their wounds. Ps. 147:3.

When she was 14, my brother's only daughter mysteriously disappeared or ran away from home. No one in the family was sure why she left. Sue (not her real name) was doing well in school. Then the father she had been very close to passed away when she was 10. In fact, Sue had been alone with him in his final moments. She had tried to resuscitate him, as she had been taught. Could she be blaming herself for his death? No one knew for sure.

In the years after her disappearance it was rumored that Sue might be living in a town south of Miami. But where? Then came Hurricane Andrew. After its rampage, the rubble of destroyed buildings and homes was mute evidence of broken dreams and unfulfilled hopes. The day after Hurricane Andrew hit—and seven years after her disappearance—Sue rang her mother's doorbell. Imagine how happy the family was to see this daughter who was no longer a 14-year-old in pigtails, but a mature young woman of 21. God often uses brokenness to fulfill His purpose in our lives. While I don't know His purpose for Sue, she is working and attending night classes at a local community college. The broken family is reunited.

Before planting his crop the farmer must break the soil with his plow. Broken clouds give rain to water the crops and cleanse the earth. Mary had to break her alabaster box before the perfume could be enjoyed. Brokenhearted Peter repented and returned with greater power than ever. God uses brokenness and trials to teach valuable lessons. Most of Paul's Epistles were written from behind prison walls, and so was John Bunyan's *Pilgrim's Progress*. Many times God allows a man or woman to be placed in the fire to test their endurance, but only to the extent they can bear.

From each trial we are to learn lessons of trust, faith, and hope. Trials are not designed to break or destroy us. Financial reverses, job loss, illness, marital difficulties, a wayward child, or other problems can destroy a person if these trials do not move them to take a firmer grip of God's hand.

My sister-in-law had given up hope of ever seeing her daughter alive again. We believe God used Hurricane Andrew to bring Sue back home and heal the brokenhearted family.

Your circumstances may seem out of control and beyond remedy. In faith, begin to focus your eyes on the Healer of broken hearts. He will take your heartaches, sadness, and shattered dreams and make something beautiful of them—in His time. Guaranteed!

MABEL ROLLINS NORMAN

NOVEMBER 13

Ponderings From the Patch

> The wisdom that comes from heaven is first of all pure: then . . . full of mercy and good fruit. . . . Peacemakers who sow in peace raise a harvest of righteousness. James 3:17, 18, NIV.

*R*aspberries! The flavor is fantastic! For me they can add pizzazz to a fruit salad, jazz up a sophisticated soufflé, or satisfy in a bowlful of cream. A raspberry patch came with my home. I marveled at how last winter's superabundant rains had quadrupled the crop—as well as the work this past summer. As I enjoy the raspberries I picked in the summer, I ponder the lessons God has taught me from His second book, nature. For example:

A few scratches are inevitable in reaping a harvest.

When I am willing to look from a new perspective, I discover hidden treasure.

The growing vines yield the most fruit.

Plants, like people, thrive on tender, loving care.

Protective gear is valuable to "get into the thick of things."

Work is accomplished twice as fast before the heat of the day.

Raspberries are best when shared with a friend.

Ponderings from the patch show life to be "berry" fruitful.

SHARI CHAMBERLAIN

NOVEMBER 14

A Pocketful of Rue

He believed in the Lord; and he counted it to him for righteousness. Gen. 15:6.

Recently I was in my favorite department store to return a raincoat that was too large. It had been purchased six weeks earlier in a branch store 3,000 miles away. I had no receipt or tags. Knowing the store's reputation for no-hassle, customer-oriented service, I was confident they would take the coat back at the full price paid a month and a half earlier.

As I went to customer service to receive my refund, I marveled again at the no-questions-asked approach used by this nationwide chain. The saleswoman made no assumptions about my returning a coat that I could have worn a half dozen times or perhaps purchased six months ago, rather than six weeks, as I stated. Instead, righteousness was "imputed unto me," and I was handed over the full amount in cash.

Humming to myself, I headed to another department, stuffing the bills into my pocket as I walked. Maybe I'd look at a new sweater for my husband. Having gone nearly the length of the store, I turned to a table display and happened to glance back down the aisle. A woman in a teal jogging suit, obviously in a hurry, brushed past shoppers with an intent expression. I made an instant judgment: Why didn't she do her speed walking out in the mall? This was a store where people wanted to browse in peace.

No sooner had I made my mental assessment than she was upon me. "Excuse me," she panted. "Didn't you just get cash back in customer service?"

After I answered yes, her next words left me staring. "Here are two dollar bills you dropped as you left the window. I thought you'd want them back."

I took the bills from her outstretched hand, grateful she couldn't read my mind. Babbling thanks for her honesty and perseverance, I realized that she carried away the warm feeling of a good deed, while I had my money, plus the rueful aftertaste of a snap judgment gone awry.

I had come to the store hoping—no, expecting—to be taken at face value and believed. My hopes were fulfilled. Obviously, I could learn something from a clothing chain and an honest woman about valuing others and believing the best.

CAROLE BRECKENRIDGE

NOVEMBER 15

Why, Lord?

Is there anyone among you who, if your child asks for bread, will give a stone? . . . If you then, who are evil, know how to give good gifts to your children, how much more will your Father in heaven give good things to those who ask him! Matt. 7:9-11, NRSV.

"*M*ommy, Mommy, *please* stop and let us get some balloons!" echo two exuberant girls as they fix their pleading eyes upon mine.

I glance at my watch, realizing that each moment's delay will cause us to be a few minutes later to our appointment. "OK, girls," I agree, "but please choose quickly."

I love to say yes to my children, simply because I feel a keen satisfaction in being able to make them happy. However, at times

I am very unpopular when the answer is a decided no. Typically I hear "Oh, Mom, *why?*"

It is during these times that I think about how God loves to say yes to His children. As a mother I may not think a balloon is very important in comparison with the concerns in my adult life, yet I still want to show my love to my children by saying yes. God treats us much the same. I'm sure that some of the things we ask for are minuscule in comparison to God's far greater concerns for the whole of His creation. Yet God does not harshly brush us off just because it may be a small matter. He knows that it's important for us, just as the balloon is of monumental importance to my girls. In fact, God's a much better parent than I am, because everything that concerns His children is no small matter to Him. He longs to give good gifts to His children.

But sometimes God says no. The no's are often difficult for us to accept. So we ask God why.

"O Lord, why?" I remember asking at the age of 16. "Why are my legs shaped like toothpicks?" Sometimes the whys in this life are more complex. As a young mother facing the death of our only son, I sobbed, "Why, Lord, why?" as I gazed upon his tender young face.

In this world of sin there will always be whys. But I have discovered that when I am tempted to ask God why He has said no, I can also ask Him why He has said yes. Why, Lord, am I so fortunate to have two healthy children? Why am I blessed with my eyesight, a warm home, and two legs to walk with? And why, Lord, did You come to this world to die for me? As if this is not enough, Lord, I have You to thank for my own salvation. Lord, You are so good to me. I am filled with the wonder of "Why?"

Dear Lord, please guide me to trust Your power to direct my life, and because I know You love me, help me to also trust the providence of Your whys.

JULIE REYNOLDS

Speeding

Happy are those whose transgression is forgiven. Ps. 32:1, NRSV.

*T*he phone rang, and I jumped out of bed. I had only one hour before the start of the shift. The commute to the hospital takes at least 20 minutes. I needed to take a shower before getting into my uniform, and I needed to read my morning devotional. Knowing that once I was on duty there would be many concerns that would occupy the time, and it would be difficult to get a chance to eat breakfast, I knew I must also browse the refrigerator to choose something to eat while driving.

Once all this was accomplished, I got into my car and headed for the highway. My car clock showed that it was 7:10, and I was not even halfway to work. There was very little traffic on this early Sunday morning, so I moved into the fast lane and began accelerating. I was speeding at more than 85 miles per hour in a 65-miles-per-hour zone. In a few moments the highway patrol signal lights came on behind me. The officer had caught me. I pulled over to the right side of the highway. He politely asked to see my driver's license and vehicle registration and returned to his car.

I sat in frozen silence. I didn't feel it was appropriate to pray to be spared from the verdict. I was sure I was about to get a ticket. I knew I had broken the law and deserved the penalty. *I will pay a good sum of money for this fine. He'll probably send me to traffic school to erase my transgression, and now I will definitely be late to work,* I thought.

When the officer returned, he asked me if I knew why he had stopped me. "I was speeding, sir," I said.

"Do you know how fast you were going?"

"Between 80 and 85 miles per hour."

"Where are you going?"

"To the Kaiser Hospital, sir."

Then the officer kindly returned my license and car registration, saying, "I do not want to blemish your driving record, for you have such a good one. But be careful." And he let me go! I couldn't believe it! He forgave me of my transgression! That is what I call *grace!* I sighed in relief and went on my way to work.

Romans 5:20 says: "Where sin abounded, grace did much

more abound." Christ came to pay for our sins because He loves
us more than we deserve.   ESPERANZA AQUINO-MOPERA

NOVEMBER 17

In Everything, Give Thanks

In every thing give thanks: for this is the will of God in Christ
Jesus concerning you. 1 Thess. 5:18.

Our 80-year-old neighbors are having a run of misfortunes.
In September their 20-year-old grandson, a brilliant
young man in his final year at the university, was killed in a traffic accident.

"God is so good," they told us through their tears. "We don't
know why this tragedy happened, but we thank Him that Tim
died instantly. He was not left to suffer and perhaps be crippled
for life. Right now, Tim loved the Lord—but who knows what
the future might have brought?"

Three months later our neighbors returned from an outing
to find their street blocked by police cars, an ambulance, fire
trucks, and emergency services. A student driver had lost control of her car and crashed into the side of their house, causing
extensive damage.

"Is anyone hurt?" was the old couple's first question. When
assured that no one had been injured, they sighed with relief.
"The house is insured, and the damage can be repaired. We're
just so thankful that no one was hurt and that we were not home
when it happened. One of us would surely have been right inside,
where the wall collapsed."

Six weeks later Mrs. Neighbor fell and broke her arm. She
suffered greatly, and her arm is still in a cast. She brushed off our
proffered sympathy by saying, "Oh, I'm so thankful it wasn't my
right arm."

The following day, as our neighbors were driving to visit a
daughter, their car seized up. For 10 days they were without
transportation while the auto was being repaired. And when they
got the $3,000 repair bill, they admitted to us in shock, "The

repairs cost far more than we expected. We are just so thankful that we have enough money to pay it."

Yes, my neighbors take Paul's command literally: "In every thing give thanks."

Let's not confine our thanksgiving to blessings bestowed. Let's try to find reasons for thanksgiving in every experience, good or bad. "Giving thanks always for all things unto God and the Father in the name of our Lord Jesus Christ" (Eph. 5:20).

GOLDIE DOWN

NOVEMBER 18

Jesus Loves You!

For God so loved the world that he gave his one and only Son, that whoever believes in him shall not perish but have eternal life. John 3:16, NIV.

During the last half of 1995 I was struck with a serious problem. I eventually fell into depression for several months, suffering from headaches day and night. I was treated by my doctor, but with no success. Although I prayed that the Lord would help me out of this unbearable situation, it seemed He was not listening at all.

Eventually I began suffering from swollen ankles, sleepiness, and tiredness until finally I could hardly put one foot in front of the other. A visit to an internist revealed that I had had a heart attack, which was the cause of the tiredness and sleepiness. In his opinion, a heart bypass operation was in store for me, but he advised me to visit a cardiologist with whom he had been discussing my heart problem.

How I prayed for a miracle! "Please, Lord, if it is Your will!" And then the miracle did happen! On the two EKGs done by the cardiologist there was not a sign of any heart attack, and my heart was functioning at 100 percent!

The astonished doctor simply shook his head. And my husband and I could not stop praising the Lord. Meanwhile, I was still in the same state of depression. One night our local pastor visited me. He was so gentle and kind that before I knew it, I started crying my heart out, giving him the details of my problem that had caused me so many tears. Instead of reading some texts to make me feel guilty and without picking up one stone to throw at me, he said to me, "Charlotte, remember, even if you forget everything else, *Jesus loves you!*" These words he said very softly and repeatedly.

I've known these words very well since I was a little girl, but that specific night was the turning point, and I grabbed the wonderful thought of Jesus, the Almighty, loving me, a great sinner. I am the apple of His eye, and my name is written in the palm of His hand!

We worship a wonderful God, my friend. Our Jesus, gentle and loving. I do not see Him as a tyrant sitting with His whip to torture me, but as a loving Father with His arms open to enfold me with love and all the goodness of life.

Jesus loves you, too!

CHARLOTTE E. DeBEER

Who Listens?

Hear, my child, your father's instruction, and do not reject your mother's teaching. Prov. 1:8, NRSV. My child, do not forget my teaching. Prov. 3:1, NRSV.

Listen, my child," Solomon says over and over in Proverbs. And I could relate. I'd taught a teen Bible class for several years. I loved "my" kids. I'd have done almost anything to help them understand God's love, to help them understand that God's plan for their lives was the one they'd want to follow if only they could see the end from the beginning. I wanted desperately to save them from the pitfalls so many others have wandered through on their way to maturity.

But as I read Proverbs, I mourned that no one would benefit from the wisdom of Solomon's first several chapters. The young couldn't grasp it. Those like me who understand the importance of his message understand because we've lived long enough to experience the consequences of avoiding his counsels.

Then God stopped me short. *When will you be any younger than you are today?* The thought thundered in the silence of my mind. After a moment's reflection to reorient my thinking He whispered, *Solomon's advice to the young is for everyone who is younger today than they will be tomorrow.*

I'll keep praying for "my" kids and doing anything I can to help them make wise choices. But this not-quite-so-young person is taking Solomon's wisdom to her own heart too.

"My child, if you accept my words and treasure up my commandments within you, . . . then you will understand righteousness and justice and equity, every good path. . . . It will save you from the way of evil" (Prov. 2:1-12, NRSV).   HELEN HEAVIRLAND

NOVEMBER 20

The Spaghetti Incident

Do for others what you want them to do for you. Matt. 7:12, TEV.

The other day a friend of mine was bemoaning the fact that she had two small sons to get ready every morning before she left for work. "You are so lucky," she told me. "All you have to worry about is getting yourself ready."

"And two dogs and a cat," I reminded her. Just that morning I had arrived at work in a more frazzled state than the mother of two. My mornings are well organized, but unfortunately my pets occasionally make last-minute changes in my schedule. I had prepared a steaming plate of left-over spaghetti—so much more interesting than a breakfast of cold cereal—and set it on the kitchen counter. I poured myself a glass of ice water and put it down by the spaghetti. I filled the ice tray and turned around to put it back in the freezer. This is when I forgot the first rule of cat owners—never turn your back on a cat in the kitchen! When I returned to the counter, Gilead was standing with all four feet in the spaghetti while playing one of his favorite games—bobbing for ice cubes in my glass. I grabbed him, washed his paws off, and put him on the floor. The spaghetti wasn't very appetizing with four little paw prints in it, and since the dogs couldn't stomach such spicy food, I decided to throw it away. When I turned around to go to the trash can, I tripped over Gabriel, one of my shelties. Hot spaghetti spilled all over his back. As I washed the spaghetti off his back, Galen, my other sheltie, helped by licking up all the spaghetti that had landed on the floor. My plans for an enjoyable breakfast had gone completely awry.

Satan wants us to feel sorry for ourselves and take our eyes off Jesus. Nobody's life is worry-free, but instead of concentrating on life's little annoyances we need to think of our blessings. We don't have to look far to see that there's always someone who has it worse than we do.

Thank You, Lord, for Your blessings, which are far greater than the inconveniences in life.

GINA LEE

NOVEMBER 21

Thanksgiving

Let not your heart be troubled: ye believe in God, believe also in me. In my Father's house are many mansions: if it were not so, I would have told you. I go to prepare a place for you. And if I go and prepare a place for you, I will come again, and receive you unto myself; that where I am, there ye may be also. John 14:1-3.

You have been hearing about it for weeks, maybe even months. It has been in all the papers, on television ads, and the topic of many conversations between friends, family, and work associates. We plan grand things "to do" during this special time. For some it means a very long trip across the country with cranky kids, few rest stops, delayed flights, snowstorms, floods, tornadoes, and lack of sleep. For others it means a short drive across town. Still others never leave the house. And in the past, a sleigh ride over the river and through the woods was all that was necessary.

You've guessed it, haven't you? From that last comment about the sleigh and the woods? I think I would welcome that mode of transportation if Grandma's wasn't so far away. Today is a bit different, isn't it? Ask almost anyone, and you'll find that getting home for the holidays is quite an event. Why do we do it? What draws us to put everything else on hold? Who is it we want to see? Or is there more to it?

I hate to admit it, but some people travel out of obligation, some out of loyalty, some out of tradition, and some are forced, but I'd like to think that most travel out of love—the nonjudgmental love that a family can give.

On Thanksgiving most differences are put aside, and we reminisce about happy times. We tell stories on each other, we laugh, we play games, we eat. We feast, not only on food, but on the abundance of love that permeates the room. We bask in the warmth of acceptance and the assurance that we belong. And we miss the ones in our family circle who are not there. Divorce, distance, and death have a way of separating us. Yet we hold in our hearts the memories that missing ones have shared with us.

God made families to love one another, just as He loves us, unconditionally. He wants us to nurture one another, pray for one another, and care for one another, just as He has nurtured, prayed, and cared for us. He is preparing a feast for us on a table many miles long. He is making a home, a mansion, for each of us. A home filled with peace and harmony forever.

"Let not your heart be troubled: ye believe in God, believe also in me. In my Father's house are many mansions: if it were not so, I would have told you. I go to prepare a place for you. And if I go and prepare a place for you, I will come again, and receive you unto myself; that where I am, there ye may be also."

When Jesus returns to gather us home, we will all be traveling out of love. The love of the Father, bestowed upon the Son, and spilled at the cross for all of us. My prayer is that each one of us is preparing now for Jesus to come. It promises to be the best Thanksgiving we've ever had!   DARLYN TOWNSEND

NOVEMBER 22

Seeing Through the Clouds

Grace to all who love our Lord Jesus Christ with an undying love.
Eph. 6:24, NIV.

I was flying a shuttle flight from Portland, Oregon, to Medford, where I live. It was a beautiful, clear day, and as I looked out my window I could see several snowcapped mountains jutting up close to our flying space. Then I noticed there were some areas where valleys lay covered with dense clouds. I felt sorry for the people living under those clouds. I was sure that while I was flying high above enjoying the bright sunshine, their view was obscured, and they were experiencing a dismal day.

I was reminded of the times I've felt life was clouded and dismal. Times I couldn't see through the clouds that enveloped me. No sunshine anywhere. Perhaps, as a pastor's wife, I've encountered a parishioner who told things behind my back that weren't true. Or I've had a disagreement with one of my children that seemed so difficult to reconcile. Then there are physical difficulties that many of us have to live with. The future looks bleak, and we don't understand why God doesn't handle things the way we think He should. We get so enshrouded in dark clouds we can't see Him.

In times like these I must realize by faith that I need the Son, and if I will just be patient I'll find that the clouds cannot linger forever. The sunshine of His presence will break through and envelop me with warmth, love, and peace. I cannot remain depressed or discouraged when I know the clouds are only temporary. God, in the sunlight of His love, is always sustaining me by His grace, even though I sometimes cannot see Him or understand why things are the way they are. Someday I will see Him, and then I'll live forever in sunshine.   ELLEN BRESEE

The Miraculous Escape

Before I formed you in the womb I knew you, before you were born I set you apart. Jer. 1:5, NIV.

Thirty days after our son was born, my husband and I traveled with him and our 2-year-old daughter to another city. The 60-seat bus in which we were riding was going at a high speed on a broad highway. Suddenly, unmindful of the oncoming bus, a careless cyclist zigzagged from the opposite direction directly toward us. Our bus driver kept honking, but the cyclist paid no attention. The driver slammed on his brakes to avoid a collision. In seconds the bus skidded to the right. The front wheels sank into the loose sand, tilting the bus to the right, throwing all the passengers to the right. Cries filled the bus.

Panic-stricken, we all scrambled out with great difficulty, fearful that the bus was about to turn over. Once outside, I realized that God's mighty hand was balancing a 60-passenger bus firmly on just one wheel. What a miracle! Everyone in the bus thanked God for His protection. Our infant son slept peacefully, undisturbed by the commotion.

I feel sure God had a special purpose for each of us in this incident. God has brought you to another day as well. Our lives have been preserved. We need to commit ourselves to Him each day and allow Him to use us to bring honor and glory to His worthy name.   HEPZIBAH G. KORE

Oh, Be Thankful!

It is wonderful to be grateful and to sing your praises, Lord Most High! It is wonderful each morning to tell about your love and at night to announce how faithful you are. I enjoy praising your name to the music of harps, because everything you do makes me happy. Ps. 92:1-3, CEV.

One afternoon I watched one of my favorite talk shows. The host has many interesting, informational topics that are often helpful. On this particular day the subject was about being happy. The special guest, a counselor, talked about people with unpleasant attitudes.

"It doesn't take much to be happy," she told the audience, "but many people don't realize that being happy comes from within. Being happy is an experience of recounting the many ways you are blessed and the many things you can be thankful for."

The counselor went on to suggest that every day we write in a journal at least five things for which we are thankful. We are blessed in so many ways, yet we fail to express our thankfulness. She challenged us to express our gratitude daily.

Could I honestly think of five things each day for which I am thankful without listing the same ones again and again? I wondered as I listened to her talk about her own experience of recording her thanks. I decided to give it a try.

I began that day, and although I have skipped a day or two here and there, I was surprised at how the list grew and grew. On some days I listed not five, but as many as 10 reasons I was thankful. This exercise in thankfulness did so much for me. I began to think more of Christ and His love. Yes, I often thank God when things go well, but am I just as thankful when things get a little tough?

Maybe you'd like to start your own "Thank You, Jesus" journal. Write down five things for which you are thankful today. Do it for several days. Just reading over your list of blessings will give you a burst of energy!

MARIE H. SEARD

Questions to Ponder

The knowledge of the secrets of the kingdom of heaven has been given to you. Matt.13:11, NIV.

*H*ave you ever wondered if there's another word for "synonym"? Why isn't there a mouse-flavored cat food? Why do they report power outages on TV? Where do forest rangers go to "get away from it all"? Why do medical doctors call what they do "practicing" medicine? If a person with multiple personalities threatens to kill himself, is it considered a hostage situation? How can there be self-help "groups"?

Questions to ponder . . . the world is full of them. The above questions came off the computer Internet superhighway. Like most such nonsense, who knows where it began and where it will end? As Festus said to the apostle Paul: "Much learning doth make thee mad" (Acts 26:24).

We can't know everything. Sometimes it seems that I just acquire a new fact or concept when it suddenly grows obsolete. And for every tidbit of truth I discover, a thousand questions pop up to haunt me. Human knowledge is growing so quickly that I'm lucky to stay current with the basics of knowledge in my own field, let alone digest the enormous amount of trivia bombarding us every day. Sometimes I'm overwhelmed by it all. I feel like crawling into a little cave beside the brook Cherith and letting the rest of the world go by. And I would, except I know what Jesus said, and His words make all the difference. He said, "Ye shall know the truth, and the truth shall make you free" (John 8:32).

The simple truth is, Jesus loves me. He died to save me. He forgives my sins. He promises me eternal life. While He doesn't always answer my questions, He has given me everything I need to guarantee eternal life. Religionists try to muck up Christianity with convoluted theories and vague suppositions, but Jesus came to simplify and to redeem. He died on the cross so I could live. It's as simple as that.

I may not have all the answers to life's questions. I may not understand all the intricacies of life. But I know in whom I believe. And I know what He commanded me to do. He said, "Repent and be baptized . . . obey My commandments . . . love one another . . ." Simple instructions from the Master, and easy to follow when I have the Holy Spirit as my guide.

And for any questions I might still have, questions for which I can find no answers, I'll have all eternity to uncover the answers in God's kingdom.

KAY D. RIZZO

NOVEMBER 26

Transformation

Come now, and let us reason together, saith the Lord: though your sins be as scarlet, they shall be as white as snow; though they be red like crimson, they shall be as wool. Isa. 1:18.

*B*are trees stood stiffly, sharply outlined against the leaden skies that cold, bleak winter day. Acrid smoke curled upward from the chimneys of dull buildings that looked down on narrow streets, punctuated here and there by potholes filled with dirty water. The last crackling-dry leaves danced wildly with city litter, caught up temporarily in the slipstream of passing cars. A depressing scene of dullness and dirt.

Then it snowed. Silently. As we slept, nature covered with a thick blanket of purest white every shivering tree, every ugly building, every muddy pothole, every dead leaf and piece of city litter. And as the sun rose, its long-fingered rays animated with a magical touch billions of minute crystals that sparkled and scintillated off every snow-covered surface. The change was nothing short of miraculous, the beauty breathtaking.

It didn't last, though. Before the day was over, passing cars had churned the city streets into a sea of brown slush. Flecks of grime from the chimneys had marred the virgin white of roofs and trees. And once more litter, now soggy and motionless, splattered roads and pavements alike.

The physical world has so much to teach us about the unseen and spiritual. Who has not marveled at the change in the life of a repentant sinner, clothed in the perfection of Christ's snow-white robe of righteousness and responding to the gentle, warming rays of God's love? Surely there is no greater evidence of God's transforming, regenerating power!

But let us always remember that in order for a born-again life to retain its pristine beauty, it must be given completely into God's hands, hour by hour and day by day, that the white robe of Jesus' righteousness might cover it continually. Otherwise our inherently sinful natures will surface once more, and our lives will be marred, no longer reflecting the beauty of the character of our Creator and Redeemer.

> I bring my life to You today,
> Sweet Jesus, Saviour, King.
> You have the pow'r and only You
> To cleanse my heart of sin.
>
> By grace I'll wear Your righteousness,
> A robe of purest white,
> Which covers my forgiven sins,
> Perfects me in God's sight.
>
> So every day this is my prayer,
> Lord, dwell in heart and mind.
> As You inspire my thoughts and words,
> Through me, please bless humankind.
>
> REVEL PAPAIOANNOU

NOVEMBER 27

Modeling

Clothe yourselves with the Lord Jesus Christ, and do not think about how to gratify the desires of the sinful nature. Rom. 13:14, NIV.

Modeling is a multimillion-dollar business. Models are used for selling everything from clothes to chewing gum. I guess when a product is modeled by a person, it sells much better.

Let me share my memories of three women who modeled Christ.

Model 1: Lillie. She grew jasmine indoors. Jasmine produces small, delicate, white flowers with a lovely scent. Not very many people experience success in growing it. One morning as I was leaving for work, she called to say that her plant was full of blooms. She had taken the time to pluck them and string them and wanted to know if I would like to pick them up on my way to work and wear them in my hair.

Model 2: Grace. I was asked to coordinate a friend's wedding. Unwisely, I also agreed to help prepare a dish for the wedding banquet. Not being very good at quantitative cooking and because of the shortness of time, I enlisted Grace's help. Unfortunately, she had a stiff neck as a result of an accident. I promised her that she would need only to supervise. It turned out that the project was larger than I had anticipated, and it took longer than I had estimated. Grace took on the responsibility of completing the cooking and delivered the food to the reception hall. When I returned from the wedding, I discovered that the kitchen was clean. I later found out that Grace had stayed up until 2:00 in the morning catching up on her own housework!

Model 3: Lena. She was 84 years old and lived across the street from me. She was nearsighted, with thick glasses, and her hands were losing their nimbleness because of arthritis. She loved to crochet, and her afghans and tablecloths were simply beautiful. One of her desires was to crochet a lace tablecloth for my dining table before she died. It is one of my prized possessions.

Time will never erase from my memory what these Christian women modeled for me. I want to pass on this kind of friendship to other women.

HEPHZI OHAL

NOVEMBER 28

What Shall I Wear?

Seek ye first the kingdom of God, and his righteousness; and all these things shall be added unto you. Matt. 6:33.

So many of us have a real fixation about what clothes we should wear. I'll admit to many sleepless nights, lying awake and wondering, *What will I wear tomorrow?* The Lord addressed our concerns when He said, "Do not worry about your life, what you will eat or drink; or about your body, what you will wear. Is not life more important than food, and the body more important than clothes?" (Matt. 6:25, NIV). Yes, we agree. But we still like to plan ahead. We want to be prepared. We want to look our best.

I read about a woman pastor in England who found a simple remedy. She purchased six blue dresses for the weekdays and one special white dress for church. She never had to think about it—she knew exactly what she would wear. Oh, how boring! We have so many beautiful, colorful fabrics and styles to choose from. I love variety! Yet I have to respect her simplicity and frugality.

There are many individuals who have extra rooms just to store their clothing, accessories, and shoes. We are bombarded with the "dress for success" message. We can agree we feel better when we have selected the appropriate clothing for the occasion. I remember several embarrassing experiences when I did not have the finances to obtain the "right" dress for the party, the college banquet, the job interview, or the corporate dinner. Whether it was lack of funds, poor taste, or being in the wrong place at the wrong time, I looked foolish!

The most important dress of my lifetime was my wedding dress. I searched for months. I needed just the right shade of ivory, the best fit, and the appropriate style for an outdoor wedding. Several of my bridesmaids helped me select a beautiful satin dress that, while significantly marked down in price, was several sizes too large. The seamstress assured me it could be altered. Just weeks prior to my wedding date she called to say it would be impossible to make the dress fit. I prayed and shopped frantically until I found the perfect dress, more beautiful than the first one I had chosen.

Jesus knows our needs. He is most concerned that we are preparing for the great wedding banquet of the Lamb (Rev. 19:7-9). God offers us Christ's robe of righteousness as the only garment we need for heaven. So "be dressed in readiness, and keep your lamps alight" (Luke 12:35, NASB).   CAROL J. SMITH

Perseverance

Blessed is the man who perseveres under trial, because when he
has stood the test, he will receive the crown of life that God has
promised to those who love him. James 1:12, NIV.

*T*he first church social event of the summer was a hike to
Bald Hill Mountain, where once upon a time a well-known
trail had led. A group of varied ages, 13 to 82, showed up at the
church parking lot, eager for fellowship and a good hike. Sharing
rides, we soon arrived at the designated starting point on the
trail. It was exciting to be on the familiar trail, which was quite
well marked, with a variety of flat, shady terrain. Part of it twisted
into narrow and slightly overgrown paths and later a challenging,
hot, and exhaustingly steep climb to the top. All of us were tired
and almost worn out. A rest period was welcomed.

After a conference between the leaders and an affirmation
from the rest of the group, we continued on the trail, rather than
backtracking. We trudged on, even though what had been a trail
was now virtually nonexistent and overgrown. We started on the
downgrade, this time in cooling shade and through densely
wooded areas. One by one we followed each other through what
was often just a hint of a trail. Much of the time we were blazing
a new trail. We went up and down, then around the side of the
mountain, holding onto rocks, roots, and branches, helping each
other and beginning to wonder if we were lost.

By our watches and an occasional glimpse of the sky, we
could see that darkness was fast approaching. Should we continue, or should we go back? Go back? No, that would be awful!
No one wanted to backtrack through that difficult terrain.
Onward we pressed, sometimes in silence and concern, but
mostly with smiles and encouragement.

Finally, around the last wooded bend, we came to a well-
marked path. We looked at one another, scratched, tired, wind-
blown, and dirty. We looked as though we had come through a
combat zone. There were relief, thankfulness, and laughter as we
continued on the well-marked path. But then—oh, no! How could
it be? Once again we were facing a dense, wooded area.
Nevertheless, we decided to press forward, and in a matter of a few

hundred feet we suddenly found ourselves on the original path. What a sense of victory! We knew we were homeward bound.

I began wondering what the Lord could teach me. Perseverance came to my mind. I could have given up, but by choosing to persevere I gained a great sense of satisfaction. In today's text I found the assurance that we are blessed when we persevere in trials and temptations and remain faithful to God. When we continue to walk with the Lord, we are assured of receiving the crown of eternal life that our God has promised to those who love Him and persevere in life's journey.

ERIKA OLFERT

The Place to Turn

Then said Jesus unto the twelve, Will ye also go away? Then Simon Peter answered him, Lord, to whom shall we go? thou hast the words of eternal life. John 6:67, 68.

In 1974 I met and fell in love with Jesus. He changed my life. Although I still had many challenges, most stemming from an unhappy marriage, I found peace and hope in my relationship with Him.

By 1982 my marriage had dissolved. When my husband moved out of the house, I moved out of the house too—God's house. I don't know why. I suppose I was angry and tired. I was hurting and feeling so unloved and unneeded. I decided I would find someone who would love me, so I stepped out into the world. No more worries about church, Bible lessons, or taking care of my body. When I left, I left everything. Instead of going to church, I went to bars. Instead of eating properly, I indulged in alcohol and cigarettes. Instead of prayer meeting, I went on dates with nice, but unspiritual, men.

To my surprise, very seldom did I have fun. I laughed, sang, and danced, but I was lonelier and angrier than ever before. And the "love" I was so desperately seeking was the very thing I had left behind, for God is love, and I had left Him in search of the kind of love the world offers. The kind that is never pure, uplifting, or lasting.

Like the prodigal son, I finally came to my senses. I fell on my knees and asked God to forgive me for my riotous living. I confessed to Him all that I had done, and He forgave me and made me new again.

I discovered that when you leave Jesus, there is nowhere else to go—no other church, no other person, no other thing. Jesus is everything. He is all we will ever need or want. Forever.

SHARYN ROBICHAUX

DECEMBER 1

A Daily Baptism

If anyone is in Christ, there is a new creation. 2 Cor. 5:17, NRSV.

*D*o you ever have trouble feeling forgiven, even when you've prayed and asked the Lord's forgiveness for something you feel really bad about? Do you ever have a sin that lurks hauntingly in the back of your mind, taunting you, nagging you, leaving you feeling shamed and unforgivable? Even though you've asked the Lord to forgive you, do you sometimes find yourself on your knees, asking His forgiveness for the same sin again, when in your mind you know that He's already forgiven you? Somehow the guilt and shame still have a hold on you.

Perhaps that's why the baptism experience is so profound and leaves one feeling so fresh and clean and new. As a child I never had trouble understanding the concept of baptism and the forgiveness of sin. The church baptistry was in our backyard. We lived on a denominational college campus in Nigeria. Previous occupants of our house had built a concrete baptistry in the yard because the church had not yet been built. I watched the baptisms with fascination. My 6-year-old friend Ricky and I would hang on to the concrete edge of the baptistry, watching persons being lowered into the water, then coming up radiant and happy.

It would be my job to clean the baptistry the following week. Ricky and I knew that lots of sins had been washed off in the water, because by the next day the water always had a thick green scum on it. There were numerous frog eggs and other non-descript gelatinous masses too. If we didn't let the water out right away, we knew that we would get hundreds of little black wigglers in the water. There was no doubt in our minds. The water was full of the sins that had been left behind by the candidates. We used to share philosophical discussions about whether the water would be dirtier if 12 "not-so-bad people" were baptized as opposed to six "really, really wicked ones."

As we watched the baptisms take place in the little concrete tank that year, Ricky and I drew some conclusions about baptism. While our logic was slightly flawed, the conclusions are valid even today.

1. All sin is the same. It's always filthy if you hold on to it long enough.

2. The water was always slimy, even after some rather respectable people had been baptized. You can never tell by looking what kind of secret sins people have.

The beautiful part of the baptism was that no matter how scummy the water was by Monday, the people who had been baptized always came out so radiant and clean. I remember those baptisms and the glow on people's faces.

Later on it occurred to me that what we really need is a baptism experience every morning. If we could picture God washing away all of our sins by burying us in the water and raising us to a new life, leaving all the slime behind us every time we ask for forgiveness, maybe we wouldn't have such a hard time picturing ourselves clean and whole in Jesus. Perhaps if we practice mental imagery of our baptism as part of our morning devotions it would help take away those secret, nagging guilt feelings and allow us to start our day as new creatures in Christ Jesus.

SALLY PIERSON DILLON

Water on the Train!

Then God opened her eyes and she saw a well of water. Gen.
21:19, NIV.

*D*ecember 24—I had less than eight hours to complete
my Christmas shopping. I stumbled out of bed with the
determination that I would get to the Pentagon City Mall before
the crowd of last-minute shoppers converged on it. After having
devotions, I ate a light breakfast, got dressed, and left.

At 9:30 I was headed south on the Metro. As I rode along, I
silently engaged myself in conversation with the Lord about not
being able to go home for Christmas. I had been unable to get a
confirmed seat on a flight to the Caribbean for a price I could afford. I had tried relentlessly since October to get a seat at a reasonable price, with no success. I wondered why God hadn't
answered my prayer in the affirmative. Hadn't He heard my desperate prayer for a seat?

These thoughts quickly disappeared when I arrived at the
mall. I was surprised to find the place practically empty! I quickly
got the two gift items I needed and headed to the bakery shop
for a cinnamon-raisin croissant. I ate it, then headed for the train.
As I boarded I silently resumed my conversation with the Lord.

"Lord, that croissant was sweeter than I thought. I need some
water badly. I wish I had some to drink now."

I changed trains at the Gallery Place station. As I sat waiting
for the Red Line to Takoma Park, I again thought about the water.
I was thirsty. When the train pulled into the station, I boarded the
middle car. Normally I would get on the last car to avoid walking
so far to get to the escalators when I got to Takoma Park. I saun-
tered toward the middle of the car and sat down in a vacant seat.
As I sat down, I rested my shopping bag on the seat next to me. A
thought came to mind, and I pulled the shopping bag toward me
to retrieve my receipts. As I pulled the bag closer I was filled with
amazement at what I saw tucked away in the corner of the seat—
a 16.9-ounce bottle of Crystal Springs water! *Water on the train!
Someone must have forgotten this!* I thought.

I picked it up. It was cold. But wait a minute . . . the seal was
unbroken. Then the thought flashed into my mind: *God has an-*

swered my prayer! My heart filled with gratitude and praise for the water. I broke the seal and drank some. God knew I needed water, and He supplied the right amount, at the right temperature, and at the right time. No doubt it was the Spirit who guided my steps to that car and that seat. I was again reassured of God's love and concern for me, even in the simple things of life.

ANDREA A. BUSSUE

DECEMBER 3

Relax!

Commit thy way unto the Lord; trust also in him; and he shall bring it to pass. Ps. 37:5.

his is the Connection," said Marianne, an experienced caver, as we hunkered down to the entrance of this connecting passage that joined two major parts of the cave. "The ceiling is low, so you'll have to turn your head sideways while you push through on your belly. I've gone through here dozens of times, so I'll go first."

Then it was my turn as she called instructions from the other end of the passage 20 feet away. "Try to stay on the up side of the passage floor. . . . Push toward me, and—most of all—relax," Marianne instructed.

With my right arm stretched in front and my left arm dragging behind, I tried to follow her directions, but kept slipping toward a drop-off. "I'm slipping," I told her, trying to sound brave. But I didn't want to get stuck in that long, narrow crack.

"Keep pushing toward me, and relax," she encouraged.

When my left knee slipped to the edge of the crack, I tensed instinctively and jerked it back. At the same time, my head hit a rock hanging from the ceiling, clamping my helmet tightly over my face. "Marianne," I called in muffled panic through the stuffy air inside the helmet. "You gotta help me!"

"I'm trying to," came her voice from the other end of the passageway. "But you've got to follow my directions and relax."

Yeah, right, I thought. *Follow your directions and get stuck in this cold, muddy tunnel for the rest of my life.* I felt like crying, for I realized I was powerless to stop my slide on the slippery slope to imminent entrapment.

Then I did a desperate, foolhardy thing—I gave in to her instructions and relaxed. Immediately my arm slipped into the crevice and stuck tight. My left knee—and then my whole leg—followed my arm into the black void. As I quietly set a personal best for unabashed panic, the most amazing thing happened. My left leg suddenly dropped through that long, tight crevice. Then my left arm. Both hung free in some sort of vacuum. And . . . sliding to the left like that had suddenly given me enough room to reach back with my right hand and push the helmet off my face. I blinked at a smiling Marianne in the beam of my headlamp.

The "floor" on which I was lying was actually a "ceiling" for a room underneath. My boot and gloved hand needed only a few seconds to find anchor points on the rough calcite wall. From these I easily and quickly pushed my prone body through the muddy ooze of the Connection to join my cave guide at the other end.

Jesus is a guide who can tell me how to get to the other side of any difficult place through which I must pass. For He's been through them all. My Lord has promised that when I "relax"—trusting in His counsel instead of my own instinctive reactions—He will get me through the tight places of my life. Knowing this, whenever I encounter a real-life Connection, I can trade panic . . . for peace.   CAROLYN RATHBUN-SUTTON

DECEMBER 4

Proclaim Him Beautifully

You are a chosen race, a royal priesthood, a holy nation, a people for God's own possession, that you may proclaim the excellencies of Him who has called you out of darkness into His marvelous light. 1 Peter 2:9, NASB.

*O*ne of the many things I appreciate about my church is the pleasure of getting together in fellowship with other women. None of these women are gossipers, or cliquish—they're just plain nice to be around.

On one such occasion a group of us got together for breakfast. As we chatted, Betty recalled her recent experience with music. "I bought a new music tape," she remarked, "and I decided I didn't like it at all. It sounded so 'tinny.' Then I happened to be over at Joanie's house one day, and she had such lovely music playing. I asked her what it was, and do you know, it was the same tape I had!"

Betty had our attention now. "What made the difference?" I asked.

"It was my tape player," she responded. "It made the music sound of poor quality, while Joanie's gave it a lovely sound."

The Bible tells us that we are all part of a people for God's own possession, and that we are to proclaim the wonders, the excellencies of Him, our God. That seems pretty reasonable to me. God is our Creator, our Redeemer, and I know in my own life I can trace His guidance and protection, His loving care, from the moment of my conception. As we each grow in our life experience, many of us appreciate more and more the wonderful qualities of our Father in heaven.

My desire is that I won't fail to give that proclamation in my own life, that I can somehow represent Him in such a way that others will be attracted to Him too. I want my witness of Him to be a lovely sound, not a "tinny" sound that might misrepresent Him. I want to be an instrument in His hands for good, never for wrong or evil. I hope that you do too.   MARILYN KING

DECEMBER 5

Never Forgive

If you do not forgive others, neither will your Father forgive your trespasses. Matt. 6:15, NRSV.

A Nobel laureate survived the tragic terror of Nazi labor camps, having spent 11 months as a teenager in the hell called Auschwitz. Lending his articulate voice to the cause of

Holocaust remembrance at an Auschwitz memorial service, Elie Wiesel spoke emotionally of his experience. And although he has won the world's most prestigious recognition for fostering peace, Wiesel nevertheless prayed that God would not have mercy on those who had not shown mercy to Jewish children.

What would you have done had you survived Auschwitz and been invited to speak? Could you have prayed a more forgiving prayer? Would you—like Jesus—have prayed for God to forgive them because they knew not what they did? Perhaps the crucifiers did not know Jesus was the Son of God, but most certainly the Nazi tormentors did know exactly what they were doing. No pleading ignorance there!

I wonder what God thought of that prayer, He who knew about all the atrocities committed in all the Nazi camps. Had God forgiven those torturers?

What about the text above? Must we forgive any crime, even though the perpetrator has not asked to be forgiven? Hard questions, these.

It is no easy commandment, this order to forgive. But the *how* to forgive is a whole other matter, demanding a sermon all its own. So teacher that I am, I'll give you an assignment: research on your own the way to be able truly to forgive. Whether you are struggling with forgiving someone who stole $10 from your wallet or with forgiving the atrocious deaths of 6 million Jews, you and I and Elie Wiesel all have one need in common—the need of a forgiving Saviour. And since we all share this need, we had better make it our business to be forgiving. There is no other plan. WILMA McCLARTY

DECEMBER 6

Beauty Beyond Imagining

No eye has seen, no ear has heard, no mind has conceived what God has prepared for those who love him. 1 Cor. 2:9, NIV.

My grandmother Magdalena used to entertain me with stories from her life. She was a true master storyteller.

She could describe events and paint places with such beauty that they became part of my own life. My favorite stories, which I asked her to tell me over and over, were of the time when she was a young girl living in the Alps of northern Italy. Who could resist these interesting stories that were sprinkled throughout with descriptions of a place that sounded as beautiful as heaven?

When she described her town, my grandmother would say, "My village is very beautiful. High, snow-covered mountains touch the blue, blue sky that is often decorated with lacy white clouds. Lovely forests of tall, leafy trees surround it, and around the borders of the forest run small brooks of snow runoff. In the summer the valleys are adorned in a thousand colors with the most beautiful flowers. The few houses are tall and dark with thick granite walls. My aunts and cousins live in the town, and my parents' house is there, where they planned to return one day."

As a girl I often imagined visiting that old stone house, gathering flowers in those valleys, and playing by the banks of the streams. I would visit the nearby houses, most of which belonged to uncles and aunts, and get to know all these relatives. What a lively imagination I had, fed by my grandmother's stories!

Once, when I was a teenager, I heard my father kindly say, "Grandmother, each time you tell us one of your childhood stories your imagination seems more vivid, and the descriptions of your village become more beautiful. I'm sure if you went back there now you'd be disappointed to find nothing but an ordinary little town."

I always dreamed of visiting this place I had imagined so often. But I never could find it on any maps until one day an aunt gave me the exact name of my great-grandfather's birthplace. Limone, in the Piemonte region of Italy. When my husband and I had the opportunity to visit Europe, we made sure to visit this small Italian village, so familiar from the stories I'd heard in childhood.

We arrived in Limone, using a map bought in the area. It was such a small town that it didn't appear on any of the larger maps of Italy. As we arrived, it seemed to me that I was coming to a place I already knew, except that it was much more beautiful than I'd ever imagined. I don't ever remember seeing such a majestic display of nature. I was in a place spoken of and imagined so many times, but my grandmother's descriptions and my own imaginings had failed to grasp the reality. Walking through the stone streets of the village, looking at the high mountain peaks and dark forests and the summer flowers in all their splendor, and hearing the murmuring of the brooks, I remembered 1 Corinthians 2:9.

How often we think of heaven and of the promise of Christ's returning to take us home with Him—and we try to imagine what that will be like. I believe that the descriptions in God's Word are only pale shadows of what it will be like. How very, very beautiful it will be to live forever "in my Father's house," where there "are many rooms" (John 14:2, NIV), for there we will be forever with Him.   EUNICE PEVERINI

DECEMBER 7

The Painter's Portrait

We all, with unveiled face, beholding as in a mirror the glory of the Lord, are being transformed into the same image from glory to glory, just as by the Spirit of the Lord. 2 Cor. 3:18, NKJV.

No matter how many art museums and galleries I have visited in various parts of the world, I remain fascinated by the huge diversity of colors, styles, and subjects chosen by painters to express themselves. Each painting subtly reveals something about its creator.

Recently, in the art section of the newspaper, I read about a local artist who declared, "Every day I paint my portrait." The columnist who wrote the article verbalized what many artists and poets feel: "A work of art is the statement made in paint, pencil, clay, stone, or words by the artist. It is that person's life, using the chosen media to express it" (*Cyprus Weekly*, Mar. 15-21, 1996).

As I reflected on the artist's words, I thought about God and how He has displayed His artistry magnificently in nature. And yet He has preferred to paint His portrait in human lives. He is the master painter, and we are His chosen medium. God uses unimaginable variation in His creative artistry. No two of His "portraits" are alike. Each has his or her own personality, talents, and style that reflect the Artist in a unique manner.

As the earthly artist works diligently to get just the right color mix, the correct light reflection and shadow, and the perfect expression on the face in a portrait, the heavenly Artist also works untiringly with us. God paints from the inside out. Through His Holy Spirit our thoughts, our motives, and our aspirations are purified. The inner life commands the outer actions.

God did not merely begin to paint His portrait in us when we were born, or even when we became reborn into Jesus. His brush strokes continue to change us from what we were before into what He wants us to be today. The apostle Paul gives us insight into this process in 2 Corinthians. As we contemplate our Lord, we are being transformed into His image by His Spirit.

It may take years, and even centuries, before the works of a painter are truly appreciated. But artists do not give up. They continue to generate art. God is just as relentless as He applies His creative power to us. He does not give up because you and I are not now all He wants us to be. He patiently produces His art within us, knowing that if we allow Him creative freedom to work in our lives, in time we will emerge as the masterpiece He has designed us to become—a portrait of Himself.

JOYCE NEERGAARD

DECEMBER 8

It's an Emergency!

Sometimes there is a way that seems to be right, but in the end it is the way of death. Prov. 16:25, NRSV.

During the four years I worked at the emergency room admitting desk, many times I witnessed a sick child being brought to the emergency room by a young, concerned parent. Most of the cases involved nonemergency medical care for a cold or the flu, with or without runny nose, coughing, and fever.

During the usually long wait, the child would invariably whine for a snack. "Later," would be the parent's reply. "Now!" the child would wail. Big crocodile tears, pouting, or a temper tantrum followed. Mom or Dad would give in, snatch the child up in a fit of anger, and head for the snack bar. The child would return, munching on a large candy bar and quite often sipping a carbonated soda with caffeine. In the majority of cases the happy child even forgot how ill he or she was for a time. Then, cranky and tired of doing nothing, there would be more whining, and Mom or Dad would pull out another candy bar to quiet the child.

Well, the kid won again, I'd say to myself. Unfortunately, the kids almost always won. A few whines or tears, a strong will, an embarrassed mom or dad too tired to fight, a sleepy child, and the "sick" one got to eat lots of junk. Of course, the hospital snack bar had some nutritious snacks to choose from, but the kids got what they wanted. What they were used to having. And the parents wondered why their kids were always sick.

Sometimes we feed on the wrong stuff when the right choices are within our grasp. Sin-sick, we settle for quick (and oftentimes junky) fixes for what really ails us. And yes, we also wonder why we can't shake what's wrong with us. If we would open our hearts, minds, and souls, we could be filled with Jesus Christ, our Lord and Saviour. IRIS L. STOVALL

DECEMBER 9

A Special Friend

A true friend sticks closer than one's nearest kin. Prov. 18:24, NRSV.

Friends . . . How we all need friends! Some of us have few friends, while others have quite a few. Some are "casual" friends, while others are "heart" friends.

I have a special heart friend. She has been there for me through thick and thin. She knows my fears, my desires. When I've needed a shoulder, she has always been there for me. I have other heart friends, but she is extra-special, a special gift. The Lord gave her to me, so to speak. As I think about her special attributes, her gentle strength, I praise God for her friendship. "Every good gift and every perfect gift is from above" (James 1:17).

I am also blessed to have a Friend such as Jesus. He is a very special heart friend of mine. No matter the time or place, I have His constant companionship. In times of sadness He wraps His comforting arms around me, and in times of joy I have sensed His smile. There are also times when I've seen His sense of humor.

For me to think of my special Friend on that cross, bearing my sins and my punishment so I can live, I am very much aware of how special He is! I realize my unworthiness, but Jesus has said He is not ashamed to call me a member of His family (Heb. 2:11), and "I will put my trust in him" (verse 13).

To be forgiven and adopted into God's family, to have a Big Brother who is also a very special friend, I am indeed blessed beyond what I may imagine.   KATHY ISAACS

DECEMBER 10

Before I Called

It shall come to pass, that before they call, I will answer; and while they are yet speaking, I will hear. Isa. 65:24.

During a bitter and difficult separation that ended in divorce, I decided to move out of the house that held so many painful memories. Being single now was a challenge, one I had not faced for more than 15 years. Finding money to pay first and last months' rent and the security deposit for a new place meant "robbing Peter to pay Paul."

One December morning, after I had finally gotten moved, the thought occurred to me while driving to work that I needed at least $300 to get back on track with my bills. I hadn't yet prayed about the matter, just thought about it as I drove along. When I arrived at work about 20 minutes later, I noticed two unmarked envelopes on my desk. One contained five crisp $100 bills, and the other a note stating that $1,000 had been applied to my daughter's account at the college where she was a student. This was verified. There were no names on the envelopes except mine. I was going through some very difficult times financially, emotionally, and otherwise, and God knew I needed the assurance that He had not forgotten me. Tears filled my eyes as I sought a private place to let them flow and to thank Him for this special blessing that marked the beginning of my day at work.

I knew it was God who had done this, because I had spoken

to no one about my need. God already knew. I had received more than I needed, but more important, I was assured of God's love and concern for one such as I. I was reminded of the promise in Hebrews 13:5: "I will never leave thee, nor forsake thee." God never promised that life would always be peaches and cream, flowery beds of ease, or one mountaintop experience after another. Without the valleys, the mountaintops would have no significance. Without hard times, we would not appreciate the good.

God hears our every prayer, often before we even speak it, because He knows our needs and the desires of our hearts. Isaiah 65:24 is very precious to me: "It shall come to pass, that before they call, I will answer; and while they are yet speaking, I will hear."

Indeed, He heard my prayer that day before I had uttered it. He read my heart, assessed the need, and supplied it all before I even asked. What a mighty God we serve. With experiences such as this, my love for Him and my faith in Him continue to grow day by day.   GLORIA J. FELDER

DECEMBER 11

A Future Without Fear

No lion shall be there, nor any ravenous beast shall go up thereon, it shall not be found there; but the redeemed shall walk there: and the ransomed of the Lord shall return, and come to Zion with songs and everlasting joy upon their heads: they shall obtain joy and gladness, and sorrow and sighing shall flee away. Isa. 35:9, 10.

One wintry Saturday afternoon while living in Montana, we decided to drive the Cooke City Highway, a road that runs along the northernmost border of Yellowstone National Park to Red Lodge, Montana. The weather was cold but sunny, as Montana's winters often are, a perfect climate for the wildlife from the park, which sometimes can be seen feeding along the road when the snow is heavy.

We were rewarded on this day by the display of a herd of buffalo with their young, as well as a couple moose, some coyotes, and numerous blackbirds. We had almost reached the snow-bank that signaled the end of the snow-plowed road when we noticed five or six coyotes below us in the valley. Two of them were just sitting, looking toward the road. One coyote was pacing back and forth, one was lying in the snow, and one was standing, looking intently beyond the road. It seemed to us to be a little strange, since usually they are trotting busily in the snow, looking for mice or whatever else they can catch for food.

Suddenly our son cried out, "There it is!"

"There it is, but what is 'it'?" questioned my husband.

"Look! There against that rock! An elk!"

We stopped the car, and sure enough, a very old bull elk was backed up against the rock. His head was lowered, his bones stuck out pitifully; he was barely a skeleton of his former elegance. His eyes were clouded over, but they were obviously trying to see the danger, trying to recognize the source of his fear. He swayed slightly as if he were about to fall. He was not disturbed by our stopping to look at him. His horns were still beautiful, still lowered in a posture of defense. He once had been a magnificent specimen of an animal, his legs strong and full, his eyes brightly surveying the landscape, making known his presence by the proud lift of his head and his marvelous bugling.

We gazed in awe, knowing that the coyotes were aware of his presence, aware of his slender grasp on life. They knew that if they waited long enough they could make a meal of him without any effort on their part. Obviously he had heard their howling; he knew they were waiting, and he challenged them to attack him while he still had breath in him. He was waiting for death, but determined to fight to the end. What a tragedy!

I am reminded of the text in Isaiah that promises there will be no "ravenous beast" in the earth made new. Isaiah goes on to say that "the redeemed shall walk there . . . with songs and everlasting joy upon their heads . . . and sorrow and sighing shall flee away." There is no better promise than that. We need not fear, whatever happens to us. We can look forward to everlasting joy, and even the wild beasts shall be tame there. But even more comforting is the part that says "sorrow and sighing shall flee away." There is no mother on this earth who has not known sorrow, some more intensely than others, but never without sighing. The promise of all of this having fled away and songs and everlasting joy taking its place is a promise more precious than gold.

JEAN REIFFENSTEIN ROTHGEB

God's Wonders

One generation will commend your works to another; they will tell of your mighty acts. They will speak of the glorious splendor of your majesty, and I will meditate on your wonderful works. Ps. 145:4, 5, NIV.

I have a Thanksgiving cactus and a Christmas cactus that I leave in their pots and set outdoors in the summer in a cluster of ferns that surround the north foundation of my house. When the danger of frost nears, I bring them in. One year each had bloomed properly where it had been placed near an east window.

One bright February morning I looked at the drapes at the window and was shocked to see a very large, beautiful yellow butterfly clinging there. Apparently a caterpillar had climbed onto one of the cactus plants in the summer and made its cocoon, or chrysalis, supposedly until a safe warm spring day. But the climate changed when the plant was brought inside. The warm sun through the window and the proximity of a radiator had fooled that little body inside the cocoon into thinking it was spring. It had been hidden so well that I was unaware of the little home it had made for itself.

I was very familiar with the marvelous workings of God's wonders. As a second-grade teacher, I had often found the striped caterpillars on the milkweed plants and kept them in a little cage, feeding them fresh milkweed leaves until they grew big enough to shed their skins for a beautiful green chrysalis with little gold dots circling its top. Then in 10 days a beautiful monarch butterfly would emerge. So I understood how a big yellow butterfly could appear in my house in the winter.

What a wonderful world God has created. A tiny egg on a leaf can, in three more steps, become a beautiful butterfly. And part of that metamorphosis is a creepy, crawly caterpillar. God can take a sinner like me and change me into a being that can love and serve Him. All I need to do is surrender my sinful self to His care and complete control, just as that caterpillar left its destiny to God.   MAXINE McADDO

DECEMBER 13

A Woman of Resolve

"It's all right," she said. 2 Kings 4:23, NIV.

ut you can't possibly go away then," Melissa said in her most grown-up voice. "You'd miss the *Nutcracker* ballet." With her little feet planted squarely on the carpet and her arms crossed over her chest, she was the picture of determination.

Usually I spent holidays with family and close friends. At Christmastime the *Nutcracker* was, to all intents and purposes, virtually a tradition. However, I'd been invited to speak to a women's group late in December. It would mean leaving home for three days between Christmas and New Year's Day.

"You're right. I will miss the *Nutcracker* ballet," I replied. "We'll have dinner together on New Year's, so you can fill me in."

"But it won't be the same!" she wailed.

How could I explain to her that my soul felt drawn to these women who were struggling with issues of abuse and discrimination? These women undoubtedly had never attended a *Nutcracker* ballet. These were women who needed help in trying to make sense of pain and disappointment.

"It's not fair!" Melissa pouted.

"You're right again," I agreed. "It's not fair, and I must go anyway." With a chuckle I added, "Find me a Bible verse that says life is fair, and I'll reconsider."

An interested expression crossed Melissa's face, a cross between intrigue and resignation. "I'll bet there isn't one, or you wouldn't have said that!" Then she added, "Find *me* a Bible story that says it's OK to leave when your family wants you to stay!" The twinkle in her eyes told me she was only teasing.

"The story of the Shunammite woman," I replied.

Melissa ran to get the Bible and turned to 2 Kings. In her clear (and now sweeter) voice she read the story. Because her son had just died, the woman of Shunem had decided to solicit the help of Elisha. Obviously, her husband wasn't excited about her leaving on the trip.

"'Why go to him today?' he asked. 'It's not the New Moon or the Sabbath,'" he said (verse 23, NIV).

However, there was no discussion, no nasty recrimination,

no conforming. She simply responded, "It's all right."

"There you have it, Melissa," I said. "She knew it was the right decision for her. She was compelled to go. I must meet my speaking appointment."

The example of the Shunammite woman provides a model for women everywhere. When the Holy Spirit prompts us to follow a certain course of action, let's state with quiet conviction, "It's all right," and proceed.

"So, Melissa," I said, "do we have a date for New Year's Day?" We did.

ARLENE TAYLOR

DECEMBER 14

From the Inside Out

Woe to you, teachers of the law and Pharisees, you hypocrites! You clean the outside of the cup and dish, but inside they are full of greed and self-indulgence. Blind Pharisee! First clean the inside of the cup and dish, and then the outside also will be clean. Matt. 23:25, 26, NIV.

From my Michigan home I wondered what duties might lie before me as I prepared to go on a mission trip to help build a school in Panama. I could never have guessed all that was involved in the building process, and what I would learn.

The first day I found myself standing in the hot sun painting electrical boxes for lights and switches. Where we were, near the city of David, the rainy season lasted all but three months of the year. A special paint was used to prevent the metal from corroding. Until the second day of painting, I hadn't thought about how many electrical boxes there were. I was continually supplied with more, of various sizes and shapes, that needed to be painted, inside and out.

As the job became more tedious and the sun became hotter, the question crossed my mind *Is all this painting really necessary? These boxes will be tucked away in the walls, and who will ever know if they're painted or not?* Fortunately, my conscience kept me going, and my supply of unpainted boxes did eventually run out.

In the days that followed, I was occupied with other jobs that no one would ever see either. As the walls of block buildings went up, we put in metal rods for reinforcement. We also poured cement around all the rods, whether they were horizontal or vertical, for greater stability. Another job I had was surveying both sides of the walls to patch holes in broken blocks and fill cracks between them. After we finished the buildings, someone else would come and plaster the walls, covering all the patchwork, inside and out.

People looking at the finished school would never know about the painted electrical boxes, cemented rods, or patched holes. But when the rain falls, the winds blow, and the earth quakes (as it does there), the buildings will stand because we did the inside job right.

I learned that it's the same with us as we build characters that will stand the test of time and circumstances, lasting into eternity. It's an inside job too!   DONNA MEYER VOTH

DECEMBER 15

Shooting Prayers

Pray without ceasing. 1 Thess. 5:17.

As a friend and I were being shown to a booth in one of our favorite restaurants, we passed a young woman. I noticed tears on her cheeks, and my heart was touched. From where I sat in the next booth to hers, I could see her profile and her tears.

"Dear God, I don't know what her problem is, but please bless and help her."

From time to time as my friend and I ate our lunch, I continued to "shoot" prayers at the girl. Suddenly she turned and smiled at me. My heart seemed to leap for joy! After a while she got up, and as she passed us, she looked right at me and smiled again.

Praise You, God! Praise You—it works! I thought.

Since reading a booklet about "shooting" prayers at people, I've tried the practice. I confess that the above incident is the only one to which I've had a visible response. But that doesn't stop me. When I hear sirens, I pray, "Please be with whomever and whatever." A car at the side of the road—flat tire or open hood—brings a "please help them, Lord."

There are the truckers and other drivers on our busy streets and freeways; the police and firefighters; the ambulance people; the postal department folk and the repair men and women who are working to help us. Then there are the chefs, servers, and people busing tables in restaurants; the clerks, baggers, and oh, so many others with whom I come in contact, especially in our families.

In church I shoot prayers at the pastor, the soloist, and the parents of an unhappy little one. These are just a few of the ways I "pray without ceasing." You undoubtedly can think of other ways.

A favorite author of mine once wrote, "At the sound of fervent prayer, Satan's whole host trembles" (*Testimonies*, vol. 3, p. 346).

Let's keep them trembling!   PATSY MURDOCH MEEKER

DECEMBER 16

Son of God, Son of Man

The Word became a human being and lived here with us. John 1:14, CEV.

*B*oth human and divine; the baby Son of God was also the baby son of humanity. I do not always understand divinity, but I do understand humanity and therefore love Him all the more.

I think He cried when He was hungry or needed His swaddlings changed. When He was comfortable, He snuggled close in Mary's arms and smiled up at her as nourishment flowed from His earthly mother to the Creator of all things. In a chair fashioned in Joseph's carpenter shop, His earthly father gently rocked his little son. He slept peacefully. He too needed rest.

His chubby hands reached for bright sunbeams and delighted in their changing colors, unknowing that all things bright and beautiful came from these same hands. When He was startled, Mary held Him close, comforted Him, and promised Him safety. She could not see the cruel cross. His tiny fingers found their way to His mouth, and He sucked contentedly, making happy little sounds. The same fingers made the blind to see.

He laughed and played with His feet and toes, the pattern for which He had fashioned from the dust of the earth. He clapped His little hands with delight at birds and butterflies. These, too, He had spoken into being.

I think He fell and bumped Himself when He learned to walk. Mary soothed and urged Him to try again. His wobbly little legs became sure and strong, and thousands would follow in His footsteps!   ELVA E. SPRINGER

DECEMBER 17

Of Magi and Gifts

They opened their treasures and presented him with gifts of gold and of incense and of myrrh. Matt. 2:11, NIV.

*I*t was almost Christmas. I had so hoped to be able to leave work early, but first one thing and then another had kept me at my desk. Finally I turned off the light, locked the door, and stepped out into the fading rays of sunset. Purse in one hand, attaché in the other, I cut through the rose garden, climbed a flight of cement stairs, and walked up the hill to the parking lot. Four days at home for the holidays . . . What a treat!

In the car I reached for the ignition—and remembered. My umbrella was still sitting on the filing cabinet. Oh, well, I wouldn't need it tonight. The rain had cleared off, and blue skies had been forecast for the next couple days. So why did I feel compelled to retrieve the umbrella? There were two others at home. The feeling persisted: *Go back for the umbrella.*

This is ridiculous! I said to myself. Nevertheless, I turned off the engine and retraced my steps. The walkway leading to my office acted like a wind tunnel. Leaves swirled at my ankles. Rounding the corner, I saw her, leaning against my office door, face in her hands. Every line of her body spoke of grief. The keys in my hand clanked together, and she looked up.

"I've been praying you hadn't left yet," she said simply.

We went into my office. Her husband had just called to say he wouldn't be coming home that night. As a matter of fact, he didn't plan ever to come home again. He'd found someone else. Her words were halting and filled with pain. Her questions were unanswerable. She hadn't known about the affair; truly thought the second business was just taking more time. Why had he waited until now to tell her?

Only those who have experienced such a crisis can really understand the shock, devastation, and initial hopelessness, especially in the midst of a subculture that reveres marriage and decries divorce. We wept together, prayed together, held each other's hands. And then she was ready to leave. She would stay at a friend's home for the next few nights.

"Knowing that you survived a divorce will help me to get through the holidays," she said.

Once again I turned off the light, locked the door, and stepped out into the wind tunnel. We walked up to the parking lot, arms around each other.

"I now know how Mary must have felt receiving gifts from the Magi," she offered as she paused by her car. "Thank you for your gifts of time, understanding, and empathy."

What a wonderful sentiment, to be classed with the Magi! Each one of us always has a gift we can share. In the car, I reached for the ignition. I'd received this opportunity to give because I'd gone back for the umbrella. *The umbrella!* It was still sitting on the filing cabinet.

I didn't need it.

ARLENE TAYLOR

The Christmas Wastebasket

Unto us a Child is born, unto us a Son is given. Isa. 9:6, NKJV.

*I*t was 1951, and it was going to be a very limited Christmas. The hospital bills were large; the paycheck was small. It would take three years to pay for this child, but she was worth every penny. She was our first, she was healthy, and she was ours.

Our Christmas gifts to loved ones would be meager, and there wasn't going to be any money to pay for gifts for each other. We had already decided that, my husband and I. There would be one small gift for our new baby girl, born in October, but we were adults and we could understand if we didn't get something for each other.

Since I didn't work and had no money of my own, I had no choice but to keep my promise. I bought some bricklike paper and used it to cover a small table to set the even smaller Christmas tree on. Then I put our few gifts from relatives under the tree.

On Christmas morning I found on the table a wrapped package that hadn't been there the night before. It was oddly shaped and addressed to me. It felt light in weight, but I couldn't imagine what could be shaped in that fashion. And we had agreed we wouldn't get anything—I knew we didn't have the money. Then I opened it and found—a wastebasket. Not just any wastebasket; it was blue—my favorite color—and it had a large red ribbon painted on the side. It had cost all of 45 cents!

Now this might not seem like much to those of us today who have computers, cars, stereos, houses, and more in our affluent society, but that Christmas wastebasket meant a great deal to me. It was a gift of love, given with sacrifice, since every penny was very dear to us. I treasured and kept the wastebasket for many years, until the bottom fell out and I finally had to discard it, since it could no longer serve its purpose.

God too gave a Gift to us, a very dear Gift, on that Christmas morn so long ago. It too was given with much love and sacrifice. Do we really treasure that Gift?   LORAINE F. SWEETLAND

DECEMBER 19

The Spirit Is So Wonderful

Remember the words of the Lord Jesus, how he said, It is more blessed to give than to receive. Acts 20:35.

*T*he commercials are almost overwhelming, but underneath is a sweet, sweet spirit seldom shown by so many people at any other time of the year. Merriment, songs, goodwill! The way husbands, armed with sizes, colors, preferences, go shopping en masse. A sight of this magnitude is seen only during the Christmas season. Clerks trying to guess sizes according to verbal descriptions of shapes and forms (both idealistic and real). I think clerks could write fascinating stories related to Christmas shoppers, as well as the recipients.

There are two sides to the Christmas holidays. One side maintains it is of pagan origin, commercial and irreligious, that justifies their nonparticipation. The other side loves to show its love through gifts of the heart and the hands, believing that Christmas is commercial only if the person chooses to make it so. The spirit of giving, unselfish acts, and a display of love to those less fortunate do something for the giver as well as the receiver. Even the richest of people benefit from the spirit of giving, of thinking of other people. What other event causes such universal goodwill?

It is a given: I need to set a budget for my Christmas shopping and stay within it. To go deeper in debt can be a folly that I will regret for a long time. The question is What are the most things I can make for the least amount of money that will still be in good taste?

Father, help me to think of others, both rich and poor, for they all need Thy love and the manifestations of love from their fellow men and women. May I in some way point them to You and to Jesus, the greatest Gift ever given.

FONDA CHAFFEE

DECEMBER 20

Angel Drop

He who has begun a good work in you will complete it until the day of Jesus Christ. Phil. 1:6, NKJV.

As I stood at the crest, the intermediate ski slope, Angel Drop, rolled down the mountain before me. Even in the semidarkness I detected moguls, the "bumps" around which experts love to maneuver. I was no expert, only determined. I stood a moment longer, enveloped by the thrill of skiing this big slope. No longer afraid, I felt both daring and confident. After skiing four nights during the season, I'd graduated from beginning slopes to intermediate ones.

I thought back to the second night, when I'd skied Snow Park, the hardest beginner slope. A small child rammed me from behind, knocking me flat. I couldn't walk without pain for more than a month. The third night I was afraid to return to Snow Park. I stood at its base looking up, lecturing myself. "If you don't go on this slope now, you never will, and you'll never learn to ski." This get-back-on-the-horse principle worked. I chose to ski Snow Park the entire night, s-l-o-w-l-y. But it took a while to overcome the fear of people skiing behind me.

After that moment on the top of Angel Drop, I spent the rest of the season skiing mostly intermediate slopes. When our church group drove to West Virginia near the end of the ski season, I even ventured a black diamond—an expert slope. I skied all the way down on my feet, albeit very slowly. My desire to learn to ski was being fulfilled!

As I stood on Angel Drop that night, stars sparkling overhead, lights of the nearest town twinkling in the distance, stillness blanketing us all, I realized that my spiritual growth has been similar to learning to ski. At first, all I had was a desire for God. As I grew spiritually, I progressed to the years of following all the rules because I *had* to, worrying so much about "technique" that I never caught on that Christianity can be fun and exciting. Then, as on my first excursion to Angel Drop, where I discovered a bigger and better slope than ever before, I glimpsed the first tiny inklings of an intimate relationship with Jesus and experienced the first forays into the realm of *real* prayer.

It's taken time to progress as a skier. And it's taken time to grow in Jesus. But I am doing both, sometimes slowly, but at least growth has been constant. I'm discovering the joy of being unafraid to ski down a big slope. And I'm discovering the joy of being in connection with God, hearing His voice.

I have a ways to go. But one day I plan to ski down double black diamonds—the hardest expert slopes. And one day I know that Jesus will keep His promise to complete His work in me. I look forward to both. SHERRY MANISON

The Ultimate Gift

"A virgin will have a baby boy, and he will be called Immanuel, which means "God is with us." Matt. 1:23, CEV.

Have you ever stopped to wonder, What does Christmas
    really mean?
What do we truly see when we view the manger scene?

A mother, a baby, the sheep and oxen mild?
The shepherds, angels, Wise Men, the lovely Christ child?
The sweet baby Jesus, with such an innocent face,
The beautiful epitome of God's loving grace.

The humble shepherds who watched for the sign,
And with God's help knew it was just the right time.
Thousands of majestic angels who came from above,
Bringing true meaning to Christmas, God's matchless love.

Strains of the melodious, angelic voices,
As the whole world in awe and wonder rejoices.
The Wise Men traveling, came from afar,
Intently following God's celestial star.

God in His wisdom had set her apart,
As Mary pondered it all in her heart.
God's ultimate Gift to us had come,
The sweet baby Jesus, God's only Son.

LILLIAN MUSGRAVE

Friendship With Jesus

Jesus said to her, "Everyone who drinks of this water will be thirsty again, but those who drink of the water that I will give them will never be thirsty. The water that I will give will become in them a spring of water gushing up to eternal life." John 4:13, 14, NRSV.

*T*heologians could probably tell them best, but the stories of how Jesus befriended women bear repeating! Jesus had a wonderful way about Him, a wonderful way with people. He could put them at ease, winning their hearts and their confidence in one conversation.

Thus it was with the Samaritan woman at Jacob's well. Jesus showed a marvelous disregard for custom and status and prejudice when He initiated His noonday talk. He was a respected teacher. After a lifetime of multiple husbands, respect was the last thing given to this woman. He was a man who could earn a living as a carpenter. She was a woman, little more than property during those times. He was a Jew, the Son of David, and she was a Samaritan, despised by Jews for the mixture of her blood lines.

Jesus was out to make a definite point, one that would echo from His time to ours. He befriended this sister and poured living water into her soul. The sad, arid desert of her heart began to bloom with His saving grace. The true love of salvation brought her to life, and all the substitutes she had lived with were seen for what they were and instantly abandoned. Jesus let her know she was priceless. To God, to Him. Then He gave her His priceless truth—first her own salvation, then the announcement of His mission to earth. He announced it to an audience of one, to a woman who knew sin and its stain. He befriended her, saved her, and made her a true sister.

The story was not lost. An evangelistic spirit engulfed her, launching an immediate, successful campaign. "Come see a man!" she told her neighbors, those she'd spent a lifetime avoiding, those who had pointed fingers and called her a disgrace. Now the stories and the gossip and the condemnation didn't matter. She'd met a Man, a Saviour, a Friend. She had been healed from the inside out. He told her everything, showed her there was more to life on earth, promised her redemption and eternal life. He answered all her questions and met her every need. She had a Friend—for life.

Thank You, Father God, for allowing Your only Son, Jesus, to come to earth to show us what a loving God You are.

KYNA HINSON

Beyond the Road to Bethlehem

Does not the Scripture say that the Christ will come from David's family and from Bethlehem, the town where David lived? John 7:42, NIV.

The road you take to Bethlehem leads through that little town
Where once Emmanuel stooped low and laid aside His
  crown
To tread love's airway route to earth. There, wrapped in
  swaddling clothes,
God's tiny infant Gift was placed in trusting, sweet repose.

We linger at that manger where the angel star had led,
And long to stay, because we fear the treacherous road
  ahead
That leads away from Bethlehem. But we must hasten on
And find His footprints; follow in the path where He
  has gone.

We trace them to the wilderness; we meet temptation's
  power
And sense we're not alone, for He is with us in this hour.
We feel the lure of wealth; perceive the perils of our pride,
But footsteps of our faithful Friend are ever there to guide.

We follow to the Jordan; feel its cleansing in our soul,
And revel in His promises that He will make us whole.
We rest upon the slope where Jesus multiplied the food,
And feast upon His words, as when He fed the multitude.

Then, treading in His steps where once He healed the
sightless eyes,
We too find healing in His words, "I say to thee, arise!"
Now on the troubled Galilee, our soul midst waters deep
Can feel the calm of trusting peace where Jesus fell asleep.

His steps lead to Gethsemane; it brings us to our knees.
We see again His prostrate form and hear His an-
guished pleas
For strength to journey forward to the brink of
Calvary's hill.
His prayer is heard; with courage we arise to do His will.

Now bloodstained sandals mark the pathway; soft earth
bears the trough
Where once the heavy beam was dragged beside Him
and cast off.
In awe we bow before His cross, more beautiful by far
Than all the mountains round about; more glorious than
the star.

Yes, dark the road from Bethlehem, but faith lights up
our way;
Christ's footprints guide mid gathering storms, and we dare
not delay.
His nail-pierced hands are reaching out in welcome
just ahead;
With open arms He's waiting on the path He bids us tread.

The road to Bethlehem is mirthful with glad hearts aglow;
With evergreen and holly red; with sprigs of mistletoe.
It rings with songs and laughter; hopes of children, shep-
herds, kings;
And all the world is blest with joys the Christmas sea-
son brings.

So take the road to Bethlehem, but do not linger long;
Search out His footsteps; share them with the restless,
querying throng.
Dim glows the star at Bethlehem, but do not count it loss—
Upon our path in splendor beams light shining from
the cross.

Take now His footsteps; walk by faith the path that
Jesus trod.
'Twill surely lead from Bethlehem by Calvary, to God.

LORRAINE HUDGINS

DECEMBER 24

Treasured Gifts

There are different kinds of gifts, but the same Spirit. There are different kinds of service, but the same Lord. 1 Cor. 12:4, 5, NIV.

I have always loved Christmas. As a child I would lock myself in my bedroom and make small gifts for my loved ones, wrap them, and put them under the Christmas tree with great pride, knowing I had done my best. Kneeling beside the tree, I would look for the packages with my name on them. I would turn them and shake them with hopeful anticipation, wondering what treasures were inside. Would they contain something I had written on my wish list?

As an adult I've found that the gifts I have come to treasure most have been gifts made specifically for me: two handmade quilts, throw pillows, crocheted pot holders, and an oil painting, each made by loving people at different churches we pastored through the years. And then there have been the special gifts made by my own children that I have especially treasured: pot holders, an apron, ceramic figurines, wall plaques, and the list goes on and on. The gifts are special because the persons making them gave unselfishly of themselves, wishing only to show their love and bring happiness and joy to others.

Each year we put up our Christmas tree the weekend after Thanksgiving. The only thing we put under it is the Nativity scene—until just a couple days before Christmas. We want to draw attention to the most precious, important Gift God could ever have given the world in the gift of His Son, Jesus. Jesus unselfishly gave of Himself each day as He ministered to the sin-sick and physically sick. He made children and women feel welcomed, loved, accepted, and important.

May we dedicate ourselves to following His example of giving of ourselves, not just at Christmas, but each day of the year. Give a gift of encouragement or a listening ear, take a shut-in shopping, baby-sit for a young mother so she can go out, or start a telephone ministry to latchkey children in your church. Whatever your gift, if you pray about it God will show you how to put it to use sharing Christmas all year long.

CELIA MEJIA CRUZ

DECEMBER 25

No Room in the Inn

She brought forth her firstborn Son, and wrapped Him in swaddling cloths, and laid Him in a manger, because there was no room for them in the inn. Luke 2:7, NKJV.

*I*n 1978, shortly after my husband and I graduated from Andrews University, our family decided to visit my sister and her family in Arizona. We also wanted to see the magnificent Grand Canyon before returning to the mission field. We asked many people whether it was necessary to make motel reservations near the Grand Canyon. All of them said no, there were many inns and motels nearby.

We left the campus with great anticipation. It was a long drive from Michigan to California, where we were to board a plane for Bangkok, Thailand, to resume our mission work. When we arrived at our destination, we looked for a place to lodge for the night. We drove around. We asked. We knocked. We searched. We begged. We prayed. We did all we could to find a place to spend the night, but to no avail. The only answer we received was "There's no vacancy."

Finally we found a place. It was beside the road, hidden from motorists, under the tall pine trees. It was our car. We parked and decided where each of us should sleep. The girls would have the back seat, our son could lay on the back window ledge, and my husband and I would doze in the front seats. So much for a motel room, but we managed to make the best out of a bad situation.

Thank God, my three children never uttered a word of complaint, even though we felt cold and uncomfortable during the wee hours of the morning.

Two thousand years ago the Babe of Bethlehem, our precious Saviour, came to our world to dwell among us, to show the love of our heavenly Father. Jesus and His earthly parents were also told "There's no room in the inn." As we celebrate His birthday during this festive season, may it be that when He knocks at our heart's door, we will gladly welcome Him and say with rejoicing, "Come in, Lord Jesus! There's plenty of room for You in my heart!"

OFELIA A. PANGAN

DECEMBER 26

You're Famous!

You are a chosen people, a royal priesthood, a holy nation, a people belonging to God, that you may declare the praises of him who called you out of darkness into his wonderful light. 1 Peter 2:9, NIV.

I was visiting my "adopted" family in Huntsville, Alabama. On our way home from church my little sister and I occupied ourselves with conversation as we endured the 35-minute drive home. As we began talking, she looked very intensely at me and asked, "Terrie, are you famous?"

I smiled and asked her what prompted that question.

"Well," she said quite seriously, "you know a lot of people, and people ask you to speak and sing everywhere! So are you famous?"

"No, Ashley," I answered as I thought of lights, camera, action—not to mention money—"I'm not famous."

She looked me directly in the eyes and said with confidence, "You're famous to me!"

My eyes became misty as we embraced. . . . *You're famous to me.* And we all are famous to God. As adults the challenge to realize our greatness through Christ is ever present. How quickly we forget! The stress of professionalism, the pressures of singleness and marriage, the war between good and evil, and just the common everyday living of life make it appear at times that we are insignificant and unimportant. Yet 1 Peter 2:9 tells us that we have been specifically selected and are of a sovereign priesthood. We belong to the God of the universe! We are the apple of His eye. He lovingly holds our lives in His hands and has special plans for each of us (Jer. 29:11).

Fame is defined as widespread public recognition. The next time you feel lost in the crowd, remind yourself that you are known, loved, and thought of by the King of kings and Lord of lords. And in the words of Ashley, you're famous!

TERRIE E. RUFF

DECEMBER 27
What Does Your Wallet Say?

As a father has compassion on his children, so the Lord has compassion on those who fear him; for he knows how we are formed, he remembers that we are dust. Ps. 103:13, 14, NIV.

Last Sunday my husband, Kim, and I shopped at an outlet mall near Richmond, Virginia. At a traffic light on our way out, I spotted a wallet on the ground.

"Wait!" I said, jumping out of the car. I gathered the strewn contents and jumped back in. Opening the wallet, I found a driver's license belonging to Sharon. "She must be so worried," I said. "Poor thing!"

"Let's stop at a phone booth and call her," Kim suggested.

So we pulled over and dialed the phone number on her checkbook. It turned out to be a business number.

"I guess I'll have to try her tomorrow morning," I sighed.

"Maybe there's a home number in there," Kim offered.

So I began "snooping" through the wallet. I felt kind of uncomfortable going through a stranger's things, but also fascinated. From her driver's license I discovered that Sharon is one year younger than I am, one inch taller, and five pounds heavier. From the business cards she carried I guess she likes Japanese food and has friends who work for the government. She must prefer one particular airline, because she has a frequent flier card. And she likes to buy books, because she belongs to a book club. I never did find Sharon's home phone number, but as I looked through her papers and photos, I began to feel that I sort of knew her. Here was a person I've never met who has likes and dislikes, people who matter to her, budgets and dreams.

On Monday I called Sharon's work and told her I had found her wallet.

"I can't believe you have it!" she squealed. "Oh, there are still good people in the world. God bless you!"

She explained that she had placed her wallet on the car roof while putting her baby girl in the car seat. Then she forgot it was there and drove away.

I packed Sharon's wallet in an envelope and slipped in a gift copy of *The Bible Story* for her baby. After all, by now she felt like a friend. And since finding Sharon's wallet, I'm beginning to understand a little better how God can love each of us. He looks deep into every corner of our wallets—and our hearts. He understands us. He knows us intimately, and He loves us deeply.

And as we look at those around us and see what and whom they care about, we will grow in love toward them too.

LORI PECKHAM

DECEMBER 28
Ringing Out the Will

So teach us to number our days, that we may apply our hearts unto wisdom. Ps. 90:12.

Only a few hours left in the old year, and I envision Father Time in his travel-worn robe, standing critically before me, his hourglass almost spent. His bony fingers seem to clutch a blue-clad document bearing my name. His voice crackles as he reads:. "'As a Christian growing cold, I declare this to be my last will and testament: to distribute my talents among succeeding faithful Christians.

"'I leave my helpfulness to whoever is willing to experience the

444

joy of sharing. I leave my enthusiasm to my overworked pastor. I leave my contagious smile to someone who has found Jesus and wants to share her joy. I leave my encouragement and concern to those who are burdened to help the young. I leave my spare time to anyone who needs a few more hours for acts of kindness.'"

Page after page he reads. "'I write this will because of my neglect, my spiritual life is starving.'"

"But I didn't write that will!" I interrupt.

"Yes, you did." His bony finger punctuates his words. "By your actions." The sun touches the horizon, and Father Time begins to fade.

"Wait!" I scream. "Don't leave me now!"

"You've another chance," he calls back. "A new year is before you."

I bristle and snap on the television. *What are you doing tonight?* A small voice within me awakens warmth. *How about the widow across the street?* I fumble with the gift of perfume in my pocket. The inner voice persists. *Do you remember the story of the Good Shepherd who left His comfortable home to search for His lost lamb?*

"Stop it!" I shout.

He didn't rest until it was safe in His arms, the voice continues.

A lump gathers in my throat. I picture myself as the lost lamb. Suddenly I long, more than all else, to be found by my Shepherd. I go to the kitchen and bake some cookies for my neighbor. My eyes fall on a tinseled package: the Raggedy Ann doll I neglected to donate.

Your opportunity, the little voice whispers. *Pick it up.*

Mechanically, I obey and hurry across the street.

"Here's something from my oven."

My neighbor smiles.

"Oh, yes! And this is for your little girl."

Her smile broadens.

Nervously, my hand goes into my pocket. I hand her my brand-new bottle of perfume and leave, almost abruptly. I don't want her to see my tears. She couldn't possibly understand my newfound joy. I hurry across the street. A tiny person seems to trail me. Clad in his happy-new-year banner, he's holding something that looks suspiciously like a brand-new hourglass.

Not a moment to lose, I reflect. *I have so much to do this year!*

LORRAINE HUDGINS

DECEMBER 29

Goodbyes

He will wipe every tear from their eyes. There will be no more death or mourning or crying or pain, for the old order of things has passed away. Rev. 21:4, NIV.

*H*ave you ever said so many goodbyes that you were emotionally exhausted? I have. Last week we flew to Portland, Oregon, for a final visit with our daughter, Carlene. In two weeks she moves to Florida—3,000 *miles away*.

The first goodbye came at Matthew's graduation, where the family had gathered to celebrate. Farewell was said by four boys to a school, classmates, and friendships that will never be revived again on this earth because of distance. And a particularly difficult goodbye was said to the talented teacher who had mentored Matthew for five years.

We also said goodbye to the church that had nurtured this family through their years of attendance. More goodbyes followed Jamison's baptism that afternoon—to Pathfinder leaders, Sabbath school teachers, and others who had mentored him to this point. That evening several families gathered at Carlene and Brian's home for sundown worship around a crackling fire, followed by swimming, volleyball, hide-and-seek, and spa fun—the last time friends would gather at this beautiful home that had hosted so many parties like this.

On Sunday one of the most difficult goodbyes had to be dealt with. Goodbyes for women who have been best friends are never easy. Carlene bade her best friend goodbye. The quiet tears in glistening eyes, the avoidance of eyes, the inability to communicate told of the secret pain we shared as these women embraced for the last time.

Now I faced the reality of the goodbye I would say to my daughter on the next day. Although I knew I would see her, her husband, and the boys again, I felt my heart would break at the thought of the 3,000-mile distance between us. Tears bathed not only my eyes, but my soul. How much more could I endure?

That night we went for a final walk in Carlene's lovely country neighborhood and soaked in the spa one last time. Both of us were aware of the final parting the next morning, but neither of us spoke of it.

Somehow we got through the airport goodbyes. Now, although I realize it will never be quite the same, I am growing toward an acceptance of what had to be. But I *never* again want to go through so many goodbyes. How I long for a day, a time, and a place where we can be with the ones we love—where we can enjoy their company at will and never be separated again. No! Never part again! Why not bow your head with me right now and ask God to prepare you for that day?

NANCY L. VAN PELT

DECEMBER 30

One Can of Mock Chicken

Put on the full armor of God. Eph. 6:11, NIV.

In the early days of our marriage the only part of our budget that posed a problem was the weekly "food allowance" of $10. In 1960, if wisely spent, $10 was adequate, but I dreaded the amount of time associated with outlining menus and carefully planning purchases.

During one time-consuming food shopping expedition, a nice-looking gentleman approached me as I was studying the shelves of the various meat substitute products. "Have you tried the new 'mock chicken'?" he asked. "I'm the sales representative for this area. Would you like to buy a can?"

I calculated I'd have about $2 left after I paid for the groceries already in my basket. "How much does a can cost?" I cautiously asked. "I'll have about $2 left; will that be enough?"

"I'm not sure," he hedged. Then with a disarming smile he added, "But I'm certain you can afford it. Just give me your address, and I'll deliver a can tonight."

At 9:00 that night I answered a knock on our apartment door. There stood the salesman, still smiling, holding an enormous frozen drum about the size of a five-gallon gas can. "Here's your can of mock chicken!" he said, plopping the drum inside our apartment and slapping a pink bill on top of it. He swiftly turned and raced down the apartment steps into the wintry night.

I picked up the bill and stared in disbelief! *Sale: 50-pound can of mock chicken. Total amount due: $50.* I had been duped by a crafty salesperson. I kept asking, "How could I have been so naive and gullible?" It took three months to sell the bulk of the 50 pounds of mock chicken to sympathetic friends.

Satan also is a crafty salesperson who lurks in the "supermarkets" of our lives. We never meet him by chance. He knows we're potential customers, so he waits for us to stop and ponder temptations. Then he approaches in a disarmingly innocent guise. "Go ahead and buy it. You can afford it," he whispers. And just as I agreed to that long-ago purchase because I thought I understood the situation and could handle the cost, we also agree to "buy." It's only after we're committed that we discover the product we had in mind differs greatly from the product the devil has in mind for us—and the cost is always enormous! We discover we're in trouble; we've been duped! We cry, "How could I have been so naive and gullible?"

There is only one way to vanquish this crafty salesperson. We must put on the whole armor of God every morning, knowing we will meet this "salesperson" during our busy day. I have confidence in this armor, because Satan cannot come near while I am wearing it. When he whispers, "Go ahead, buy it; you can afford it," I can't hear him, because my "helmet of salvation" fits so snugly on my head, and my "sword of the Spirit" drives him away.

Today, as you kneel before the Lord, ask Him to clothe you with His armor. Then go forth into the activities of your day with confidence!
ELLIE GREEN

Stay in Touch

I will pour water upon him that is thirsty, and floods upon the dry ground. Isa. 44:3.

I am not a New Year's resolution person anymore. I believe I've had my share of broken resolutions and ought to consider myself cured. However, there is one New Year's resolution that has become almost second nature. Not because of any great success on my part. To the contrary. This New Year's resolution grows out of an inner need and can be summed up in 16 words: "This year I want to get up early enough each morning to spend time with God." So when I wake up, I remind myself, *As soon as I get dressed, I will sit down and read—I mean, as soon as I get dressed and make the beds—I mean, as soon as I get dressed, make the beds, and find the things I need to take to the office—I mean as soon as I . . .*

I do have the best intentions, but all too often I find that the most I accomplish in the morning rush is to keep the peanut butter sandwich out of my hair when I open the car door. Let me share a poem that I keep in my Bible. The author is unknown to me, but the message keeps reminding me of the importance of keeping my appointment with my heavenly Father.

I got up early one morning, and rushed right into the day.
I had so much to accomplish that I didn't have time to pray.
Problems just tumbled about me, and heavier came each task.
"Why doesn't God help me?" I wondered. He answered, "You didn't ask."

I wanted to see joy and beauty, but the day toiled on, gray and bleak;
I wondered why God didn't show me. He said, "You didn't seek."
I tried to come into God's presence; I used all my keys at the lock.
God gently and lovingly chided, "My child, you didn't knock."

I woke up early this morning and paused before entering
the day.
I had so much to accomplish that I had to take time to pray.

Prayer is the heartbeat of the soul. Just as the heart supplies
every tiny part of our body with vital nourishment, prayer is the
channel through which God sustains and strengthens us and provides for our spiritual nourishment. Where there is no communication, there is no relationship. Where there is a relationship,
there is security and contentment.

"Keep your wants, your joys, your sorrows, your cares, and
your fears before God. You cannot burden Him; you cannot
weary Him. He who numbers the hairs of your head is not indif-
ferent to the wants of His children. . . . His heart of love is
touched by our sorrows and even by our utterances of them. Take
to Him everything that perplexes the mind. Nothing is too great
for Him to bear, for He holds up worlds, He rules over all the affairs of the universe. Nothing that in any way concerns your peace
is too small for Him to notice. There is no chapter in our experience too dark for Him to read; there is no perplexity too difficult
for Him to unravel" (*Steps to Christ*, p. 100). He loves you.

BIRTHE KENDEL

Scripture Index

14:3 . . . . Oct. 17
14:6 . . . . Sept. 9
14:26 . . . . . . Jan. 30
15:5 . . . . Apr. 4
15:12 . . . . . June 11
16:13 . . . . . . Aug. 15
16:24 . . . . . . July 5
20:25 . . . . July 9

ACTS
12:10 . . . . . Nov. 10
20:35 . . . . . Dec. 19

ROMANS
1:12 . . . . Feb. 7
3:23 . . . . . . Aug. 25
8:26 . . . . . . May 17
8:28 . . . . . . Apr. 10
8:28 . . . . . . Oct. 13
12:6 . . . . . . Oct. 20
13:11 . . . . . July 14
13:14 . . . . . Nov. 27

1 CORINTHIANS
1:25 . . . . . . May 28
2:9 . . . . . . Dec. 6
4:1 . . . . . . Aug. 12
7:14 . . . . . Sept. 26
7:16 . . . . . Aug. 28
9:14 . . . . . Oct. 19
12:4, 5 . . . . Dec. 24
12:7 . . . . . . Jan. 8
13:4-7 . . . . May 27
13:7 . . . . . Sept. 2
13:12 . . . . . Feb. 24
13:12 . . . . . Oct. 24

2 CORINTHIANS
1:3, 4 . . . . . Apr. 11
2:14, 15 . . . . Apr. 24
3:18 . . . . . . Jan. 7
3:18 . . . . . . Dec. 7
5:17 . . . . . . Jan. 2
5:17 . . . . . . Dec. 1
9:8 . . . . . . Mar. 13
12:9, 10 . . . . May 31

GALATIANS
3:28, 29 . . . . Feb. 6
3:29 . . . . . July 18

5:22, 23 . . . . Oct. 11
6:7 . . . . . . July 28
6:9 . . . . . . May 13

EPHESIANS
2:8 . . . . . . Aug. 29
3:20 . . . . . Mar. 23
3:20, 21 . . . . June 28
4:29 . . . . . Feb. 18
4:32 . . . . . Feb. 22
5:1, 2 . . . . June 5
5:2 . . . . . . Feb. 14
5:18, 19 . . . . May 4
5:27 . . . . . Sept. 23
6:7, 8 . . . . Jan. 18
6:11 . . . . . Dec. 30
6:18 . . . . . Feb. 20
6:24 . . . . . Nov. 22

PHILIPPIANS
1:6 . . . . . . Apr. 28
1:6 . . . . . . Dec. 20
1:19 . . . . . Sept. 16
2:5-7 . . . . . Mar. 28
4:6, 7 . . . . Aug. 20
4:7 . . . . . . Aug. 10
4:11, 12 . . . . May 24
4:13 . . . . . Oct. 5
4:19 . . . . . May 8
4:19 . . . . . Sept. 19

1 THESSALONIANS
4:16 . . . . . Mar. 21
4:16, 17 . . . . June 1
5:16, 17 . . . . Mar. 31
5:17 . . . . . Dec. 15
5:18 . . . . . Aug. 16
5:18 . . . . . Nov. 17

2 THESSALONIANS
3:3 . . . . . . May 21

2 TIMOTHY
1:7 . . . . . . Oct. 9

TITUS
3:5 . . . . . . July 22

HEBREWS
1:14 . . . . . Jan. 15

2:13 . . . . . . Oct. 21
2:18 . . . . . . Jan. 19
4:7 . . . . . . June 30
4:16 . . . . . . Jan. 3
6:1 . . . . . . Mar. 20
10:22 . . . . . Aug. 3
10:25 . . . . . Jan. 13
10:35, 36 . . . . July 30
12:1 . . . . . Mar. 16
13:5 . . . . . Feb. 2
13:5 . . . . . Sept. 7

JAMES
1:2 . . . . . . July 16
1:5 . . . . . . May 7
1:12 . . . . . Nov. 29
1:17 . . . . . Feb. 15
1:17 . . . . . Sept. 3
3:17, 18 . . . . Nov. 13
5:16, 17 . . . . June 15
5:16 . . . . . July 4

1 PETER
1:19 . . . . . May 18
2:9 . . . . . . Dec. 4
2:9 . . . . . . Dec. 26
3:12 . . . . . May 15
4:12, 13 . . . . Sept. 4
4:16 . . . . . Oct. 8
5:7 . . . . . . May 1
5:7 . . . . . . May 23
5:8 . . . . . . May 12
5:8 . . . . . . Aug. 26
5:8, 9 . . . . Oct. 15

2 PETER
1:2, 3 . . . . . Mar. 10
3:18 . . . . . Mar. 29

1 JOHN
1:9 . . . . . . May 3
3:1 . . . . . . Feb. 3
4:19 . . . . . Oct. 12
4:10 . . . . . Sept. 24

REVELATION
3:17 . . . . . Jan. 12
3:20 . . . . . June 18
7:9 . . . . . . July 31
8:4 . . . . . June 19